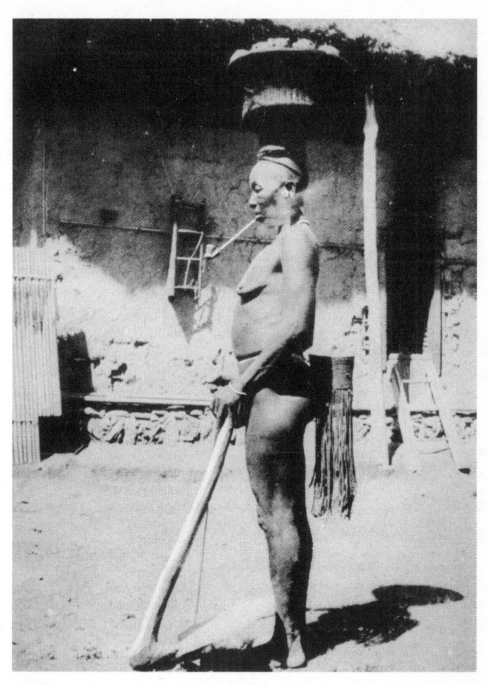

Frontispiece

A Woman of Zhoaw Village, home from the farm.

CONTENTS

WOMEN OF THE GRASSFIELDS

A study of the economic position of women in
Bamenda, British Cameroons

Phyllis M. Kaberry

Routledge
Taylor & Francis Group

LONDON AND NEW YORK

First published 1952 by Her Majesty's Stationery Office, London

This edition first published 2004
by Routledge
11 New Fetter Lane, London EC4P 4EE

Simultaneously published in the USA and Canada
by Routledge
29 West 35th Street, New York, NY 10001

Routledge is an imprint of the Taylor & Francis Group

Preface to this edition © 2004 Mitzi Goheen

Printed and bound in Great Britain by
TJ International Ltd, Padstow, Cornwall

British Library Cataloguing in Publication Data
A catalogue record for this book is available from the British Library

Library of Congress Cataloging in Publication Data
Kaberry, Phyllis Mary, 1910–1977
Women of the grassfields : a study of the economic position of women
in Bamenda, British Cameroons / Phyllis M. Kaberry.
p. cm
Originally published: London : H.M. Stationary Off., 1952.
With new pref.
Includes bibliographical references and index.
ISBN 0–415–32000–3 (pbk. : alk. paper)
1. Women – Cameroon. 2. West Cameroon (Cameroon) – Economic
conditions.
HC995.Z7 W475 2003
330.96711 22   2003058424

ISBN 0–415–32000–3

WOMEN OF THE GRASSFIELDS

Focusing on the chiefdom of Nso' in the Bamenda 'Grassfields' of British Cameroon, *Women of the Grassfields* is an extremely significant work of anthropology and gender studies. Phyllis M. Kaberry's fieldwork was prompted by the conditions in Bamenda in the 1940s when, despite considerable natural resources, there was underpopulation, very high infant mortality, and the status of women was low. By examining the social and economic status of women in the region, Kaberry produced a rich and engaging study of Nso' politics and kinship as well as the texture of both men's and women's lives.

First published in 1952, the book is central to the development of anthropology in its concentration on women's lives and the situating of gender in the larger context of local culture and the particular historic conditions. Kaberry, a true participant observer, also advanced the methodology of ethnography by giving her informants a real voice.

Mitzi Goheen's new preface explores the book's continued relevance since its first publication and its influence on later research and writing on Cameroon for scholars from a wide range of disciplines.

Phyllis M. Kaberry (1910–1977) was educated at the University of Sydney and was reader in Social Anthropology at University College London for twenty-six years. She is the author of *Aboriginal Woman*, also available from Routledge.

ROUTLEDGE CLASSIC ETHNOGRAPHIES bring together key anthropology texts which have proved formative in the development of the discipline. Originally published between the 1930s and the 1980s, these titles have had a major impact on the way in which anthropology, and most particularly ethnography, is conducted, taught, and studied.

Each book contains the text and illustrations from the original edition, as well as a new preface by a leading anthropologist explaining the book's contribution to the development of anthropology and its continuing relevance in the twenty-first century.

ABORIGINAL WOMAN
Sacred and profane
Phyllis M. Kaberry

WOMEN OF THE GRASSFIELDS
A study of the economic position of women
in Bamenda, British Cameroons
Phyllis M. Kaberry

STONE AGE ECONOMICS
Marshall Sahlins

THE MAASAI OF MATAPATO
A study of rituals of rebellion
Paul Spencer

THE SAMBURU
A study of gerontocracy
Paul Spencer

HUNGER AND WORK IN A SAVAGE TRIBE
A functional study of nutrition among the southern Bantu
Audrey Richards

CUSTOM AND POLITICS IN URBAN AFRICA
A study of Hausa migrants in Yoruba towns
Abner Cohen

PREFACE TO NEW EDITION

It is truly gratifying to see Phyllis Kaberry's important book republished in a series that will make it available and bring it to the attention of a wide audience. First published in 1952 by Her Majesty's Stationery Office, *Women of the Grassfields: a study of the economic position of women in Bamenda, British Cameroons* has long been essential reading for anyone interested in the Grassfields of western Cameroon. Kaberry's careful and detailed ethnography has provided critical background for research and writing on Cameroon for scholars from a wide range of disciplines. (History: Chem-Langhee (1984, 1989); Engoteyah and Brain (1974); Fanso and Chilver (1990), Lafon (1982), Mzeka (1980), Price (1979), Rowlands (1979); Fine Arts: Koloss (1992); Political Science: Bayart (1979), DeLancey (1989), Jua (1989); Economics and Development Studies: Koopman (1989), Lewis (1980); Anthropology and Women's Studies: Aletum and Fisiy (1989); Ardener (1975), Diduk (1989), Fisiy and Geschiere (1991), Geschiere (1986), Goheen (1996), Guyer (1981), Nkwi (1987), Rowlands and Warnier (1988), Shanklin (1999), Wendi (1990)). This list is far from complete, but it does give some insight into the importance of this work. In addition to its importance to research, *Women of the Grassfields* also provides a significant and detailed local history. At the time of its first publication and even today, the Nso' people see this work as an accurate account of the time; Kaberry provides enough detail and frank analysis to make her perspective (and those of her informants) clear. When I first went to Nso' in 1979 I was impressed and surprised by the accuracy of Kaberry's ethnography; after almost twenty-five years of doing field research in Nso' I am still in awe of her work. This is not only because she was a brilliant ethnographer. *Women of the Grassfields* contains perceptive insights into theory and practice that in retrospect seem prescient, and locate this book as a pioneering work in anthropology and women's studies. It is a pleasure and a privilege to introduce a new edition of this classic ethnography.

In the mid-1940s, Phyllis Kaberry traveled to the highlands of western Cameroon, commissioned by the International African Institute to write a report on the social and economic position of women. After a survey of the entire Bamenda Grassfields, she settled in the chiefdom of Nso' to begin research. By this time, Kaberry was already an accomplished and distinguished scholar, an anthropologist highly respected both for her scholarly writings and for her careful, detailed field research. With extensive publications and substantial field research experience in Aboriginal Australia and New Guinea, Phyllis had an established reputation as a leading scholar of Oceania, the region that composed the focus of her university studies.

Although she had not done field research in Africa, her reputation as a scholar and her research on women made Phyllis Kaberry an obvious candidate for this project. Her academic training and credentials were impeccable. She took her first degree in anthropological studies with an emphasis on history at the University of Sydney. Here distinguished anthropologists of Melanesia and Aboriginal Australia mentored her, most notably Raymond Firth, Ian Hogbin and A.P. Elkin. She completed a Master's degree with First Class Honours, and by 1935 had two papers published in *Oceania*. In 1936, at Firth's suggestion, she moved to the London School of Economics to prepare her doctoral thesis under the supervision of the eminent anthropologist of Melanesia, Bronislaw Malinowski.

By 1939, Kaberry had completed her doctoral thesis. It was published almost immediately under the title *Aboriginal Woman: Sacred and Profane*. In this book, she argued that the then typical view of Aboriginal women as outside the sphere of the sacred was not an indigenous one. On the contrary, she proved that women in Aboriginal society held important sacred and ritual positions and participated in creating sacred art. This work emphasizes the need to focus more field research on women's subjective lives and perspectives. It also demonstrates the importance of sustained long-term field investigation to discern local or indigenous taxonomies and paradigms. Kaberry expands and develops these themes in *Women of the Grassfields*.

Phyllis Kaberry's investigations in Australia and New Guinea, which in addition to her book included a number of published articles, foreshadowed two additional themes that would become central to her field research in Cameroon. First, she was deeply concerned with the natural environment in its relationship to human populations. Second, she was adamant that local people be given their own voice and not be objectified as "text." This theme remains salient in current discourse on anthropological field research, but it was not a widespread concern in the 1940s.

As noted earlier, Phyllis Kaberry's field research on women and her distinguished publishing record made her, from the perspective of the International African Institute, a perfect candidate for the job. However, to her, this charge to travel and do research in Africa initially seemed less than perfect. Her research interests in the 1940s were in New Guinea, and she planned to do field research there after World War II. It evidently took some hard talking and strong persuading before she agreed to take on the African project. Her decision to take on this research project and make the journey to what was then the British Mandate, shortly to become the United Kingdom Trust Territory, of Southern Cameroons was to have far-reaching and lasting effects. Some of these are important to our understanding of the significance of Kaberry's field research and writing, and the importance of *Women of the Grassfields* in shaping future research in a number of fields and disciplines.

The first is a personal and professional shift in her primary research focus from Oceania to the highland Grassfields of western Cameroon. This region and its peoples remained an abiding passion and research interest for the rest of her life. She made two fourteen-month field trips to Nso', the first in 1945–6 and the second in 1947–8, after a brief return to London to present her report to the International African Institute. She was determined to spend as much time as possible in the Grassfields and stayed closely in touch with a number of her Nso' informants, many of whom had become close friends. Kaberry was promoted to a Readership at the London School of Economics in 1951. She now had to take on all the accompanying obligations of teaching and administrative duties this entails. Determined to revisit the Grassfields, in 1958 when she received a Leverhulme Fellowship, she returned to Nso'. This time Elizabeth (Sally) Chilver, an Oxford historian anxious to study colonial administration in place before it disappeared, accompanied her. Phyllis's passion for the Grassfields was contagious, and Sally too became enthralled by the region. Thus began a long collegial friendship and a collaboration that produced twelve jointly written articles between 1960 and 1974 (see "Publications relating to the Grassfields by Phyllis Kaberry and Elizabeth Chilver" in the Bibliography). Kaberry and Chilver also collaborated in the research and writing of *Traditional Bamenda*, a locally published book that became a classic on the Bamenda Grassfields (Chilver and Kaberry (1968)). This book was the result of their concern that an adequate basis for social and historical studies of the region was needed, one that would be made available locally. *Traditional Bamenda* is remarkable in its breadth and detail. In this book, Chilver and Kaberry cover the entire Grassfields in what is today the Northwest Province of Cameroon. The Grassfields constitute a distinct culture area composed of a number of chiefdoms of varying size and complexity. Overall the Grassfields chiefdoms described by Chilver and Kaberry range from the small village chiefdoms of Widekum to the expanding conquest-states such as Nso'. While these chiefdoms are linguistically and ethnically diverse, they share a number of features, including the centrality of chieftaincy, the importance of men's secret societies, and an emphasis on title and rank as significant political attributes. *Traditional Bamenda* records singularities and commonality in these diverse chiefdoms in detail; it accomplishes the aim of the authors to provide a comprehensive local history. When one considers the terrain covered and the diverse languages spoken in the region, this is a truly astonishing work.

It is not difficult to see why Phyllis Kaberry developed an attachment, even a passion, for her research in Nso' and for the region in which it is situated. The high Grassfields Kaberry entered in 1945 is an area of proud beauty and sweeping landscapes. It is easy to fall in love with the sheer beauty of the region. Here, mountains rise to heights of 1,700 meters, plunging into deep valleys and ravines. During the rains, outcroppings of granite and dark thunder clouds stand in stark contrast to the sun shafts dancing on the tall grass as it bends and sways in the winds of a gathering storm. In the dry months a thin layer of red dust hangs in the air and colors the landscape. During the rainy season waterfalls cascade down the sides of the steep hills, becoming more sedate with the changing season. The spectrum of greens covering the hills and valleys is various, from the light green of the high grass on the hillsides to the deep, rich forest green of raffia bushes lining the streams in low-lying ravines. However, the breathtaking vistas and spectacular scenery do come at a price. There are few flat places and even today few decent roads. To walk about on the slippery red clay paths and roads in the rainy season is to assault one's ankles and knees and at times to put one's life in jeopardy. With astute accuracy, local people speak of walking as "trekking." Phyllis must have covered hundreds of miles of steep terrain on foot, trekking to every corner of the region from village to village before she settled in Nso'.

Despite the physical difficulties, she fell in love with the region, and Nso' people, men and women alike, loved her. From the beginning of her first research trip she was an energetic and committed participant in Nso' life. Deeply engaged with the lives of the women she was studying, Phyllis became an advocate for them with both the traditional and colonial authorities, all of whom she was unafraid to confront. This book as well as her subsequent publications reflect her determination to help women farmers fight both the destruction of their crops by cattle and the men who turned a blind eye to their problems. She was concerned, and rightly so, with the early signs of the commodification of land, a practice that went against Nso' land tenure rules and undermined women's access to farmland. She used her influence with the colonial office to promote the appointment of Elizabeth O'Kelley as Principal Adult Education Officer for women. Ms O'Kelley introduced a number of labor-saving devices; the most important of which were hand-operated corn mills women could afford and control. Dried corn is hard and difficult to grind into the corn flour that is a staple of the Nso' diet; the introduction of these corn mills helped alleviate much hard work. Phyllis continued her advocacy role throughout her time in Nso'; she saw herself as a peer and a friend to the Nso' women. She accompanied them to the farm and participated actively in all aspects of their life.

Phyllis Kaberry's enthusiasm for the Bamenda Grassfields in general and the chiefdom of Nso' in particular, and her commitment, even devotion, to the people there formed a central leitmotif of her research from the mid-1940s until her death in 1977. Her productive collaboration in field research and writing with Elizabeth (Sally) Chilver was another. Their joint work to support both scholarship on Cameroon and Cameroonian scholars has remained central to networks of communication that span three continents. They actively encouraged a number of Nso' people to pursue a higher education; several of these now teach at the University of Yaounde. Local scholars and local histories were also encouraged and supported. There is now an organization called The Kaberry Research Centre whose central mission is to encourage the writing of local histories and collect writings on the Grassfields to make these available for research.

The immense value of Kaberry's work to research on the Grassfields and beyond in Cameroon should be clear by now. *Women of the Grassfields* also became an important work for feminist writing and development research. Its early focus on women, and its implicit message that gender roles are contextual, socially constructed and negotiated as well as central to understanding African society *writ large* have become central tropes of women's and gender studies in Africa and beyond. While examining "women's role" in Nso', Kaberry found that women's role or position or status cannot be understood outside of the overall social institutions and political economy. *Women of the Grassfields* originally was to be a study of the "position of women." Kaberry took the work far beyond this narrowly conceived project. This book is a comprehensive historical ethnography in a regional setting describing the structure of Nso' politics and kinship as well as the texture of both men's and women's lives. It is one of the earliest studies of the social construction of gender demonstrating on-going negotiations over the meaning of gender roles. At a very early time, Kaberry points out the necessity of situating gender (or women's roles) in a larger context constructed by both local culture and the particular historical contingencies. Here we see in some detail how the meaning of gender is often contested and always negotiated. Kaberry is one of the first anthropologists to demonstrate women's agency. We see this in her earlier work in Australia. It becomes a central trope of gender roles in *Women of the Grassfields*. Much of her subsequent research in Cameroon continues this theme. It is no surprise that her work has become a cornerstone of feminist research and writing on Africa and beyond.

Kaberry takes gender into the heart of our understanding of Nso' political economy; *Women of the Grassfields* clearly transcends her original charge to study "women's position" in the Bamenda Grassfields. This book is significant in a number of ways, most of which are mentioned above. Its early focus on women's lives and Kaberry's arguments about the social construction and centrality of gender in political discourse may be central tropes in feminist studies today, but these were unique ideas at the time this book was written. The same is true of her methodology. She insists on giving her informants a voice and does not view them merely as "text." Her dedication to long-term field research is based in part on her insistence that it is critical to learn the local language and discern meaning in local categories and taxonomies. She was a true participant observer with a keen eye for detail. And she was devoted to the people of Nso' among whom she lived and worked. Phyllis Kaberry received a number of awards in recognition of her outstanding field research and academic achievements, including the Rivers Medal and the Wellcome Medal of the Royal Anthropological Institute. But her most prized honor was bestowed by the *Fon Nso'* in 1958 when she was given the title "*Yaa woo Kov*" (literally translated as "Queen of the Forest"). In her eyes and those of the Nso' people with the bestowing of this title she became a "*wir Nso'*," a true Nso' person. Phyllis Kaberry was a classic (and classy) anthropologist who set high standards for field research and scholarship. All of these attributes combine to make *Women of the Grassfields* a classic work.

Mitzi Goheen
2003

Acknowledgement

I would like to thank Shirley Ardener for her help with this preface, and Sally Chilver for her great help, guidance and friendship over the past twenty-five years.

Bibliography

(Except where otherwise noted, this Preface was based on unpublished notes and conversations with Elizabeth (Sally) Chilver and Shirley Ardener and on my own fieldnotes.)

References cited in the text

Aletum, Tabuwe Michael, and Cyprian Fonyuy Fisiy, *Socio-Political Integration and the Nso' Institutions, Cameroon*. Yaounde: Institute of Human Sciences, 1989.

Ardener, Shirley, "Sexual Insult and Female Militancy." In Shirley Ardener, ed., *Perceiving Women*. London, Malaby Press, 1975.

Bayart, Jean-François. *L'état en Cameroon*. Paris: Presses de la Foundation nationale des sciences politiques, 1979.

Chem-Langhee, Bonfen. "Southern Cameroons, Traditional Authorities and the Nationalist Movement 1953–1961." *Afrika Zamani* 1, nos. 14–15 (1984): 147–63.

Chem-Langhee, Bonfen. *The Shuufayship of Bernard Fonlon*. Yaounde: University of Yaounde, 1989.

Diduk, Susan. "Women's Agricultural Production and Political Action in the Cameroon Grassfield." *Africa: Journal of the International African Institute* 59, no. 3 (1989): 358.

DeLancey, Mark W. *Cameroon: Dependence and Independence*. Profiles: Nations of Contemporary Africa. Boulder: Westview Press, 1989.

Engoteyah, Tambi and Robert Brain. *A History of the Cameroon*. London: Longman, 1974.

Fanso, Verkijika and Elizabeth Chilver. "Nso' and the Germans: Contemporary Documents and Oral Traditions." Unpublished manuscript 1990.

Fisiy, Cyprian and Peter Geschiere. "Judges and Witches, or How is the State to deal with Witchcraft? Examples from Southern Cameroon." *Cahiers d'études africaines* 118 (1991): 135–56.

Geschiere, Peter. "Hegemonic Regimes and Popular Protest: Bayart, Gramsci and the State in Cameroon." In Wim M.J. van Binsbergen, Filip Reyntjens, and Gerti Hesseling, eds., *State and Local Community in Africa*. Centre d'Etude et de Documentation Africaines, 1986.

Goheen, Miriam. *Men own the Fields, Women own the Crops: Gender and Power in the Cameroon Highlands*. Madison: University of Wisconsin, 1996, 1999.

Guyer, Jane I. "Household and Community in African Studies." *African Studies Review* 24, nos. 2/3 (1981): 87–138.

Jua, Nantang. "The Petty Bourgeoisie and the Politics of Social Justice in Cameroon." In Peter Geschiere and Piet Konings, eds., *Proceedings/Contributions, Conference on the Political Economy of Cameroon: Historical Perspectives*, 737–55. Leiden, University of Leiden, African Studies Centre, 1989.

Koloss, H.J. "Kwifon and Fon in Oku," In Erna Beumers and H.J. Koloss, eds., *Kings of Africa*, 33–42. Maastricht: Foundation Kings of Africa, 1992.

Koopman (Henn), Jeanne. "Food Policy, Food Production and the Family Farm in Cameroon. In Peter Geschiere and Piet Konings, eds., *Proceedings/Contributions, Conference on the Political Economy of Cameroon: Historical Perspectives*, 531–55. Leiden: University of Leiden, African Studies Centre, 1989.

Lafon, Joseph. "An Address on the Occasion of the Episcopal Consecretation of Rev. Father Cornelius Fontem Esua, First Bishop of Kumbo." Unpublished manuscript, 1982.

Lewis, John Van Deusen, ed., *Agricultural Marketing in the Northwest Province, United Republic of Cameroon*. Yaounde: USDA/USAID, 1980.

Mzeka, N. Paul. *The Core Culture of Nso'*. Agawam: Paul Radin, 1980.

Nkwi, Paul Nchoji. *Traditional Diplomacy: A Study of Inter-chiefdom Relations in the Western Grassfields, Northwest Province of Cameroon*. Yaounde: University of Yaounde, 1987.

Rowlands, Michael J. "Local and Long Distance Trade and Incipient State Formation on the Bamenda Plateau in the Late 19th Century." *Paideuma: Mitteilungen zur Kulturkunde* 25 (1979): 1–20.

Rowlands, Michael J. and Jean-Pierre Warnier. "Sorcery, Power and the Modern State in Cameroon." *Man* 23, no. 1 (1988): 118–32.

Shanklin, Eugenia. "Anlu Remembered: The Kom Women's Rebellion of 1958–61." *Dialectical Anthropology* 15, nos. 2–3 (1999): 159–82.

Wendi, Bernadette. "The Cameroonian Woman in Development." *The Activator, Newsletter for the Association for Creative Teaching, Northwest Province* 4/1 (January 1990).

Publications relating to the Grassfields by Phyllis Kaberry

1950 "Land Tenure among the Nsaw of the British Cameroons." *Africa* 20(4).

1952a "Nsaw History and Social Categories." *Africa* 22(1).

1952b *Women of the Grassfields*, London: Her Majesty's Stationery Office.
1957a "Myth and Ritual: Some Recent Theories," *Bulletin of the Institute of Classical Studies* 4. London.
1957b "Primitive States" (Review Article). *British Journal of Sociology* 8.
1959a "Nsaw Political Conceptions." *Man* LIX:206.
1959b "Traditional Politics in Nsaw." *Africa* 29 (4).
1960   "Some Problems of Land Tenure in Nso'." *Journal of African Administration* (10).
1962a "The date of the Bamum-Banso War." *Man* LXII (20).
1962b "Retainers and Royal Households in the Cameroon Highlands." *Cahiers d'études africaines*. III-II, 10.
1969. "Witchcraft of the Sun: Incest in Nso'." In Douglas and Kaberry, eds., *Man in Africa*. London: Tavistock.

Publications relating to the Grassfields by Phyllis Kaberry and Elizabeth Chilver

1960   "From Tribute to Tax in a Tikar Chiefdom." *Africa* 30(1).
1961a (Editors) *The History of Custom of Ntem*. (pamphlet). Oxford: Oxonian Press.
1961b "An Outline of the Traditional Political System of Bali-Nyonga." *Africa* 31(4).
1962   "Traditional Government in Bafut." *Nigerian Field* 28(1).
1963a "The Peoples of Bamenda." *Cameroon Students' Journal* 1.
1963b "Historical Research in Bamenda." *Abbia* (4).
1965   "Sources of the Nineteenth-Century Slave-Trade: the Cameroon Highlands." *Journal of African History* VI(1).
1967   "The Kingdom of Kom in West Cameroon." In Forde and Kaberry, eds., *West African Kingdoms in the 19th Century*. London: Oxford University Press.
1968   *Traditional Bamenda*. Buea: Government Printing Office.
1970a "Chronology of the Bamenda Grassfields." *Journal of African History* XI(2).
1970b "The Tikar Problem: A Non-Problem." *Journal of African Languages* 10.
1974   *Western Grassfields (Cameroon Republic) Linguistic Notes*. Occasional Paper no. 29, Institute of African Studies, London.

Phyllis Kaberry: unpublished material

(a) British Library of Political and Economic Science (LSE) London. Original field-notes, notes from administrative records, and correspondence, with a handlist by David Price.

(b) National Archives, Buea, Cameroon. Quarterly Reports 1945–88; Report on Farmer-Grazier Problems in Nso', 1959.

(c) Epitomes and transcriptions of Kaberry's and joint field notes on particular topics have been compiled by E.M. Chilver for MESIRES and local research groups. These include compilations on Nso' clans, installation rituals (Nso' and Mbot), on particular groups (Tang-Mbo, Bafreng, Big Babanki, some Ndop chiefdoms) and a report to the Bali History Society.

PREFACE

IN 1944 the International African Institute was consulted on the question of organising a field study of the peoples of Bamenda with special reference to the position of women. Its attention had first been drawn to this matter by Dr. Margaret Read, a former research Fellow of the Institute, following enquiries made of her by the Chief Commissioner, Eastern Provinces, during her visit to Nigeria as a member of the Commission on Higher Education in West Africa. The need for such research had been reported by the Cameroons Development Corporation, and shortly after a despatch was addressed by the Governor of Nigeria to the Secretary of State for the Colonies, in which he drew attention to conditions in the Bamenda division of the Cameroons under British mandate, where, despite considerable natural resources, there was under-population, and social obstacles to opportunities for economic development and educational advance were apparent. Among factors thought to be in part responsible for the situation were a very high infant mortality rate to which social factors might be contributing, and a low status of women.

The Governor transmitted with his despatch two reports, one by a lady education officer and one by the Senior Resident, Cameroons Province, in which the need for appointing more women educationalists was urged in order to assist the adaptation of a backward society to changing conditions, and in particular to assist the people in meeting the new forces which were impinging on them. The Governor pointed out, however, that educational workers could not hope for even a moderate degree of success without the assistance of a social anthropologist to provide information which would enable them to guide and assist the people aright. The first essential, therefore, was a study of the general social and economic conditions of the people themselves. He therefore requested that a grant might be made from the Colonial Research Fund to enable such investigations to be carried out.

The Colonial Social Science Research Council, to which the matter was referred, recommended after consultation with the International African Institute that direction of the research should be entrusted to the latter and a grant for this purpose was made to it from the Colonial Research Fund.

The Institute was fortunate in securing the services of Dr. Phyllis Kaberry, who had already carried out anthropological field work in North-Western Australia and in New Guinea, and had given special attention to the status of women among the peoples studied. She had held research and teaching fellowships in the Universities of Sydney and Yale and her publications included a book based on her Australian studies entitled *Aboriginal Woman* (Routledge, London, 1939). In January 1945 she left for West Africa and worked for an initial period of 18 months among the Nsaw and other peoples of Bamenda. Returning to England in July 1946 she presented an interim report on her findings and in January 1947 resumed her field studies for a further period until April 1948.

The present work embodies Dr. Kaberry's full report on the particular aspects of social life which she was invited to study. This is, however, provided within the framework of a comprehensive account of the social and economic life of the peoples of Bamenda. One of its most striking contributions at once to the theoretical analysis of social relations and to the factual knowledge needed by administrators is to be found in her study of the system of land rights among

xvii

the Nsaw and other peoples where the village communities are linked in a centralised political system. She shows first how the titular ownership of chiefs is, in the routine of production and consumption, traditionally quite subsidiary to *de facto* control by the head of a kin group, and that both are subject to strong customary obligations, breaches of which evoke opposition, non-co-operation and defection that are held to be morally justified. She shows too that, though in relation to the rest of the tribe and the chief, land is regarded as held by the men of a lineage under the authority of their head, yet in the domestic context women, as wives of these men, exercise real control over land use by virtue of their rights as producers over the crops they grow. Any proposals or actions directed towards changes in the allocation and use of land or in farming techniques must reckon with this series of rights which are at each level limited by moral standards and practical restraints.

Dr. Kaberry reaches her more general conclusions, however, after a vivid presentation of the daily life and manifest attitudes that she observed during her long residence in Bamenda villages. The reader, whether scholar, administrator or layman, will appreciate both her account of actualities of life in the Bamenda highlands today and her study of the cultural forces, traditional and new, that underlie them and are helping to shape the future.

DARYLL FORDE,
Director, International African Institute.

INTRODUCTION

AT the beginning of 1945 I undertook, at the request of the Government of Nigeria, to make a survey of the economic and social position of women in the Cameroons Province and in Bamenda in particular. For the reasons which I have already discussed in an earlier report, my work was eventually confined to Bamenda.

The terms of reference for my research were broad, but how broad was not at first, I think, generally recognized. The activities of the Bamenda woman are many-sided and cannot, without distortion, be abstracted from the context of tribal life and placed in a cultural vacuum. Their investigation entails, primarily, a study of economic, kinship, religious and political institutions. The need for the same breadth of approach holds equally for the presentation of the results of research. In other words, ones starting point is not the women but an analysis of a particular aspect of culture. On that basis one may then proceed to examine in more detail the way in which the structure and organization of rights, duties and activities within a group of institutions affect the position of women. All this has implications for the type of generalization that can be formulated and for the planning of anthropological fieldwork in the future.

In the first place, this handling of data yields a series of statements on the role of women in particular segments of tribal life. Generalizations at this level are valid, significant, and of value to those concerned with the problem of raising the status of women and promoting their welfare. An attempt to go beyond this and, by a species of anthropological or moral arithmetic, to decide whether the position of women in general is high or low, or good or bad is, in my opinion, likely to prove profitless. I have made this point with almost monotonous regularity in all my reports. It is repeated here because one still finds in the questionnaires of such bodies as The United Nations Trusteeship Council a demand for broad generalizations on the position of women in such and such a territory. Clearly, the replies to such questions are at best superficial, at worst distorted, and almost invariably contradictory. Let me give two examples which I found embedded in the Government files. A missionary who had spent many years in Bamenda asserted that " the women of this Division have achieved a remarkable degree of freedom and independence contrary to notions abroad ". Another missionary of a different denomination but also of considerable experience of the country stated : " The status of women is alarmingly low. The main causes of this are considered to be the dowry system and polygamy—especially in its extreme form as practised by local chiefs, village heads and prominent men of the tribe ". As a further contribution to this diversity of opinion it is not inappropriate to cite those given me by some women of Nsaw. " Woman is an important thing, a thing of God, a thing of the earth. All people come forth from her." And this statement—also made by the wife of a polygynist : " A woman is a very God. Men are not at all. What *are* men?" Sometimes the answer to this rhetorical question was—" worthless ! " Again, in response to my inquiry why people mourned four days for a woman and only three for a man, the men offered the explanation : " A woman is one who bears the people (of the country). Women are very important. Women are like God, because they bear children." It should be noted, however, that to the people of Nsaw even God has his limitations and is not omnipotent.

Obviously some of the commentators had in mind certain activities or customs which they regarded as an index of the general position of women. But, if allowance is made for this and the judgment is taken to refer primarily to a particular practice such as marriage payments or polygyny, it is still of little value unless it is shown to be based on a detailed knowledge of the institution concerned and its interlocking relationships with other aspects of tribal culture.

With the economic aspects of polygyny and marriage in general I shall deal later in this book.[1] It should be stated at the outset, however, that it is not the task of the anthropologist to produce a policy, despite some tendency to regard him as a species of medicine man called in to diagnose a disease in the body-social and to prescribe a cure when traditional remedies have failed! And this brings me to a point which was raised earlier in connection with the planning of anthropological research. It should be clear from the preceding discussions that there is no short cut to the study of women. Generalizations on their status and roles are the end-product of an intensive process of investigation into the social organization or into a particular set of institutions of a tribe. In the framing of projects for research much would be gained, I think, if the terms of reference recognized this fact and indicated more precisely the scope of fieldwork entailed. In other words, instead of defining a research project as " a survey of the economic and social position of women ", I would substitute for this " a survey of the economic and other aspects of social organization ". Or, if the object of particular interest were the position of women in marriage and the family, then the terms of reference should be broadened to include a study of marriage and the family. This is not an attempt to expunge or to exclude the women from the picture. On the contrary, it seeks to provide a broad and reliable basis for valid generalization on their role and status by ensuring that all the relevant factors will be taken into account and that their particular problems will be placed in a perspective where integral relationship with others are made evident.

As far as the presentation of my own material in this book is concerned, I have confined myself to an examination of the economic position of women, not merely because the terms of reference for my research laid emphasis on this aspect, but because problems in this field are in some ways the most pressing and the most difficult of solution. They affect not only the women but are bound up with the role of agriculture in the economy, the system of land tenure, pastoral and trade development, the introduction of new occupations, and so forth. Women, as wives, mothers and daughters, produce most of the food and spend the greater part of the day on the farm. In this sphere of activity they enjoy considerable independence and have well defined rights; and it is in this sphere that there has been less change than in others. For example, the influence of Missions, Native Courts, and especially of Reviewing Officers is modifying marriage law in such matters as freedom in the choice of a spouse, custody of children and divorce,—questions with which I hope to deal in another publication. But Christian women, not to forget the pagans, still continue to farm and still accept in principle and largely in fact the traditional division of labour between the sexes. The placing of agriculture in the foreground for detailed analysis reflects, then, its importance in the life of the women. Changes introduced in this field will affect not only the status and position of women in marriage and the family, but will radically modify the economy and the general standard of living.

---

[1] This report was submitted as a manuscript to the International African Institute at the end of March 1951, and a copy was later sent to the Government of Nigeria. Since then the text has been revised for publication in book form: Chapter 1 has been shortened and some of the later chapters have been re-arranged and reorganized

In what is to follow we shall endeavour to approach problems along broad sociological lines. We shall be concerned with ecological conditions,—the type of natural resources, the traditional means of exploiting them, the range of economic needs, and the bearing of all such factors on the division of labour between the sexes. In discussing land tenure we shall not be content to list the women's rights to usufruct, but shall view it as a functioning system. Nor can this subject be dissociated from the more general problems which affect not only the women but all members of the community,—namely, soil conservation, the return for labour in terms of harvest yields, and the extent to which these have to be supplemented by the purchase of extra quantities of food.

Finally, while analysing as fully as possible particular disabilities under which the women labour, account will also be taken of the contribution of the men and its implications for the functioning of the economy as a whole. For, in the long run, the alleviation of the lot of the women is bound up with the welfare and general improvement in the standard of living of the community, of which they form but a segment.

Before bringing this introductory section to a close I should like to discuss the conditions under which my fieldwork was carried out in order to indicate the nature, range and limitations of the material I collected and the extent to which it constitutes a reliable basis for generalization.

Originally it was intended that I should make a survey of the Cameroons Province, that is Bamenda, Mamfe, Kumba and Victoria Divisions. But after almost a year in Bamenda I realized that a survey of even a selected number from its 23 Native Authority Areas would demand all the time I had available and, ideally, much more. An attempt to cover the other Divisions would yield little reliable data for valid generalization. Such a survey would have fallen into the category of tribe-trotting, but not scientific fieldwork. With the consent of the Government of Nigeria, I therefore spent my second tour in Bamenda.

The reasons for my choice of Nsaw (Banso) as a centre for intensive study have already been discussed in earlier reports and require but brief mention here. The Tikar are the largest ethnic group in Bamenda and are subdivided into a number of independent chiefdoms, differing in size, language, political structure, and kinship organization. Nsaw is the largest of these and, like most of the Tikar, is patrilineal whereas Kom, an area which I seriously considered as a centre for intensive investigation, is matrilineal. Secondly, the political structure of Nsaw still retains many of its traditional features but other aspects of the culture have been and are being modified under the influence of Missions, the Administration, schools, the expansion of trade, medical services, the presence of immigrant Fulani and Hausa, and transients who travel the main motor road which passes through the capital, Kimbaw. There is a Roman Catholic Mission in the charge of European priests at Shisong, some 2 miles from Kimbaw, and also a maternity clinic run by the nuns at the convent closeby. The Mission has its school at Shisong and a smaller one in Kimbaw, where the Basel Mission also has a school in the charge of an African headmaster. There is a hospital and dispensary with an African dispenser, a U.A.C. store and a large market.

I reached Kimbaw on the 4th April 1945 and, by courtesy of the Basel Mission, stayed until the end of October in their Resthouse which was in Veka'akwi area and within about 3 minutes' walk of the nearest compound. At my request the Administration kindly seconded one of the Court Messengers to act as my interpreter, guide, philosopher and friend; and for the first three months I had lessons in Lamnso from Benedict Somo (an ex-schoolteacher) his wife, and another woman. Father Stokman lent me grammar which one of the Roman Catholic Missionaries had compiled and it proved most helpful. At the beginning of November I trekked north, but did not spend much time in Nsungli as, according to the *Intelligence Reports*, its social structure and economy appeared to be similar to that of Nsaw and I was anxious to reach the forest peoples to the north in Mbembe and Mfumte. After 7 weeks I returned to Kimbaw, and I spent about a month there before visiting the outlying village of Vekovi, where I had reason to believe fewer changes had occured in the traditional system. In March I spent a week in Djottin-Vitum, a conquered village of Nsungli extraction, and then passed on to Kom where I had three weeks. An illness cut short my stay in the Bafut N.A. and I returned to Kimbaw at the end of April 1946. I remained in Kimbaw until the end of June, but lived in a hut in one of the larger compounds (hut 13 in Mbonyaar Compound of Sketch Plan, App. D).

In July I returned to England for leave and to write my Preliminary Report; and I reached Bamenda again in January 1947. After a fortnight's stay in Kimbaw, I began a long trek on foot through Ndop to Bamenda Station; and then, from Nyen (in Meta) through the other Widekum tribes of the west and so north to Aghem and Fungom. Again, I planned my survey on the basis of information in the *Intelligence Reports*, and selected the village of Teze in Ngie for a month's fieldwork before spending brief periods in the other tribes. Dates and length of stay are given in an Appendix, but I did not reach Bamenda Station until August. After a week in Bali I went back to Kimbaw, with the object of obtaining some quantitive data—budgets, farm measurements, and recording of diaries. I took over the hut which I had occupied in my first tour, and lived there from September to March 1948.[1]

Fifteen months, all told, were spent in Kimbaw and other villages of Nsaw, but unfortunately the period was not a continuous one. After my first tour there was a long interruption lasting almost fifteen months before I returned to Kimbaw, and this proved something of a linguistic setback. However I was able to work alone with the women none of whom, with two exceptions, had even a knowledge of Pidgin-English. I spent most of my time on the farms and in the compounds; I never summoned people for formal interviews to my house, though many came to visit and gossip. As far as possible I avoided " paying " for information, but from time to time I made presents, usually in kind—salt, cloth, trinkets, soap, tobacco, and so forth—to those who assisted me and who became my friends. Needless to say gifts poured into the house, mostly in the form of farm produce, fowls, eggs and fruit, and for these I made a return. Where I was recording budgets of the individuals concerned I made a somewhat reluctant note of our mutual transactions!

Much of the material in this book is drawn from my Nsaw notebooks, and most of the African terms and texts are in Lamnso. I have used the orthography recommended by the International African Institute with one or two exceptions, namely *wv* for bilabial *v*, and *fh* for bilabial *f*. Most final vowels in Lamnso are palatalized and the sound sometimes approaches the German *ich* and sometimes *y*. Both are recorded in my notebooks since individuals varied in their pronunciation, but in this text I have employed the phoneme *y*. There are two *o* sounds : *ɔ* represents the vowel as in " hot ", and *o* the vowel as in " caught ". For the spelling of place-names I have adopted the current anglicized version: Nsaw for *Nso*, and Kimbaw for *Kimbo*.

---

[1] Full details of my itinerary are given in Appendix A.

ACKNOWLEDGEMENTS

It is difficult to know where to begin and where to end in making my acknowledgements to all those who gave me assistance and hospitality during my fieldwork. First of all, however, I should like to express my profound sense of gratitude to the Government of Nigeria and the Colonial Research Committee for making possible the opportunity and privilege of undertaking research in Bamenda. The investigation was financed by a grant from the Colonial Development and Welfare Fund and was carried out under the auspices of the International African Institute. I am deeply indebted to the Director, Professor Daryll Forde, for his advice, encouragement and unfailing interest in my work, and to Mrs. B. E. Wyatt, Secretary, for her many acts of kindness while I was in the field and here in London. I should also like to thank Professor Margaret Read who, after her return from Nigeria in 1944, first whetted my curiosity about the Cameroons. Over a luncheon table, strewn with maps, she " sold " me Bamenda in an hour. I say " sold ", but after a few months in the Cameroons there was never a more voluntary and enchanted captive to the landscape and its people than myself.

Before leaving London I also had the good fortune to meet Miss G. Plummer (then Deputy Director of Women's Education Nigeria) and Mr. W. E. Holt (then Senior Education Officer, Cameroons), both of whom gave me valuable information and advice. The Department of Education, Nigeria, was particularly interested in my research in relation to its bearing on problems of girls' education and I became its special *protegée* while in the field. I should like to express my thanks to Mr. R. Davidson (Director of Education), Mr. T. Baldwin (then Deputy Director), Miss G. Plummer, Mr. W. E. Holt, Mr. B. Cozzens, Miss A. Spence, Mrs. J. Sandiford and other members of the Department for their help and hospitality.

In the British Cameroons Government Officials all co-operated to facilitate my research, to organize transport, and to extend generous hospitality. By anthropological standards my two tours were long, and without the friendship and encouragement of Officials, and not least the opportunity for stimulating discussions, I should not only have been deprived of many pleasures but should have lapsed into that state of staleness which is apt to beset even the experienced fieldworker after the first eight or nine months. I should like to record here my gratitude to all those with whom I came into contact, and in particular to Mr. A. Bridges (then Resident of the Cameroons Province) and Mrs. Bridges, Mrs. P. G. Harris, Mr. W. Aston-Smith (S.D.O., Bamenda), Mr. C. Mayne (then S.D.O.), Mr. Brayne-Baker (S.D.O.), Mr. F. Kay (then S.D.O.), Mr. J. Stapleton (then A.D.O.) and Mrs. Stapleton, Mr. W. Newington (S.D.O. Kumba) and Mrs. Newington, Mr. J. Pedder (then S.A.O.); Mr. S. E. Gwilliam (S.A.O.), Mr. J. McCulloch (then Vet.O.), and Dr. D. McLaren (S.M.O.).

During my first seven months in Kimbaw and again for three months in 1946 the Basel Mission most generously allowed me to occupy their comfortable Resthouse. I thank them and the other Missionaries of Bamenda who gave me hospitality and who performed many acts of kindness. My nearest European neighbours were the members of the Roman Catholic Mission at Shisong, two miles from Kimbaw. The Rev. Father Stokman took a keen interest in my work, lent me a Lamnso grammar which he had compiled, found my first Lamnso teachers for me, and at all times was ready to help and advise. Mother Camilla and the other nuns at the convent were my very good neighbours and made my existence almost a sybaritic one with their regular gifts of vegetables, strawberries and cream. Last and not least my warmest thanks are due to Mr. and Mrs. Paul Gebauer of the

American Baptist Mission for their kindness and the pleasant days I spent in their company.

My greatest debt is to my African friends and acquaintances in Bamenda without whose courtesy, trust and co-operation my research could not have been carried out. They endured my questioning and my " 'satiable curtiosities " about every detail of their lives with forbearance, humour and patience, and never made me feel an intruder. To single out individuals from among the hundreds whom I met is perhaps invidious but, inevitably, there were people in Nsaw whom I came to know well over my long stay in that country and who greatly assisted me in my work. I should like to express my thanks to the Fɔn of Nsaw, the Queen Mothers, the Councillors and Court Officials; to Mr. Vincent Lainjo (then N.A. Treasurer), to my interpreter and friend, the late Benedict Tata, and to my first teachers of Lamnso, Mr. Benedict Somo and his wife Christina Lambiif. I lived in the Veka' akwi area of Kimbaw and now take the opportunity of thanking my friends at Djem, Mbonyaar, Kinga, Menggu, Ka and other compounds who saw me almost daily over many months and always made me welcome. Mr. Sylvester Ndjodzeka kindly lent me his house at Mbonyaar and he, the Fai, and other members of the compound made me feel at home and one of the family. Finally, I should like to record my appreciation of my two stewards, Mr. Michael Keng (of Oku) and especially Mr. Daniel Mbinkar Tatah, who not only looked after me but helped me in my work.

If this book throws some light on the problems of the women and contributes in any measure to our understanding of their values, courage and wisdom it will have gone a little way towards discharging my debt to them for the confidence and friendship which they so generously extended to me.

P.M.K.

London, 1951.

Chapter I

THE PEOPLES OF BAMENDA

DISTRIBUTION OF MAIN ETHNIC GROUPS

BEFORE we examine the economy of Bamenda and its bearing on the position of women, a somewhat detailed account of the history, ethnic character and distribution of the peoples is necessary since very little information has been published. The total population of the Province as given in the Annual Report for 1948 is 301,000; but this is estimated from figures for adult taxable males, the last census having been taken in 1931. The people are negroid, with possibly a northern strain in some of the Tikar tribes. They vary considerably in physique; but, in general, those of the uplands appear to be taller, wirier, and of better build than those of the forest, where malaria, filaria, yaws, goitre and elephantiasis are prevalent.[1]

Apart from the analysis of the Nkom language by the Rev. Father Bruens,[2] very little linguistic research has been done in Bamenda. The Basel Mission has translated the New Testament into Bali, and the Roman Catholic Mission has made some study of the language of Nsaw and produced a catechism in Nkom. The languages of Bamenda have hitherto been classified as Benue-Cross River (or semi-Bantu) and the Tikar placed in the Bafumbum-Bansaw group. But, in a recent set of articles dealing with a reclassification of West African languages,[3] Greenberg has suggested that Bali, Bafut and Ndob (and presumably this would be extended to the dialects spoken by other Tikar peoples in Bamenda) are Bantu. But a definitive classification must wait on further research, as well as the publication of the results of the linguistic field survey of the northern Bantu Borderland now being carried out from the French Cameroons.

Until 1949, Bamenda was organized into 23 Native Authority Areas (see map in Appendix), but these did not in all cases coincide with ethnic boundaries. In Fungom, for example, there are a number of villages which differ in dialect, culture and provenance,—some deriving from the French Cameroons, some from the Benue Province. In the Ndop N.A. there are 12 small chiefdoms which neither linguistically nor culturally form a homogeneous unit, though 10 of them point to Ndobo in the French Cameroons as the centre

---

[1] As far as I am aware there are no anthropometric data for the British Cameroons. Dr. Olivier has made a preliminary survey of the principal tribes of the Southern French Cameroons, and he includes a very small sample of 21 men and 13 women from the Tikar at Fumban. Vide, " Documents anthropométriques pour servir à l'étude des principales populations du Sud-Cameroun," Bulletin de la Société d'Études Camerounaises, 1946, Nos. 15–16, p. 64.

[2] A. Bruens, "The Structure of Nkom and its relations to Bantu and Sudanic," Anthropos, Band XXXVII–XL, 1942–45.

[3] Joseph H. Greenberg, " Studies in African Linguistic Classification. 1. The Niger-Congo Family," South Western Journal of Anthropology, vol. 5, No. 2, 1949, pp. 5–7. Greenberg has classified the West Sudanic nucleus, the Benue-Cross River, the languages in the British Cameroons, as well as some to the east, as Niger-Congo. Within this family he has tentatively distinguished 15 genetic sub-families; and to one of these—the Central Branch—the languages of Bamenda belong. This group includes, among others, the Cross-River languages, Munshi, Mbarike (Zumper), Jukun-Kyentu-Nidu, Bitare, Tigong, Batu, Ndoro, Bantu (Bafut, Ndob, Bamun, Bali, Banyen, Banyang, Ngami), and Mambila. In Bamenda, the Mbembe of the north appear to have linguistic affiliations with the Tigong; the Aghem claim to have migrated from Munshi; Badji (or Badjong-Pai) in Fungom is said to be of Zumper origin; while the Widekum may be affiliated with the Banyang in Mamfe.

1

from which they emigrated. In Nsungli,[1] where there were the three Native Authorities of War, Tang and Wiya, the position is more complicated since the villages which belong to any one of these units do not occupy a continuous stretch of territory, but are interdigitated among villages belonging to the other two sub-tribes.

Some of the administrative units in the northern and western forests (as in Mbembe, Ngie, Meta and Esimbi) reflect to a much greater extent similarities of dialect and custom; but, while there is some consciousness of a common cultural heritage, the people themselves have never recognized a central political authority. It is perhaps only in Nsaw, Kom, Bum and Bali, where strong consolidated kingdoms had been created prior to the arrival of Europeans, that the existing Native Authorities corresponded fairly closely to the traditional system of organization.

Following upon the proposals made in 1948 by the Administration, 22 out of 23 of the Native Authorities agreed to federate into four groups, each with its own central treasury and council.[2] Bali remained outside this reorganization since none of the Authorities could be persuaded to become members of a group in which it was included. Traditional hostility dies hard: the people have not yet forgotten that in the last century Bali conquered villages in the south and south-west, exacted tribute, and, under the Germans, received recognition as a suzerain power. They are fearful of domination: as one ruler phrased it—" if you federate with Bali, you might just as well cut your own throat! " Such an attitude is no doubt unduly apprehensive today, but the appointment of the Fɔn of Bali as a member of the Eastern House of Assembly in 1946 has, if anything, reinforced it.

So far we have discussed the relation between administrative units and ethnic grouping, and attention has been directed to those differences of dialect and custom which are stressed by the people themselves. But, if traditions of migration and broader linguistic and cultural similarities are adopted as criteria, the peoples of Bamenda fall within five main groups:

(a) Tikar,
(b) Widekum,
(c) Mbembe,
(d) Bali,
(e) Aghem.

To these must be added the Hausa and Bororo (or Pastoral) Fulani who have entered the territory in increasing numbers since the advent of British rule. The former tend to congregate in the large market villages; while the latter pasture Zebu cattle on the hill tops of the plateau, more especially in Nsaw, Nsungli, Kom, Bafut, Fungom and in Ngwo.[3] It is difficult to arrive

---

[1] The term Nsungli is not the name of a particular tribe, but is applied to the War, Tang and Wiya groups by the Nsaw. It derives from the Lamnso word for chatterers, nsuŋnin. Since, however, these three groups present marked similarities of culture and dialect in contrast with neighbouring peoples I have, for the sake of convenience, retained Nsungli as a classificatory term for them. This has been and still is the practice of the Administration in its Reports.

[2] The groups are (i) North-Eastern Federation (Mbembe, Mfumte, Misaje, Mbem, Mbaw, Nsungli); (ii) North-Western Federation (Fungom, Bum, Kom, Aghem, Beba-Befang, Esimbi); (iii) South-Western Federation (Ngwo, Ngie, Ngemba, Meta, Mogamaw); (iv) Nsaw-Ndop-Bafut Federation; (v) Bali. Bamenda, formerly a division of the Cameroons Province, became a Province in July, 1949. The Province now contains three divisions, namely Bamenda, Wum and Nkambe.

[3] No census has been taken of the Fulani and Hausa; but, according to the Annual Report for Bamenda, 1947, there were among the former about 1,500 payers of jangali (cattle tax)— a rough approximation to the number of adult Fulani men. There were 156,870 cattle in the Province.

at even an approximate estimate of the numbers of the five main groups, the more so since, as mentioned previously, Native Authority Areas are not ethnically homogeneous. For example, among areas which are predominantly Tikar there are small bands of Mambila origin (as in Mbaw); villages of Mbembe and Zumper origin in Fungom; a Chamba (Bali) village in Ndop, and Widekum villages in Bafut. In giving some idea of the relative numerical strength of the main ethnic peoples I have disregarded these small enclaves, since I have no data on their size.[1]

TABLE I

Ethnic Group	Native Authority Area	Density Per Sq. Mile	Estimated Population of Groups in 1948	Percentage of Total Population
TIKAR ..	Nsaw (Banso)	40		
	Kom (Bikom)	62		
	Bum	14		
	Bafut	60		
	Ndop	69		
	Wiya ⎫	7	175,000	58.1
	Tang ⎬ (Nsungli) ..	40		
	War ⎭ ..	68		
	Mbem ⎫ (Ntem) ..	44		
	Mbaw ⎭ ..	10		
	Fungom	20		
WIDEKUM ..	Ngemba	47		
	Ngie	91		
	Ngwo (Ngunu)	60		
	Mogamaw	74	83,000	27.5
	Meta (Menemo) ..	100		
	Esimbi (Age)	23		
	Beba-Befang	87		
MBEMBE ..	Mbembe	14		
	Misaje	42	22,000	7.2
	Mfumte (Kaka) ..	23		
BALI	Bali (Bani)	14	14,000	4.8
AGHEM ..	Aghem (Wum)	17	7,000	2.4
Total ..		43	301,000	100.0

HISTORY

(a) *Tikar*. As may be seen from the list above, the Tikar are numerically the most important. Nsaw, which constitutes a centralized political unit, has a population of 32,000 and is the largest. It is followed by Kom with 18,000, and Bum with 5,000. The Ndop N.A. has 35,000 but, as indicated earlier, it is a congeries of small chiefdoms which differ in dialect and custom and have, on an average, 1,500 to 4,000 members. The same applies to Bafut and Fungom.

[1] The percentages given in the Table have been worked out on the basis of population figures in the Government Files of 1945. In the Widekum group, Beba and Befang are frequently linked together but should be regarded as two sub-tribes. In Mamfe, there are the Widekum-Menka tribes, which are culturally related to the Widekum of Bamenda and which number about 10,000. There are about 10,500 Tikar settled in the French Cameroons. Since the writing of this report, further figures on the estimated population of the Bamenda Province have been made available in the Colonial Office Report for 1950 p. 236, Table 3. The figure given is 286,200, but as this may well be an underestimate and, as the next census is due in 1952–53, I have made no alterations in the Table above.

3

According to their own traditions, the various groups of Tikar settled in Bamenda came originally from Tibati, Banyo, Kimi and Ndobo—all in what is now the French Cameroons. Material on the history of earlier migrations is lacking, though Mr. Hawkesworth in his *Assessment Report of the Bafut* has made the statement that the Tikar, under a chief called Mbum, migrated originally from Bornu to the territory, which now bears that name near Ngaundere. The French anthropologists incline to the view that the Tikar derived from the Mbum, and that the separation occurred many generations ago at a point somewhere between Ngaundere and Tibati. From there they settled in a vast plain watered by the Mbam River and its tributaries, the Mape and the Kim.[1]

About 300 years ago, increasing Chamba pressure, internal dissension, and a desire for new land resulted in the splitting off of small bands. Some of these were under the leadership of sons of a Tikar ruler, who were later to arrogate to themselves the title of *Fɔn* (Paramount Chief or King).[2] They travelled west and south-west and eventually reached what is now Bamenda, but the sequence of their migrations is confused. Among the earlier were those coming from Ndobo to the Ndop Plain in the south of the Province, where small, politically autonomous villages were constituted some six to ten miles apart. None of these units was sufficiently strong to dominate the others; hostilities over land, murder and enslavement characterized their relations; and even the Fulani and Chamba raids in the last century failed to bring about some semblance of political unity or federation, though from time to time asylum was granted by one village to refugees from another.

Mbaw, Mbem, and Nsungli in the north-east of Bamenda were also the scene of early Tikar migrations from the French Cameroons. Settlements were made below the escarpment in the area formerly known as Ntem; but, at a later date, three main groups, whose descendants were to constitute the sub-tribes of Wiya, Tang and War, went up on to the Nsungli plateau and founded a number of small villages. In each sub-tribe one Village Head claimed the title of *Fɔn* and supremacy over the others; but even before the advent of the Germans his authority had been challenged by some of the component villages intent on asserting their autonomy. From Mbwot (most senior of the War group) a large band split off and travelled south into Nsaw, where some remained to establish the villages of Nkor and Djottin-Vitum and their offshoots—Dom, Din, Mbinon and Lassin.[3] The main body of migrants under the leadership of their *Fɔn* journeyed farther west, subdued earlier settlers, and founded the centralized kingdom of Bum.

Bafut, Nsaw, Kom and Fungom[4] were probably the last of the large scale

---

[1] *Vide*, E. H. Hawkesworth, *The Assessment Report on the Bafut Area of the Bamenda Division*, 1926, para. 15; and I. Dugast, *Inventaire Éthnique du Sud-Cameroun* (Mémoires de l'Institut Français D'Afrique Noire, Centre du Cameroun Série, Populations; No. 1, 1949), p. 129.

Dr. Jeffreys has made a special study of tribal migrations in Bamenda, and it is hoped that his information will soon be made available. I myself did not make intensive inquiries into this subject; but, in the course of discussion with *Afɔn* and Village Heads, I found that some details of migration, which were mentioned in *Reports* written 15 to 20 years previously, had already been forgotten.

[2] As a matter of convenience in this book I have employed the Nsaw term for paramount chief namely, *Fɔn* (pl., *Afɔn*), but there are dialectical variations of it in other Tikar groups.

[3] The *Afɔn* of Djottin-Vitum informed me that their ancestors found earlier settlers on the site of the present village, and that they conquered them. Little is known about the indigenous inhabitants; but, in one of the Government Files, there is a note to the effect that remnants of this population are to be found today in the Fonfukka Valley. The people of Djottin-Vitum speak a dialect called *Nooni*.

[4] In the Fungom N.A. there are five Tikar villages (Fungom, Mme, Nyos, Kuk and Kung) which, like Kom, are matrilineal. The first four may have been originally an offshoot of the Kom.

4

Tikar migrations to Bamenda. The Kom, who are matrilineal, defeated a number of patrilineal groups in the surrounding area (Nchang, Ake, Mejang, Basaw) and made them tributary. The sub-tribes which today constitute the Bafut Native Authority were earlier migrants who passed through the Ndop Plain on the way to their present territory. They comprise Bafut (which claims seniority over the rest), Babanki, Bafreng, Babanki-Tungaw, Bambili, Bambui and Bamenda.

The Nsaw, according to the history given to me by the Fɔn and most of his Councillors, settled first at Kovifem, some 12 miles to the north-west of their present capital of Kimbaw. There they prospered, multiplied and dispersed over the land to the south and south-west. There too they were joined by small bands from other Tikar groups which had settled earlier in what is now known as the Nsungli area, the Ndop Plain and the Bafut N.A. These became voluntary allies, but some of their leaders elected to maintain a semi-independent status as m'tar. They possessed, and still possess, among other privileges a right to retain the skin of leopards; and they were, and still are, under no obligation to give a daughter in marriage to the Fɔn. They became the founders of clans whose members regard themselves as " the true people of Nsaw ", in contradistinction to the people of conquered subtowns of alien origin (see below). Some of the other leaders of groups who were voluntary allies were assimilated into the Fɔn's own clan as distant clansmen or duiy, and they became the founders of important sub-clans. Among these were the ancestors of three high-ranking councillors (vibai), namely Fai-o-Ndzendzef (from the Tang clan in the Nsungli area), Fai-o-Tankum (from Mbaw), and Fai-o-Luun (from Kiluun in the French Cameroons). In the last century, as a result of constant Fulani raids, the reigning Fɔn decided to move his capital to the south. He subdued the Chief of Nkar who, until that time, had held much of the land in the vicinity of Kimbaw and to the south-west. He then defeated a number of villages in the north-west whose founders had come originally from the Nsungli area. These were Djottin-Vitum, Din, Dom, Lassin, Mbinon, Nkor and Nser. By the time the Germans arrived the Fɔn had consolidated his kingdom and established a centralized machinery of government.[1]

(b) *Widekum.* I have classified the eight patrilineal tribes of the west and south-west of Bamenda as Widekum since the majority give the village of Widekum on the Mamfe border as the place from which they migrated to Bamenda many generations ago. Ngie and Esimbi deny such an origin and may represent an earlier stratum of settlement. The former claim a common origin with Meta and Mogamaw, but assert that Widekum split off from Ngie! The Esimbi recognize no affiliations at all with the others; but, apart from differences in dialect, their culture is similar.

The pattern of migration bears a strong resemblance to that in Nsungli, Mbem and Fungom. Small bands established their villages over the tribal territory and became politically and economically autonomous, although they acknowledged descent from a common tribal ancestor whose name is frequently that of the tribe (e.g. Øngiɛkum for Ngie, kum meaning lineage head; and Ungwo for Ngwo). The genealogies of some of the Village Heads in Ngie go back ten to twelve generations, and in Meta eight to ten.[2] One Village Head in each tribe was recognized as senior to the others in that he took the leading

---

[1] For another version of the settlement of Nsaw consult M. D. W. Jeffreys, " Nsaangu's Head," *African Studies*, March 1946, and his article on " Death of a Dialect," *African Studies*, 1945. See also M. D. W. Jeffreys and P. Kaberry, " Nsaw History and Social Categories," *Africa*, XXII, 1952.

[2] The genealogies of the Village Heads of Asarabiri (Ngwo) and Benakemø (Esimbi) are much shorter, being 6 in the one case and 4 in the other.

role in the sacrifices to the tribal ancestor and the gods of the earth;[1] but, according to statements in the Government Reports as well as those made to me by informants, it is now several generations since there has been an assembly of all villages of one tribe for the performance of such rituals. Prior to European control inter-village fighting and slave-raiding were frequent, and the only instance of concerted action in Ngie seems to have been for defence against the aggression of Bali in the last century. It was unsuccessful. Most of the tribes, with the exception of Ngemba and part of Ngwo and Meta, inhabit the forest since an advance to the uplands was checked by the Tikar and Aghem. Bebadji (Beba) was for a long time tributary to Bafut and was influenced by Tikar culture before it finally broke away and moved to its present site. Farther north, villages of Befang and Esimbi were harried by the Aghem and compelled to send drums of oil as tribute. German subjugation of the Widekum forest areas was piece-meal and in some cases was undertaken at the instigation of Bali, from whose suzerainty villages in Meta, Mogamaw and Ngie revolted between 1904 and 1912. Beba-Befang and Esimbi were not visited by the Germans until 1907; villages were burned, and many of the population scattered to form isolated compounds, especially in Esimbi.

(c) *Mbembe*. The term Mbembe has been applied by myself to the group of three tribes, Mbembe, Mfumte and Misaje, which inhabit the rather lowlying forest areas of the north and north-east of Bamenda. With the exception of the two villages of Bebe Ketti and Bebe Jatto, they comprise small patrilineal groups who are of mixed origin and who settled in their present territories about four or five generations ago. The people of Misaje possibly originated from Kentu, but have been influenced by Tikar culture. In Mbembe itself, the first settlers were probably from the Upper Donga and established themselves in Akwadja. They were followed by others from the Wukari Division who were probably Tigong and who crossed the Donga farther to the west and founded the village of Ako, from which, at a later date, small bands migrated to what are now the villages of Mbandi, Akonkaw, Andi, Jevi and so on.[2] Some of the villages in Mfumte, e.g. Lus and Kwaja, claim to have come from Akwadja in Mbembe to their present site; while others again allege that they are Tikar from the French Cameroons.

The villages consist of fairly compact clusters of compounds and, prior to the advent of the Germans, they were frequently on hostile terms with one another. Their political and kinship organization is very similar to that of the Widekum, although linguistically they differ markedly from the other ethnic groups of Bamenda. Their linguistic affiliations to the Mbembe—speaking people of the Cross River have not yet been investigated. They apparently offered little resistance to a German expedition in 1910 which came to collect labourers and taxes; and were left to pursue their own way of life, apart from the suppression of warfare and slavery. During the British regime they have, until recently, been only " lightly administered " owing to lack of communication by motor road and remoteness from administrative head-

---

[1] The most senior Village Head in Ngwo, namely that of Asarabiri and its hamlets of Nkun, Geminggi, etc., maintains a more elaborate court than the Ngie Village Heads. He claims a right to a portion of game killed in his village-area, and to services in housebuilding and the provision of firewood. His authority is, however, limited to his clan and its effective exercise appears to depend on an exceptionally forceful personality rather than on the sanctions of tradition.

[2] *Vide*, R. Newton, *An Intelligence Report on Mbembe and Nchanti Areas of the Bamenda Division of the Cameroons Province*, 1935, paras. 11–17; and 91–97. Mashi and Munkap, in the Fungom N.A., claim to derive from Bebe Jatto and Ketti, but no longer follow matrilineal descent. In Mbembe, the villages of Berabi and Abonkwa claim an origin from Bamum, while Mbiribwa asserts that it came from Ntem (Tikar).

6

quarters. Medical facilities have been non-existent; and the solitary mission school in Mbandi had no pupils at all when I visited the area at the end of 1945. The American Baptist Mission has met with more success in Mfumte.

(d) *Bali* (or *Bani*). The Bali are a patrilineal people who are reputed to be a branch of the Chamba-Leko of Adamawa.[1] Owing to increasing Fulani pressure at the beginning of the last century, they left Koncha under their leader Gawebe and journeyed south to Tibati. From there they proceeded to make war upon the Bamum and eventually entered Bamenda from Bagam. Some were mounted on horseback, and they harried Bafreng, Bande, and Bafut before passing on to what is now Bali-Nyonge, some 16 miles to the west of Bamenda Station.[2]

In 1889 the German explorer, Zintgraff, reached Bamenda from Tinto (Mamfe) and he stayed for four months at Bali-Nyonge, where he was well received by the *Fɔn*, Garega, who was a grandson of Gawebe. He returned again in 1890 with a trading expedition, but the Tikar *Fɔn* of Bafut was hostile and two messengers were killed. The following year a punitive expedition was carried out in which it was alleged about 1,000 Bali took part. A treaty was concluded with the *Fɔn* of Bali by Zintgraff in which the latter was recognized as exercising suzerainty. But, in return, the *Fɔn* was " assured of the establishment, recognition, and protection of his position as paramount chief over the surrounding tribes of the northern hinterland of the Cameroons ". From the neighbouring tribes a regular tribute was raised, part of which was given to Zintgraff for expenditure on administration.[3] In 1901, the Germans set up a military and administrative post at Bamenda Station, and soon after this some of the tributary villages began to refuse allegiance. The Government continued to support Bali however and, when a new *Fɔn* succeeded to office in 1905, his position as paramount chief over 31 villages was confirmed. But charges of oppression were made continuously and after 1909 some of the villages were granted independence.[3] The Bali assisted the Germans in the first World War, but the British gained control in October 1915. Many villages attempted to break away from Bali and were punished; but, by 1920, it was realized that the problem of political relations in Bali required investigation, and an *Assessment Report* was made by Mr. W. E. Hunt (Now Sir William Hunt) in 1925. Bali was an early centre for missionary activity, the Basel Mission making it their headquarters in 1903, although at first they were more successful in securing converts and school pupils in Mbengwi in Meta. The New Testament was translated into Bali and used in other parts of Bamenda where the Mission carried on its work. Today, many of the people in Bali are Christian (Protestant and Roman Catholic); many have received some schooling; and many are prosperous carpenters, tailors and traders. The Bali market is one of the largest in the Province and is attended by men and women from over twelve miles away. Most of the people wear European clothes of some description; a number have built substantial houses of sun-dried mud brick, and have even begun to agitate for a little town-planning!

---

[1] W. E. Hunt, *Assessment Report on the Bali Clan of the Bamenda Division*, 1925, para. 7. Their original language was Mubakaw, but in Bamenda they adopted Mungaka, which is possibly a fusion of Bati and Bamum dialects. The account of their history in Bamenda is taken from the *Report* cited above. For a discussion of the Chamba in the Benue and Adamawa Provinces, see C. K. Meek, *Tribal Studies in Northern Nigeria*, 1931, Vol. 1; and C. L. Temple *Notes on the Tribes, Provinces, Emirates and States of the Northern Provinces of Nigeria*, 1919, pp. 79–80.

[2] *Vide* W. E. Hunt, *op. cit.*, paras 17 and 34. After a number of forays the Bali split up into six sections. Two, Bali-Nyonge and Bali-Gansin, remained in what is now the Bali N. A. Area; the Bali-Bagam and the Bali-Gasho submitted to Bagam; the Bali-Kumbat went to the Ndop Plain; and the Bali-Muti went north to Kentu through Aghem.

[3] *ibid.*, paras. 19–25.

(e) *Aghem.* The Aghem, or the Wum as they were called in some of the Government Reports, claim that their ancestors came from Munshi and that they passed through Esu in Fungom on their way to their present site on the tableland, some 4,000 feet above sea-level. Their principal village is divided into ten large sections under Section-Chiefs (*Batum*), one of whom is regarded as senior to the others. They were all originally matrilineal, but a few genera-tions ago one of the *Batum* quarrelled with a sister's son and instituted patrilineal descent, inheritance and succession in his own section. His example has not been followed by the others and their kinship system resembles that of the matrilineal Tikar villages of Fungom. Prior to the arrival of the Germans the role of the Aghem in the north-west was similar to that of Bali in the south-west. They conquered the neighbouring forest peoples of Befang and Esimbi, but they did not evolve the highly centralized system of government characteristic of Bali, Nsaw, Bum and Kom.

SOCIAL STRUCTURE

POLITICAL ORGANIZATION

Among the Widekum and Mbembe peoples the village, as already men-tioned, was the political unit and the village head had very little executive authority. The political structure of Bali and most of the Tikar chiefdoms is basically similar to that of Nsaw. A paramount chief, with the assistance of councillors, rules the country and, under the traditional system, depended for the enforcement of his orders and justice on one or more secret societies. These societies still exist but no longer act as a police force though they are still feared by non-members. In Nsaw much of the former structure remains intact though stripped of many of its functions and some account of it is given here.

It will be remembered that Nsaw includes a number of villages of alien origin conquered in the last century. These villages became tributary to the Fon-Nsaw but in many ways retained independence in the management of their own affairs. Their chiefs were permitted to keep the title of *Fon*, but succession to office was contingent on ratification by the Fon-Nsaw. In the system of rank the latter is of course paramount. Next to him in precedence is the Fon-Mbiami (a Nsaw sub-chief), followed by the Fon-Nkar and the Fon-Ndzerem (a *Fon* whose ancestor sought sanctuary with Nkar when his people were harried by the Fulani in the last century). Below these are the *Afon* of the conquered villages of the north-west. Each sub-chief has his own set of councillors, court officials and *ŋwirɔŋ* society.[1]

The Fon-Nsaw has his palace in Kimbaw: it comprises his own inner courtyards, dwelling huts, kitchens and stores. In front of this section lies a large courtyard (*Takɔbu*) where the *Fon* hears cases and discusses public affairs with his advisers. Separated from this by small antechambers is a piazza (*mandɔngai*), flanked on one side by the quarters of the *Fon's* wives, and on the other by those of the *ŋwirɔŋ* society, members of which are called *nʃilafsi* and act as personal attendants, messengers and, in the old days, as police.[2] The governing body of this society is called *Ye-ŋwirɔŋ* (literally, Mother of

---

[1] To simplify orthography in this book I have not italicized Nsaw titles when prefixed to proper names —e.g. Fon-Nsaw (*Fɔn* of *Nso*), and Fai-o-Ndzendzef (the *Fai* of *Ndzɔndzɔf*). A very brief account of Nsaw history is given in my article on " Land Tenure Among the Nsaw of the British Cameroons," *Africa*, XX, 1950. See also correspondence between Dr. M. W. Jeffreys and myself in *Africa*, XXII, 1952.

[2] Members of the *ŋwirɔŋ* society are recruited from the first-born sons of court officials (*atanto*) and of all other *nʃilafsi;* and also from the first-born sons of all male and female kin of the *Fon* at six generations' remove.

8

Ngwirong) and is comprised of several high ranking councillors with the *Fɔn* as president. Close relatives of the *Fɔn* are not permitted to join the society, but they have an association of their own—*ŋgiri*—and headquarters at the far end of the piazza.

The management of the palace, the guardianship of the *Fɔn's* wives, and control of food and wine stores are in the hands of court officials, the *Atanto*, whose title means " Fathers of the Palace " and who are all of *n/ilaf* status. They have an important voice in the arrangement of the marriages of the *Fɔn's* daughters and grand-daughters, though they are not allowed to wed such women themselves. Their compounds are in the vicinity of the palace; they are in constant attendance on the *Fɔn*; and, by reason of ease of access to him, wield considerable influence. The *Fɔn's* Councillors proper are, however, the *Vibai* (sing.—*Kibai*), the most senior of whom, Fai-o-Ndzendzef, also assists in the sacrifices carried out annually to the ancestors and to God at Kovifem. The High Priest (*Tawɔŋ*), the High Priestess (*Yewɔŋ*) and the numerous Queen Mothers, (*Aya*; sing.—*Ya*) also assist in the government of the country and the hearing of cases. In rank they come next to the *Fɔn*, but play a less prominent role in secular affairs than the *vibai*.[1] Upon the succession of a *Fɔn* the title of Queen Mother (*Ya*) is conferred upon his mother; or, if she is dead, then upon a ' sister ' or ' daughter ' of the *Fɔn* providing her mother is of *m'tar* status (see p. 5). In addition, there are other women of royal lineage who bear the title of *Ya* in commemoration of the mothers of previous *Afɔn*. They are treated with reverence by all Nsaw people, including men of rank; they have large compounds, servants, and their own raffia and kola plantations.

In the old days the *Fɔn* had his military organization (*mandjɔŋ*) which was divided into two sections—*yam* and *baa*. Most of the villages to the north and north-east of Kimbaw belonged to the *yam*, and those to the south and south-west to *baa*. Each village had its own club house (*laf mandjɔŋ*) under a *Ta-mandjɔŋ* (Father of the *Mandjɔŋ*); adult males automatically became members and met regularly for wine drinking, hunting, and of course gave military service when called upon. Kimbaw itself was divided into two sections, *yam* and *baa*, each having its own club house in the environs of the palace, and its own *ta-mandjɔŋ*, and supreme commander, *nfoomi*. The Society has been shorn of its military functions but it still exists for purposes of recreation, hunting and tax collection!

Local Organization. Bamenda villages may be anything from one to five miles apart and they vary widely in size. The smallest have little more than a few score inhabitants; the largest, including Kimbaw, Aghem, Bali and some of the Ndop village-areas, have over 3,000; while, in the great majority, population ranges from 300 to 800. In the 1947-48 figures for adult taxable males in Nsaw, 47 villages were listed; but it is worth pointing out that 14 of these only became tax-paying units in 1942-1943 and that their population is small by Nsaw standards in that it varies from just under 100 to just over 500. Of the remaining Nsaw villages, there are 15 with a population from 500 to 1,000; 7 with a population from 1,000 to just over 2,000; and, finally, Kimbaw with

---

[1] There are 13 *vibai* who act as Councillors to the Fon-Nsaw. In the case of 4 (Ndzendzef, Tankum, Yuwar, and Luun) the office has been vested in their respective lineages since the settlement at Kovifem; a fifth councillorship (that of Tsinlaa) was created by the *Fɔn* who fled to Tauwvisa from Fulani raids; while those of Ndzendzeftsen, Do-e-Ngven, and Do-e-Run were established when Kimbaw was made the capital. The late *Fɔn* during his long reign, which lasted from 1910 to 1947, appointed 5 others—Tankumkui, Sob, Mbisha, Ngandzen, and Nkavikeng—who are still looked upon as *parvenus*. There are 7 important *Atanto* (sing., *tanto*) who live in Kimbaw and whose lineages have been entrusted with the office for many generations. The late *Fɔn* raised other individuals to this status, but most of them live outside the capital.

9

approximately 4,800.[1] Nsaw occupies an area some 700 square miles in extent and the density is about 40 to the square mile; but, within a radius of some two hours' walking distance from Kimbaw, the density must be well over 100. In this particular region there are 17 villages with a total population of nearly 15,000. The pressure on arable and residential land is considerable and, for many years, there has been a drift to the fertile areas near Kwanso, Shiy, and south of Mbiami.

In most Tikar tribes and in those influenced by them, houses are square structures of wattle and daub surmounted by a pyramidal thatched roof. The usual size is 12 feet square, some being a little more commodious. Immediately under the roof is an attic, which is usually approached through a small aperture in the top of the front or side wall, and which is reserved mainly for the storage of grain and firewood. The traditional style of hut lacks windows, and has a sliding door of raffia poles raised a few inches or a foot above ground-level. A hearth of three or four stones occupies the centre of the floor, while ranged around the walls are beds, and racks for pots, baskets and other utensils. Women and small children have stools of cane, and usually there is a larger and finer one kept hanging on a peg for visitors of rank or importance. At the back of the hut (but sometimes outside) is placed a grindstone; and ranged along the outer walls under the eaves are raffia bins for dried grain, bundles of thatching grass, and heavy firewood. Chickens are kept in coops of wattle and daub, or in cane boxes where available. Failing these shelters, they roost inside with the family at night. In many Tikar villages near the main roads, Africans are beginning to build their huts from sun-dried mud brick,—à practice which results in a great saving of raffia poles. These houses often have windows and doors of plank, are rectangular in shape, and in some cases are lined inside with mats of raffia pith. Christians have displayed most initiative in adopting this style of architecture, but their wives are usually confined to the traditional type of kitchen, where they sleep with their young children and where they are sometimes joined by the head of the household when the weather is particularly inclement. On the highlands nights are often very cold, firewood is scarce, and the crowded though ill-ventilated snugness of the old-style hut is preferred to the spacious and draughty atmosphere of a modern dwelling. In Mbembe and Mfumte, hut-walls are made from layers of clay bound with palmnut fibre; in Ngie most of the huts are round, but have a raffia or timber framework mudded over and surmounted by a roof thatched with palmleaf mats.

In all Bamenda tribes each married woman generally has her own hut which she occupies with her unmarried children. If her husband has no other wives he may for some years possess no special dwelling of his own; but, when circumstances permit, he builds one in order to have space for his belongings and the entertainment of his guests. Adolescent sons may share this with him, but as soon as possible they take over a vacant hut and in any case they will, when they marry, construct one for the bride.

Dwelling and store huts face on to a central courtyard and nearby are small kitchen gardens, plantain groves and sometimes kola trees. The size of a compound varies widely throughout Bamenda: in Mbembe, Mfumte, Nsungli, Bali and Aghem one which has been established for several generations may

---

[1] For tax assessment Kimbaw is divided into the two *mandjɔŋ* sections of *yam* and *baa*, but both are under the immediate surveillance of the *Fɔn*. The figures for population are approximate and are based on those for adult males who pay either the head-tax or income-tax. I have also included Hausa and other strangers such as Bamum, but not the Fulani. There are some 770 Hausa living mainly in Kimbaw, Jajiri, Mbiami and Lassin; and some 800 Bamum in Mbiami, Mbo-Nso, and Kifom. There are a number of small villages beside the 47 mentioned in the text above; but, for payment of tax, they combine with large villages in their vicinity. All told, there must be from 50 to 60 independent villages.

contain anything from 10 to 20 houses; while in Nsaw that of a senior Council-lor such as Fai-o-Ndzendzef has 103 and extends over some 4 acres of ground. But in many tribes, even among the Tikar, compounds are smaller and inhabi-ted by the compound head, his wives, married sons and perhaps younger married brothers. The Ngie kinship group which constitutes a co-residential unit is even more limited in size, since a man, at marriage, normally leaves the parental compound and builds one of his own on land allocated to him by his father. In those Tikar tribes where rank is stressed the apartments of a lineage head are trellised off from the rest of the compound; and the graves of his predecessors, where sacrifices are performed, lie in his small inner courtyard. But in most of the forest tribes even a village head lacks such privacy and his hut may be only a little larger than that of an ordinary villager. A rough plan of some Kimbaw compounds is given in Appendix D.

As a general rule Bamenda villages form fairly compact clusters of compounds, but much depends on the lie of the land and whether the women also have rough shelters on the outlying bush farms, where they live for weeks at a time during the season of heavy work. Where the forest is relatively dense, as in parts of Widekum, compounds are dispersed in small clearings. The system of land tenure will be discussed in detail in a later chapter, but it should be pointed out that it is only rarely that a village is subdivided into territorial units or wards under Ward Headmen appointed at the will of the paramount authority.[1] More commonly, sections of residential land are vested in the heads of lineages and occupied in the main by their male dependants, except in some of the matrilineal groups where the individual may elect to reside with his father, wife's father, or a friend until he inherits the house or compound of a mother's brother or elder brother. Much depends on personal inclination, amicable relations with kin and neighbours, good health, availability of farmland, occupation and, nowadays, propinquity to co-religionists in the case of one who has become a convert to one of the Christian sects or to Islam. For example, out of 33 male householders in the zɔŋafə Section of Aghem, only 6 were living near a mother's brother; 14 were near their father; 4 were with a wife's father; and 9 were with a friend or a stranger. The strength of the tie between a man and his father, the considerable economic independence of a man after marriage, and his right to receive the major part of the marriage payment for his daughters—all these factors operate against the emergence of the matrilineage as a localized unit.

In the patrilineal tribes, on the other hand, the pattern of residence is more uniform. Where compounds are small, the male members and unmarried females of a number of adjacent compounds are related as a rule by agnatic ties and, for certain purposes, come under the authority of one of the compound heads who acts as lineage head. In Nsungli and Nsaw, where compounds are frequently large, some 4 to 10 families may have their huts grouped round a rectangular courtyard. The elementary family emerges as a clearly defined residential, social and economic unit, producing nearly all the food it requires and exercising a certain amount of control over its own affairs. But male members of these families, as well as unmarried females, are related to the compound head by patrilineal ties and may therefore be regarded as consti-tuting the major part of a co-residential patrilineage. The women, who at

---

[1] The Ndop villages of Bamessi and Bamungo are divided into 4 and 6 wards respectively, each ward having its own headman. The Bamessi term for ward head, tientüa, is obviously a dialectical variant of the Lamnso tantee, " Father of the Village." The tientüa settles minor disputes, particularly over compound boundaries, and has a place on the Fɔn's council. The Bali term for ward head is nkɔm and he may have under his supervision at least 9 compounds. In Aghem, a ward is called akɔn, and a ward head, t/o-akɔn. The position of Ward Head in both Bali and Aghem is not hereditary, and the same is true of the office of compound head (mokubɛ) in Aghem.

marriage go to live with their husbands, pay frequent visits, sometimes continuing to work plots on the land of the lineage; and they may, in old age or when widowed or divorced, return to live permanently in the parental compound.

(a) *Nsaw Lineage Organization.* In Nsaw the average size of a lineage is difficult to compute since it may number anything from 20 to 70 members; but frequently a lineage head (*fai* or */e*) had under his direct surveillance from 3 to 10 adult married males who stand in a relationship to him of sons, brothers, brothers' sons, and more rarely father, father's brothers and grandsons. Sometimes a man goes to live in another part of the village or even in a different village. The reasons for changes of residence are various: pressure on building-space, particularly when an individual has more than one wife and many adolescent sons; desire for better farm land; care of distant raffia plantations entrusted to him by the lineage head; ambition to have a compound of his own and to become the founder of what may ultimately be a sub-lineage; prolonged illness, constant misfortune, or quarrels. It should be stressed, however, that even though he builds his compound many miles away a man still remains under the authority of the lineage head and is known merely as a compound-owner, *ngaalaa*, whatever the number of his wives and children.

If a compound in Nsaw prospers and at least two generations have lapsed since its foundation, the title of sub-lineage head, */e*, may, with the consent of the *Fon* and of the *fai* of the parent lineage, be conferred on one of its members. The new */e* then has rights of inheritance to the property (*vitsø*) of the members of his group (*ki/εεr*: *pl*, *vi/εεr*), arranges the marriages of the women; but is expected to make a token gift of firewood each year to the *fai* of the parent lineage as a symbol of subordinate status. After a lapse of four generations, the title of *fai*, indicative of senior status, may be granted;[1] after five generations, marriage is permitted between members of the two lineages.[2] But a man may not select a wife from the lineages of his mother, his mother's mother, and his mother's mother's mother.

When a woman is given away in marriage with the consent of the *fai* of her lineage, she is referred to as a *wiiy o nøøne* (a woman who enters the house) or a *wiiy o foone* (a woman who is given). Her children belong to her husband's lineage; and, when he dies, she is expected to marry the member of his lineage who has been selected by her late husband's *fai*; or at least to remain in the compound, unless she is very old. On the other hand, if she " marries " without the consent of the *fai* of her lineage, she is termed a *wiiy o t/εmin* (translated into Pidgin-English as a woman who is stolen, although Lamnso for stolen is */ɔŋ*). Efforts are made to secure her return; but, failing success, any children whom she bears belong to her own father's lineage. Normally they remain with her until they no longer require her immediate care, that is, until about the age of 6 years. Sometimes they are not claimed until later, but the *fai* of the mother's lineage has the right to arrange the marriages of the girls. If an unmarried girl becomes pregnant, the child belongs to its mother's father's lineage and will address the mother's father by the term for 'father'. An illegitimate child of a married woman (*wiiy o nøøne*) belongs to her legal husband.

---

[1] It should be noted that in the Nsaw lineage organization the genealogical relationships between the founders of the component lineages of clans are rarely known.

[2] The title of */e* is sometimes used as a matter of courtesy for men who have established their own compounds and have one or more married sons living with them. But it is not associated with any rights over kola and raffia plantations, nor with the giving of female dependants in marriage. It may also be applied to married sons of the *Fon*, and to ex-officials of the *ŋwirɔŋ* society. The son of a High Priest may also be granted the title of *fai* and its attendant privileges by the *Fon*.

Nsaw patriclans are dispersed and the number of their component lineages varies widely from three to twenty-two. In the latter case some of the lineages are only three generations in depth, in so far as descent is traced back to the first man who was granted the title of *le* or *fai*; a parent lineage from which others have hived off may be ten generations in depth. In some of the large patriclans there may be two or three *afai* who are almost equal in status, although in matters of etiquette the seniority of one is recognized. In this case each *fai* is the head of a lineage from which several other lineages have stemmed off, and so may be regarded as head of a sub-clan. Social relations tend to be frequent and intimate among members of a sub-clan, though in the absence of geographical propinquity ties may weaken.[1] In theory, the sub-clan head may demand a gift of firewood from the heads of the component lineages; in theory, he has a voice in the selection of their appointment to office; and he would, in any case, be present at their installation. From time to time the lineages assemble for sacrifice (*tati fɛ taŋri ntaŋri*); and, in times of disaster or the death of the clan head, the heads of all component lineages would participate in a joint ritual.

Once a man is appointed a *fai* (or a *le*) his personal name is no longer used except by his superiors in rank.[2] He is a *talaa*, father of the compound, to all its members irrespective of age and generation. He has the right to call on all his dependants for assistance in the clearing and cultivation of his farm (*lu-sum*), and in bridge and house construction. He inherits, with minor exceptions, the raffia and kola trees planted by male members, as well as such types of property as livestock (sheep, goats and fowls), clothes, guns and money. He arranges the marriages of all women of the lineage, with the exception of the first born; he receives the major part of the gifts made by their husbands, and has first claim on their services.[3] He acts as intermediary between the living and the ancestors; and, finally, he settles minor disputes. Despite the spread of Christianity, greater mobility of population, and opportunities for the attainment of a large measure of economic independence in the pursuit of new and relatively lucrative occupations, the authority of a lineage head over his dependants is still considerable. One of the main factors in this is his control of land, but full discussion of the subject must be deferred until a later chapter.

Before we touch on the rights and responsibilities of kinship heads in other Bamenda groups, attention should be drawn to the strength of ties with maternal kin among the Nsaw. There is much visiting among matrikin and joint participation in ceremonies connected with birth, marriage, death, and the various societies. The individual is believed to come under the influence of the ancestors of his or her mother; and, in consultation with a diviner,

---

[1] A Kimbaw man in discussing the closeness of ties between a sub-lineage in Kimbaw and a parent lineage in Memfu said: " If he (a man) goes and sees a thing in Memfu, he then takes and eats (it). If a man from Memfu comes to Ka (i.e. the compound of that name in Kimbaw), he sees something, he then takes and eats it, because it is a thing of that which is one (that is, the sub-clan).

Wu du yɛn kifa e Mmfu (Memfu), *wu nin li a yii. Wir o fɛ Mmfu wi e Ka, wu yɛn kifa, wunin li a yii, bifɛɛ ki dzən kifa ke lo ke mo'ɔn.*

[2] Character and not seniority in age is the main criterion for the office of lineage head in Nsaw. If there are no male members in a lineage, a man may be selected from another lineage in the same clan; or, more rarely, the firstborn son of a woman of the lineage may be appointed, though I was given no actual instance of this. If none of the males has yet reached puberty, a woman of the lineage may be appointed to act temporarily as lineage head until one of the boys has attained adolescent status. I was also told that, in the absence of suitable candidates, the son of an unmarried woman of the lineage might succeed to the office.

[3] When a *fai* dies his widows are inherited by his successor; but if a man who is not a *fai* or a *le*, that is, a *wir o fɛtər*, dies the widows are allocated by the lineage head to male members of the compound, usually to the deceased's brothers.

sacrifices may be offered to them in the event of sickness or misfortune. Again, when a man succeeds to the position of *fai* or *ʃe*, he not only goes ceremonially to the head of his own clan or sub-clan, but also to the head of his mother's lineage, whom he refers to as *tar-yewor* (father of our mother). He takes with him salt, oil, fowls and firewood, the last a symbol of submission. The *tar-yewoʃ* then performs a special sacrifice (*tʃu melu*) and invokes the blessing of the ancestors. On occasion, sacrifices are also offered to the ancestors of the patrilineages of the mother's mother and even of the mother's mother's mother. The officiant priest is always the head of the lineage involved, while the *fai*, on whose behalf the sacrifice is to be performed, presents the fowl, sheep or goat required for the rite.

Finally, a man has rights of usufruct in land belonging to the mother's lineage; he receives assistance from her kin and may be sure of a welcome and hospitality when visiting them.[1] As one youth explained to me: " People of your mother know how to look after you more than those of your father. Perhaps it is because they are going to take a child of a woman from there (that is, a child of a woman of their own lineage) to give away in marriage."[2] This last statement is probably a rationalization, since in most patrilineal tribes of Bamenda ties with maternal kin are very close and, as a rule, friendly. But it serves to draw attention to a custom which distinguishes Nsaw from the rest of the Tikar peoples. A lineage head has the privilege of arranging the marriage of a first-born daughter of any female member of the lineage; he also has a major part of the marriage gifts, and first claim on the services of the husband selected for the girl. In the case of the *Fɔn* and *Vibai*, this privilege is extended to grand-daughters and other descendants, and illustrates the way in which rank influences kinship affiliation in Nsaw.

All descendants of the *Fɔn* down to the fourth generation are referred to in general usage as *wɔnto* or children of the palace, but exact generation level may be indicated by prefixing to this the term for child, *wan*. Thus a great-grand-child would be described as *wanwanwanto*. The *Fɔn* gives away in marriage not only his own daughters and grand-daughters, but also the first-born among his great-grand-daughters and his great-great-grand-daughters. At the fifth generation his descendants are called *duiy*, a word probably derived from the verb, *du*, to go and indicating a more distant relationship.[3] A first-born son of any man or woman, who is at six generations remove from the *Fɔn*, may be taken as a servant (*nʃilaf*), and a first-born daughter as a wife for the *Fɔn*.

All those related to the *Fɔn* by the ties discussed above are referred to as *wiri e Fɔn* and may be regarded as a limited kinship group consisting, firstly, of all agnatic descendants of a *Fɔn*; and, secondly, of all other cognates of a *Fɔn* down to the sixth generation. Often a son or son's son of the *Fɔn* is granted the title of *ʃe* or *fai*, and he may become the founder of a lineage within the *Fɔn's* patriclan or even of a sub-clan, as in the case of the ancestor of the

---

[1] When a youth spears his first game, he takes the animal to his *fai*, who tells him to take it to the *tar-yewɔf* (that is, the father of the mother of the boy). He is instructed to hand over the next game he kills to his own father; and, on a third occasion, to hand game over to the mother's mother's father.

[2] The Lamnso text is: *Wir ye-wɔn a ki mo lei fɛ wo ʃaa vɛ tar-ɔn. ɣansemosi bo dzə bifa a yii li wan o wiiy fo fo bo djuur.*

[3] Among *wir duiy* distinctions may be made on the basis of closeness of relationship to the *Fɔn*. An individual who is at 5 or 6 generations remove from a *Fɔn* may be described as *duiy-nto* (*duiy* of the palace) or *duiy-ʃiŋgwaŋ* (*duiy* of the salt), that is one who in time of need begs salt and other necessaries from the *Fɔn*. One who is more distantly related may be described as *duiy-kikəŋi*, that is *duiy* of the plant emblem of the *Fɔn* which is carried by his messengers. A relative, who has " gone far " and who no longer wishes to recognize a kinship tie with the *Fɔn*, is referred to as *duiy-mɛnkiŋi*, a *duiy* who turned his face away. He is a " strong head (*taf kitu*) " attempting to achieve *m'tar* status.

councillor, Fai-o-Yuwar, who was a son of a *Fɔn* who reigned at Kovifem in the early days of Nsaw settlement. In addition to those lineages which trace direct agnatic descent from a *Fɔn*, there are the sub-clans of three of the senior councillors, Ndzendzef, Tankum and Luun, whose ancestors came from other tribes but who elected to become affiliated to the *Fɔn's* own clan and assumed the status of *wir duiy*.

Some of the other important *vibai* are the heads of *m'tar* clans but, whether they are *duiy* or *m'tar*, *vibai* have privileges similar to those exercised by the *Fɔn* in the matter of marriage. A *kibai* selects husbands not only for his own daughters but also for the first-born among his grand-daughters and great-grand-daughters. He has also the right to inherit the property of a first-born daughter's son and that of the first-born son of any grand-child. At the fifth descending generation he may take a first-born daughter as wife, and a first-born son as a servant (*n/ilaf*).[1]

As may be inferred, Nsaw kinship is complex and I hope to deal with it in greater detail in a later publication; but, before we leave it, attention should again be drawn to the fact that, although the lineage organization is patrilineal and although a wider range of contacts and activities is influenced by patrilineal affiliations, in some situations an individual places particular emphasis on his tie with his mother's patrilineage and acts as a corporate member of it. If he is a son of the *Fɔn*, he frequently goes to reside, after marriage, with his mother's father. If he is related to the *Fɔn* or to a *kibai* through his mother, then he is brought up in his father's compound and regards himself as a member of his father's lineage, having with its others members residential, economic and religious relations. But, in times of hardship or financial emergency, he may beg assistance from the *Fɔn* or the *kibai*, as the case may be; and, if he quarrels with his own *fai*, he may repudiate his patrilineal connections and assert that he is only a *wir duiy* or a *wan kibai*. This fluidity of kinship affiliation is to some extent reflected in linguistic usage where the term *kfɵɵ* has a wide range of meanings and may apply to such groups as the family, kindred, or lineages or clans of the father, mother, father's mother or mother's mother. If an exact distinction is sought it may be qualified in the following ways: *kfɵɵ ye laf*—group of the house, i.e. elementary family; *kfɵɵ ye laa*—group of the compound, i.e. co-resident patrilineage; *kfɵɵ ye ku'un*—great group, usually the clan of the father, but sometimes that of the father's mother or mother, where either is politically and socially more important than the former. In the case of a man descended through his mother's mother from the *Fɔn* or a *kibai*, her lineage may be referred to as *kfɵɵ ye ku'un*; but, where this is not so, the mother's mother's lineage is spoken of as *ram* (a term which is also used for a runner from a plant), and kinship relation is unlikely to be recognized in the succeeding generation except in the case of a *fai* or */e*.

(*b*) *Kinship Organization in other Bamenda Tribes*. In the other patrilineal Tikar tribes (where I had only a brief stay), the kinship system appears to be similar in many respects to that of Nsaw in so far as the lineage head (usually referred to by a term equivalent to Lamnso *Talaa* (Father of the Compound) allocates land and inherits the property of his male dependants, particularly

---

[1] In 1946, I attempted to make a census of the *Fɔn's* wives and counted 84. To this should be added at least another 10 who carried water for his household and whom I did not see. Among the 84 there were 15 who had not reached puberty and who were referred to as *wɔn wiinto* (children of a *Fɔn's* wife). They were being trained to become wives of the *Fɔn*, and their marriage would not be consummated until several years after they had menstruated. Among the adults, whom I personally questioned, 23 were daughters of *n/ilafsi;* 2 were daughters of *atanto* (also of *n/ilaf* status), and 10 were grand-daughters of *duiy*. The remainder had either been given by sub-chiefs or else voluntarily by men of *m'tar* status. Incidentally, only those *wɔnto* (sons of the *Fɔn*) whose mothers are *m'tar* are eligible for the office of *Fɔn*. The same qualification is also necessary for other dignitaries of royal status, such as the High Priest, High Priestess and Queen Mother.

livestock, money and such trees as kola, raffia, mangoes, and oil palm where these are cultivated.[1] In return, however, he is expected to assist them in procuring wives, but it is he who arranges the marriages of all women of the lineage and claims a major share of the marriage payment. In Ndop and Bafut, the *Fɔn* has the right to take a first-born daughter of any family not closely related to his own as a wife.[2] As in Nsaw, a woman is not consulted about the marriage of her daughter, but in Bamessi the consent of the mother's mother is important; she is treated with great respect, and may demand some assistance from her grand-daughter's husband. Again, in this community (as well as in Bangola and Bamungo), when the mother of a lineage head (*tiɛnda*) dies, he appoints either a sister or a daughter to act in her stead as the " great mother ", and to perform minor sacrifices which do not entail the offering of a fowl. Finally, as in all Bamenda tribes, he is the intermediary between his dependants and the lineal ancestors; indeed his function as priest is one of the main sanctions for his secular authority and an important factor in the cohesion of the lineage.

Among the Mbembe, Mfumte, Ngie, Ngwo, Esimbi, and possibly some of the other Widekum peoples, the lineage organization provides the framework of the political structure. Clans tend to be localized and, as a rule, most of the lineages in any one village are segments of the patriclan of the village head. In the Mbembe villages which I visited,—namely, Akonkaw, Mbandi, Jevi, Ako and Akwadja, there were from three to five major patrilineages (*ndu*) named after their founders: e.g. *Ẑafiya* (people of Afiya), *Ẑienka* (people of Nka), and so on. One lineage is senior to the others and its lineage head (*afa*) acts as village head. It is said that patriclans were once exogamous, but nowadays intermarriage is permitted between members of some of the component lineages.[3] Each major lineage has under its control a tract of arable land which is allocated to individuals by the lineage head; in addition it is associated with a locality in the village. Most of the compounds established in such an area are occupied by men and unmarried women who are members of the lineage, though from time to time residence is changed if there has been illness or misfortune. Each compound (*yapɔre*) has its compound head (*ŋwuriku*) who has under his authority his younger brothers and sons. Traditionally he had a claim to their services and earnings; but, in return, was expected to assist them with their marriage payments. However, in the Government Report of 1935, it was stated that the pattern of economic co-operation was being modified;[4] and, when I visited the region in 1945, the evidence I collected indicated a growing desire on the part of the younger men to have full control of such resources as palm bush.

---

[1] Titles, corresponding to the Lamnso term, *talaa*, are *telaa* (Wiya); *tufu* (Bamungo); *tifo* (Bamessing).

[2] Among the Tikar, as well as the Bali, the *Fɔn* has the right to take as a wife a female twin, unless she is closely related to him. Twins are regarded as a blessing from God and the term for them is often " Children of God." It is also noteworthy that in all the Tikar tribes, with the possible exception of Nsungli, Fungom and Mbem, the *Fɔn* has a right to a share of the marriage payment on the first-born among his grand-daughters and, in some cases, the first-born among his great-grand-daughters.

[3] In Akonkaw village I was told that a man might not marry a woman belonging to a major patrilineage of his mother; while in Mbandi the restriction applied only to the minor patrilineage of the mother. In most Mbembe villages there is a lineage called *kepinthɔre* or *kupinsiri*, the head of which has important ritual functions. He was described to me as a " medicine man "; and, to Mr. R. Newton, as one who in times of epidemics or droughts prepared a special " medicine " to sprinkle on the roads leading to the village. Members of *kepinthɔre* may marry individuals belonging to any of the other lineages.
Vide, R. Newton, *An Intelligence Report on Mbembe and Nchanti Areas of the Bamenda Division*, 1935, *paras*. 277–279.

[4] R. Newton, *op. cit.*, para. 225.

16

The lineage organization of Ngie, Ngwo, Esimbi, and probably of the rest of the Widekum group, appears to be basically similar to that of Mbembe. For instance, in the Ngie village of Teze, where I spent a month, most of the people, apart from some women who have married into the village from outside, are members of the patriclan of the founder and are known collectively as " children of *Uføømbøiy*," *buŋə Uføømbøiy*, or sometimes as the " children " of his son, *Andjo'føiy*. There are five major lineages (also named after their founders) which, according to genealogies collected from lineage heads, are only from three to six generations in depth. Obviously some ancestral names have been forgotten; while the names of others are recalled only after a considerable amount of head-scratching, contradiction, and requests for assistance from the Village Head! Fission has occurred in all the lineages, and the head of a minor segment either bears the title of lineage head, *kum*, or is referred to as an " important man of the lineage ", *wva'eku*. The title for village head was originally *kum*; he was *primus inter pares*, and was assisted in the direction of village affairs and the settlement of cases by the heads of other lineages. Nowadays he often calls himself a *Fɔn* in imitation of Tikar chiefs, but he is indeed a *Fɔn fainéant*!

A lineage head acts as mentor to his dependants, performs sacrifices, and has a right to a portion of the larger game caught by them. But he has little in the way of economic privileges, as compared with his Tikar counterpart; and, in matters of marriage, he is consulted but has neither the final voice nor a lien on the marriage payment, though he may be given a sheep or a goat. It is noteworthy that in most of the Widekum group a woman has the right to veto the marriage of her daughter; and a suitor therefore usually makes sure of her consent before he approaches her husband. Marriage may occur within the clan, the exogamous unit being a lineage some three to four generations in depth.

Among the matrilineal groups—Kom, Aghem, and five villages in the Fungom N.A.—the matrilineage is rarely a co-residential unit, since many men elect to reside after marriage with their father, an affine or a friend. The lineage head has ritual and advisory functions; and, among the Kom and Fungom, he usually has a tract of residential and arable land under his control, which he allocates among kin and those strangers who approach him with a request for a plot. He has no rights, in virtue of his office, over the property of members of his lineage.

The term for matrilineage in all three groups is very similar and derives from the word for buttocks and that for house, and may be translated as " buttocks of the house ". As one man explained to me: " all people come out from there!" In Kom it is *sa'əndo* or *sassəndo*; in Aghem, *sɛh'əndugu*; and in Fungom Village, *sassɛndɛ*. In theory, the matriclan is the exogamous unit, but marriages sometimes occur when the parties belong to different lineages in different villages and are unable to trace a genealogical relationship. As a rule, a man in Kom obtains financial assistance from his own father for the marriage payment; but, if this is not forthcoming or if he is a younger son, he seeks the help of a mother's brother.[1] When his own daughter marries, a large part of the marriage payment is handed over to him; another portion is given by the groom to the girl's mother, who in turn divides some of it among her mother, sisters, brothers, and mother's brothers. If a lineage head happens to be own brother or own mother's brother he receives his cut; otherwise he must be content with any gift which the groom makes to him as a matter of expediency and courtesy.

---

[1] In Aghem and Fungom villages a man looks first to his mother's brother or, failing him, to an elder brother for assistance.

Chapter II

ECOLOGY

BAMENDA, or the " Grassfields " of the Cameroons, lies about 280 miles by motor road north of the port of Victoria. It is bounded on the east by the French Cameroons; on the north by the Adamawa Province; on the north-west by the Benue Province; and on the West by the Mamfe Division. It lies between 9°45 and 11°10′ east longitude and 5°40′ and 7° north latitude, and is some 6,932 square miles in area. Its dominant geographical feature is the high grassy plateau which sweeps from the north-east and east over the centre of the Province at an average height of 4,500 feet above sea-level. Above this again hills and ranges rise another 1,000 to 2,500 feet to culminate in Mount Oku at 7,000.

Except for the forest clad slopes of Mount Oku, there is very little timber on the plateau, though at one time it probably fell within the belt of high forest. Local methods of cultivation and the annual burning of vast tracts of country have gradually denuded the region of most of its trees. Green hills trace a clear line against the skies; but, in the shallow valleys and on the rising ground, the landscape presents an aspect of alternating woodland and meadow. Compact villages are overshadowed by groves of tall dark kola trees; along the streams are plantations of raffia; and beyond the compounds, with their red walled huts and grey thatch, lie strips of cultivated ground which impose their small regular patterns on hill-top and slope.

In the north the plateau drops precipitously into the lowlying forests of Mbembe which slope down to the Donga River—the northern boundary of Bamenda. In the north-west it descends more gradually into the orchard bush of Fungom; while in the west and south-west it again plunges into hill-forest, where the Ngie build their compounds in small clearings in the steep valleys, or perch them precariously on narrow ledges of rock on the sheer slopes.[1] A description given of travelling in parts of New Guinea might be aptly applied to ones progress through Ngie and Beba in the wet season, for it is indeed a matter of " up on one's hands and knees, and down on one's backside!"

The southern escarpment at Nsaw and Oku rises sharply from the Ndop Plain—a relatively lowlying area with an average elevation of some 3,000 feet above sea-level. This region of Bamenda is sparsely covered with small timber and scattered oil palm, and is punctuated by massive outcrops of basalt and granite. Under another name the plain might be regarded as extending west across the Province to Batibo, but it is broken by the Babanki Pass—a spur which runs out from Mount Oku to link the central tableland with the high grasslands which lie behind Bamenda Station and stretch south into the French Cameroons. Bamenda Station—the administrative headquarters—is situated on the edge of the escarpment of this more southern range and, to the traveller returning from trek in the outlying parts of the Province it seems a miniature metropolis with its cluster of European houses, its old German fort (now functioning as a district office), its hospital, school, post office, police station and cemetery! At the foot of the hill sprawls Abakpwa—a mixed

---

[1] At Ngwo on the western boundary there is a tract of grassy upland at some 5,000 feet above sea-level. In the east of the Province, Mbem and Mbaw lie below the escarpment.

community of Hausa and members of surrounding tribes. Here the Roman Catholic and American Baptist Missions have their headquarters, while close to the African market a U.A.C. caters for the material needs of the populace. All roads converge on Bamenda Station: from Santa in the south on the international boundary, 12 miles away; from Mamfe, 90 miles to the west; from Bafut and Njinikom in the north; and from the east one which passes through Nsungli and Nsaw and which will eventually encircle the whole Province.[1] According to the last report (1950) this ring road (130 miles) is almost completed.

The Province is well-watered: streams in the east—the Nun and the Mbam—flow into the Sanaga River in the French Cameroons; the Donga, Katsina Ala and Metchem flow west to join the Benue in Nigeria; while the Ma and the Momo flow into tributaries of the Cross River in Mamfe. The rainfall varies between some 65 inches in Nsaw and 124 inches in Kom.[2] The wet season begins about the end of March and finishes early in November, the heaviest precipitation occurring between August and mid-October. From December until March the harmattan from the north envelops the country in a dim red haze of dust. As might be expected, temperatures vary considerably. On the Grassfields it rarely rises above 84° F. in the shade in the hottest time of the year; while during the rains it often drops to 65° F. during the day and much lower at night,[3] when one is glad to huddle over log fire or brazier, and sleep beneath four blankets. Mists drive down the valleys; gales carry away branches and beat down groves of plantain; and houses are frequently struck by lightning. In the lowlying forest areas and on the plains one is reminded that Bamenda is, after all, only some 6° north of the Equator. Afternoon temperatures soar to 92° F. in the shade; nights encourage mosquitoes and other insects, but bring little respite to human inhabitants of the region.

Bamenda has frequently been cited as one of the most fertile areas of West Africa and certainly one that offers great potentialities for development. In the low forest belt, which fringes the north and west of the plateau, oil palm flourishes; on the uplands there is not only excellent pasture, but also a soil and climate favourable to the production of coffee, pyrethrum, linseed and quinine, not to mention local subsistence crops.[4] No survey has yet been made of the Province, but the following figures, though only approximate, convey some idea of the variation in natural resources. It has been estimated that out of a total area of just under 7,000 square miles, there are some 3,000 square miles of arable land (including hill-grazing); some 1,432 square miles of pasture (not devoted to agriculture); and some 2,500 square miles of forest.[5] Existing forest reserves totalled only 508.5 square miles in 1948, or 7% of the Province. Until a survey has been made, figures are apt to be misleading; but the area under cultivation has been placed at some 220 square miles.

---

[1] Until the end of 1945 the main road east of Bamenda Station terminated at Ndu in Nsungli; but since that date it has gradually been extended north and, by the middle of 1948, had reached Misaje. It will pass through Bum and link up with a road which is under construction north of Bafut at Befang. In 1948 there were some 220 miles of motorable road in the Province, as compared with 165 in 1945. The great majority of Bamenda villages can only be approached by native footpaths.

[2] Between the years 1944 and 1948, the annual rainfall at Bamenda Station ranged from 87.35 inches to 115.13 inches; and at Banso (Kimbaw, in Nsaw) from 63.09 to 78.13 inches. *Vide, Report on the Cameroons under United Kingdom Trusteeship,* 1948, p. 151.

[3] At Bamenda Station in 1945, the minimum mean air temperature was 48.7° F. and the maximum 81.2° F. *Vide, op. cit.*

[4] A sugar-crusher has been installed at Ndop, and sugar cane is bought from the surrounding area. Cakes of brown sugar were sold at about 5d. a lb. in 1948.

[5] *Report on the Cameroons, op. cit.,* p. 78.

In general, much the same range of food stuffs is grown throughout Bamenda, —namely, cereals, tubers, plantains, pulses, gourds, greens and sugar cane; but there is some variation in their importance in particular areas. Maize (*Zea Mays*) is grown everywhere and is one of the preferred foods except in Ngie, where cocoyams and plantains take its place as staples. Guinea corn (*Sorghum Vulgare*) was at one time cultivated in large quantities in most tribes except those to the west, but its production has fallen off in late years owing to the difficulty of enlisting the help of small children to scare away the birds which ravage the crop. Bulrush millet (*Pennisetum Typhoideum ?*) is confined to Mbembe; while finger millet (*Eleusine Corocana*) is grown only in Nsaw and a few villages in Nsungli.

Almost equal in importance to maize as a staple is cocoyam (*Colocasia Antiquorum*) which is harvested during most of the year and planted at any time during the rains. Yams (*Dioscorea Dumetorum*) and the native white carrot called *rizga* in Hausa (*Coleus Dazo*) are a sustaining contribution to the food supply from October to February; while sweet potatoes (*Ipomoea Batatas*) eke out slender resources in January and again before the harvest of corn in August, since they are planted twice a year in some tribes. Irish potatoes were introduced during the German regime and of late years their production has increased in all tribes, with the exception of the forest areas and the remote north-west. Cassava (*Manihot Utilissima*) is also of recent adoption and, though it does not rank high in terms of native food preference, it is valued because it is easy to cultivate, is resistant to locusts, and a standby when farm and larder would otherwise yield nothing.

Next in importance are the various pulses,—dwarf, lima and sword beans, pigeon and cow peas, the leaves of the latter being used as an alternative to other relishes such as native spinach (*Solanum Nodiflorum*), okra (*Hibiscus Esculentus*), and *egusi* (*Lagenaria Vulgaris*). Groundnuts (*Arachis Hypogea*) and bambarra nuts (*Voandzeia Subterranea*) flourish chiefly in the lowlying areas such as Ndop and Mbem. Where available in sufficient quantity they may form part of the relish; but more often they serve as sweets for the children *and* adults. The Hausa express groundnut oil in small quantities, but it is expensive and rarely within the means of the local inhabitants. In addition to these crops, there are plantains, bananas, avocado pears, mangoes, sugar cane, pumpkins and peppers. Within the last few years a number of Africans have begun to grow oranges, grapefruit, guavas, pawpaws, soya beans, cabbages, tomatoes and pineapples; while in Kom and the Metchem Valley brown rice has done particularly well and finds a market among road labourers and Europeans. Of increasing importance as cash crops are castor seed and coffee (mainly the Arabica variety), some 14 tons of the latter being exported in 1947,[1] while in 1950 two co-operative societies marketed 18 tons.

The list is by no means exhaustive, but the diversity of the foodstuffs already mentioned gives some idea of the economic potentialities of the Province, though it should not be taken to imply that the present standard of living is a relatively high one. A number of factors operate to keep production at subsistence level and even below it in certain cases. Not all parts of Bamenda are equally fertile and this factor, linked with losses caused by depredation of pests, birds, wild animals and sometimes cattle; inadequate methods of cultivation and storage; and, finally, soil depletion result in a period of seasonal scarcity in many tribes. Fortunately, some villages have a small surplus of grain—in particular Ndop, Mbaw, Misaje, and also Bamum in the French Cameroons, and this is disposed of in the large markets along the motor road

---

[1] *Vide, Annual Report, Bambui*, 1947.

or just off it. Methods of agriculture and standards of nutrition will be discussed later. Here we are mainly concerned with the general distribution of resources and its bearing on the development of trade and the division of labour between the sexes.

In this respect, the short period of scarcity in foodstuffs accounts for but a small proportion of the total volume of trade which is such a feature of Bamenda economy. Much more important is the dependence of some 70% of the population of the uplands and plains on the people of the forests for a supply of palm oil.[1] Palm oil is a most valuable nutritional element in the diet and is used everywhere as a sauce or relish for porridge and boiled tubers which are of stodgy consistency, and require considerable lubrication for their passage down the throat. The oil is produced, as a rule, by men of the forest tribes and is bought up by middlemen from the surrounding areas, who then retail it, usually in small quantities ($\frac{1}{4}$ or $\frac{1}{2}$ pint), in the central markets. The uplands and plains people, on their side, derive much of their cash income from the sale of kolas (which grow well in Nsaw, Nsungli, Oku and Bali), livestock, honey, tobacco, and various tools and utensils.

MEAT

As in other parts of Africa, the diet is deficient in first class animal protein. The forest areas are better off for game and fish especially in the dry season. On the uplands and plains a little game and fish is sold in the markets at certain seasons, but for the great majority these are luxuries. A few bush rats transform an ordinary repast into a banquet! Nowadays, the Fulani occasionally sell what I should judge to be their more decrepit beasts to local butchers, who retail them at a considerable profit. But their main customers are those in the higher income group, and the average householder thinks twice before he spares threepence or sixpence for a few ounces of offal or poor beef. Though fowls, sheep, goats, and pigs are reared, they are killed as a rule only for sacrifices, ceremonies, house-building, or to honour a special visitor.

HANDICRAFTS

Finally, the environment provides materials for housing, utensils, furniture, tools, weapons and ornaments. On the uplands and plains, the houses have a framework of light poles which are obtained from raffia palm midribs. There is only a small trade in this commodity among neighbouring villages, and the great majority of men depend on gifts from relatives and friends though it may take them two years to accumulate a sufficient number to build a house.[2] A man may cut thatching grass anywhere, but if he requires extra bundles he buys from someone who has a surplus to dispose of. Raffia, besides providing poles, is also tapped for wine; but here again the sale is limited as a rule to the village of production or to neighbouring villages. In the forest areas, where there is little raffia, oil palm is tapped for wine.

Deposits of clay are worked in Bamessi, Bali, Mbembe, Mfumte, Misaje, Mbem, Meta, Esimbi, Munkap and Fungom villages. With the exception of Mbem and Munkap, pottery is a woman's craft, while pipe making is in the hands of the men. In the forest villages a woman makes what she requires for the house, keeping a few extra ones which she will barter for small necessaries

---

[1] The most important centres for oil production are Misaje, Mbembe, Mfumte, Bafut, Mogamaw, Ngie, Meta, Esimbi and some of the Fungom villages near the Katsina Ala River. A little oil palm grows in Lassin, Ndop, and Bali, but in the latter area oil is not manufactured. The method of expressing oil is described later.

[2] One informant who had just built a house estimated that he had used 500 raffia poles for the walls and about 150 for ceiling and roof. A house built of sun-dried mud bricks thus represents a saving of some 500 poles.

in cases of emergency. In Meta and especially in Bamessi, nearly all women fashion large quantities of pots in the dry season, disposing of some in the home market. Pots sold outside the village are carried and retailed by the men. Blacksmithing is a male craft and, like pottery, is confined to certain villages, the most important being Bamungo, Oku, Mbembe, Mfumte, and some of the Fungom villages of the north-west. Nowadays, smiths smelt down scrap iron instead of ore for their knives, spearheads, matchets and hoes. Other specialist occupations are the manufacture of caps, bags, baskets, mats, umbrellas, stools, hoe-handles, wooden food receptacles, mortars, fishing nets, and so on,—some tribes having a reputation for finer work than others and exporting a large quantity of their goods over the adjacent region.

The amount of cloth woven is negligible and poor in quality. Hand-woven Hausa cloth from Northern Nigeria is imported and worn by boys and men as a loose loin covering; but most women are content, or have to be content, with a small strip of cloth or beaten bark for a pubic covering; while in other areas a string fringe or a bunch of leaves suffices. Nowadays, many of the men buy European cloth, singlets, shorts and overcoats; while the wrap or dress has become of the badge of Christian womanhood. Finally, there are ornaments of which camwood is of the most traditional importance. It is pounded up by the women and smeared over the skin for festive occasions. Beads and coils of wire (for necklaces) are prized by the women of some tribes, and the more sophisticated flaunt disused cartridge cases in their pierced ear-lobes; or buttons or screws in their lower lip.[1]

TRADE

We have already surveyed in brief the nature and distribution of natural resources and types of production. For their role in developing trade the main points may be summarized here. Agriculture is carried on at subsistence level by the vast majority of inhabitants and, apart from very small quantities of grain brought in from Bamum and Maidaguri, Bamenda may be regarded as self-sufficient in foodstuffs. Within Bamenda, however, most of the tribes of the uplands face a period of scarcity from April to the end of July; while others, who live in the plains, notably Ndop, are able to plant maize twice and may have a small surplus. But it should be emphasized that there is no deliberate cultivation of additional plots with the object of disposing of the crops in the markets.[2] Most families consume all that they produce and a small surplus is in the nature of a windfall. In a good year a Bamessi woman may be able to hand over to her husband 30 to 70 lbs. of maize to sell, or perhaps the same quantity of groundnuts. The following year she may have at most only a few pounds; or may even have to buy a little extra food for the family.

Most of the petty trade in foodstuffs is in the hands of the women. The quantities involved are small and bring in only a few pence. Most women do not trade regularly, but only when they need the cash for the purchase of a pot, basket, hoe-handle or seed. Those who depend on trade for all household necessaries buy maize, cassava or beans, cook them in various ways or make flour, and retail the product at a small profit. Men who traffic in maize or groundnuts buy up small quantities from a number of individuals until they have accumulated one or more bags (20 to 60 lbs.), which they sell

---

[1] In Aderi, some of the women only had a pubic covering of plantain leaves. In Nsaw, wives of the *Fon* and Councillors wear no covering at all.

[2] In a recent verbal communication from the Senior Agriculture Officer I learnt that, within the last year or so, a few returned soldiers have settled in Ndop and are cultivating maize for export to the plantations in the south.

in the large markets of Kimbaw, Bamessing, Bali and Bamenda Station.[1] A more recent development is for traders to take Irish potatoes and cabbages to the coast.

For other items of diet—game, beef, fish, sheep, goats, pigs and fowls, condiments, oil, tobacco, kolas, beer and wine—Bamenda is self-supporting, though nowadays most people prefer European salt to the locally-made potash.[2] But, as noted earlier, oil palm has a very limited distribution with the result that some 70% of the population are dependent on middlemen for their supply of oil. Moreover, while purchases of food are made only occasionally, most householders buy a little oil every week or fortnight. Again, groundnuts and tobacco only thrive in certain villages, so that the purchase of small quantities of these—the one a sweetmeat for children, the other a solace for adults—is a recurrent item in most family budgets.

Bamenda, regarded as a unit, possesses all the materials it requires for housing, tools, utensils and furniture. But many of these things are manufactured by specialists in certain tribes or sometimes only in certain villages in a tribe. Bamessi pots are exported as far north as Nsungli and west to Bali: Bamessing pipes are smoked in Ngie; and women of Mfumte wield hoes made in Oku. The main imports (excluding European articles) from outside Bamenda are camwood (from Mamfe forests); a little tobacco from the French Cameroons and Nigeria; *kamwa* or rock salt from Nigeria; and, especially important, Hausa cloth, some of which is sold by Hausa traders, but much by local Africans who make journeys to Adamawa and Northern Nigeria, taking with them oil or kolas. A more recent development is the enterprise shown by some men in purchasing a few head of cattle from the Fulani and driving them to Nigeria.

Finally, there is the general trade in European articles—cloth, kerosene, soap, salt, lamps, matches, thread, needles, ornaments, buckets, and a wide range of miscellaneous goods. Some of these are obtained from the U.A.C. at Abakpwa and Mamfe, but most come from Calabar. Besides the traffic in kola, oil, livestock, potatoes and cabbages across the Provincial borders, there is also the export of coffee, castor seed and palm kernels.[3]

In nearly all branches of trade, the people of the uplands and plains display particular initiative, a fact which is linked possibly with more intensive culture contact and their accessibility to the main motor roads; but also, to a great extent, with a lower degree of economic self-sufficiency as compared with the peoples of the forest. The latter, on their side, are usually self-supporting for foodstuffs, oil, supplies of fish and game. Many of the tribes have no markets at all; in others only one or two villages have small markets where a limited range of articles is disposed of. Attempts to establish markets in such villages as Kamini (Misaje), Jevi (Mbembe), and Fungom have met with no success. It is significant, however, that Ngie forms a notable exception in having a

---

[1] On the 28th May, 1946, I made a rough count of the number of female and male traders in the Kimbaw market. There were 228 adult women and 160 adolescent and small girls— total 388 (exclusive of 15 Fulani women). In the main market place there were about 1,375 male traders (exclusive of some 50 Hausa). The largest number of those dealing in any one commodity were 138 for shelled groundnuts, 119 for bags of corn, 110 for palm oil, and 93 for kolas. There were 305 engaged in general trade.

[2] In Nsaw there has been, for many years, a law forbidding the keeping of pigs, but an exception has been made in the case of a mixed farmer and one or two other individuals, who have built styes. It is mainly men of the central and western groups who breed pigs, more especially in Meta, Ngie, Esimbi, and Aghem. In Ngie pigs are kept in stone-pens, and fed on cocoyam and the waste from the oil pits.

[3] In 1947 some 575 tons of palm kernels were exported from Bamenda, and some 120 tons of castor seed. Rice is disposed of locally and consumed mainly by strangers from Nigeria and by Europeans.

BI

market attended by large numbers of people, particularly women. In this tribe food is often scarce, handicrafts are poor, and such things as pots, pipes and iron tools must be obtained from outside. Elsewhere in the forest, most household necessaries are obtained by the women through private barter with friends and neighbours; and only rarely by competitive barter in a market. The men, as a group, are reluctant to venture far afield, though two or three days' journey would enable them to sell their fowls or oil at a much larger profit. There is still very little desire for European goods; and, in fact, were it not for the need to accumulate goods for marriage payments it is doubtful whether they would bother to produce as large a surplus of oil as they do now, despite the keen demand for it in the rest of Bamenda.

MARRIAGE PAYMENTS

And this brings us to the custom of marriage payment and its importance for the development of trade. Its bearing on the status of women and rights to custody of children will be discussed in a later article. Here I wish to emphasize its function in stimulating production. Too often it has been condemned as a custom which imposes a heavy burden on the enterprising young man who wishes to secure a wife and set up a household and family of his own. The handing over of large numbers of livestock, which may be used again by the recipient as a marriage payment on his new wives or those of his dependants, has frequently been regarded as a profitless and perpetual exchange of goods which might otherwise be directed to improving the standard of living of the donors. It is true that in some tribes the payment is exceptionally high; that everywhere is has increased over the last 15 years; and that isolated individuals have difficulty in obtaining a wife. But, if the subject is viewed in broad economic terms, it would seem that, so far from cramping individual initiative, it is on the contrary often one of the main incentives to economic activity on the part of men, always bearing in mind that it is the women who carry out most of the agriculture and thus contribute to the subsistence of the household. To accumulate the necessary goods or cash a man must either act as middleman or else produce articles which he can sell. Even when he has obtained one wife, he will probably cast his eye about for another since prestige depends to a great extent on the possession of a large compound filled with wives and children. In this respect it is significant that those who enjoy a regular wage as mission or government employees or who follow a lucrative trade such as butchering, once they have built a better style of house and acquired a few European clothes and other articles, are tempted to secure more wives, even though they may be Christians. But even when men are content with one wife, they must often assist their younger brothers and especially their sons to secure brides.

A regular marriage payment is customary in all the Bamenda tribes with the exception of Nsaw, where a series of gifts and services is made to the wife's kin throughout her lifetime and even after her death if she has borne children. The cash value of the articles handed over elsewhere varies considerably from some £5 or £6 in Bamessi and Esimbi, to £10 or £15 in most other tribes. In Ngie it is much higher and constitutes a serious problem. Usually it is reckoned in one unit of value—goats, " shovels ", the so-called " Bikom " cloth, or drums of oil. But while the greater part of the marriage payment consists of a certain quantity of one of these things, the balance is made up of salt, cloth, daneguns, iron rings, fowls, cowries, pigs, sheep, goats, cash and even—as recorded in one matrimonial case—" ladies' underwear "! Besides these items, there are also the subsidiary gifts of meat, oil, and salt made at the request of female relatives and junior kinsmen of the bride. Sometimes there are two categories of payment (a) the marriage payment proper; and (b) the small marriage payment or what is known as " expenses " in Pidgin-English.

In other tribes again, there is (c) a third category of gifts made specifically to the bride's mother who distributes a portion among her own brothers and sisters. As a rule it is only the value of the gifts in the first category which is refunded in divorce.[1]

Nowadays in such areas as Bali, Ndop, Bafut and Meta, marriage payment is frequently made in cash and only a small balance in oil, livestock, salt, and so forth. Regular wage-earners or relatively wealthy traders are spoken of as " gentlemen of the town " and, in keeping with their status, are expected to disburse more. In Bamungo (Ndop), for example, I was told that an " ordinary man " would pay about £6, a " gentleman " about £10! In Nsaw, where a series of gifts of no set value is handed over during many years of marriage, increasing demands for cash and cloth are made on men in the higher income bracket. They may be sought after as prospective sons-in-law, as illustrated by one case which I have in mind. The man concerned is an ex-servant of the *Fɔn* and, in the old days, would probably have possessed two wives at most. He is, however, a successful butcher and has acquired fourteen. He is a pagan, and does not provide them with clothes; but his expenditure on salt and oil, as well as grain in times of scarcity, is a by-word in the village and gives him the stamp of the ideal husband in the eyes of many Nsaw women and their parents. Some of the younger men are becoming disgruntled by the importunacy of their affines, and many are beginning to keep a record of gifts and services with a view to producing it as evidence in the event of divorce. One man whom I knew was taught to write by an African schoolmaster, and the first use to which he put his new accomplishment was to make such a list. His wife had left him a few months previously and he had decided to divorce her.

The time taken to accumulate the marriage payment varies, much depending on the age at which betrothal takes place, the number of sisters for whom marriage payment has been obtained, the energy of the fiancé as producer and trader and, finally, the resources of the group of male kin who assist him. As I have mentioned earlier, the majority of oil-producers in the forest are content to wait the arrival of middlemen from adjoining tribes on the uplands and plains such as Aghem, Nsungli and Bali. With his earnings from oil, a Ngie or Esimbi man buys livestock (sheep, goats or pigs) which he either keeps for breeding or hands over immediately to his fiancée's relatives. In Mfumte, where specially wrought shovels are the main article of marriage payment, a man may buy these direct from a smith; or else he may collect scrap iron and take it to the latter who smiths it into shovels for a small fee. As a rule, a few articles (goats, sheep, or fowls, or small quantities of oil or cash) are handed over from time to time over a period of several years. In some cases the payment is not completed until the birth of the first child. Those who immediately benefit from the transaction are the father and senior male kin of the bride; but, more important for our discussion here, is the resulting expansion of trade.

This may be more fully realized if we consider a man's annual commitments apart from the accumulation of marriage payment. An Esimbi man, for example, probably spends no more than 3s. or 4s. on tools and utensils; some 5s. on cloth; and another 10s. for miscellaneous expenses, including a head tax of 4s. All told, the cash outlay is in the vicinity of some 20s. to 25s. per annum for a man with a wife and child. An estimate of income is difficult

---

[1] In the old days, marriage exchange was practised widely throughout the Province. Sometimes slaves were given in exchange for wives, or a female slave might be bought and retained as a wife.

It should be mentioned here that in all tribes there are preliminary gifts before and immediately after betrothal which take the form of palmwine, camwood, firewood, meat, and so forth. In nearly all areas men are expected to do some work at housebuilding, farm clearing and harvest for their wives' relatives.

to compute since the last assessment was made in 1932; but, on the basis of this and comparative data from other oil-producing tribes of Bamenda as well as my own material, it seems likely that from 30 to 40 gallons of oil are produced in a year.[1] Of this, about 10 gallons would be consumed by the household, leaving some 20 to 30 gallons for sale at 2s. to 3s. 6d. a gallon according to the season.   In short, it yields an income between £2.10.0 and £3.10.0 This may be supplemented by occasional sales of fowls and baskets.   It should be noted here that on the uplands, where oil costs from twopence to fourpence a cigarette-cup (about a ¼ pint) most households can only afford this quantity a week; whereas, in Esimbi, a woman may use 3 pints a week, and in Ngie about 1½ to 2 pints.   Besides the heavier consumption of oil in a forest household a certain proportion is used by the women to barter for necessaries—a little tobacco, salt, and extra food.

The income from oil may be pitifully small; nevertheless it is in excess of a man's needs, as traditionally conceived, and provides the small surplus which may be set aside as a contribution to marriage payment for another wife for himself or for a younger brother or adolescent son.   Without the incentive to accumulate wealth for this purpose both before and after marriage, the temptation for the average male to sink back into a state of bibulous lethargy would, I think, prove overwhelming, particularly in view of the fact that the women provide most of the food and, as yet, there is little demand for European articles.   In fact, the ideal existence, as sketched by the Chinese poet, Wang Chi, in the seventh century A.D., would strike a responsive chord in the breast of the Esimbi or Ngie man:

> " 'Tell me now, what should a man want
> But to sit alone, sipping his cup of wine ? '
> I should like to have visitors come and discuss philosophy
> And not to have the tax-collector coming to collect taxes;
> My three sons married into good families
> And my five daughters wedded to steady husbands.
> Then I could jog through a happy five-score years
> And, at the end, need no Paradise."

As it is, the Ngie or Esimbi man contrives to spend a good deal of time over his cup of palmwine, cracking kernels in the village-shelter, recounting the erstwhile glories of his tribe, bemoaning the tribulations of the present—in particular, the payment of tax, the disrespect shown by the younger generation, and the increasing stubbornness of womenfolk.   Of course, in time, the demand for European articles such as clothes, tools, utensils and furniture, will intensify as it has done on the uplands and plains near the main roads; but, for the present, the majority are content with what they can earn by local trade. Very few think it worth while to headload palm kernels into the U.A.C.; and very few take their oil and fowls to the big markets, a few days' journey distant.   Even some of the returned soldiers, whom I met in Ngie and Esimbi, showed the same lack of enterprise.   Having used much of their savings to procure a bride at inflation rates, they seemed content to sit back, crack kernels, drink wine and wait for something to turn up.

DIVISION OF LABOUR

In the preceding discussion I have endeavoured to indicate the general distribution of resources, types of production, the need to accumulate marriage payment, and the bearing of all these factors on the development of trade. It should be already clear that it is primarily the men who require a cash income, for in Bamenda the women do not traditionally wear cloth, and their

---

[1] Oil becomes scarce from about August to November, when heavy rains make it difficult to climb the slippery trees.

needs do not extend beyond the provision of farm tools, house utensils, a few ornaments, and the occasional supplementing of food-supplies. In the forest areas, men purchase the more expensive items such as hoes, leaving the women to obtain the other necessaries by bartering a little oil, pots, baskets, or food, as the case may be. On the uplands and plains, many men also assume responsibility for these, as well as providing the more costly items. Consonant with the financial commitments of the men is the general tendency for them to concern themselves with those crafts, or with the management and control of those resources, which yield a cash income. Notable exceptions are firstly, pottery (except in Mbem and Munkap) which is in the hands of the women; and, secondly, the expression of palm oil in Ngie and to some extent also in Mogamaw. But, even in these regions, any surplus over and above what is required for household needs and petty barter is disposed of by the men and the profits retained by them. Moreover an important supplement to income in Ngie is the breeding of fowls, a task to which the men devote considerable time, carrying the birds in small coops to the farms where the women turn up insects and grubs as they hoe.

Likewise, the lucrative trade is the hands of the men. Women may sell small quantities of foodstuffs, pots, or baskets in their own village; but there are obviously difficulties and disadvantages in the married women leaving their homes and children to carry heavy headloads of pots, kerosene tins of oil, bags of grain, and crates of kola nuts to other villages, and even to Adamawa or the French Cameroons. I am of course referring chiefly to the uplands and plains. In the forest areas, where most men are reluctant to undertake long trading journeys, the present division of labour whereby the women carry out most of the farming is less consistent with the pattern of economic needs. But, outside the forest belt, there is some validity in the argument of the men that if they were to do more farming they would not have the time to earn money for the household, as well as to perform the heavy and strenuous tasks such as housebuilding, hunting, clearing of high bush, cutting of thatching grass and big firewood. This is not to deny that the men have more leisure than the women, in the sense that they work less consistently; but it is doubtful whether any additional assistance they might give to the women in their slack periods would make an appreciable difference to the size of farm yields, granted present methods of cultivation.

I stress this point since the European observer, confronted by the spectacle of women bending over their hoes through the day while a number of men may be seen lounging in the compounds, are apt to regard the division of labour as not only inequitable but as an exploitation of the female sex. Such an attitude, however, fails to take into account the contribution made by the men in the heavier tasks, more especially in the dry season; and, secondly, the onus on them to earn money for household necessaries. Often this latter responsibility entails the making of long trading journeys,[1] and it is only within the last few years that new avenues have opened for earning a steady income— tailoring, bricklaying, carpentry, coffee-growing, as well as increased opportunities for employment in public works. In addition to their main occupation, most men do a small trade in various articles as opportunity offers,—thatching grass, firewood, honey, tobacco, game, plantains and fowls. It is worth noting here that, while the women are responsible for most crops, many men look after plantains and tobacco. When the women perform this task they usually

---

[1] In 1933 in Nsaw, it was estimated that of 2,339 men dealing in kolas some 75 per cent made journeys to distant markets, the remaining 25 per cent confining their buying and selling to local markets. *Vide*, W. M. Bridges, *Banso Re-Assessment Report*, 1934, *para*. 197. The division of labour is discussed more fully in Ch. VI. Some comparative figures on the men engaged in other occupations are given in Appendix B.

have the right to any small profits which may accrue. The existing division of labour will, however, require more detailed treatment in terms of particular problems affecting the status, position and welfare of women. But, for the present, I have avoided as far as possible making any judgments as to whether the lot of the women is a hard one. Instead I have concentrated on attempting to relate the existing division of labour to ecological conditions; on placing it, in short, within an economic framework. Such a background will, I trust, provide the perspective for the detailed analysis of agriculture which is to follow. But, before we consider methods of cultivation, labour, leisure, farm yields, and general standard of living, it will be necessary to discuss the system of land tenure. I make no apologies for describing it in detail, for it is basic to the agricultural economy in which the women perform so important a role.

Chapter III

LAND TENURE

AN upland landscape in Bamenda has something of the intimacy and enchantment of parts of the English countryside: hills rise to skies soft and luminous with white cloud in April and May; the young grass is a vivid green after the rains of March; while here and there on the slopes, a darker note is struck where a small grove of kola trees marks the site of a long abandoned compound. Along the valleys there are lush plots of cocoyam, maize and sugar cane which thrive in black alluvial earth; while on the hill sides the soil has oxidized after burning and turned to vermilion, brick-red or tawny orange. The small raised beds give a quilted appearance to the fields, which are separated from one another by deep trenches or slender lines of acacia and other saplings. The colours have a simplicity and clarity of tone that is not often seen in the Tropics.

The sense of an ordered existence which is patterned in the farms on the hill sides and valleys is also present in the villages, with their neat rectangular compounds and groves of plantain and kola. The impression is of long, undisturbed, and secure settlement which contrasts sharply with that given by villages in the forest of Ngie and farther west into Mamfe. Here, away from the main motor roads, small patches of cultivation are almost lost in the tangle of undergrowth, while compounds are isolated in little clearings walled with oil palm. Even in Mbembe, where compounds cluster compactly on narrow ridges, the village seems to maintain but an insecure foothold: to be precariously islanded amid the forests which sweep up to within a few yards of the huts and the struggling paths, which lead down to the water supply.

Yet whether in the forest, plain, or on the high upland, the principles of determining residence and cultivation of land vary but little. The woman, who has worked on her plot during the day, returns to her hut to prepare some of the food she has harvested and to store the rest. But often a group of women who have been cultivating adjacent plots come home to the same compound or to adjoining compounds. In other words, there is a close relation between, on the one hand, the fragmentation of arable land into small plots; and, on the other, the subdivision of the village into large compounds or groups of small compounds.

In an earlier chapter a brief outline of local organization was given and the structure of the village was analysed in terms of its component kinship units. We saw, first of all, that in the patrilineal tribes the nucleus of a large compound, or sometimes of a group of small compounds, consisted of men and unmarried women who belonged to a patrilineage; and, secondly, that in most tribes, with the exception of Mbembe and some in the Widekum group, lineages of different clans to live together in a village. They are under the political authority of a Village Head, who is usually the descendant of the first settler or of the most senior man of a small band of first settlers in the locality. Where the village is the largest autonomous political unit, he may exercise a titular claim to all land within the village boundaries, but the implications of this are political rather than economic. The right to reside in a village and cultivate its land is contingent on obedience to the Village Head and conformity to custom. Strangers who wish to settle must, therefore, obtain permission from him and, if he consents, he will either allocate them vacant plots or direct them to one of the lineage heads. Where villages are knit together into a centralized political system as in Bum, Kom, Nsaw and Bali, it is the *Fɔn* who asserts a titular claim to all land in his territory. But it should be stressed that, for an understanding of the functioning of land tenure, titular ownership is of subsidiary importance compared with the *de facto* control exercised by the heads of kinship groups within any one village. The residuary rights of the paramount authority find expression, as a rule, only in certain circumstances, as for instance when a lineage dies out. Unless political obligations have been flagrantly disregarded, any attempt on the part of a titular owner to reclaim land held for generations by a particular lineage would provoke bitter resentment and opposition, and would be regarded as a breach of moral right and, indeed, of custom. It is under modern conditions that such a contingency is likely to occur when, for example, there is any question of demarcating grazing grounds for Fulani cattle, or of leasing land to a mission or to the Government for a dispensary, a demonstration plot, school, and so on. On the whole, the populace recognizes the value of such " good works "; but if only the paramount authority has been consulted, as has occurred in one or two instances, then the general attitude is that the rights of the *de facto* occupier have been infringed.

TYPES OF LAND TENURE

My information is most detailed for Nsaw; elsewhere, my visits were of short duration but, from inquiries which I made and from data in the Government Reports, it would seem highly probable that the great majority of tribes in Bamenda possess a system of land tenure which closely resembles that of Nsaw.[1] *De facto* control over land is exercised by the heads of lineages or extended families and, in some cases, this is also extended to oil palm, raffia and kola trees planted by male dependants. A deviation from this system is found among a few of the Widekum tribes, of which Ngie may be regarded as typical. There, *de facto* control is vested in married males, but the lineage head would appear to have residuary rights in the event of landholder dying without male issue or brothers to inherit. Finally, there is a small group which includes Ngwo (Widekum) and some of the Fungom villages where residential land is vested in family heads, but arable land is allocated among lineage heads by the Village Head. Aghem is somewhat anomalous in that it is the Section Head (*Batum*) who allots arable land to those residing in his section.

NSAW LAND TENURE

We have already described how the Nsaw first settled in Kovifem and its vicinity and how, as their numbers increased, they dispersed over the territory to the south and south-west, where they either found unoccupied land or else earlier settlers from other tribes, from whom they " begged " allotments for compounds and farms. Shisong (two miles from Kimbaw, and now the headquarters of the Roman Catholic Mission in Nsaw) and the land to the south and south-west of it were held by the Fon-Nkar, but much of the land in Kimbaw was claimed by early Nsaw migrants, notably *Do*, *Kilam*, *Kiyɛɛr* and, later, *Santo* and *Tsɔnkinkar*. When, after a large-scale attack by the Fulani some 5 generations ago the reigning *Fɔn* decided to shift his capital to Kimbaw, he chose for the site of his palace land which, until then, had been held by

---

[1] *Vide*, C. W. Rowling (Acting Commissioner of Lands, Nigeria), *A Study of Land Tenure in the Cameroons Province* (mimeographed report), 1948, p. 11, *parq*. 24. Much of Mr. Rowling's material is based on Government Intelligence and Assessment Reports, as well as court records of disputes. But, in the section dealing with Bamenda, some of the material from my own field reports has been incorporated. For a short account of Land Tenure among the Nsaw of the British Cameroons, see my article in *Africa*, vol. XX, No. 4, 1950.

Fai-o-Kilam, who was reputed to have been a ' son ' of the *Fɔn* and a black-smith.[1] The *Fɔn's* followers—*Vibai*, *Atanto*, and other lineage heads—approached the first settlers and were given tracts in Kimbaw and on the surrounding hill tops. Among the most important of the big landowners was Fai-o-Do of the large *m'tar* clan (*Vɛ-Do*)[2], who at the time had rights over the area now known as Veka' akwi and much of the valley extending north-east towards Ketiwum and Kishi. His descendant, who now lives at Ketiwum, still has *de facto* over a small section of Veka'akwi and a strip on the north side of the main road. The site of his predecessor's compound in Kimbaw is marked by an abandoned grindstone which cannot be removed without the *fai's* permission, but the land is farmed by a daughter of the *Fɔn*.

After the *Fɔn* had conquered Nkar, Ndzerem, and the villages of Nsungli extraction in the north-west and west, he became the overlord of all Nsaw territory; those of his people who, until that time, had enjoyed considerable independence, notably the Fon-Mbiami, were left in possession of their land but held it subject to his over-riding authority. In the past he had the right to dispossess any rebellious or criminal man, and to resume control of any area already allocated to a lineage head should he require it for purposes of his own or for some project of value to the country. In practice this was rarely if ever done; but, under modern conditions, the existence of the residuary rights of the *Fɔn* is evident whenever there arises the question of demarcating grazing ground for Fulani cattle or of leasing land to a Mission or the Govern-ment. He is under a moral obligation to consult the owners, to obtain their consent, and to secure some compensation for them if they stand to lose financially; but, in the last resort, his authority to carry through the transaction is not disputed by the bulk of his people. In general, however, it may be said that the *Fɔn's* claim to the overlordship of Nsaw lands is a titular one, and represents the territorial aspect of his political power. Residence in Nsaw is conditional upon submission to the *Fɔn* and adherence to the laws of his country. For this reason strangers from other tribes who wish to settle must first obtain his permission before they formally approach some lineage head with a request for a house-site and farm plots.[3]

The *Fɔn* also has certain areas reserved for his own needs: the site of the palace, which has already been described, and a water-supply near by, which may only be approached by deputed servants and wives; a hill slope on the other side of the valley where thatching grass for his huts is cut; hunting grounds at Mbokum; and, finally, several plots of arable land near Kimbaw amounting to some 22 acres, which are cultivated in rotation by his wives.[4] The best of the grain is removed to his storehouses for his personal use. His wives have separate farms of their own elsewhere, some on land belonging to the lineages of their parents, some demarcated for them by various *afai*. In addition, there are also tracts near the villages of Bamgam and Waasi (near

---

[1] When the *Fɔn* took over his land, Fai-o-Kilam moved to another part of Kimbaw; but he and his successors were restless individuals, and they later went to Vekovi and then to Melim. He was described to me by one *fai* as " a man who walked with his house in his hand." Fai-o-Santo and Fai-o-Tsenkinkar were also ' sons ' of the *Fɔn*; while *Kiyøør* belonged to the *m'tar* clan of *Mbitiɛ*.

[2] In Lamnso, when reference is made to a particular clan or lineage as a unit, the particle —*vɛ*—is prefixed to the proper name, and may be translated as " people " or " those of "; e.g. *Vɛ-Do*, people of *Do*; *Vɛ-Djɛm*, people of *Djɛm*.

[3] An exception is made in the case of people from Oku which, although it now forms part of the Ndop N.A., is a sub-tribe of Nsaw. Oku people are referred to as ' brothers ' and are free to settle without asking permission of the *Fɔn-Nsaw*.

[4] The land in Kimbaw, vested specifically in the *Fɔn*, is small compared with that held by some of the *afai*; but it was explained to me that the first *Fɔn* to live in Kimbaw had a smaller compound and fewer wives than his successors.

Jajiri) which, although vested specifically in the *Fɔn*, may be regarded as common land in so far as anyone who is unable to obtain sufficient land from kin or friends, is free to cultivate, without asking permission or paying a pepper-corn rent of a basket of grain at harvest. Apart from these areas, the rest of Nsaw territory is divided, subject to the ultimate authority of the *Fɔn*, among lineage heads some of whom, the sub-chiefs, the more important *vibai*, and village heads, enjoy an exceptional position in terms of the large tracts which they control.[1] But it should be stressed that the Village Head, by virtue of his office, has no titular claim to all the land within his village boundaries. He is the *Fɔn's* delegate and, as such, he is responsible for the maintenance of order, the transmission of the *Fɔn's* commands and the hearing of minor disputes, including those over land. But, where a case is not settled to the satisfaction of both parties, there is always the right of appeal to the Council of the *Fɔn* or, nowadays, the Native Court. However, in addition to being *Tantee* (Father of the Village), he is also a lineage head and it is by virtue of this position that he administers and allocates among his dependants certain tracts of land in the village and its vicinity, to which his ancestors laid claim in the past and which have been retained for the use of the lineage.[2]

Although the pattern of existing tenure is intricate the principles determining it are simple enough. In most cases a *fai's* land does not form one continuous tract. This is partly due to historical circumstances, partly to methods of cultivation. Sometimes a *fai* moved to another village where he acquired new land without in any way invalidating his rights to land he already held in the ancestral settlement. Again, when the number of dependants of a *fai* increased, he might find that he required more farm land, particularly if provision were to be made for fallowing. But it sometimes happened that blocks adjacent to his own had already been allocated by himself or his predecessor to other settlers, and he had therefore to search farther afield. Moreover, the Nsaw grow a variety of crops which require different types of soil and different elevations; finger millet and *rizga* do best on the dry hill tops, while maize and cocoyam thrive in the moist rich soil of the valleys. It is only rarely that a single original holding includes both types of land. I know of only one example in Kimbaw, that of Fai-o-Djem, whose compound is built on the outskirts of the village and who owns the adjacent land, which extends east up the valley as well as on to the surrounding hill tops. There is sufficient land for all his dependants and only one of these, for particular reasons, has borrowed a plot from a stranger. He is a Christian with a large family of four sons and four daughters. About four years ago he noticed that crops growing near Kingomen (4 miles to the east) were particularly fine and, as there was plenty of uncultivated land nearby, he asked the owner to lend him a plot for guinea corn and finger millet. He told me that he was bearing in mind the needs of his sons in the future. After marriage they would of course have rights to plots on the land of their own lineage; but the amount of good soil is limited and the Kingomen land may well prove a welcome

---

[1] Fai-o-Ndzendzef has large tracts of arable land in Kimbaw, Mba', and Shup which amount to some 7.7 acres. He has others at Mbam (north of Kimbaw) where his ancestor first settled when he came from Nsungli to join the reigning *Fɔn* at Kovifem. The original compound has long since disappeared; but the farm land is in the charge of the *fai's* delegate who is known as the *Ta-Ngvɔn* (Father of the Land) and who grants permission to those wishing to cultivate. A gift of grain is made to him at harvest and stored until required by Ndzendzef in the event of a shortage in Kimbaw.

[2] Character and not seniority in age is the main criterion for eligibility to any position of authority in Nsaw, though usually a married man has a better claim than one who is single. In the choice of a *Tantee*, an office vested in the lineage of the first settlers, the opinion of members of the lineage is given particular weight; but, in addition, that of senior lineage heads in the village would also be taken into account, and in any case the *Fɔn* must ratify their decision.

32

addition unless, in the meantime, the landholder decides to reclaim it for his own group. However, as I have already pointed out, the position of Fai-o-Djem is exceptional. The wives of men who have recently settled in Kimbaw (including those of a newly appointed *kibai*)[1] must beg land from strangers, or else obtain plots from the heads of their lineages who may live several miles away in other villages.

Usually the transfer of a tract of land from one *fai* to another involved also the transfer of the privilege and duty of performing sacrifices to the god of the earth (*nyooiy*) at a stone altar, either near the compound or in an outlying field; but, in some cases, the original holder continued to carry them out himself. Opinions varied on the subject of whether there was one god or many. Some people said there was only one god (*nyooiy*) and his blessing might be invoked on specific localities by the performance of sacrifices at local altars. Others suggested there were many gods and pointed to the existence of a plural for the term for god (*anyooiy*); but they were in agreement that one of the gods, though unnamed like the rest, was supreme. This god created the first human beings and is associated with the earth (*nsaiy*) and its fertility. Reference is made to him in such phrases as " God knows (*ki nyooiy*) "; or " God forbids (*ʃɛm nyooiy*) "; or " a thing of God (*kifa ke nyooiy*) "; or in the term for twins who are called " children of God (*wɔn nyooiy*) ".

Once a year, at the end of December when the *Fɔn* has given permission to his people to harvest their finger millet, he makes the journey along the route, which once linked Kovifem with the royal raffia plantations at Mba', south of Kimbaw. Minor rituals are carried out at altars along the path, which has been cleared in preparation by the women beforehand. But it is at Kovifem that the *Fɔn*, with the *Yewɔŋ*, *Tawɔŋ* and Ndzendzef, performs the major sacrifice to his ancestors and to *nyooiy* to ensure the fertility of all Nsaw land and Nsaw women.[2] He is accompanied by many of his followers, and usually takes the opportunity to visit the more northern villages where there is feasting and rejoicing in his honour. The tie between *nyooiy*, the earth, and the people who live on and cultivate the earth, is a close one and is expressed in moral and ritual terms. The rituals carried out at Kovifem, and in other localities in Nsaw by lineage heads who have *de facto* control of tracts of land, are an expression of dependence on the supernatural, of gratitude for a plentiful harvest, and also of peace among the people. This last is important since, without it, the efficacy of the rituals may be endangered. Quarrels affect the growth of the crops; and therefore harmonious relations with the source of the earth's fertility, *nyooiy*, may only be restored by a settlement of the dispute and atonement by sacrifice.[3]

No land may be pledged or sold in Nsaw, though the same does not apply to raffia and kola trees. But it should be noted that ownership, that is *de facto*

---

[1] The *Yelaa* of a *kibai*, who had decided to reside in Kimbaw, had to go far afield. She had some plots 6 miles away in Tabessob, her father's village; and other plots, " begged " from strangers, at Kingomen and Meluf.

[2] Unfortunately, I did not see this ritual as it would have involved my being absent from Kimbaw during the period when the women were harvesting millet. But, on several occasions, I was present when lineage heads offered sacrifices to *nyooiy* after the harvest of millet, or just prior to it in the case of one *kibai*. Incidentally, one way of discovering the original owner of an area is to inquire who formerly sacrificed for the land (*tʃu ngvɔn*). But the answer may require checking since a *fai* is sometimes reluctant to admit that his ancestor " begged " (*lɔn*) the land from someone else. This is partly a matter of prestige; but also partly due, under present unsettled conditions, to the fear that he may be deprived of it.

[3] In some cases, an outburst of bitter quarrelling in a compound may be attributed by the diviner to the fact that *nyooiy* requires a sacrifice. One *kibai*, whom I knew, was having trouble with bickering among his wives, and called upon the former landholder to perform the rite. Peace was restored!

control by *afai*, is not contingent upon cultivation. There are some areas in Nsaw which have never been farmed; and others which have only been brought under the hoe within the last twenty years or, in some cases, even more recently, although they have been vested in certain lineages for five or more generations. This principle must be clearly distinguished from that which determines the individual's right to *usufruct* of a *particular* plot allocated to him or her by a lineage head. Here, quite apart from the observance of rules and the fulfilment of kinship obligations, rights are dependent on continuous cultivation, allowing of course for periods of fallow. But, as long as a person requires the plot, it is left to him or to her to determine the period of grass fallow. Should he or she leave the village and not return to cultivate the plot, and should it be required by another person of the lineage, then the *fai* resumes control and re-allocates it. This brings us to the subject of individual rights of usufruct and, in particular, those of the women.

At first glance the system of land tenure may seem inflexible and one likely to operate in a manner adverse to the interests of the women in that, although they do all the farming, they have no legal control over the plots of land which they require for their various crops. Certain questions automatically arise: does the system involve preferential treatment for one sex, class, or age group in the community, or does it confer rights of usufruct upon all women by virtue of their kinship, affinal, local and political ties? Again, once farm plots have been allocated, what security of tenure do the women possess; what freedom do they enjoy in lending sections to others; and what voice have they in determining who shall take over a plot, once they have decided to abandon it permanently? The answers to many of these questions hinge on a knowledge of the Nsaw kinship system; but an analysis of land utilization and control throws in its turn, considerable light on the balance achieved between the power of the *Fɔn* on the one hand and the rights of lineage heads on the other; on the status of members of the lineage (including women) *vis-à-vis* the lineage head; on the factors making for cohesion within the lineage and on those which are productive of tension and fission. Here, we are attempting primarily to isolate the economic functions of kinship groups and their bearing on the position of women, but two points should be borne in mind: firstly, a change in the present system of land tenure by, for example, a re-allocation of arable areas among lineage heads, or by the introduction of individual ownership, would have consequences extending beyond the sphere of economics. It would, in short, entail a profound modification, dislocation, and perhaps even destruction of existing political, religious and kinship obligations. Secondly, an attempt to establish a sharp dichotomy between the rights of the women and those of the men is, in some respects, an artificial process and one contrary, in general, to Nsaw attitudes, though a statement which I shall quote in a moment might appear to give the lie to this. But, on the whole, it is consonant with Nsaw values to investigate rights to land in terms of an individual's status *qua* membership of particular kinship groups, and not *qua* sex. Let us probe more deeply into the nature of ownership of land by *afai*, the rights and responsibilities by which, in the last resort, it must be defined as a functioning system.

THE CONCEPT OF OWNERSHIP

I am going to quote four statements which were made to me at different times. At first sight they appear to be contradictory, but they were accurate within the contexts in which they occurred; and, moreover, they may be reconciled if the concept of ownership is analysed at all levels. They are as follows:

(a) " Men own the land; women own the crops." (*Vilum kɛr ngvən; viki kɛr vifa ve yi.*)

34

(b) "A woman only owns a farm; she does not own the earth (land); a lineage head owns the land. A lineage head, he alone owns the land; a 'son' (or a 'daughter') of the compound does not own the land." (*Wiiy kɛr adzə sum tʃatʃa; bo wu yo kɛr nsaiy (ngvən); ngvən kɛr fai. Fai, win mo'ɔn, kɛr ngvən; wan o laa la yo kɛr ngvən).

(c) "Farms, kola trees and raffia ought not to be given away, because these are things of the lineage." (. . . . . *bifɛɛ vəni dzə vifa ve kføø*.)

(d) "A lineage head only has the power to give a new place (one not already allocated) to a stranger. A place, which people are cultivating, he ought not to give to a stranger." (*Wu kɛr vitavi adzə wu fo kirə ke fii'ki e wir o sən. Adzə kirə ke wiri si lime la wu yo adzə fo e wir o sən.*)

The first statement—" men own the land; women own the crops ", or in a variant form such as " women cannot inherit land; only men own the land "— was made to me on a number of occasions, not only in Nsaw, but also in other parts of Bamenda. One particular instance will serve to underline the distinction which the men had in mind. In 1945, a land dispute came up for review in the Native Court and the putative plaintiff was a woman who was acting on behalf of her sick father, a *fai*. She won the case, but soon afterwards it was bruited round the village that the Reviewing Officer had not understood that she was only acting as her father's representative, and he had assumed that she was the *de facto* owner of the plot in question. Various friends of mine were disturbed lest it should serve as a precedent; and they pointed out that, if her son were astute, he might be tempted to claim the land on the score that it has been recognized in Court as his mother's. But, it was asserted emphatically, women do not own land; they only control the crops. It is true, as we shall see later, that a woman sometimes lends a friend a small section, but this is a personal arrangement between the two women and has no validity in a court. For example, if a woman called A. has a large plot she may give her friend B. permission to cultivate a section of it. If, at a later date, another woman called C. begins to encroach on B.'s plot, B. cannot take the matter to the council since she only received rights of usufruct from A., who has no legal authority. The procedure followed in such a case would be for A. to make the trespass known to her husband (or to her own father if the plot is on the land of his lineage) who would then order C. to go away. Should this fail, A.'s husband would report the matter to the *fai* who allocated the land in the first instance. If the case were taken to court, the *fai* might be plaintiff against C., or else A.'s husband would appear as plaintiff and call on the *fai* as his witness.

But, in the statement quoted above, the main distinction drawn is between spheres of influence. All women manage their crops; and all women, by virtue of their sex, are ineligible for the office of *fai* or *ʃe* in which control is vested.[1] But although all men are eligible for such an office, only a few attain it. And this brings us to the second statement; " a woman only owns the farm; she does not own the land. A *fai* owns the land; a 'son' or 'daughter' of the compound does not own the land." Here it is necessary to define more precisely the meaning of the terms *sum*, *ngvən*, and *nsaiy*. *Sum* is a farm plot; *nsaiy* is the earth or soil; and *ngvən* is land, but more especially arable land and is used, for example, in the phrase *tʃu ngvən*—to sacrifice for the land and ensure its fertility. The verb, *kɛr*, has a number of cognate meanings—to hold, have, own, or manage; and the connotation depends on the context. In the

[1] In the case of a lineage having no *adult* or adolescent males to succeed to the position of *fai* or *ʃe*, a woman is sometimes appointed by the head of the clan or sub-clan to act as trustee, until one of the boys comes of age and can assume responsibility. For example, in a sub-lineage of Yuwar in Mbam, a woman has been chosen for this role by Fai-o-Yuwar, the sub-clan head resident in Kimbaw. She is a titular *ʃe*, performs sacrifices, and administers the family property, including land, kolas, and raffia.

statement quoted above—*wiiy kɛr sum* (woman has the farm)—there is no implication of absolute control, but rather of management of a farm plot while it is in her hands. Neither she nor a male dependant of the lineage has, ultimately, any legal claim to its disposal. It is the fai (or /e) who administers the property of the lineage; that is, he makes the original allocation of plots among members of his lineage and among his sisters' children, and also among more distant relatives, affines, friends or strangers who approach him with a request for land. Whatever temporary arrangements the beneficiaries may make about the use of their plots the *fai* has, in the event of a dispute, the over-riding voice; and, moreover, he retains the privilege of reclaiming allotments. I should say the legal privilege since, as we shall see, he is under a moral obligation to exercise this only in certain circumstances.

And this brings us to a consideration of the obverse aspect of his authority—his responsibilities. Although it is left to a *fai* to decide whether distant kin, affines, friends or strangers should be granted plots, he should do so only when it does not prejudice the interests of his dependants, or deprive them of land which is necessary for their subsistence. Secondly, he should look to the future and safeguard his patrimony for the next generation. For example, kola trees and raffia plantations may be sold or pledged, but male dependants should be consulted; and it is done only in cases of necessity and never on a large scale.[1] Kola and raffia are "things of the lineage"; they are its capital or, as one man put it, "the source of salt and oil", the means by which money is obtained to buy necessaries. Though a *fai* reaps the major profit from the sales of the produce (nuts, wine, poles), he is expected to assist his dependants in times of emergency. But land, while it is in a different category in so far as it cannot be pawned or sold, should also be husbanded and care should be taken that, when it is lent to non-lineage members, it is reclaimed after a certain lapse of time. For it is recognized that there is a tendency for land which is cultivated for many years by an affine or stranger to become permanently alienated. This danger is particularly obvious in the case of certain beneficiaries such as the wives and daughters of the *Fɔn* and of *vibai*, and there are usages designed to circumvent such a possibility.

In the first place, most important lineage heads (but not *atanto*) are given a daughter or grand-daughter of the *Fɔn* (*wanto* or *wanwanto*) as a wife. This woman cultivates a number of farm plots, but there is always one special area, perhaps 1½ acres in extent, which is reserved specifically for her use by the *fai* and which is called the *sum-wanto*. However, when she dies her daughters (who come under the authority of the *Fɔn*) are not permitted to go on farming it, though they have rights of usufruct to the other plots of their dead mother, the *wanto*. Two reasons are given for this custom: in the first place, a *fai* is usually given another *wanto* as a wife, who then takes over the *sum-wanto*; but, secondly, even if this does not happen for some years, there is the danger that if daughters of the deceased woman worked the *sum-wanto* the land might eventually pass into the hands of the *Fɔn*.

A similar attitude underlies the custom whereby, in a *m'tar* lineage, the woman appointed to be *Yelaa* (Mother of the Compound) should never be the daughter of a *kibai* or the *Fɔn*, since it is feared that her senior kinsman may be able to secure a hold on *m'tar* property, in this case arable land. Likewise, in *m'tar* lineages, it is only in exceptional cases that a man whose mother is a close relative of the *Fɔn* or a *kibai* succeeds to the office of lineage head, since both these personages have certain rights of inheritance in the property of cognatic

---

[1] I was told by one man that nowadays, when a *fai* or a /e decides to abandon a compound, he may try to sell the kola trees. Such an action provokes disapproval and is regarded as selfish (*kingan*), since he should leave the trees for his brothers and sons if he does not want to look after them.

descendants. In the appointment of a *fai* or a */e*, the members of the lineage, and sometimes the head of a senior branch, have the deciding voice; but the *Fɔn*, through his delegates, is able to influence the decision and, in some cases, he may exert pressure to secure the election of a man related to himself through maternal ties. When this happens, the head of the *m'tar* lineage concerned is said to have " scorched his head " (*fh/wi kitu kfə*), since the affairs of the lineage come within the orbit of the *Fɔn's* influence by virtue of the kinship tie. I heard of several cases, but for one of these there was some justification and I shall describe it here, since it throws considerable light on the lineage system and the rights of *m'tar* vis-à-vis the *Fɔn*.

Many years ago, a Christian was designated to be */e* of a *m'tar* sub-lineage but he refused on religious grounds, since he would not be able to perform the sacrifices for the compound. A pagan was appointed but, after a time, he ran away and left the compound without anyone in immediate authority, though the sub-clan head, who lived in a distant village, occasionally visited and collected the kola nuts from the trees belonging to the sub-lineage. The men left behind in the compound were Christians, with the exception of one youth who, through his mother, was a relative of the *Fɔn*. In 1947 he was selected to be */e* by the *Fɔn's* delegates. Some people said that, in view of the history of past appointments, there was no alternative short of taking a man from another lineage of the same sub-clan. And one man pointed out that the new */e* was at fourth generation remove from the *Fɔn* and was, therefore, more likely to come under the influence of his mother's father who was, in fact, a *fai*. But the head of another lineage of the clan, to which the */e* belonged, was more critical. He admitted that the head of the sub-clan did not bother to look after the people of the compound, and the *Fɔn* had therefore taken a ' son ' of his own and put him on the stool. But, he asserted, " it is not correct (*bo ki yo dzə titi*) ", and he went on to explain why. " When they take a *wir duiy* (to be *fai* or */e* in a *m'tar* lineage), he then earns things only to give them to the *Fɔn's* side (group). All his people (dependants) will then turn back, as if they were of the *Fɔn's* lineage. Those men all enter the *ŋgiri* society.[1] If they catch a leopard, they cannot keep the hide and the head in their compound. They bring it, and give it only to the *Fɔn*. (*A li wir duiy wu nɛna a kɛŋ vifa a fo adzə Fɔn mbüf. Wir adzəm lo nɛna binkir adzə dji kføø Fɔn. Wir e /o'i a wi ŋgiri laa adzəm. Awinni ko baa adzə la yo dzə lɛm djuf wina kitu kfə e awinni laa. Awinni wi /o fo adzə Fɔn*).

The usages which I have described above not only illustrate the jealousy with which *m'tar* lineages seek to preserve their status, but they also make clear the validity of the sharp distinction drawn between the titular ownership of land by the *Fɔn* on the one hand, and the *de facto* control by *afai* on the other.

Among those who frequently request the loan of a plot from a *fai* are the wives of the *Fɔn* (*vikinto*). Refusal is difficult in view of their rank; and, moreover, if the land is not for the moment required by his dependants a *fai* is able to do a favour and perhaps gain a friendship which may be of use later. But sometimes an ambitious man does so at the cost of evicting a non-relative who has farmed a plot for many years and whose household may temporarily suffer some hardship until she can find another. Such an action is likely to provoke disparaging comments even among his own kin, who feel that a moral principle is at stake although their own interests may not be immediately affected. Criticism becomes more acute when a *fai* grants to a wife of the *Fɔn* particularly fertile plots which might well have been offered to women of his compound. One case will illustrate the issues involved.

---

[1] The *ŋgiri* society has its quarters (*laa*) near the palace, and its membership is drawn solely from among male members of the *Fɔn's* kin. The society meets for recreation, and for the performance of certain rituals and masked dances.

There is a *fai* of a long established *m'tar* lineage whom I shall refer to here as *Fai-o-Bum*.[1] He is a man of middle-age who has a number of wives and is notorious for the way in which he neglects his duties to his dependants, even to the extent of failing to carry out important rites at the harvest of finger millet. Like other *afai*, he has several plots (*ʃu-sum*) reserved for his own maize, and one of these is on especially fertile alluvial land. After a period of fallow the surrounding area was brought under cultivation early in 1946, but he did not bother to have his own plot cleared and sown with grain. Instead, he lent it to a wife of the *Fɔn*. Feeling ran high in the compound and his action was condemned even in the presence of non-relatives. One of his older wives discussed the matter angrily with her friends, pointing out that there were many children in the compound who would need good land later, and that the *Fɔn's* wife in question already had several farms. She concluded her remarks by saying that the *fai* was a very bad man (*wir o bi feyi*).

A younger brother (actually father's brother's son) of Fai-o-Bum was equally outspoken in his criticism. John, as I shall call him in this book, was a Christian with a large family. His late father had been the *fai*; and his late mother, the *Yelaa*, had been entrusted with the management of the *ʃu-sum* and had worked the strip adjacent to it. John condemned the *fai's* action because, as he pointed out, the *ʃu-sum* is "a thing of the lineage" and "a farm of very strong magic" (*wu dʒə sum o kifu ke ʃiib ke tavin ki*). At the time for planting maize, the *fai* should perform rites on the *ʃu-sum* in the early morning and then return to the *ʃu-fai* (his own house) where he scrapes off shavings from a piece of *mɛnkan* wood (ebony?) on to a basket of seed, which has been kept by the *Yelaa* and is known as the "corn of God" (*ŋgwasaa-nyooiy*). She plants a little of this with her own hand on her own farm, and then on the *ʃu-sum* adjacent to it, distributing the rest of the medicated seed among the women of the compound who sow it and other seed on the *ʃu-sum*. Now, these rites are believed to influence the crops planted on all the land held by the lineage; for, just as the *fai* is the representative of the lineage, particularly in the ancestor cult, so his farm, the *ʃu-sum*, symbolizes the farms of his dependants. John, though a Christian, was not bigoted and his view was that, while his kin and Fai-o-Bum remained pagans, the *fai* should fulfil his ritual duties to his people. "It is good that the pagans should ask God to help them; and it is good that the *Fai* should ask God to help his people." But, demanded John, how could the *Fai* perform the necessary rites seeing that he had lent the *ʃu-sum* to a wife of the *Fɔn*? John had no fears for the success of his own crops, but he understood the sense of insecurity engendered among his pagan kin. At one stage in our discussion he remarked acidly: "the *Fai* does not look after the things which we eat. He washes his body and then goes to drink palmwine. He only drinks palmwine. Some *afai* cut thatching grass; ours does nothing at all!"[2]

There was another element in this situation which also aroused resentment. Not only had Fai-o-Bum lent the *ʃu-sum* but he also ran the risk of losing it. It was explained to me that after a time the *Fɔn's* wife might bring her daughter to farm there and this might prove to be the thin edge of the wedge, whereby a block would be prised off the land of the lineage to pass into the hands of the *Fɔn*. John himself had had to face such a contingency himself and he men-

---

[1] Some of the information which I received was given to me in confidence and, where this is so, I shall use pseudonyms for any individuals concerned.

[2] Sometimes one *fai* criticizes another for lack of responsibility. On one occasion a *fai*, who was a friend of mine, spoke with keen disapproval of the conduct of the head of a sub-clan: "Fai-o-X is proud (literally, feels his body is different). He does not look after the people here at all. He only likes to eat the things here. If there is no sub-lineage head here to gather the kola nuts then the people (of the compound) go and give (the nuts) to him. He then sells them and eats. (*Fai-o-X yu wunə djee. Bo wu yo lei fɛ wir fɛn yɛ. Wu kɔŋ a yii adzə vifa fɛn. A bo ʃe yo dzɛ fɛn a koiy biy, a nɛna a du fo win. Wunin fii'ni nɛna yii*)."

tioned it to me in illustration of the care which must be observed in lending a plot to a *Fɔn's* wife. He had allowed one to use a small farm for two years; but, at the end of that period, he said she must go as his own wife wished to cultivate it in the following season. His real motive was that he did not wish the woman to secure a foothold.

I have described this incident in some detail because it brings out clearly that, behind the respect and obedience which dependants (not excluding the wives) express towards the *fai*, there is also a strong sense of their own rights and of his corresponding obligations. It is the responsibility of a *fai* to perform all the sacrifices deemed necessary for the security and welfare of his group; to look after their interests and not merely to further his own ambitions; to act as trustee rather than as selfish consumer; and to keep his patrimony intact as far as possible for his successor and his dependants. It should be stressed here that Fai-o-Bum is a-typical in his conduct and is considered so by a number of people in Kimbaw. As my friends phrased it, with a gift for understatement which is almost English: " his ways are different (*li dzə djee djee*)! " In the incident described above, some of the senior men of the compound protested to him about his action but he was adamant. It was said that in the old days his dependants might have asked the *Fɔn* to remove him from office on the score of his neglect of a wide range of duties. But now, they explained, things are different and the best they could hope for was that the next *fai* would be a better man. Fai-o-Bum is in his late fifties and may reasonably be expected to join the ancestors soon! In the meantime he runs the risk of incurring the anger of ancestors and bringing misfortune on himself and his children. He may also forfeit the allegiance of some of his male dependants who, when they find the conditions become increasingly intolerable, may set up compounds elsewhere. When a *fai* is lacking in moral sensibility, these two sanctions usually operate as restraints on his behaviour. But in the case of Fai-o-Bum they seemed ineffective and already some of his male relatives living in a neighbouring compound had taken the first steps towards a permanent break. One of the issues involved was land and I shall refer to it later in this book.

One further point should be considered, namely rights to a house-site in a compound. A man is allotted an area by the *fai* and when he wishes to build another dwelling he normally has no difficulty in obtaining permission to utilize vacant land nearby.[1] When he dies, his widow continues to occupy her hut, and his adolescent sons may take over their father's hut. But if he has no male issue the hut reverts to the *fai*, who either allocates it to another member of the compound or allows a stranger to live there. But in this last case, once the hut has fallen into decay, another may not be built without the express consent of the *fai*; whereas in regard to a member of the lineage this would not be required.

WOMEN'S RIGHTS TO USUFRUCT

So far we have looked at ownership in terms of the *fai's* rights and the circumstances in which they are exercised. We shall now consider the rights of the women and the extent to which they compare favourably with those of the ' sons ' of the lineage head.

Most Nsaw girls grow up in the compound under the authority of the head of their father's lineage, marriage being patrilocal. At an early age they begin to importune their mothers for a pocket-handkerchief plot where they may cultivate a few plants of *rizga*, millet, sweet potatoes, or maize. Sometimes

---

[1] When a man builds his first hut in the compound, the landholder, who is usually the resident *fai*, kindles the first fire, pours a little palmwine in libation, and invokes the blessing of God and the ancestors on the new householder.

a group of such midget farmers takes over ground no longer considered worth farming by their mothers; and there, in company, they experiment, learn and compete with one another. More often, however, a woman marks out a small plot on her own farm for her daughter. By the time a girl is 14 or 15 years old she assists her mother regularly on the main farms, and has two or three for which she is directly responsible and which she regards as her own. They increase in size or number, and it often happens that she is put in charge of outlying farms if her mother is old or sickly. Two individuals may together cultivate about 1.9 acres, or more if there are young children to be fed in the household. A married woman with no children, or only one or two, works a total of some 1.3 acres.

When a girl marries, at the age of seventeen or later, she is under no compulsion to surrender her plots and, if she is living in the same village, she generally continues to work them, to assist her mother, and to receive help in return. Even when her husband belongs to another village where there is plenty of land, she is reluctant to abandon her own plots which she had farmed for several years and for which she has a certain sentimental attachment. But particularly important is the companionship of her mother, sisters, and friends who offer a refuge and a respite from the strangeness of her husband's village. If she lives only some three or four miles away, she may return several times a week to tend her old farms, sometimes remaining the night with her mother. What I wish to emphasize here is that her sex in nowise places her at a disadvantage *vis-à-vis* male members of the lineage. As long as she cultivates her plot she is under no obligation to cede it to a kinsman. Let me quote one instance among many. Yirbongka is a woman past child-bearing who enjoys good health and has five surviving children, some of whom live in Kimbaw. Her marriage was, from the Nsaw point of view, illegal in that it took place without the permission of her *fai*. After a number of years she returned to her father's compound, which was close by. During her marriage, however, she had continued to farm some of the plots allocated to her in her adolescence, one of them being a large strip of fertile alluvial land near the compound. In her possession of this she enjoys an advantage over some of her brother's wives. Yet, there is no question of her surrendering it, nor did I ever hear the others express jealousy. She is dignified, good-tempered, kindly, and respected and liked by the rest of the compound, including the *fai*, who often makes her the recipient of his confidences. When she dies, or perhaps before that, she may give some of her plots to her son's wife, some to her daughters; and perhaps others again to other members of the compound. Those not allocated by her personally would return to the common pool until re-allotted by the *fai* himself.

If, however, a married woman lives far away from her parental compound and is not prepared to make the journey, her plots will either be taken over by her mother or sisters; or, if they are not required by them, they revert to grassland and are at the disposal of the *fai*. Should she at a later date become a widow or divorce her husband and desire to return to her parental home, she resumes cultivation of her old plots if they have not been re-allocated and providing the *fai* agrees; or she may be granted others in their stead.

As a general rule, a married woman finds it convenient to have her farms on the land of her husband's lineage. When a man marries, his *fai* demarcates an area for him and, in addition, his own mother may make one or two of her own plots available for the bride. As the size of the family increases, a woman requires a larger area and, if it is available in her husband's village, she prefers to work it rather than to make a long journey to her mother's village. Care of her children and heavier responsibilities lead her to conserve her time and energy as much as possible. Granted a choice of plots, the decision rests with her. As one woman explained to me: " I have given up my farm at Nkar (some 10 miles away). My husband was unwilling because the ground was good; but I had delivered three children and was tired ".

Besides rights of usufruct in land of the father's lineage, a man and a woman enjoy almost similar rights in regard to plots on land of their mother's lineage. That this is a matter of the privileges of kinship and not a favour secured through friendship is brought out by the fact that no gift of maize is demanded at harvest. My first interpreter, Benedict Tata, told me that his wife was working a large plot at Tabessob, which had previously belonged to his mother and was part of the land of her lineage. When I asked if he had first to obtain his mother's brother's permission, he said " No! If it is my mother's farm (*sum*), I do not have to beg permission from any man at all. I am cultivating it, (*afɛn dzə sum yewor la m yo dzaa lɔn fɛ wir ɣɛ. Mɛn aa limlimin*) ". But, while I encountered other examples of this, they were for obvious reasons few in number. Usually a woman obtains sufficient land for her needs from the *fai* of her husband or her father; and it is only when she has a large family and also is living near her mother's father that she is likely to capitalize, as it were, her ties with him.

When her husband's land is poor or inadequate and she lives far from her own kin, she may " beg " plots from some *fai* in the village or from her women friends. This is more likely to occur in Kimbaw than in other villages because of a large population and increasing pressure on local land reserves; and, finally, the tendency for a number of men to take up residence there rather than in their father's village. This is particularly true in the case of ex-servants of the *Fɔn* and sons of the *Fɔn*. Sometimes it is left to the woman herself to approach a *fai* with a supplicatory gift of food and " beg " that he demarcate a plot for her; sometimes her husband may take a calabash of palm wine and make the request. If the *fai* has vacant land either he or his delegate marks the boundaries, and the woman is then free to plant her crops providing she observes the rules for a traditional rest-day, when the hoe must not be wielded. At harvest she presents the *fai* with a basket of grain (never tubers); but if the yield has been poor, he is content with a few cobs and may even waive these. The gift is a formal acknowledgement that right to usufruct is dependent on the good-will of the landholder. Often the husband supplements it by small offerings of salt, tobacco, and wine in order to keep the relationship " sweet ", and perhaps obtain a little more land when the first plot reverts to fallow. When a person has cultivated a plot for many years, more especially in the case of an affine, no demand for the pepper-corn rent may be made, but it is understood that the original conditions of transfer still remain in force.

Sometimes a village head (*tantee*) has an exceptionally large tract of land, of which outlying portions have never been cultivated and he will permit another *fai*, who is a close friend in a neighbouring village, to take over a large block for allocation among his own dependants. The original holder does not surrender his claims to it, but, where it is unlikely he will require it for his own kin, such land tends to be regarded as belonging to the beneficiary *fai*. For example, there is one block on the boundaries between Kimbaw and Kingomen which was granted to Fai-o-Djung in Kimbaw by a *fai* in Kingomen some 20 years ago. The dependants of Fai-o-Djung still cultivate it and, while admitting it is a loan, feel secure in their tenure and do not envisage the possibility of eviction. One man has obtained permission to plant raffia there; and the women decide among themselves who shall farm. For instance, an inherited wife of Fai-o-Djung, an old woman, has decided that her son's wife is to take over her plot; a widowed sister of Fai-o-Djung has " given " hers to a friend in the adjoining compound, which belongs to a sub-lineage of the same clan as that of Fai-o-Djung.

Both a man and a woman have, then, a number of alternative means for obtaining land. Moreover, as is apparent from earlier remarks, an individual expects to retain the usufruct of plots received from the heads of the lineages of both parents. Normally a woman, once she has been granted plots, continues to farm them for the rest of her life, often transmitting them to her sons or daughters. It is left to her to decide the period of grass fallow, which may be from 3 to 6 years, and may extend to 10 or more without invalidating her position as temporary occupier. She regards the plots as her own, jealously safeguards her boundaries, is quick to report any encroachment; and, finally, she rests secure in the knowledge that, without due cause, she will not be dispossessed during her lifetime. When these facts are taken into account, the two statements—" women own the farms " and " women do not own the land "—are not contradictory but refer to different types of ownership or, rather, different sets of rights. Even when a new *fai* succeeds to the position of compound head he is morally bound to leave his dependants in possession of plots allocated to them by his predecessor. This principle is usually observed for, " a *fai* only has the power to give a new place (one not already allotted) to a stranger, a place which people are working he ought not to give a stranger." The circumstances in which a person might be called upon to forfeit his claims will be discussed later. But it should be pointed out that a *fai* should only evict a dependant who has committed a serious breach of duty. Action for any other reason is likely to be regarded as arbitrary and would provoke the just question: " Where have I erred ? I have not spoilt anything. Why are you angry ? (*M si djai ka ? Bɔ m yo bivirne kifa. Aa ki bani feya ?*) Nevertheless if a *fai* persists in reclaiming a plot against the wishes of his dependants there is nothing to be done about it, as the following incident will illustrate. Unfortunately, Fai-o-Bum again figures as the villain of the piece, or as one who frequently acts in a way contrary to Nsaw values.[1]

One day I arrived at John's compound to find him perturbed and rather angry about a plot which was a short distance from his house and which had lain fallow for five years. He told me that his wife, Mary, and also two inherited wives of Fai-o-Bum, had been given these by the late *fai* long ago. John had intended clearing it but had just discovered another man (to whom he at first referred as a " stranger ") had forestalled him. John said he was going to ask the man who had given him permission and report the matter to Fai-o-Bum. It was then that he made the statement which I have quoted several times previously to the effect that a *fai* has no power to re-allocate a plot which a person is farming. He also admitted that the stranger was in reality a ' brother ' who had gone to live in Ketiwum. He was particularly incensed because he had rendered him many services such as looking after his kola trees and mangoes.

When I next met John and asked him about the dispute he said ruefully that he had given way, since his ' brother ' was the elder and he did not wish to quarrel.[2] Moreover, the two inherited wives of the *Fai* had apparently made no strong objection to surrendering their plots, which were adjacent. Without their support his position was weak, but he still considered that his rights had been infringed and he cherished a grievance.

---

[1] Fai-o-Bum was in some respects a likable person, rather astute, and always courteous to me. I regret that I must so often cite actions (or sometimes lack of action) which place him in an unfavourable light; but, as every anthropologist knows, a breach of custom is often one of the means by which a deeper insight into values and attitudes is obtained. Fai-o-Bum, by his lapses from Nsaw standards of conduct, often provided this!

[2] It is significant that John, in his first outburst of anger, deliberately referred to his father's brother's son as a " stranger "; that is, he temporarily repudiated the relationship. Later in a calmer mood, he emphasized the kinship tie as a reason for ceding his claim.

It remains to discuss the circumstances in which a *fai* has legal and some moral justification for withdrawing rights of usufruct from a beneficiary who is a kinsman. Two examples will bring out the principle involved. Not far from Bum there was a small compound which had been founded by a father's brother of Fai-o-Bum. The compound head had only the status of *ngaalaa* (as he was still a dependant of Bum), but on account of his age and the fact that he had one married son, Maximilian, and another, Dwemfe, he was sometimes addressed as */e* as a matter of courtesy. (*fɛ gɛ'ɛr gɛsin*). About a year before my arrival he contracted a serious illness, but although Fai-o-Bum passed the compound almost daily on his way to drink wine at one of his clubs, he rarely called in to enquire after his ' son ', to sit with him, and to hear his dying wishes. However, once the *ngaalaa* was dead, the *Fai* made a prompt appearance in the compound and seized the livestock, clothes and money to which he was legally entitled; but he discovered that Dwemfe had hidden his father's dane-gun because he was angry about the neglect shown by the *Fai* previously. The *Fai* persisted in his attempts to secure possession of the gun, but was reluctant to take the matter to court because of the publicity which would be thrown on his own unfatherly conduct towards the dying man. But in 1949 he ordered Dwemfe to relinquish two farm plots which were large and at a convenient distance from his compound.

The reactions of the other dependants of Fai-o-Bum are of particular interest here. John and some of the wives of the *Fai* admitted that Dwemfe had legitimate cause for grievance in the callousness and lack of care which the *Fai* had displayed when the *ngaalaa* was dying. But, while they recognized the hardship which the *Fai's* decision entailed for Dwemfe's wife, they did not question the *Fai's* right to reclaim the land; and, in fact, they regarded his action as inevitable once it was clear that the breach would not be healed. In the dry season of 1947, Dwemfe's wife had only a little over 0.33 acre for cultivation and, by the end of the year, Dwemfe was buying grain for the household. Fortunately, his income was somewhat above the average and, moreover, he had taken steps to improve his position for the coming year. Through his mother he was a distant relative of the *Fɔn*, and in formal conversation he repudiated his ties with the *m'tar* lineage of his father and stressed that he was a *wir-duiy*. He was on very friendly terms with a relative of his mother who lived in a compound not far away; he attended the weekly *djaŋgi* there, and cultivated the friendship of its *fai* who, in February 1948, lent him a fairly large plot of land.

In another incident, which concerned the same compound, Fai-o-Bum appeared in a better light. Dwemfe's brother, Maximilian, was a Christian who was a somewhat cantankerous and idle fellow, although he had a wife and three children to support. At different times he had been entrusted with the care of stands of raffia by their owners and had profited from the perquisites which went with the task, namely some of the wine and also the poles, which are cut away when the palm is tapped. In each case he skimped his duties and lost the job. Eventually, his own *Fai*, Bum, put him in charge of one stand of raffia, but again Maximilian performed the task in a negligent fashion and at last said he wanted to give it up. Fai-o-Bum was very angry and threatened to deprive Maximilian's wife of her farm plots,—a course of action in which he had the support of some of the men of the compound. The *Fai* was reported to have said: " If you give up one thing, you give up all " (*a mati ki mo'ɔn, a mati vidzɔm*); and my informant went on to explain that a man cannot accept one thing (such as farm land) from his ' Father ' (the *Fai*) and, at the same time, refuse others (in this case, the care of a small clump of raffia and the perquisites which went with it). A man should be grateful for anything the *Fai* may give him. In the end, the *Fai* relented over the land out of pity for Maximilian's wife Rebecca. " She weeps before the *Fai*: ' Where is her ground ? She has two children. Where is her work ? ' Then the *Fai* says: ' Go and work! ' (But) he is estranged from Maximilian. Maximilian's conduct is not good. The *Fai* will tap the raffia. Maximilian is always having quarrels." (*Rebecca wu tɔŋ fai : ' win nsaiy yelia ? Wu kɛr wɔn a baa. Lim dzɔ fɛ ? ' Nɛn fai suŋnin : ' duri a lim ! ' Wu mɛŋ Maximilian. Li o Maximilian bo wu yo bɔŋ. Fai wu wi rɛŋ ruu rɔ. Maximilian sa nsa ɣansidzom*).

It remains to consider the rights of a woman to lend à plot or a section of a plot to others for a short period. This type of arrangement, as pointed out earlier, is to be distinguished from the right of a *fai*, since it is a matter of mutual convenience and is not legally binding on either party. Nor does the new farmer hand over a basket of grain at harvest. The practice indicates, however, the confidence which the men repose in the judgment of the women, and their recognition that the women, as farmers, should in most cases be left to decide the use to which the land is put. Even when a woman has received plots from her husband, she does not necessarily consult him first and he generally supports her in the event of a dispute. For instance, Mary, the wife of John, gave a woman friend in a neighbouring compound permission to cultivate a small area. In the following year she withdrew the right, not because of any quarrel, but because she deemed it expedient to resume control. The woman's husband begged John to reverse Mary's decision, but John's reply was " Mary has refused. The matter is closed. (Mary *wu binsine. Ki maini*)."

The motives which influence a woman to make a plot available to another may be those of friendship, a desire to help one in need, or to make a return for past services. Sometimes it happens that, in an area which has lain fallow for several years, all the women begin cultivation in the same season except for one individual. Yet her patch with its tall grasses will then become a sanctuary for pests and small animals which will ravage the crops on the surrounding farms; and, out of consideration for the farmers, she may allow one to take over the plot for the year.

There are two other practices which throw light on the woman's rights. In the first place *rizga* is often planted on the high hill-tops where other crops do not thrive. The plots are extremely small (two or three hundred square yards or even less) and the *fai* does not bother to demarcate the boundaries. Instead on an appointed day, the women of the compound, under the leadership of the senior wife of the *fai*, ascend the hill. Each pegs out a claim sufficient for her needs and, if there is any bickering, the senior wife steps in to quell it. Sometimes finger millet is planted the following year, but after that the land usually reverts to grass fallow for 8 or 10 years.

In regard to the farm plots allocated by her husband or her father, we have already seen that she often chooses who is to cultivate them once she has decided to surrender them permanently. She would, in such a case, designate certain kin only: a son or daughter, a husband's brother's son or daughter if the land belongs to her husband's lineage; or a son, daughter, brother or sister, if the land belongs to her own father's lineage. Again and again I encountered instances of this, and the pattern of tenure which emerges is that a certain number of farm plots tend to remain in the hands of a segment of the lineage—a man, his sons, and daughters, and his sons' sons. Of course, if a woman leaves her husband she forfeits any rights to plots received from him and also the standing crops, providing the marriage has been contracted legally,— that is, with the consent of her own *fai*. On the other hand, if she has lived with her husband without the consent of her own *fai* and has only the status of a *wiiy-o-t/ɛmin*, she may harvest her crops, but runs the risk of a stormy encounter

44

with an irate husband.[1]   The possibility of such a brawl was brought out rather cynically on one occasion when a woman who was a *wiiy-o-t/ɛmin* told her friend that she was thinking of leaving her husband.   Her confidant advised her to wait until she had harvested her crops!

SYLVAN RESOURCES

Methods of cultivation and rights to disposal of crops will be discussed in detail in later chapters; but, before bringing our survey of land tenure in Nsaw to a close, some account must be given of control of kola trees and raffia. Like land, these are regarded as the property of the lineage, and their management is vested in the *fai* or */e*.[2]   If a man plants kola or raffia trees he enjoys the fruits of his labour, but at his death they are taken over by the *fai*, and not by his own sons or brothers.   This applies also when they have been planted on the land of another *fai* from whom, in the first place, permission must have been obtained.   The landholder, in this case, would have no right to a gift of produce nor any right to the trees.   There is, however, one minor exception to the rule of inheritance.   A man or a woman may plant one or two kola trees and a small raffia stand in the name of a son, who is then assured of rights of usufruct to the produce.   But when the son himself dies the trees are inherited by the *fai*.   Women do not own kolas or raffia, but an exception is made for a *Ya* or *Yewɔŋ* who is often given a little raffia and a few kola trees by the *Fɔn* for her own use during her lifetime.   At her death they are taken over by the *Fɔn*, who may entrust the care of them to her son.

A *fai* often superintends his own trees and plantations—weeding, gathering the nuts, tapping the wine, and cutting away the midribs.   But he normally entrusts the care of some of his property to one of the members of the lineage; or, if it is in another village, then to a kinsman or friend living there.   The man in charge (*ngaaruu*) is allowed to keep some of the wine, providing he supplies the *fai* with some on request.   If he is entrusted with a few kola trees, he weeds them and gathers the nuts, receiving in return some of the small ones—a hundred or so.   Much depends on the generosity of the *fai*.   It is exceptional for a *fai* to manage all his sylvan resources; when this does occur, he is regarded as mean and selfish.   In the gathering of the nuts, those present in the compound help the *fai* and, it must be admitted, help themselves to a few which they either conceal in their loin cloths if they are men, or which they rush to hide in a corner if they are women!   The *fai* reaps the major monetary profit; but, on the whole, this is equitable since he usually has several wives and many children for whom to provide, as well as his other dependants in times of emergency.   Nowadays, owing to the rise in the cost of living, some *afai* are tempted to skimp their responsibilities; but it should be recognized that the pursuit of new and relatively lucrative occupations has given some of the younger men a considerable measure of economic independence and security.   This is particularly marked in areas outside Nsaw where regular marriage payments are made and where there is now less tendency for male dependants to look to their lineage head for assistance in this matter.   In Nsaw, the general trader, carpenter, fruit-grower or coffee-planter often enjoys a larger income than many a *fai*.   He is able to meet the needs of his own wife and children, besides helping poor relatives and even a financially embarrassed *fai*.   But complications may arise over inheritance.   The question is whether costly tools of trade or livestock such as pigs and cattle, or plantations of fruit

---

[1] The divorced husband does not relinquish his claims to the plots: he may allocate them among other wives, or allow them to revert to grassland until he acquires a new wife; or, more rarely, he may permit a younger brother's wife to make use of them.

[2] In the case of the compound (mentioned on p. 37) which for some years lacked a resident */e*, the produce of the kola trees was taken by the sub-clan head who lived in another village. But, once a new */e* was appointed in 1947, he had no further rights.

trees and coffee are to be placed in the same category as the other sources of wealth traditionally inherited by a *fai*; or whether they are to be regarded as personal property over which the owner has full rights of disposal. At least one coffee-planter expressed the fear that his sons would not be allowed to inherit his plantations, and he was anxious to know if he might make a will bequeathing them specifically to his children.

The problem is a difficult one and not confined to Nsaw. Both mixed farming and the cultivation of cash crops may well prove an important factor in raising the standard of living; but each entails some financial outlay, as well as expenditure of initiative, time, and labour. It seems only fair to those who are prepared to take the risk and branch out in new fields of economic enterprise that they should have some measure of security in regard to land tenure and the disposal of their property after death. Despite the strength of lineage ties and the fact that the lineage still functions as a corporate unit in many spheres of social life it is true to say, I think, that concern for the future of his sons and a desire to make provision for their welfare has become one of the dominant motives of the average Nsaw man.

But once the principle is recognized that the *fai* or */e*, by virtue of his office, has no claims to the inheritance of semi-permanent crops, then increased cultivation of coffee, or groves of orange, grapefruit, avocado pear, or mango-trees may well create problems in the sphere of land tenure itself, since the land involved would, to all intent and purposes, become vested in the farmer and his heirs. Once a *fai* becomes aware of this possibility he may well refuse in the first place to grant permission for their cultivation, since he already exercises this right in regard to another permanent crop, namely raffia. No difficulty need arise so long as relations between the *fai* and the cultivator or his heirs remain amicable; but, if a quarrel occurs and the *fai* decides to resume control of the land, what is to happen to the crops? A sale of the crops might take place; but, if the *fai* himself does not want to buy them, then any prospective purchaser would want security of tenure. Renting and sale of land were forbidden by Nsaw law but, granted the development of a system of leasehold, the way is open for an abuse of his privileges on the part of the *fai*, unless explicit provision is made for the consultation and consent of the members of his lineage in any questions affecting a transfer of land. Moreover, a *fai* himself might begin to cultivate permanent cash crops on lineage land, which was not allocated or which had been abandoned by its farmer users, with the result that the area for subsistence farming by his dependants would increasingly diminish. On the other hand, there is the possibility that members of a lineage might form a co-operative for the cultivation and ownership of cash crops, or for the rearing of cattle. These problems are not confined to Nsaw but are likely to arise also on much of the uplands and plains, since in none of these regions is there a system which approximates to individual tenure.

SUMMARY OF NSAW SYSTEM

I have discussed at some length the functioning of the Nsaw system of land tenure in order to show its flexibility and the degree of economic security which it affords to farmers under subsistence conditions; and I have also analysed the new problems that are arising from the development of permanent cash crops. In the mass of detail, however, the main features have perhaps become blurred and require some re-emphasis before we turn to other types of land ownership in Bamenda. In the first place, control of residential and arable land is vested in a number of patrilineage heads (*afai* and *a/e*): that is, in the last resort, the Nsaw court recognizes that the authority to allocate or withdraw rights of usufruct to farm plots and residential sites resides in such

coffee are to be placed in the same category as the other sources
traditionally inherited by a *fai*; or whether they are to be regarded
l property over which the owner has full rights of disposal. At least
-planter expressed the fear that his sons would not be allowed to
plantations, and he was anxious to know if he might make a will
g them specifically to his children.

blem is a difficult one and not confined to Nsaw. Both mixed
d the cultivation of cash crops may well prove an important factor
he standard of living; but each entails some financial outlay, as well
ture of initiative, time, and labour. It seems only fair to those
repared to take the risk and branch out in new fields of economic
that they should have some measure of security in regard to land
l the disposal of their property after death. Despite the strength
ties and the fact that the lineage still functions as a corporate unit in
res of social life it is true to say, I think, that concern for the future
and a desire to make provision for their welfare has become one of
ant motives of the average Nsaw man.

e the principle is recognized that the *fai* or *ʃe*, by virtue of his office,
ims to the inheritance of semi-permanent crops, then increased
of coffee, or groves of orange, grapefruit, avocado pear, or mango-
well create problems in the sphere of land tenure itself, since the land
ould, to all intent and purposes, become vested in the farmer and
Once a *fai* becomes aware of this possibility he may well refuse in
ace to grant permission for their cultivation, since he already exer-
right in regard to another permanent crop, namely raffia. No
eed arise so long as relations between the *fai* and the cultivator or his
in amicable; but, if a quarrel occurs and the *fai* decides to resume
the land, what is to happen to the crops? A sale of the crops might
; but, if the *fai* himself does not want to buy them, then any
purchaser would want security of tenure. Renting and sale of
forbidden by Nsaw law but, granted the development of a system
d, the way is open for an abuse of his privileges on the part of the
explicit provision is made for the consultation and consent of the
f his lineage in any questions affecting a transfer of land. More-
himself might begin to cultivate permanent cash crops on lineage
h was not allocated or which had been abandoned by its farmer
the result that the area for subsistence farming by his dependants
easingly diminish. On the other hand, there is the possibility that
f a lineage might form a co-operative for the cultivation and owner-
crops, or for the rearing of cattle. These problems are not confined
ut are likely to arise also on much of the uplands and plains, since
these regions is there a system which approximates to individual

OF NSAW SYSTEM

discussed at some length the functioning of the Nsaw system of land
order to show its flexibility and the degree of economic security
ffords to farmers under subsistence conditions; and I have also
e new problems that are arising from the development of permanent
. In the mass of detail, however, the main features have perhaps
urred and require some re-emphasis before we turn to other types
nership in Bamenda. In the first place, control of residential and
l is vested in a number of patrilineage heads (*afai* and *aʃe*): that is,
resort, the Nsaw court recognizes that the authority to allocate
w rights of usufruct to farm plots and residential sites resides in such

It remains to discuss the circumstances in which a *fai* has legal and some moral
justification for withdrawing rights of usufruct from a beneficiary who is a
kinsman. Two examples will bring out the principle involved. Not far from
Bum there was a small compound which had been founded by a father's
brother of Fai-o-Bum. The compound head had only the status of *ngaalaa*
(as he was still a dependant of Bum), but on account of his age and the fact
that he had one married son, Maximilian, and another, Dwemfe, he was
sometimes addressed as *ʃe* as a matter of courtesy. (*fɛ gɛ'ɛr gɛsin*). About a
year before my arrival he contracted a serious illness, but although Fai-o-Bum
passed the compound almost daily on his way to drink wine at one of his clubs,
he rarely called in to enquire after his ' son ', to sit with him, and to hear his
dying wishes. However, once the *ngaalaa* was dead, the *Fai* made a prompt
appearance in the compound and seized the livestock, clothes and money to
which he was legally entitled; but he discovered that Dwemfe had hidden
his father's dane-gun because he was angry about the neglect shown by the
Fai previously. The *Fai* persisted in his attempts to secure possession of the
gun, but was reluctant to take the matter to court because of the publicity
which would be thrown on his own unfatherly conduct towards the dying man.
But in 1949 he ordered Dwemfe to relinquish two farm plots which were
large and at a convenient distance from his compound.

The reactions of the other dependants of Fai-o-Bum are of particular
interest here. John and some of the wives of the *Fai* admitted that Dwemfe
had legitimate cause for grievance in the callousness and lack of care which the
Fai had displayed when the *ngaalaa* was dying. But, while they recognized
the hardship which the *Fai's* decision entailed for Dwemfe's wife, they did not
question the *Fai's* right to reclaim the land; and, in fact, they regarded his
action as inevitable once it was clear that the breach would not be healed.
In the dry season of 1947, Dwemfe's wife had only a little over 0.33 acre for
cultivation and, by the end of the year, Dwemfe was buying grain for the
household. Fortunately, his income was somewhat above the average and,
moreover, he had taken steps to improve his position for the coming year.
Through his mother he was a distant relative of the *Fɔn*, and in formal conversation he repudiated his ties with the *m'tar* lineage of his father and stressed that
he was a *wir-duiy*. He was on very friendly terms with a relative of his mother
who lived in a compound not far away; he attended the weekly *djaŋgi* there,
and cultivated the friendship of its *fai* who, in February 1948, lent him a fairly
large plot of land.

In another incident, which concerned the same compound, Fai-o-Bum
appeared in a better light. Dwemfe's brother, Maximilian, was a Christian
who was a somewhat cantankerous and idle fellow, although he had a wife and
three children to support. At different times he had been entrusted with the
care of stands of raffia by their owners and had profited from the perquisites
which went with the task, namely some of the wine and also the poles, which
are cut away when the palm is tapped. In each case he skimped his duties
and lost the job. Eventually, his own *Fai*, Bum, put him in charge of one
stand of raffia, but again Maximilian performed the task in a negligent fashion
and at last said he wanted to give it up. Fai-o-Bum was very angry and
threatened to deprive Maximilian's wife of her farm plots,—a course of action
in which he had the support of some of the men of the compound. The *Fai*
was reported to have said: " If you give up one thing, you give up all " (*a
mati ki mo'ɔn, a mati vidzɘm*); and my informant went on to explain that a man
cannot accept one thing (such as farm land) from his ' Father ' (the *Fai*) and,
at the same time, refuse others (in this case, the care of a small clump of raffia
and the perquisites which went with it). A man should be grateful for anything the *Fai* may give him. In the end, the *Fai* relented over the land out of

pity for Maximilian's wife Rebecca. "She weeps before the *Fai*: 'Where is her ground? She has two children. Where is her work?' Then the *Fai* says: 'Go and work!' (But) he is estranged from Maximilian. Maximilian's conduct is not good. The *Fai* will tap the raffia. Maximilian is always having quarrels." (*Rebecca wu tɔŋ fai: 'win nsaiy yelia? Wu kɛr wɔn a baa. Lim dzə fɛ?' Nɛn fai suŋnin: 'duri a lim!' Wu mɛŋ Maximilian. Li o Maximilian bo wu yo bɔŋ. Fai wu wi rɛŋ ruu rə. Maximilian sa nsa ɣansidzom*).

It remains to consider the rights of a woman to lend a plot or a section of a plot to others for a short period. This type of arrangement, as pointed out earlier, is to be distinguished from the right of a *fai*, since it is a matter of mutual convenience and is not legally binding on either party. Nor does the new farmer hand over a basket of grain at harvest. The practice indicates, however, the confidence which the men repose in the judgment of the women, and their recognition that the women, as farmers, should in most cases be left to decide the use to which the land is put. Even when a woman has received plots from her husband, she does not necessarily consult him first and he generally supports her in the event of a dispute. For instance, Mary, the wife of John, gave a woman friend in a neighbouring compound permission to cultivate a small area. In the following year she withdrew the right, not because of any quarrel, but because she deemed it expedient to resume control. The woman's husband begged John to reverse Mary's decision, but John's reply was "Mary has refused. The matter is closed. (Mary *wu binsine. Ki maini*)."

The motives which influence a woman to make a plot available to another may be those of friendship, a desire to help one in need, or to make a return for past services. Sometimes it happens that, in an area which has lain fallow for several years, all the women begin cultivation in the same season except for one individual. Yet her patch with its tall grasses will then become a sanctuary for pests and small animals which will ravage the crops on the surrounding farms; and, out of consideration for the farmers, she may allow one to take over the plot for the year.

There are two other practices which throw light on the woman's rights. In the first place *rizga* is often planted on the high hill-tops where other crops do not thrive. The plots are extremely small (two or three hundred square yards or even less) and the *fai* does not bother to demarcate the boundaries. Instead on an appointed day, the women of the compound, under the leadership of the senior wife of the *fai*, ascend the hill. Each pegs out a claim sufficient for her needs and, if there is any bickering, the senior wife steps in to quell it. Sometimes finger millet is planted the following year, but after that the land usually reverts to grass fallow for 8 or 10 years.

In regard to the farm plots allocated by her husband or her father, we have already seen that she often chooses who is to cultivate them once she has decided to surrender them permanently. She would, in such a case, designate certain kin only: a son or daughter, a husband's brother's son or daughter if the land belongs to her husband's lineage; or a son, daughter, brother or sister, if the land belongs to her own father's lineage. Again and again I encountered instances of this, and the pattern of tenure which emerges is that a certain number of farm plots tend to remain in the hands of a segment of the lineage—a man, his sons, and daughters, and his sons' sons. Of course, if a woman leaves her husband she forfeits any rights to plots received from him and also the standing crops, providing the marriage has been contracted legally,— that is, with the consent of her own *fai*. On the other hand, if she has lived with her husband without the consent of her own *fai* and has only the status of a *wiiy-o-tʃɛmin*, she may harvest her crops, but runs the risk of a stormy encounter

with an irate husband.[1] The possibility of s rather cynically on one occasion when a wom her friend that she was thinking of leaving advised her to wait until she had harvested he

SYLVAN RESOURCES

Methods of cultivation and rights to dispos detail in later chapters; but, before bringing Nsaw to a close, some account must be given o Like land, these are regarded as the property o ment is vested in the *fai* or */e*.[2] If a man plan the fruits of his labour, but at his death they a by his own sons or brothers. This applies als on the land of another *fai* from whom, in the f been obtained. The landholder, in this case, of produce nor any right to the trees. There i to the rule of inheritance. A man or a woman and a small raffia stand in the name of a son, usufruct to the produce. But when the son hi by the *fai*. Women do not own kolas or raffia *Ya* or *Yewɔŋ* who is often given a little raffia for her own use during her lifetime. At her d *Fon*, who may entrust the care of them to her

A *fai* often superintends his own trees and the nuts, tapping the wine, and cutting away entrusts the care of some of his property to on or, if it is in another village, then to a kinsman in charge (*ngaaruu*) is allowed to keep some of the *fai* with some on request. If he is entruste them and gathers the nuts, receiving in retu hundred or so. Much depends on the genero for a *fai* to manage all his sylvan resources; wh as mean and selfish. In the gathering of the pound help the *fai* and, it must be admitted, they either conceal in their loin cloths if they hide in a corner if they are women! The profit; but, on the whole, this is equitable si and many children for whom to provide, as times of emergency. Nowadays, owing to th *afai* are tempted to skimp their responsibiliti that the pursuit of new and relatively lucrativ the younger men a considerable measure security. This is particularly marked in are marriage payments are made and where ther dependants to look to their lineage head fo Nsaw, the general trader, carpenter, fruit-grow a larger income than many a *fai*. He is able t and children, besides helping poor relatives an *fai*. But complications may arise over inherit costly tools of trade or livestock such as pigs a

[1] The divorced husband does not relinquish his clai among other wives, or allow them to revert to grassla more rarely, he may permit a younger brother's wife to

[2] In the case of the compound (mentioned on p. 37) */e*, the produce of the kola trees was taken by the sub-c But, once a new */e* was appointed in 1947, he had no fi

trees and
of wealth
as person
one coffe
inherit h
bequeath

The p
farming
in raising
as expen
who are
enterpris
tenure a
of lineage
many sp
of his so
the domi

But on
has no
cultivatic
trees may
involved
his heirs.
the first
cises this
difficulty
heirs rem
control o
take pla
prospecti
land wer
of leaseh
fai, unle
members
over, a *f*
land, wh
users, wi
would in
members
ship of ca
to Nsaw
in none
tenure.

SUMMAR

I have
tenure in
which it
analysed
cash cro
become
of land
arable la
in the la
or withd

44

45

men, as long as they remain in office. But, as the previous discussion has shown, a purely legalistic approach to ownership is inadequate for an understanding of the functioning of the system and the underlying attitudes. The concept of ownership has moral as well as legal connotations; it involves trusteeship and responsibility. From this point of view it is just as misleading to speak of a *fai* as ' owning ' the land as it would be to regard him as ' owning ' his dependants. He is primarily a father to them (*talaa*), promoting their welfare, exercising his authority for the benefit of the group as a whole, and granting to its members the means necessary for their subsistence. Just as it is almost inconceivable to a Nsaw man that a father should deny food to a child while it remains under his care, so likewise it is opposed to Nsaw values that a *fai* should deny land for subsistence to any one of his dependants while such an individual remains under his protection and authority. According to ancient Nsaw custom (*li o Nso fɛmbi*), a good *fai* keeps everything in order (*naŋsin vifa vidzəm*). "He concerns himself with the building of houses for his ' children ', and when they go to cut grass he accompanies them and encourages them."[1] Then, as one *fai* pointed out to me, " my ' children ' will call me a good lineage head, because I know how to help them. I cannot sit down (doing nothing) because I am a lineage head (*wɔn vɛmi a lo a yɔŋ mo fai o djuŋe, bifɛɛ m ki sə awinni. Adzə la m yo a dzə'am dji mo fai*)."

The system of land tenure is, apart from other considerations, of the utmost importance for an understanding of the persistence of the lineage as a corporate unit even under present day conditions, when the spread of Christianity and decisions in the Court in regard to marriage and the custody of children have done much to undermine the influence of the lineage head. Prestige is closely bound up with the number of families which live in a *fai's* compound as well as others which, through lack of building space, have been compelled to take up residence elsewhere but retain economic and other social ties with him. A compound in which the membership has gradually dwindled away and where houses are in a state of bad repair is referred to in terms of disparagement which reflect on the *fai* himself. A *fai*, then, does not wilfully drive away his male dependants even when they have become converts to Christianity. As long as they give allegiance in other than spiritual matters he is prepared generally, and is indeed willing, to grant them house-sites and farm land. They, on their side, are content to respect and obey him in affairs which do not involve any conflict with their religious principles. The advantages, from their point of view, are twofold: in the first place, there is the companionship of brothers and other close kin with whom ties of affection and common interest have been forged during early life; and, secondly, there are rights of usufruct to farm land. It is true, as we have seen, that in Nsaw no man need be landless: there are a number of alternatives for obtaining farm plots. But normally most of these are utilized in only a subsidiary degree, since a man's claims are strongest and most clearly defined in regard to the land of his own lineage. Apart from those areas which may be allotted to him specifically by his *fai*, he usually takes over, or expects to take over later, some of the more fertile and accessible plots cultivated by his own mother.

And this brings us to another feature of the Nsaw system. While in theory plots may be re-allocated at the will of the *fai*, in practice they tend to remain

---

[1] The above is a free translation of the Lamnso text given me by a *fai*. It ran as follows: " *Kɛmbiki wu ku tatini e wan laf. A yi lo kar wuiy, waa lei. Wu du fo, du a banri—'vena kar wuiy t/ɛr t/ɛr!* "

The *fai* concerned also said a woman describes a *fai* as a good man when " he buys salt, buys oil, buys a hoe, buys a stirring rod for porridge." If her mother comes to visit, he cooks a good relish (fowl) and gives it to her. When she goes she finds something (that is a gift) has been put in her bag. Then she goes away rejoicing for a good lineage head (*/ɛ 'ɛri fɛ fai o djuŋe*).

in the hands of the individual and the descendants of the individual to whom they were first granted. In short, the allocation of land to a member of the lineage (male or female) carries the implicit assurance of security of tenure. If a change is to be made the *fai* endeavours to obtain the consent of the erstwhile farmer. Furthermore, once a person no longer requires certain plots, he or she is often permitted to decide who shall take them over. The choice is confined to members of the compound or of the lineage living elsewhere; but, within these limits, there is scope for the play of preference for some individuals as against others.

Finally, as we have seen, a woman as a member of her lineage enjoys all the advantages of a man in respect to rights of usufruct throughout her span of life. Even after marriage her rights are nowise infringed and these, with her skill as farmer, give her considerable economic independence. Should she leave her husband or decide to leave his compound when she becomes a widow, she is able to obtain plots on the land of the lineages of either of her parents and grow the crops with which to support herself. As a wife or a daughter, she assumes full responsibility for the management of her farms and, in practice, she is free to lend sections to her kin and friends. When she decides to abandon them it is customary for her husband to give weight to her opinion on the issue of who is to take them over; if she is the wife of a *fai* the matter may be left in her hands.

As far as differential rights on the basis of rank and age are concerned, it should be stressed that these do not penalize, under present conditions, the newly-married woman or the woman of low status. Granted residence in the village of the lineage of the husband and amicable relationships between him and his *fai*, the main factors determining the total acreage farmed by a woman are her age, the size of her family, her good health, and energy. A *Yelaa*, a senior wife, or a wife who is a daughter or grand-daughter of the *Fɔn*,—all these derive some advantage from their rank, not in the amount of land which they cultivate but often in the possession of large fertile plots within easy access of the compound. As far as the *fai* himself is concerned, he usually has two or three farms (*/u-sum*), divided into strips, for each of which a woman or adolescent girl of the compound is responsible. The *fai* takes the best of the maize (sometimes the best of the guinea corn and finger millet when these are planted); but a woman has full rights to any tubers, gourds, greens, and legumes which she has sown on her strip.

It remains to point out how far the Nsaw system of land tenure may be regarded as typical for Bamenda. In the eastern and central areas my visits were brief and I only had time to make general inquiries among the *Afɔn*, Village Heads, Councillors, and individual men and women whom I encountered in the compounds and on the farms. But among the Mbembe, the Bali, and most of the Tikar (Nsungli, Ndop, Mbem, Kom, Bum, and the villages of Bentsan, Mashi, Fang, Fungom and Esu in the Fungom N.A.), the general principles would appear to be similar to those operating in Nsaw: namely, titular ownership by the *Fɔn* or, in the less centralized forms of political organization, by the Village Head; *de facto* control of tracts of arable and residential land by lineage heads, or heads of extended families (as in some of the Ndop villages).[1] The majority of women work plots on land belonging

---

[1] The Bafut group would appear to differ from the rest of the Tikar tribes in that *de facto* control of tracts of arable land is vested in delegates of the *Fɔn*, who re-allocate plots among individuals after a period of fallow. (*Vide, Bafut Assessment Report*, 1926, para. 211).

My own superficial inquiries confirmed this account, but the week I spent in Bafut was one of illness rather than of fieldwork and I am inclined to discount their value. It is highly probable that the patrikin of a *Fɔn's* delegate have rights similar to those enjoyed by the patrikin of a lineage head in Nsaw; and that it is only matrikin and non-relatives, who hand over a basket of grain at harvest and who must seek permission to re-cultivate after a period of fallow.

to their husband's lineage; but where these are inadequate for their needs they exercise rights of usufruct to plots belonging to their mother's lineage. In Kom, where lineages are matrilineal, the system of tenure is reversed in that the individual has a prior claim to the land of his own matrilineage, and a subsidiary claim to that of his father. There are grounds for assuming that, within the formal framework of lineage control, there is considerable flexibility in the functioning of such systems, and scope for the play of individual preference in the management of plots and the transmission of rights of usufruct. Such data are, however, difficult to obtain in the Courts or from Court Records of land disputes, and herein lies the relevance of the detailed study and presentation of the Nsaw system of land tenure, since it may suggest lines of investigation elsewhere. Of especial importance are the following points:

(a) a clear definition of the responsibilities as well as the rights of lineage heads, and the bearing of this on the concept of land ownership and control;

(b) the considerable freedom enjoyed by the women in the running of their farms, in the granting of temporary loans of areas to kin and friends; and in the transmitting of their rights to close kin, once they have decided to abandon the plots permanently;

(c) the extent to which plots, once allocated to a man by his lineage head, are handed on to his sons and sons' sons, so that particular areas tend to become vested in the smaller segments of the lineage; and,

(d) the tendency for isolated plots and even outlying tracts of land to become permanently alienated, once they have been lent to non-kin and not reclaimed for the use of the lineage within the first generation.

OTHER TYPES OF LAND TENURE IN BAMENDA

There are two other types of tenure which differ in certain respects from the *Nsaw* type and which are confined to the west of the Province. The crucial factors would appear to be a looser form of lineage organization, in the sense that the lineage head has less authority over his male dependants; and, secondly, the relative scarcity or abundance of arable land. The *Ngie* type (see p. 30), in which *de facto* control is vested in married men, occurs in some of the Widekum tribes of the west and south-west, where density of population is fairly high for Bamenda (between 70 and 100 to the square mile), and where the land is less fertile.[1] In the third or *Ngwo* type, which is found in the west and north-west, where there appears to be plenty of fertile land, the Village Head either allocates tracts of arable land among lineage heads, or leaves it to the women to farm where they will, only intervening in the event of a dispute.

NGIE TYPE

My information on *de facto* control by married males, that is, family heads, is most detailed for the village of Teze in Ngie, where I spent one month from March to April 1947. The country is mountainous and heavily forested in the narrow valleys, where the people build their villages. The yield from crops grown in the vicinity of compounds which are overshadowed by oil palm is poor, and the women go far afield, even to the hill-tops for most of their farm plots. Stretches of level ground are rare, and rough terraces of stone are constructed at intervals to prevent earth and plants from being washed

---

[1] The system obtains in Meta (Menemo) according to the investigations I made during a fortnight's stay in the village of Nyen; and also, according to the *Mogamaw Intelligence Report*, 1932, para. 83, in Mogamaw. It possibly extends to the Widekum-Menka N.A. in Mamfe. Unfortunately, I have no information at all on the Ngemba, who live on the uplands.

away in the rains. There is a patrilineage system but, unlike most areas of Bamenda, patriclans are localized in villages and not dispersed over tribal territory. A number of men belonging to a patrilineage occupy a group of neighbouring compounds in a clearing, which takes the name of the founder of the lineage, e.g. *eku-Ebanek; eku-Et/ebøiy* or *eku-Enyøku*. Usually the lineage head, *kum*, lives in one of the compounds but, in some cases, either he or his predecessor has moved to another part of the village, leaving a brother or eldest son in charge of the ancestral settlement. But, at intervals, he returns to perform sacrifices.[1] The reasons for a change of residence are sickness, quarrels or, more frequently, a desire for better land for plantain groves which are cultivated within easy access of the compound. The *kum* acts as a mentor in matters affecting his group by virtue of his role as intermediary between it and the ancestors. But, as mentioned earlier, he does not assist *all* his dependants in their marriage payments, and he has no deciding voice in the arrangement of marriages of women born to the lineage. In economic transactions his power is very limited: he has no lien on the services of his group; if he receives assistance, he is expected to make a specific return for it. For instance, there was a young man who occasionally carried palm kernels to Mamfe for his father's brother, but he did this as a favour and pointed out that he was permitted to be the lover of the girl betrothed to his uncle. It should be noted here that the Ngie women enjoy sexual freedom before and after marriage, but their lovers are expected to perform various services for the husband.

When a man marries, his father gives him a compound-site, some plots of arable land, and a few palm trees. The Ngie say that, if two married brothers continued to share the same compound and work the same palm trees and land, they (and their respective wives) would quarrel, and that to avoid this contingency they become, at marriage, economically independent not only in relation to each other, but also in respect of their father and the lineage head. A married man is free to pawn or sell his palm trees *and* his land to men of the *same* tribe, without any reference to the lineage head, though normally he would consult his father or his father's successor. Such transactions appear to be common: for, on the one hand, there are the heavy commitments of a large marriage payment which is rarely paid over in full before marriage; the provision of lavish feasts and gifts at the birth of a child; the payment of tax, and so forth. On the other hand, there are individuals (polygynists with many daughters, or men in government employment) who have a small surplus of cash or livestock and who are glad to avail themselves of the opportunity to increase their landholding or their number of palm trees by a loan or outright purchase. When a plot is pledged, the new farmer has *no* right to any palm trees growing thereon; but it is understood that he will have sufficient time to plant and harvest at least one season's crops. The pledge, in theory, is indefinitely redeemable; but, if many years have elapsed, there may be attempts at sharp practice, the farmer claiming that he originally bought the plot and did not receive it in pawn. Examples of this were found in the court records of land disputes.

It remains to consider what rights and what security of tenure the Ngie woman has under a system, in which *de facto* control is vested in family heads. Until her marriage, a girl works on her mother's farms, but sometimes she is allocated a strip by her father, or may be permitted to take over one of her mother's plots. Once, however, she goes to live with her husband, her father may bring pressure on her to surrender her claims if he requires additional land for a new wife or for a recently married son. It is true that she may threaten to apply ritual sanctions if evicted against her will; but such a step

---

[1] The man left in charge of the settlement is known as *Wva-eku*, a title which is also applied to men who have left the ancestral settlement and founded compounds elsewhere.

would entail drastic consequences in creating a permanent breach between her and her kin. And, in any case, her claim has no legal standing in the court. In this respect a Ngie woman is at a disadvantage as compared with a Tikar woman who, as long as she requires a plot, is not expected to cede it to a brother's wife or a father's wife. In Ngie, it is a woman and not a man who is expected to surrender a plot should the father require it. The man, in short, has privileges which are not granted to his sister, in that once he is married he may pledge, sell, or bequeath at will land allocated to him by his father.

The ritual sanctions which a Ngie woman may employ do not derive from her status in the lineage, but rather from the association between women and the fertility of the earth; and they may be regarded as a compensatory device whereby she strengthens her position in regard to land. On the larger farms are small heaps of stones (usually placed at the foot of an old tree), where offerings of food such as *egusi*, beans and oil, and a little water are made to the God of the Farm (*Nyugə Bwəm*) whose blessing is invoked on the crops before planting. Usually a woman who is a senior wife of the land-holder performs the rite; but sometimes she is his middle-aged married daughter, and she will eventually teach the ritual and grant the right of performance to one of his wives. It is left to her to make the selection, and in return she receives a gift of meat, plantains, and other cooked foods.

The power of a woman to render the land fertile or barren enters as a factor into transactions in land for, unless her consent is secured, any crops planted by the new cultivator will not prosper. This sanction is of particular importance in relations with her husband, since she may threaten to invoke it should he attempt to pledge or sell farm plots which she regards as essential to the subsistence of the household. Should he, despite her opposition persist she has one further sanction, namely desertion. It is significant that, although a man allots to each wife a certain number of palm trees in the sense that she becomes responsible for the extraction of oil from their kernels, he is under no moral obligation to consult her if he decides to pawn or to sell them. It is true that she may be left without oil for cooking and for barter, but her opinion carries no weight. Palm trees are " a man's thing ", and a woman cannot affect their productivity in the same way as she influences that of the earth by her ritual powers.

With the keen competition for accessible fertile land there is very little lending of plots, and certainly a woman may not, even in practice, grant temporary rights to a friend without the explicit consent of her husband. In this regard she has considerably less freedom to lend and to borrow than a woman of Nsaw and other Tikar tribes. Apart, then, from the purchase of additional plots by her husband or their holding in pledge, she has not many alternatives for obtaining extra land. There are certain boulder-strewn slopes which are so barren that anyone is free to cultivate them without requesting permission from their owner, once sacrifices have been performed. It is indicative of the shortage of land that some women are prepared to expend the labour of excavating stones from these slopes, in order to plant a few cocoyams and greens in the tiny pockets of soil. A mother and married daughter, or two married sisters, usually plant some of their crops on plots belonging to both, and then divide the harvest. The desire for companionship and assistance is satisfied through this arrangement and, at the same time, some insurance against the failure of the crops on the farms belonging to one of the women is provided.

When a woman is left a widow, she retains the plots allocated to her by her late husband, providing she remains in the compound. She also continues to express oil from the kernels of the palm trees, which were singled out for her use during his lifetime; but profits from the sale of surplus oil are put aside as a contribution for her son's marriage payment. If there are no sons, her husband's successor (a brother) would take the money and assume complete control of palms and also arable land at her death. Needless to say, if she marries a man who does not belong to her late husband's lineage she forfeits all rights. Normally, inheritance of the compound is from a man to his eldest son, or failing issue then to his brother. In Meta, it is the unmarried son (even if he is the youngest) who inherits, on the grounds that married sons have already received compound-sites, palm trees, and allotments of arable land. If there are neither sons nor brothers, property goes to the lineage head, and never to a daughter or daughter's son. This practice reveals the residuary claims of the lineage head to property of male members of the lineage.

NGWO TYPE

The last category, the *Ngwo* type, differs from the *Ngie* type in two important respects: firstly, land cannot be pawned or sold; and, secondly, the Village Head exercises *de facto* control over arable land. But it should be noted that compound-sites, small adjacent kitchen gardens, and plantain groves are handed down, as in Ngie, from father to son, except in Kung village, where inheritance is matrilineal. In the allocation of arable land two methods are followed. In Esimbi, Beba and Befang (all northern Widekum) women living in the village farm where they like, usually having some moral claim to re-cultivate plots which have lain fallow. Disputes are settled by the Village Head or his senior wife. In Ngwo (also Widekum) and in the Fungom villages of Kung, Zhoaw and Munkap, the Village Head, in consultation with lineage heads, decides every few years or so which tract of bush is to be cleared. He then allocates strips among the lineage heads, and it is left to the wives and daughters of such men to demarcate the boundaries of individual plots. Mashi (in the Fungom N.A.) presents a slight variation of this pattern: it is alleged that the subdivision of tracts of arable land among lineage heads took place many generations ago; but the Village Head has some very large areas and, when one of these is to be brought under cultivation by his own dependants, he grants temporary rights to the other lineages on the grounds that large-scale clearing affords some protection against the ravages of wild animals and other pests. In Aghem, the Section Head (*Batum*) fulfils a role similar to that of a Village Head. He has under his control a large area of arable land and grants rights of usufruct to those resident in his Section. The actual demarcation of boundaries is, generally, a matter for arrangement among the women, sometimes under the supervision of a *Natum* (' Mother ' of the *Batum*). Inheritance of houses and plantain groves is matrilineal; but, if the legatee fails to take up residence, they are taken over by the *Batum*.

Oil palms and raffia (where grown) are individually owned, and may be pledged or pawned in all the areas mentioned above, with the exception of Aghem, Beba and Esimbi.[1] In Beba there is an abundance of wild palms and each man is free to cut palm kernels where he pleases. In Esimbi, the same practice obtains with the exception of Benakemø Village where, two years ago, the Village Head and his council decided to allocate a certain number of trees to each compound-head for his own exclusive use. Men had complained that, with the increase in the cost of living, they could not always obtain sufficient palm kernels at certain times of the year, more especially when the tax fell due! In Aghem, all the Section Heads, with the exception of two who are of foreign extraction, have a monopoly of raffia.

---

[1] In Ngwo raffia is individually owned, but if a man wishes to plant raffia on outlying bush he must first obtain permission from the Village Head.

Chapter IV

METHODS OF CULTIVATION

THE women of Bamenda practise shifting cultivation but the length of time for which an area is worked and the rest period depend on the type of crops, the fertility of the soil, and the availability and accessibility of other land. In the village of Laikom in Kom many women leave ground to fallow after two years; in Kimbaw, where population is denser, large farms near the compounds may be utilized for five or six years, and kitchen gardens for even longer. While a certain amount of planting occurs in most seasons, it is towards the end of November and the beginning of December that a start is made with the clearing of extensive plots which will in March be sown with maize and which will inaugurate the new agricultural year. At this time the rulers or village heads in many tribes perform sacrifices to the gods of the earth and to the ancestors for the fertility of land and women, and for the general welfare of the people. In addition to these rites there are others associated with particular crops—maize, finger millet, and guinea corn—which may be carried out by lineage heads or individual farmers prior to planting and again at harvest.

Throughout most of Bamenda there is an eight-day week, and short periods are reckoned in weeks or sometimes moons, though the latter are not named. There are terms for the dry season and the wet season, the Nsaw making further distinctions between the beginning of the dry season, its peak, the first rains, and so forth. In general, however, the cycle of agricultural activities itself constitutes a calendar for the dating of events. So a woman, who has died just before the planting, weeding or harvesting of a particular crop, is said " to run from the planting of corn;" or " from the weeding of millet ", or " from the harvest of guinea corn ", as the case may be.[1]

By November, the uplands have paled to yellow or deepened to bronze and vermilion; the tall grasses make islands of the small fields of green guinea corn or the tawny stubble of maize. Fires, lit in the early morning or evening when it is cool, sweep across the slopes and hill tops, flare against the night sky, and illumine the country for miles around. They fulfil several purposes: in the first place, men and boys follow in their wake to hunt game; secondly, they facilitate the labour of clearing and form firebreaks around the highly combustible village huts; and, finally, they destroy undergrowth adjacent to the farms which would otherwise harbour the pests that ravage the crops. The annual burning of wide tracts of country is undoubtedly one of the causes of erosion, but it is difficult to see how any large-scale clearing could otherwise be carried out while the only tools are matchet and hoe. The alternative is the protection of farms by fencing, but the scarcity of timber makes this impracticable at present.

TOOLS

Farming implements are few and primitive. A woman's chief tool is her hoe (Pidgin-English, *sɔfri*, a contraction of shovel) which is 8 to 10 inches wide

---

[1] For instance, in Nsaw, a person may ask: " When did your child die ? ", to which the reply may be: " millet was being eaten just before he died." This may provoke the query: " Then he ran away from millet porridge ? " (*Wano kpu yan ka ? Vɛ lo yi saar bo kpuun. Wuu bɛne nyiŋe fɛ kiban ke saar a ?*)

at the top, about 12 inches in length, the sides curving gradually to a point at the base. It is attached to a knee-jointed handle which, in most tribes, is some 20 to 24 inches long so that hoeing is something of a back-breaking task.[1] Men use a matchet for clearing or planting, and a small mattock for the weeding of raffia palm. European axes are treasured possessions, but not all men can afford to buy them. Besides her hoe, a woman invariably carries a small farm knife, bought for a halfpenny or a penny, and this, with a calabash, a bag or a basket, and a walking stick, constitutes her equipment for a day's work. For solace she may take her pipe, a few strands of tobacco, a flint or a little container for glowing charcoal. In Nsaw, Ndop, and Oku most women prefer bags woven from the bast of raffia palm, but at harvest the crops may be carried to the compound in cylindrical baskets.[2] At the time of sowing, women place their seed in a small basket, which holds about a pint and which is tied to the waist by a piece of string. In Zhoaw it rests like a little bustle on the buttocks, and to it is attached a long fringe which swishes provocatively as a woman walks! Finally, in the wet season, an umbrella is just as much an indispensable part of ones paraphernalia for a journey as it is at any time in England. The Nsaw type is a square convex cane article with a criss-cross of bars inside, so that it can be fitted on the head and thus leave the hands free. In Kom, and farther to the west, it is long and cowl-shaped to protect both head and back. A European umbrella is owned, as a rule, only by the wealthier and titled among the men, and some of the well-to-do prostitutes. In regard to the latter it has almost become the distinguishing mark of their profession for, as one man pointed out to me, " What husband would spend fifteen or twenty shillings on a European umbrella for his wife when he can procure a locally-made one for fourpence! "

The day begins early for most people in Bamenda. Soon after sunrise, if not before, the smoke from the hearth-fire seeps up through the thatch; water is put on to boil for the porridge; and maize is ground, or vegetables are peeled. In Ngie, however, the women leave at dawn for their farms and often there is no time to cook a morning meal. The family goes hungry or finishes the cold remnants of the supper taken the evening before. On the uplands where temperatures are low, the women go forth much later, saying in explantion that they must wait until the sun shines brightly and has some warmth in it. In general, it may be 8.30 a.m. or 9.30 a.m. before they saunter off in ones or twos. The men loiter in the compound, do a little desultory sweeping, gossip, complete their toilet, and go off to visit their friends. Small children scamper about, often burdened with babies not much younger than themselves. They go to the stream in groups to fill water-calabashes; they consume the midday meal which has been put aside for them; and eagerly await the return of their mothers in the late afternoon or at dusk. The women bring in roots, greens or plantains, as well as the inevitable bundle of kindling which is sufficient for only two meals. Everywhere on the uplands firewood is a problem and is regarded as one of the many " troubles of women " (ngɛɛsi se viki). In Bali, Mbembe, Mfumte, and other tribes, many women have small huts at the farm and they only return to the village on market days, Sundays, if they are Christians, or at the slack season.

ORGANIZATION OF WORK TEAMS

While most agricultural activities are the concern of the women, the clearing of trees and heavy bush is undertaken by the men. For a large area they may

---

[1] In Zhoaw, and some of the other Fungom villages, hoe-handles are much longer and the women do not have to bend their backs to the same extent.

[2] The shape, size and workmanship of baskets vary considerably throughout the Province, but further details must be postponed for another report.

organize a working team (Pidgin-English—*djaŋgi*) consisting of the land-holder, kin and friendly neighbours, and the task is accomplished in one or two days. In recompense the beneficiaries provide food and wine or beer. If the plot is a small one a husband or son may do the job alone. At the harvest of maize, finger millet, and guinea corn, the men lend a hand; but, in general, it may be said that their contribution, while important, makes few demands on their time, and it is doubtful whether they spend more than 10 days at the outside on such tasks throughout the whole year. Often it is left to the women to cut away the tall grasses and low undergrowth (with the exception perhaps of Mbem, Mbaw and Mbembe where the men engage in more farmwork). In extenuation of this lack of marital co-operativeness it should be pointed out that, from November to March on the uplands, most men cut and carry large bundles of thatching grass from the hill slopes, about a mile or so from the village. During the same period they also bring in heavy timber obtained from the areas which have been burned off recently. Thus one man in Kimbaw devoted 36 days from the 25th November to the 2nd February to cutting and transporting thatching grass; while another man spent 25 days, followed by another 17 days for the carrying of large firewood to the compound. Even lineage heads are busy at this time of the year, accumulating thatch for the repair or rebuilding of their own and their wives' huts.[1]

Throughout the Province, sisters, or else a woman and her adolescent or married daughter, commonly work together for the more onerous or monotonous tasks. The companionship is prized as greatly as the assistance, in that labour is lightened by a little gossiping over the hoe, the small snack at midday, or an occasional pipe. Outside these family relationships, however, regular co-operation among women is rare in most of the Tikar tribes. From time to time a woman gives a helping hand to a friend in her own or a neighbouring compound, who is later expected, as the Nsaw say, "to return a hand" (*siiri kiwo*). But the number of days involved is small, probably no more than ten a year on an average.[2] There is, however, a quick response to illness and sympathy takes the practical form not only of visits, gifts of food, and firewood, but also of a day's work on the farm where preparation of beds, weeding or harvesting has fallen into arrears.[3] For the cutting of finger millet a woman who has a large crop may "beg" labour and provide food and perhaps a little beer. When a bride comes to the compound all the women help her for the first day on her new farm, and are feasted by her husband. And, finally, there is the joint cultivation of the farm of a lineage head by his female kin, and women married to his male dependants. In short, in these areas most women, unless they have a sister living in the same village or daughters who have reached puberty, are thrown very much on their own resources. But, in Bamessi in the Ndop Plain, in Mbem, in some of the Fungom villages, in Bali, Aghem, and especially in the Widekum tribes, a group of women form a team which works on the farms of the members in turn.[4]

---

[1] In Mbembe, the men cut the grass, but the women help to carry it to the village.

[2] During a period of six months, when I kept the diaries of 30 women and girls, the average number of days devoted to assisting friends and affines was 4.7.

[3] As might be expected, much depends on personality. A mean and querulous woman is not neglected, since a strong sense of moral duty to a relative and, indeed, pity for anyone in distress bring kin and neighbours to her side. But there is, nevertheless, a marked difference between such a response and that aroused by an afflicted woman, who is kindly and generous. Visitors are more regular in attendance, and there are more volunteers for assistance on the farm.

[4] As far as my inquiries went, the work team as a regular institution is absent in Esimbi and Meta. I did not visit Mogamaw and I found no reference to such an organization in the Government Reports. In Befang a woman occasionally assembles a group, but the practice would appear to be as spasmodic as it is in Nsaw.

In Bamessi a working-bee is called a *tzɔ* and consists of women, who are of about the same age and who are kin or friendly neighbours. For the preparation of corn beds there may be ten or twelve individuals; for weeding only three or four. About a week's notice is given and, once a woman has received help on her own plot, she is under an obligation to fulfil a similar duty to others on pain of being reported to the *Fɔn*. The women usually work in pairs, sing, chat, and urge each other on. Towards the end of the afternoon a small repast is provided, which includes a little fish contributed by the husband. In Ngie a team (*mbu*) ranges in size from three to eight for farms adjacent to the village, but is larger for those in the bush.[1] As in Bamessi, it functions mainly for the making of beds for cocoyam and is not utilized to any extent for weeding. At harvest a woman either works alone or with the assistance of some female relative. Only a small quantity of food is brought, perhaps 3 lbs. of sweet potatoes, and a relish of greens, oil, salt and pepper for four women. The women hoe with zest, and often pointed out to me the saving in time and the pleasure of companionship. " We have joined to work because we are not strong. If we work together, we finish very quickly." On the other hand, the speed may be considered a disadvantage by the very elderly. As one woman in her fifties explained to me: "If I work alone (or with my sister or daughter) I can do so at my own pace. If I have made two beds and then my body is not strong, I may return to my house. The women in a *mbu* work quick, quick." Another alert old lady in Ngwo felt much the same, declaring that she could not keep up with the rest of the group. More rarely this attitude is adopted by young married women. There were two sisters in Teze, who cultivated together and who regarded a *mbu* as a waste of time, particularly if it had many members, for, in this case, it might be weeks before the plot of one person was tackled. Illness or heavy rains might cause further delay. In Ngwo I was told that the team would be smaller: one of four would spend one day on the farm of each of its members in turn; for the four following days each member would work on her plot alone; and then the *mbu* would resume its joint activities.

It is worth noting that regular co-operation is confined mainly to clearing and the final preparation of beds before planting: that is, to the work which is considered the heaviest and which must be done within the space of about two months. Weeding takes longer, but may be carried out at a more leisurely pace and is therefore left to the individual, apart from some assistance from a mother or sister. The distribution of the institutionalized working team in Bamenda does not appear to be associated with the occurrence of women's societies or the relative abundance or scarcity of good land, or the type of crop. In the Ndop Plain it is alleged to be spreading from Bamessi to other village areas, and there is much to be said for deliberate propaganda by schools, missions and other agencies, for its adoption elsewhere, particularly on the east and central uplands. Failing its adoption as an integral element in the organization of agricultural labour, at least more might be done to encourage the formation of working teams to assist women who are in an advanced stage of pregnancy. A feast, involving a small monetary outlay, would have to be provided and pressure might well be brought to bear on husbands to make this contribution. After all, under the traditional system, they assume responsibility for the cash expenses of the household and this further commitment demands only a little more effort in their own occupations; whereas an appeal to them to assist their wives on the farm would conflict with somewhat rigid ideas about the division of labour between the sexes. This is not to say that

---

[1] The same word is used in Ngwo; but in Beba the term is *i/ii*; in Bentsan—*ekwi'ake*; in Koshin—*tiŋala*; in Fang—*kəŋəra*; in Fungom Village—*andji'awo*; in Zhoaw—*tezam*; in Aghem—*zəm*; in Bali—*nsu*; in Mfumte—*junkap*; and in Mbem—*bofak*.

attempts to modify such ideas should be abandoned; but, under present conditions, they are likely to encounter more resistance than the course I have suggested. Already, a number of Christians have shown themselves prepared to incur new expenses for the welfare of their wives and children in the matter of payment for services at the mission maternity centre, for medical facilities, schooling, and clothing. It is, I think, largely a matter of education and of convincing them that the health of a woman and her coming-child necessitates some lightening of her labours in the period of advanced pregnancy. And the same would, of course, apply to one who has suffered a long bout of illness and needs to take things easily during the convalescence. As for the women themselves, co-operation would be forthcoming if one may judge from the response on those occasions when appeals were made, *with* the promise of a feast and wine as recompense for assistance.[1]

ROTATION OF CROPS

As I mentioned earlier, the women practise a system of rotational grass fallowing, the period varying from two to ten years depending on availability and accessibility of land, together with such personal factors as economic needs, age and health. In general, plots within a half to one mile radius of the compound are left for three or four years before cultivation is resumed. Good alluvial ground, suitable for maize and cocoyam, may be planted for four

TABLE II

ROTATION OF CROPS IN KIMBAW VILLAGE

First Year	Second Year	Third Year
maize	maize; or maize and millet maize and guinea corn millet guinea corn trifoliate yams sweet potatoes	maize; or maize and guineacorn maize; or maize and millet maize maize maize maize
finger millet	maize trifoliate yams	maize maize
guinea corn	maize	maize
trifoliate yams	maize millet millet and maize sweet potatoes	maize maize millet maize or millet
rizga (coleus dazo)	trifoliate yams millet	maize or fallowed yams or fallowed
sweet potatoes	trifoliate yams maize maize and groundnuts	millet and/or maize sweet potatoes
bambarra nuts	trifoliate yams millet	millet or maize maize

[1] While I was in Kimbaw a girl, who had been appointed health visitor, decided to have a plot cleared and bedded up for her own use. She called upon the members of her own compound and neighbours for assistance and, in return (with some help from her own mother and father's sister) provided a feast in which beer, palmwine, groundnuts, kolas, *egusi*, and meat were important items. The response was excellent, the work was accomplished in one day, and the women returned in high spirits and with warm praise for the generous scale on which they had been wined and dined.

and even six years and only abandoned when the yield is so poor that it is evident the area has become " tired ". Hill-slope land, which is drier and harder, may be cropped for only two years unless no further plots are available.

In most regions some rotation of crops is followed. In Kimbaw, where my inquiries were most intensive, trifoliate yams, *rizga*, sweet potatoes, and bambarra nuts are planted in separate beds and for one year only. In the following season corn, millet, or some other crop is substituted. But in good soil maize may be planted for six consecutive years. If the plot is ¼ acre or more, one half may be intersown with millet or guinea corn; and in the second year, one of these will be intersown with maize on the other half. Millet and guinea corn are never mixed. A chart on the previous page tabulates typical forms of crop rotation in Nsaw.

PREPARATION OF PLOTS

Throughout the Province the value of ash as a fertilizer is recognized; and in many tribes, both on the uplands and in the forest, small types of tree are planted, not only as an additional source of firewood but because they are said to " soften " the soil.[1] Refuse from the house and courtyard is also dug into the kitchen garden and, although one motive for this is a quick and convenient method of disposal, it is also said to enrich the ground.

Methods of preparing plots are very similar, but some are a little more elaborate than others and are practised mainly among the Tikar peoples. Grass is cut, left to dry, burnt, and then hoed into beds, which vary considerably in size and shape, but nearly always lie up and down the slope instead of across it. The women claim that they secure better results this way and, when it is suggested that the rain washes away the soil, they point to the ditches which are dug to overcome this disadvantage.[2] In Ngie, the hill-sides are so precipitous that many of the beds have to be shored up with sticks and stones. Cultivation is back-breaking work and requires, at times, the tenacity of a limpet and at others the agility of a mountain goat. In Nsaw (as well as in Mfumte, Nsungli, Bamessi, Bafut, Kom, Aghem and elsewhere), there is a special procedure which is often employed on the farms given over to maize and which is termed in Lamnso : *fuuni kinfuuni*. Heaps of dry grass are covered with earth and then left for a month or six weeks, after which they are set alight and left to smoulder. The soil turns a light vermilion, is rather puffy, but yields an excellent crop the first year; but it is followed by a much poorer one in the second season. It has been suggested that the method secures a large amount of grass-manured top soil in each bed, destroys pests such as wire worm, and possibly lowers soil acidity. But the burning of humus leads to a rapid reduction of fertility after the first year.[3]

As I mentioned earlier, a start is often made with the clearing of bush land and old corn farms at the close of the rainy season in November, and this continues in a somewhat desultory fashion until the end of December and the beginning of January, when the harvest of finger millet and guinea corn interrupts the work. After this, however, the pace becomes almost feverish

---

[1] In Kom, a shrub identified as *Adenocarpus Mannii* is used as a soil-recovery crop; in Oku, *Sesbania Aegyptica* fulfils a similar function. Maize-stubble is kept for kindling.

[2] In an experiment at Bambui Government Farm in 1945, local " 20-Eye " potatoes gave a better yield in beds made up and down the slope than those made across it. (*Vide, Annual Report*, Bambui, App. III).
In addition to ditches between beds, deeper trenches serve as boundaries between farm plots, and along these cassava, pigeon-peas, or small saplings may be planted as a further means of demaraction.

Vide, op. cit., 1945.

in the effort to complete yam and *rizga* plots by mid-February, and to finish off maize plots before the first heavy rains in mid-March. The women divide their attention between all three if they have no assistants, and complain of their weariness and sense of strain. But those who have young daughters are better off, since the latter assume much of the responsibility for the *rizga* and yam farms. In the forest areas (and also in the Fungom villages) *rizga* are planted in ridges; but in Nsaw special beds are prepared, and the women were in agreement that this is the heaviest type of work which falls to their lot. As one woman explained to me: " When you cut out the clumps of turf, the hoe rings and you feel a sharp pain in your shoulders. So women like to work *rizga* together ", and thus lighten the labour.[1] On an appointed day they climb to the hill-top, which is to be brought under cultivation, and demarcate their plots. On the following day, or a little later, they again go and one of the young girls who has a reputation as a keen worker makes the first cut with her hoe. Tussocks of the tough grass are hoed out and turned over; then sub-soil is dug from holes in the centre of the plot and scattered over the surface to " soften " the ground. About mid-February the *rizga*-tops are set about twelve inches apart in pairs, and thenceforward they require no further attention except for a day's weeding in June. They are harvested from October to January and are of two varieties,—*lɔŋ se sui*, which is eaten raw; and *lɔŋ se ɣa*, which is boiled.

The cultivation of yams makes fewer demands on the strength of the women. Sometimes a section of an old maize farm is requisitioned, or a small strip of bush may be cleared. More tilth is required than for maize, and on more than one occasion I heard a woman upbraiding a young daughter who was hoeing too much on the surface, and not digging deeply enough. The long type of yam (Lamnso-*kiruŋ*) is cut into slices which are then left to dry on top of small mounds before being planted at a depth of 6 or 7 inches. Two canes are stuck in and crossed to serve later as supports for the vine. Trifoliate yams are planted in separate plots and, like the long variety, are scattered over the farm to dry for three or four days, before they are placed in holes about 3 inches deep.[2] Usually they are harvested from October to January and provide an important item of diet when the maize supply is beginning to run low and must be husbanded more carefully.

Sometimes there are showers in February and the women seize the opportunity to sow some spinach, cocoyams and even a little maize, though in this case they run the risk of loss. From the end of this month until mid-March they strive feverishly to complete the re-hoeing and weeding (*/ɛvin*) of the main plots for maize, and are apt to regard it as one of the most onerous tasks since they are working against time. With the first heavy downpour in March, excitement runs through the village. It is called the " rain of the maize " (*wuu-o-ŋgwasaŋ*) and is the main topic of conversation. Children run about the compound, adults stand watching under the house eaves, and delighted old ladies revolve in graceful dance in their huts. The next day there is a general exodus to the farms to plant the grain,—the men using matchets, the women hoes. The farmer makes an incision with the hoe about 6 inches

---

[1] The Lamnso text was : " *ɣanse a gwar kisə'tin ku waa suŋ 'mbiiŋ; a waa ɣu nɣaar e mbɛ feyi. Nɛna viki kɔŋ fa tati a lim lim.*'

[2] In Nsaw, different varieties of trifoliate yam are grown and distinguished by name: *rɛ-nkuuni* (very hairy); *rɛ-ndjo'bri* (yellow flesh); *rɛ-ntɛm* (yellow flesh and similar to *ndjo'bri*); *rɛ-kiluun* (very sweet and similar to the *rɛ-mbinkar*, introduced from Ndop). Most women prefer *rɛ-nkuuni* and *rɛ-ntɛm*, because they are not so sweet as the other varieties.
There are two types of large yam (*kiruŋ*), and their vines climb in anti-clockwise direction up the stakes (*viramɛr*). The *kiruŋ-ke-okuu* is round, yellow in flesh, and not very hairy. It is preferred to the other variety, the *kiruŋ-ke-nkar*, which is about 2 feet long and very hairy.

deep, trickles two seeds into it and covers them over. Usually the plants will be about twelve to sixteen inches apart. The sowing is regarded as light and pleasant work in most tribes, and is completed within a few days. In Ngie cocoyam is the staple food and is planted in large quantities from the beginning of the rains in March and throughout most of April. In farms near the village the seed from a few cobs of corn may be intersown.

On the uplands once the maize is planted the women proceed to intersow it with spinach, cowpeas, dwarf beans, cassava, *makabo*, okra, pumpkin, gourds, *egusi*, sugar cane, peppers, and egg-plant, the last two being transplanted later. In Nsaw and Nsungli, cocoyam and potatoes may also be set; but in the Ndop Plain special beds are often prepared for these, as also for groundnuts.[1] During the latter half of April the women may relax, though they go fairly regularly to their fields and do a little weeding of *rizga* and yams. In May and June the maize requires its first weeding with a hoe (Lamnso—*/ɛpti ŋgwasaŋ*) and after this it is time to broadcast finger millet.[2] Later, special seed-beds are made for guinea corn, which is transplanted about August or September. Small plots may also be cleared in July for a second crop of sweet potatoes, but the energies of women are, in the main, given over to the second weeding of maize which is done by hand rather than by hoe (Lamnso-*tsøøni ŋgwasaŋ*).

Diet in April and May on the high grassfields is poor, and the women have a lean and hungry look. Stores of grain are slender and reserved mainly for the children, while adults depend on greens, plantains, a few sweet potatoes, and beans. In June, Irish potatoes are dug up and these, until the harvest of maize, constitute nowadays a sustaining, though somewhat monotonous, staple. As one querulous old woman complained: " Potatoes, always potatoes! I am tired of potatoes! " The people of the plains and forests are, on the whole, much better off for cereals for, in the first place, their harvest of maize comes earlier: and, secondly, many of them plant a second crop towards the end of the rains. Ngie is an exception, but Esimbi had such a large surplus in May 1947 that the women were continually brewing beer.[3]

In Nsaw, a few cobs are plucked towards the end of July for roasting, but the main harvest does not occur until towards the end of August, and gleaning (*siiri ŋgwasaŋ*) continues throughout September. Outlying farms are dealt with first, and those of lineage heads receive attention last. Usually all members of the family form a working team, passers-by lend a hand for a while, and are well rewarded with cobs for their labour. But gifts are not limited to assistants: the period is one for feasting and generosity, and the mean individual is despised. The suggestion made by one missionary that the people should be less lavish with their hospitality aroused some indignation, on the grounds that it seemed a denial of the feelings of goodwill and gratitude, which ought to be expressed after the long period of scarcity (*søø*).

In a great many tribes, including those of the uplands, rough storehouses are built on the farms and the maize is kept there until dry because there are fewer rats. In Nsaw, baskets of cobs are carried direct to the village and

---

[1] Bulrush millet (*za*) is planted about the same time as maize in Mbembe, and is never intersown with guinea corn.

[2] In Nsaw, some women plant bambarra nuts (*/ilɛŋ*) about May. Tobacco, *namma*, is sown soon after guinea corn seed-beds have been prepared. After the maize harvest in September it is transplanted, and two months later the men and women go to gather it (*kɛŋ*). The leaves are laid out in the courtyard to dry for two or four days, according to the weather, then crushed with the feet, and placed in a basket in a cool place.

[3] Although much of Ngwo is on a high plateau, there is no dearth of food. It was heartening to hear the women emphatically repudiate the suggestion that they endured a period of hunger at any season of the year.

tossed into the attic, where they gradually dry in the smoke from the hearth fire below. But leaky roofs or exceptionally heavy downpours of rain may mildew the grain; and even cats cannot entirely prevent the mice from having their fill. About November what is left of the maize is transferred to tall raffia bins, which are sealed with mud. They contain between 3 and 4½ *vegati* (cylindrical baskets) or approximately 220 to 330 lbs. The Mbembe have well constructed storehouses of clay, enforced with palm fibre. These are barrel-shaped, squat on chubby little legs, and have a thatch-cover resembling a Chinese peasant's hat.

After the harvest of the wet-season maize, beds may be hoed up in the furrows for the dry season crop and also for guinea corn, which is transplanted about this time. Thenceforth work slackens off in most tribes, but the Nsaw women are kept busy with the weeding of finger millet,—a slow and tedious job; and with the clearing of small beds for cowpeas, spinach and potatoes. From October to December yams, *rizga*, groundnuts, okra, and *egusi* are also harvested, but the millet is not gathered in until the end of December. It is regarded as a royal crop and all must wait until the *Fon* has an announcement made in the market that the harvest may begin. The heads of grain are cut with a small knife and laid out on mats to dry before they are rammed down into cylindrical baskets. The men, with the exception of lineage heads, help the women in the field and also in the transporting of the baskets (which may weigh anything from 70 to 90 lbs.) to the compound, where they are propped upside down on raffia poles. According to traditional usage pagans should not eat millet until the lineage head has offered a sacrifice to the ancestors and the spirit of the earth, provided medicine for all the members of his compound, and has contributed some meat as a relish. Some lineage heads have become lax because they say they have no money to buy meat. Their pagan dependants wax impatient, as the time passes and the unsampled millet remains stacked in tempting array under the house eaves. Unless there is an obliging anthropologist to provide the meat, they may delay for a long period until, out of sheer desperation, they are prepared to run the risk of illness and even of a bad season by eating the first fruits without the appropriate ritual.

Guinea corn matures early in January and is usually cut by the men. But, as I have pointed out earlier, its production in many tribes has decreased and its place as a staple cereal has been taken by maize, particularly when this crop can be planted twice a year.

Having described the agricultural cycle in some detail, we may now summarize its dominant features. Broadly speaking, the dry season from the end of November to the middle of March is devoted to the preparation of farm plots for tubers and maize. With the onset of the heavy rains towards the end of March, maize and subsidiary crops such as legumes, cucurbits, greens and sugar cane are planted. From May to August the women are chiefly engaged in weeding; and from August to November with harvest. The calendar on the following page lists the main activities in relation to the more important crops, but certain points should be borne in mind. In the first place, while it conveys some idea of the sequence of events, the times are only approximate. If the first rains do not fall until April, weeding and harvesting, particularly of cereals, occur much later in the year than normally. Again, the calendar is based mainly on material obtained in Nsaw and is therefore more typical of conditions on the uplands than in the forest. Finally, it should be remembered that the cultivation of finger millet, which absorbs so much of the time and energy of the women from September to December, occurs only in Nsaw. To this extent its inclusion in the chart obscures the pattern of slack periods which is typical of other economies in Bamenda.

TABLE III
CALENDAR OF MAIN AGRICULTURAL ACTIVITIES—NSAW

Month	Clearing and Preparation of beds for:	Planting of:	Weeding of:	Harvesting of:
January ..	Yam, *rizga*, sweet potato. Burning off.			Finger millet, guinea corn; yams and *rizga*.
February ..	Yam, maize, and potato.	*Rizga*, yam, sweet potato, cocoyam.		Last of *rizga*, yam.
March ..	Re-hoeing maize and cocoyam plots.	Maize, gourds, greens, legumes, groundnuts, etc.		
April ..		Cocoyam, cassava, bambarra nuts.		Few sweet potatoes.
May.. ..			Maize, yam, *rizga*.	Few sweet potatoes, beans.
June.. ..		Finger millet.	Maize, yam, etc.	Irish potatoes.
July	Sweet potatoes.	Finger millet, guinea corn.	Maize.	Irish potatoes, few corn cobs.
August ..	Sweet potatoes, cowpeas.	Sweet potatoes.		Maize.
September ..	Cowpeas; dry-season maize.	Cowpeas, greens, Irish potatoes.	Finger millet.	Maize, beans.
October ..	Light clearing of cropped-maize farms.	Cowpeas, potatoes, dry-season maize.	Finger millet	*Rizga*, yam, groundnuts.
November ..	Clearing.	Cowpeas, potatoes.	Finger millet, guinea corn.	Yams, *rizga*, sweet potatoes.
December ..	Clearing and burning off.			Finger millet, yams, *rizga*, etc.

Chapter V

LABOUR AND LEISURE IN KIMBAW

THE chart on the previous page gives some idea of the variety and also the sequence of agricultural activities throughout the Bamenda year, but it does not show the amount of time which must be devoted to each crop, the trouble entailed, the factors which lighten or hinder a task, the proportion of days spent on the farm to those spent in relative leisure or in other occupations at home.

SIZE OF FARMS

According to Intelligence and Assessment Reports, as well as estimates made by the Senior Agricultural Officer at Bambui, a Bamenda woman who has no assistants cultivates from 1.0 to 1.5 acres a year.[1] In addition to this she may have 0.75 acre under grass fallow. This last figure is based on some data from Kimbaw and is approximate, since there are obvious difficulties in measuring areas completely overgrown with tall grasses and scrub. As far as the actual area under cultivation is concerned, there are considerable variations owing to such factors as age, health, temperament, and particularly the number of children in the household. A sickly old woman with no dependants may find that even an acre is beyond her strength, and may concentrate on those plots which happen to lie within a short radius of the compound. Or a Christian widow, who engages regularly in petty trade for the provision of such necessaries as cloth, salt, oil, tools and utensils, may farm only 1.07 acres, as was the case with Sui of Djem (No. 8 in the Table below). At the other extreme there is the young woman in her early thirties who has four young children to provide for, not to mention a large and hungry husband, and who may work 1.8 acres with no outside assistance, except at the harvest of finger millet (see Yeduda, No. 6). When the working team consists of mother and daughter, the area cultivated is much larger and my Kimbaw figures give an average of 2.9 acres; while that for a working team of three is 4.25 acres. While in Kimbaw during my second tour, I devoted three months to measuring all the farms of 21 women, as well as those of the *Fɔn*, some of the nobility, lineage heads, and others. In a report to the Senior Agriculture Officer, I included details of the size of each plot, its distance from the compound, the number of years which it would be worked, the period of fallow, the type of soil, and the area under various crops. In addition there were figures for the harvest of maize, millet, and guinea corn. The report is too detailed to incorporate here, but I have extracted some data from it in order to indicate the range in variation (Table IV, pp. 64, 65 & 66)[2].

---

[1] A similar estimate has been made by Madame R. Dugast, who has written a very detailed account of agriculture among the Ndiki (Banen) in the French Cameroons. A Ndiki woman, on an average, cultivates ½ to ¾ hectare a year. Crops, tools and methods are very similar to those of Bamenda.

Vide, Mme R. Dugast: " L'Agriculture chez les Ndiki de population Banen," *Bulletin de la Société D'Études Camerounaises*, No. 8, 1944, p. 77.

[2] I should like to thank Mr. S. E. Gwilliam, S.A.O., Bambui, for permitting Damon Wirkom (artisan overseer) to help me in the measurement of Kimbaw plots; and also to thank Damon himself for his untiring co-operation. Most of the work was done from October 1947 to January 1948.

TABLE IV
FARMS OF A SAMPLE OF KIMBAW WOMEN

No.	Name (X indicates a Christian). Nos. 1–12 work unassisted	Approx. Age	No. of Dependants, Including Husband*	No. of Plots Under Cultivation	Total Acreage	Remarks
1	Biy-Djem ..	20	2	8	1.3	Only wife of Mawo of Djem. Healthy, but 6 months pregnant in Jan., 1948.
2	Dzøøndzøiy ..	28	3	10	1.4	Only wife of Kibu of Djem. Healthy. Keen worker.
3	Biy-Menggu ..	25	2	8	1.2	Only wife of Tanye of Menggu. Child often sickly.
4	Wanaka ..	25	2	6	1.2	Wife of Fai-o-Mbonyaar, who has three other wives. Healthy, keen worker.
5	Melalia (X) ..	35	2	6	1.3	Unmarried, and has 2 sons. Lives at Mbonyaar.
6	Yeduda (X) ..	35	5	14	1.8	Wife of Thomas Kintarir of Mbonyaar. Hard worker, despite serious illness in 1946.
7	Yadiy	35	4	8	1.4	Wife of Fai-o-Djem, who has 4 other wives.
8	Sui	50	1	7	1.07	Widow of brother of Mawo. Keen trader.
9	Fhshwaa ..	60	2	9	1.3	Wife of Fai-o-Mbonyaar (see above). Assisted occasionally by small granddaughter.
10	Camilla (X) ..	50	0	7	0.9	Widow of Mbonyaar. Suffers from chronic bronchitis.
11	Shemsum (*Yelaa*)	60	1	4	1.4	Senior wife of Fai-o-Mbonyaar (see above). Very wiry.
12	Yirbongka ..	50	0	5	1.2	Divorced from husband, and lives in her brother's compound at Mbonyaar. Good health.

Average acreage cultivated by one woman: 1.29 acres

* Dependants include children and the husband, where the latter has only the one wife; but, in the case of a polygynist, I have included only the children among the dependants, since the husband is a lineage head and supplies some grain from his own store; and, secondly, the burden of feeding him is distributed among his wives.

No.	Name (X indicates a Christian). Nos. 13–19 work with one assistant	Approx. Age	No. of Dependants, Including Husband*	No. of Plots Under Cultivation	Total Acreage	Remarks
13	Bertha (X) ..	45	2	8	1.7	Widow of Mbonyaar. Often acute bronchial attacks. Assisted by niece, aged 14 years.
14	Audelia (X) ..	25	3	10	3.9	Wife of Maurice Njingla of Mbonyaar. Assisted by and assists her mother. Strong, keen worker.
15	Elizabeth-Kila (X).	45	7	9	1.7	Wife of Francis Lole of Mbonyaar. Assisted by husband's niece. Male dependants buy corn in market as further contribution to household.
16	Margaret (X)..	38	7	9	2.1	Wife of Nicholas Ngee of Ka. Assisted by adolescent daughter.
17	Clara (X) ..	35	6	11	2.1	Wife of Alphonse Fannso of Ka. Assisted by adolescent daughter.
18	Yuliy	55	1	12	1.9	Wife of Fai-o-Djem (see above). Assisted by adolescent daughter. Has bad rheumatism.
19	Vindjan ..	45	8 (see remarks)	12	5.2	Wife of Fai-o-Djem (see above). Assisted by married daughter who has 4 children in a separate household. The two women divide the harvest from the acreage cited; but the daughter has, in addition, separate farms of her own. Vindjan feeds three children.

Average acreage cultivated by two women: 2.65 acres.

Average acreage per woman: 1.32 acres.

* Dependants include children and the husband, where the latter has only the one wife; but, in the case of a polygynist, I have included only the children among the dependants, since the husband is a lineage head and supplies some grain from his own store; and, secondly, the burden of feeding him is distributed among his wives.

No.	Name (X indicates a Christian). Nos. 20–21 work with two assistants	Approx. Age	No. of Dependants, Including Husband*	No. of Plots Under Cultivation	Total Acreage	Remarks
20	Kengeran ..	45	7	16	4.5	Wife of Fai-o-Djem (see above). Assisted by two adolescent daughters.
21	Elizabeth-Bika (X)	43	7	15	4.0	Wife of Vincent Kwangha of Djem. Assisted by adolescent daughter and mother.

Average acreage cultivated by three women: 4.25 acres.

Average acreage per woman: 1.41 acres.

Average acreage cultivated by one woman for whole sample: 1.34 acres.

A number of points arise for consideration. In the first place, the tendency for most women to cultivate a number of separate plots is typical, I think, of most of the uplands and plains. In the forests, I made no first-hand investigation of the problem, but, in response to my general inquiries, most informants said that they had one or two large farms for maize, and three or four smaller ones for yams, *rizga*, and other subsidiary crops. The average number of plots worked by a woman in the Kimbaw sample is eight; but as in the case of the total acreage farmed by a woman, there is a fairly wide range of variation, and much the same determining factors are involved. Shemsum (No. 11) had only four,—all within 20 minutes' walk of her hut. She had abandoned others at Kingomen, but the area left to her was still 1.04 acres since, as senior wife, she had large plots adjoining the compound. Apart from occasional acts of hospitality and an occasional meal for her husband and sister's son, she had only herself to feed. At the other extreme was Yeduda (No. 6), who cultivated 14 different plots and from them had to provide food for her husband and her four insatiable children! Nine of these plots lay within ten minutes' walk from the compound; two were within 30 minutes'; two were an hour away; and one very large tract was 90 minutes' journey over two steep hills, one of which rises 1,200 feet from the valley floor.[1]

Clearly this fragmentation of a woman's total farm holding into a number of small plots, often scattered over a wide region, entails inconvenience and a loss of time and energy. This is recognized by the women themselves, but at the same time they explain and defend the practice on empirical grounds. In the first place, certain crops such as yams, *rizga* and sweet potatoes thrive best when planted in separate beds, and the odd individual who disregards this elementary principle is treated with considerable contempt for her slipshod laziness. Sometimes the soil of one area is fairly suitable for yams, sweet

* Dependants include children and the husband, where the latter has only the one wife; but, in the case of a polygynist, I have included only the children among the dependants, since the husband is a lineage head and supplies some grain from his own store; and, secondly, the burden of feeding him is distributed among his wives.

[1] At *Ro-Kɔŋ*, the stream just below Mbonyaar compound in Kimbaw, an aneroid barometer gave a reading of 5,400 feet above sea-level. From here women, on their way to outlying farms, ascended to 6,150 feet, descended into another valley, and then climbed a hill at a height of 6,600 feet.

potatoes and maize, and in this case a woman who has a large plot may demarcate small sections for the first two; or, if it is less than ¼ acre, she may plant these in rotation over a period of 2½ years. But, where possible, a woman tries to secure some alluvial land for maize and cocoyam, and here yams and millet give such a poor yield that plots for them on higher ground must be found.

Besides two main farms for maize, most women have a number of smaller ones. Camilla Labam (No. 10) had 0.7 acre under maize, but this was distributed among 5 different plots. Elizabeth-Bika (No. 21) worked 2.8 acres of maize in 11 plots, and Vindjan (No. 19) worked 3.7 acres in 8 plots. It was explained to me that, despite the additional labour involved, this procedure was justified. Maize is the staple and the preferred food and one cannot have too much of it. Even a bumper harvest will not last during the rains, and there is usually some loss owing to mildew and rats. There is also a further reason: land around Kimbaw varies in its fertility, and it is not wise to put all ones seed into one plot and run the risk of a poor yield. Quite apart from deterioration through constant cropping of plots, others brought under cultivation after a long period of fallow may sometimes prove unsatisfactory (or " refuse " the crop, as the Nsaw say). Finally, the amount of rich alluvial land within reasonable distance of the village is limited; and, while the system of land tenure ensures that most members of a lineage, owning a tract, have a fairly equitable share, there is not sufficient for large plots for them all, and still less for non-kin. All these considerations are of relevance for any proposals to change the existing system of land tenure in Nsaw and elsewhere; and it is worth noting that women in Nsungli, who had been compelled to abandon outlying plots and plant their crops in large farms close to their neighbours as protection against cattle depredations, complained bitterly of the decrease in the food supplies.

ACREAGE DEVOTED TO SPECIFIC CROPS

According to my Kimbaw figures, a woman devotes about 77% (or 1.15 acres) of her total holding to maize and finger millet. The average area under maize is 0.9 acre, and that under millet is 0.5 acre, some of which is intercropped with maize. There is very little cultivation of guinea corn in Kimbaw itself, but an Artisan Overseer from the Department of Agriculture made some measurements of farms in the village of Tabessob, 7 miles to the south, and the average size of these was one-third of an acre. Of course the percentage devoted to all these cereals varies in individual cases, and is not constant from year to year. In Yeduda's holding of 1.8 acres, 66% was under maize and millet (0.9 acre for maize and 0.3 acre for millet), and the rest of it was given over to large plots of Irish potatoes, cocoyams and rizga. But her millet farm, though smaller than the average, gave an exceptionally high yield at the harvest in December 1947. Another woman, Dzøøndzøiy, had 89% under maize and millet, but the actual area for each of these crops was 0.4 acre and 0.9 acre respectively. The maize farm was very small, but the soil was good and gave her a yield which was commensurate with that of women cultivating a much larger area.

The maize farms, as mentioned earlier, are intersown with a host of subsidiary crops,—cocoyams, gourds, legumes, and greens. In addition to these there are the small plots for yams, rizga and sweet potatoes. Their size depends on the strength of the woman, the number of her children, and her predilection for the food concerned. Most women work only one plot of trifoliate yams—about 500 square yards—, but an elderly woman who has a strong preference for them as food may have over 1,000 square yards. The rizga farms are the smallest, because of the heaviness of the labour entailed in their preparation. One which I measured was only 88 square yards, while the largest was 666. The average size is 300 square yards. Finally, there are the beds for sweet potatoes which are made twice a year and which average about 400 square yards.

(a) *Maize:* As might be expected, much of the time during the dry season is given over to the preparation of plots for maize, whether it be the clearing of land which has lain fallow, or the rooting out of stubble and weeds from land which has been cropped earlier in September. From October 1947 to March 1948 I kept the diaries of the women and girls whose farms I also measured, and on the basis of these was able to estimate the approximate number of days devoted to various tasks. Age enters as a factor, but a woman in her thirties who enjoys fairly good health requires about 30 days to clear, to prepare special beds of the *kinfuuni* type (see p. 58 of Ch. IV), and do the final re-weeding of just under 0.5 acre of ground.[1] The actual sowing of all maize farms is accomplished in two or three days, and is followed by the inter-planting of subsidiary crops, after which women may relax a little though they still go to the farms on the traditional working days. The first weeding of corn begins about the second week in May, and anything from 14 to 21 days are devoted to it. The work is not regarded as particularly onerous, but it occurs when food is running short—a point to which I shall return later. After the weeding of yams and the sowing of millet, the women begin the second weeding (*tsøøni*) of maize which is lighter than the first, since the few weeds which have sprung up in the interim can be removed quickly by hand within the course of about 10 days. In less than a week the bulk of the harvest is done by the family, which forms itself into a working team. Gleaning is carried on spasmodically through September; and, in late November, a morning may be spent in transferring the dried cobs from the loft to a raffia bin.

(b) *Finger Millet:* Since most of the millet is inter-planted in maize, very little additional time is needed for the preparation of plots. The first weeding of maize clears the ground, and the seed is broadcast in five to seven days. The real drudgery comes with weeding, mainly during October and November, though a start may be made in August. All told, 30 days may be devoted to pulling out by hand the tares which so closely resemble the grass-like seedlings. Women who cultivate more than half an acre may take 40 days or more. The job does not require much strength but it is tedious and indeed irritating, unless seasoned with a little companionship and the opportunity for some self-pity! The harvest begins at the end of December and is likewise time-consuming, since the heads of grain must be cut off separately with a small knife. The women used to laugh at me when I asked them if they had filled a tall cylindrical basket (*kegati*) during the day, and they would reply: " Many days pass before a *kegati* is filled ". When there are no children or close relatives to help a woman, a husband (unless he is a lineage head) lends a hand.[2] On an average the harvest of half an acre takes 21 days.

(c) *Yams and Rizga:* The preparation and planting of a yam plot (some 500 square yards in area) takes from 6 to 10 days; while a *rizga* patch (300 square yards) requires 10 or more. Weeding makes few demands on time; and harvesting even less, as the crops are dug out as needed for the house. One hour may be spent in obtaining some 20 to 40 lbs.

---

[1] In this estimate, the work done by two women in one day has been counted as two days' work. Some individuals do not hoe as rapidly as others, especially if their total acreage is small. Thus Melalia (No. 5) took 4 days to clear 750 square yards of high grass; 8 days to make beds; and another 4 days for the final weeding in early March.

[2] Among the 11 men whose diaries I kept, two of them gave considerable assistance to their wives. One man spent 12 days, and the other 7 days in the cutting of the grain, besides carrying the baskets back to the compound.

One further point arises for discussion before we turn to examine the women's attitude to farming. Owing to the dispersal of plots over a wide area and the variety of crops, the planning of work demands considerable foresight and empirical knowledge. As a rule, advantage is taken of fine weather and good health to tackle the outlying farms, which may be 3 to 5 miles away; and these are finished if possible before those nearer home are attended to. But if there is rain threatening or a woman is feeling sickly, she goes to those within easy access of the compound. For some areas there is a day when the hoe must not be used and, unless there is a task which can be done by hand, she must perforce work in another area where the taboo is not observed. On the distant farms companionship is sought and two relatives or friends usually arrange to go together.

The women carry out their activities methodically, generally completing, for example, the weeding of maize before turning their attention to yams and *rizga*. They criticize those who start one thing and leave it unfinished for another, and regard them as incompetent farmers or as lazy individuals. When a woman and her daughter (or daughters) regularly constitute a working team, the mother may exercise her authority and order the others to do some task if time is pressing. But she is no martinet and generally permits them to decide whether they will assist her on the main farms or else attend to their own.

WOMEN'S ATTITUDES TO WORK

Before we consider the proportion of days spent on the farm to those at home, it is important to grasp the attitude of the women themselves to their agricultural activities, since it is a factor to be taken into account in any attempt to change or modify the existing division of labour between the sexes. The women of Nsaw were almost unanimous in declaring the preparation of the *rizga* plots to be the hardest of all; but they justified the expenditure of effort on the grounds that *rizga* is an excellent food for babies, small children and for those who are ill.. One variety is boiled and easily digested but is rarely eaten by the men. Many men do not like finger millet, declaring that it is very hard on the bowels, particularly if taken immediately before or after palm wine! They express a somewhat perfunctory sympathy over the work entailed in the weeding of this crop and even go so far as to say it is " a women's job, which is too strenuous for the men "! As for the women themselves, they regard it as the most irksome during the early part of the dry season, and on more than one occasion said to me: " now you have seen one of the troubles of women! " But the harvest is worth the effort. The grain is resistant to mildew and can be stored indefinitely. It is easy to grind; is sustaining in so far as a little porridge goes a long way; and, finally, it is an important supplement to the food supply, when maize is almost finished and there are few yams and *rizga* left at the farm.[1] It says much for the providence and conscientiousness of the women that they are willing to make the sacrifice of time, patience, and labour involved in the cultivation of this crop.

Next to these two tasks—the growing of *rizga* and finger millet—the Nsaw women regard the preparation of maize plots as one of the heaviest of their duties, and in this matter they are at one with other members of their sex in the rest of Bamenda. Outside Nsaw I had little opportunity to go to the farms; but everywhere I made inquiries about their attitudes to farm work and there was a general consensus of opinion about this phase of the agricultural activities.

---

[1] Sometimes a little finger millet is mixed with guinea corn for porridge. The Mbembe mix their bulrush millet with guinea corn.

Weeding of all crops (except millet) is regarded as a relatively light task, at least in retrospect![1] It may be done fairly leisurely during the wet season providing there is food to sustain the worker, not to mention good health. Much depends on the region. In the forest and plains the " hungry period " is short and not very intensive except in a bad year, when the harvest has been small or a delay in the onset of the rainy season has hindered the maturing of sweet potatoes, planted about February. But on the uplands and in Nsaw particularly, where I had most opportunity for watching the women at their work and hearing their daily comments, the women labour under difficulties. The weather is inclement: cold dank mists fill the valleys in the early morning the women huddle over their fires and are reluctant to go forth. They complain frequently of being off-colour, of having headaches, and pains; and, indeed, many do succumb to influenza, pleurisy and fever. The men are not very sympathetic and accuse the women of indulging in self pity (*viki |am wun feyi*); but then the men need not go out into the cold and drizzle. They may while away the morning over a fire, and wax garrulous with frequent potations of palm wine! Food is short, and instead of 2 lbs. of porridge, which is a normal breakfast in times of plenty, a woman may have only ½ lb. and a few ounces of greens on which to do a day's work in the fields. My unwittingly tactless inquiries as to what the women had had for breakfast produced such answers as " hunger clutches me tightly " (*djiŋ koo mo feyi*); or " there is only a licking of fingers at the beginning of the hungry period " (*fh/wɛm adzə /u søø*); or " my belly is heaving because I have eaten only spinach "; or " I only ate pumpkin leaves. Today is hunger ". When the women return in the evening they prepare something for the children; but, if they have no dependants, they may give way to their weariness and simply lie down and sleep. It is little wonder that, when the maize is harvested, women and children (not to forget the men) gorge themselves on slabs of porridge, and top off the meal with a few roasted cobs. A woman comments with pride on the fatness and sleekness of her young daughter, and declares joyfully: " hunger goes forth from the house! "

The statements which I have quoted express more vividly than any description of mine something of the moods and the reactions of the women to particular hardships during the period of the rains from May to the end of July. My observations confirmed that their complaints had a foundation in fact: often the women (and the men) were short of food; often they went down with the coughs and colds which spread from one member of the family to another in the confined and ill-ventilated sleeping quarters of a small hut. According to my inquiries, similar conditions also prevail in the other upland areas such as Nsungli, Oku, and parts of Kom. However, it should be stressed that the very pithiness of the women's remarks may create a picture of unabated hardship, chronic disgruntlement, and little respite from labour. This would be false. The question of the amount of leisure of which the women avail themselves will be discussed in the following section. But here it should be pointed out that hunger and illness are not always inmates of the house, though a visitation is always imminent in the period of the rains. Again, complaints about the weather, health, and food do not imply that farm work is regarded as drudgery, though it becomes a burden in certain circumstances and has its monotonous and exacting phases, as indeed most tasks have.

On the whole, the women tackle their jobs with interest, zest, and pride— attitudes which are communicated at a very early age to their young daughters.

---

[1] In Tala and Mbwot in Nsungli, groups of women meet together from time to time, after the harvest of maize, to drink beer. Outside the house they place the yellow flower of one of the worst weeds, as a sign that the men are not to enter. The weed symbolizes the " trouble " which the women have had in cultivating the maize, and emphasizes their right to enjoy the product of their industry.

As one wiry old woman, who farmed 1.3 acres, explained to me : " If I have strength, I work well. If I have eaten, I work well. I (and others like me) are happy." When the women described to me their idea of a good life, they did not visualize it in terms of a cessation of farmwork. Like the old woman I have quoted, they desired primarily good health (for themselves and their children) so that they might work well; and a husband, who would provide salt and oil, as well as extra food when household supplies ran short during the period of scarcity. For the odd woman (and I met only three in Kimbaw), who neglected her plots in the hope that a husband would buy food in the market from his regular earnings as Government employee or U.A.C. storeboy, they had contempt, *not* envy. They condemned her improvidence and laziness; they did not regard her as a superior being. Their attitude was not, I think, a matter of sour grapes. In the first place, they were ready to respect the Christian woman who, although enjoying a higher standard of living because of her husband's income, nevertheless worked hard at the farm and engaged regularly in petty trade. Secondly, they considered that idleness led to bad habits. As one friend pointed out to me: " If she sits down idly, has no work, then in a little while she is begging, and then stealing."

And here I would emphasize that the responsibility of women for agriculture is not regarded by them (or by men) as a sign of inferior status. On the contrary, it confers status and is bound up with feminine self respect and dignity. They take all the pride of an expert in their work; they value the encomiums of others; they are sensitive to charges of laziness and of having ill-kept plots. But it is worth pointing out that they have little praise for the field-drudge, for the woman who, in her absorption in her farming, has not the time for a little gossip, and who works on oblivious of the presence of her neighbours. I once heard two women (one, a Christian in her thirties, the other a pagan in her late fifties) discussing a somewhat unpopular member of the compound, as they watched her bend untiringly over her hoe. " She only looks at the earth; she does not gossip at all! She works, then passes on; she does not speak. Silent always! Silence is a very bad thing! "[1] Between the sexes there is a certain amount of good-humoured teasing about their respective duties, each minimizing the contribution of the other. If bickering develops a serious turn, a woman may fling the taunt at her husband: " a man's only work is to drink palm wine! " But the men, in their more sober moments, acknowledge the importance of the women's work; and the women, on their side, admit that the occupations of the men are complementary to their own, though less time-consuming. As one of my friends put it, when I found her grinding maize after seven in the evening, " A woman's work is never finished! " But here I must intervene to point out that, while a woman's tasks on the days that she goes to the farms do seem almost endless, she does not go every day to the farm.

LEISURE

In most Bamenda tribes there are one or two days in the week, which are traditionally regarded as rest days in that the women do not do any heavy work at the farm unless, for various reasons, weeding has fallen into arrears or there is some task requiring urgent attention. Among many of the Tikar communities one of these days is associated with the death of a *Fɔn*: the women refrain from using a hoe, and the reigning *Fɔn* remains in seclusion. Generally, market day is a day for relaxation, visiting and foregathering in the market place. An attempt in 1947 on the part of the Fɔn-Nsaw to exclude the women from the market on the grounds that they were wasting maize to

---

[1] The Lamnso text is: " *wu lei nsaiy tʃatʃa; la wu yo kɔŋ fɛ fər kinfər yɛ. Wu lim nɛna tɔssin; la yo suŋnin kisuŋnin. Kisəsə yansidzəm. Kisəsə ke bir ki feyi!* "

71

brew beer for sale, that they were not working hard enough, and that they were making assignations with young men, aroused deep resentment among the women themselves though they stood in too great a fear of the Fɔn to organize overt resistance. Their attitude was that the women were always working, that the food was theirs to dispose of as they pleased, and that many depended on petty trade to provide necessaries for the household. Fortunately, pressure was brought to bear on the Fɔn from other quarters, and the new rule was dropped—to the delight and relief of the women. In Nsaw, there are five markets which occur on different days; that in Kimbaw is on a *kaaviy*, which may be regarded as the beginning of the week. The third day is *kiloovəiy*, one considered appropriate for marriage ceremonies, and housebuilding; while the sixth day, *ngoilum*, commemorates a Fɔn's death.[1] Christians, of course, observe the sabbath and decide for themselves whether to take advantage of the traditional rest days. It should be noted that the rest days (*vi/i ve bam*) are spaced so that a woman need not spend more than two consecutive days at the farm. In other tribes the period is often longer.[2]

Nsaw women may legitimately rest from farm work on three days in an eight-day week and, if questioned why they are at home on such days, the reason given is: " it is a rest day " or " it is market day ".[3] Absence from the farm on traditional working days is, on the other hand, nearly always due to some specific reason rather than a desire for leisure: sickness, preparation of food for house-building or a marriage, a protracted visit to a bride; or, more rarely, the brewing of beer or the cooking of food to sell in the market on the following day. In theory, then, a woman spends 62.5% of the days of the year on her farm; and 37.5% engaged in matters other than farm work. What is the position in fact? It was only in Kimbaw that a relatively uninterrupted period of fieldwork enabled me to keep diaries of the activities of some of the women; and, in the discussion to follow, I shall analyse, in some detail, the data which were obtained, for they have a relevance for other tribes. As I have pointed out earlier, farm work in Nsaw is, I think, heavier than in any other area, and therefore conclusions as to the percentage of days spent at the farms may be taken as representing the maximum demands made on the time of a Bamenda woman.

On pages 75—79 I have tabulated figures based on the diaries of 30 individuals (25 adult women and 5 adolescent girls), kept from the 28th September, 1947, to the 9th March, 1948 (total—164 days), but not all are equally complete. For eleven women I have records for 160 to 164 days; for ten between 150 and 159 days; for six between 130 and 149 days; and for three between 89 and 129 days. The sample was not a random one, but was determined by the accessibility of individuals to my compound, and by the friendly relationships which I had established with most of them during

---

[1] The Nsaw days of the week are: *kaaviy, rəovəiy, kiloovəiy, nsøøri, geegee, ngoilum, wailun, ntayrin.*

[2] In most tribes, the " rest-days " are spaced so that women work for 3 or 4 consecutive days; but in Koshin they work for 6 days and rest for the next 2. In Lus (Mfumte) some of the women said to me, " we only rest when there is a death! " Actually, they were at that time (December) enjoying a slack period, and had come from the huts on the farms to spend a couple of months in the village.

[3] Audelia of Mbonyaar compound had been delayed in her weeding and preparation of yam plots by the illness of her child. When I expressed surprise that she was going to the farm on market day (*kaaviy*), she replied: " I have the sorrow of pulling out weeds, pulling out weeds, up (the slope), down (the slope). The time is passing quickly. I must go and cut the seed-yams at Dzøø-Dzəng. (*M kər məndzen me /o kipwi, /o kipwi, fɛ ta, fɛ rɔŋ. yanse si /aa feyi. M ku du kɛti run-rɛ fɛ Dzøødzəŋ.*) " A moment later, she was standing by when I asked another woman what *her* plans were for the day. Audelia interposed with the remark: " She has no illness to hinder her work as I have. She may stay here. (*Bo wu yo kər yassi wo djivir lim rə mo mo. Wu waa rəsi fɛn.*) "

my first tour. However in selecting a hut in which to live for the last six months, I chose one in Mbonyaar compound because it, and some of the compounds in the vicinity, provided me with a fair cross-section of the Nsaw community. The lineage head of Mbonyaar was of *m'tar* status and had four pagan wives. There were fourteen other adults, two of whom were also pagans, and a number of children. The Christian households included individuals of all ages and, among these, were an unmarried mother, two widows and two divorcées. The men followed diverse occupations,—tailoring, bricklaying, general trade, and manual labour for the government. Adjacent to Mbonyaar was Ka, a sub-lineage of the same clan, where I kept the diaries of two large Christian families, one male household-head being a tailor, and the other a blacksmith. Ten minutes' walk up the valley lay the compound of Menggu, an offshoot of Djem, where Tanye, a pagan trader, lived with his wife and small child. Half a mile beyond this was the outlying compound of Djem, which was entirely pagan except for one large Christian family. I recorded there the activities of the *Fai*, four of his pagan wives, two pagan monogamous households, a pagan widow living alone and, finally, the members of the Christian family. A sketch plan of the four compounds is given in Appendix D.

Usually I visited the compounds in the early morning and again in the late evening, but occasionally I missed individuals because either they were away in another part of the village, or had not returned from their farms. Whenever possible I pursued inquiries the following day, but sometimes owing to an over-sight on my part the information was not obtained. Incompleteness of records occurred mainly in the first few weeks, and more especially in those for some of the adolescent girls, whom I had not at first realized were accompanying their mothers regularly to the farm.[1] Where I have details for only two or three days in a week, I have omitted them from my calculations.

I have given three lots of figures in Tables V, VI, and VII: (i) for the period between the 28th September and the 24th December 1947; (ii) for the 25th December 1947 to the 9th March 1948; and (i and ii) for the full period. In the case of four individuals (Nos. 1, 23, 26 and 27), my information for the first period was so patchy that I have not included it, though it has been taken into account for the whole period. My reason for making the subdivision is inherent in the nature of seasonal activities throughout the year. As I have already pointed out, there is a relatively slack period after the maize harvest, in the sense that the weeding of finger millet and the preparation of small beds for cowpeas, greens, and beans can be carried on at a fairly leisurely pace, without much interruption for other tasks. On the 25th December the *Fɔn* had it announced in the market that the harvest of finger millet might begin, and thenceforward the burden of farmwork became much heavier. There is another point of some importance: the percentage of days spent by the average woman at her farm during the six months concerned may be considered as fairly typical of the whole year. In my first tour I spent from April to the end of October 1945 in Kimbaw and, although I kept no diaries, my information indicated that agriculture, at that time, had also its phases of intensive activity and relatively light work.

In my diaries I recorded for each individual the name of the farm visited, the kind of work done, and whether assistance was given or received; but the analysis of such material must wait for another report. The occasions when

---

[1] There was one woman who was at first reticent and even bad-tempered in response to my inquiries, and for a time I omitted to visit her. But, after awhile, she began to resent my seeming lack of interest in her activities, and begged me to come and see her daily, as I did the other women in the compound.

a woman spent only a half day at the farm were relatively few in number and, in this report, have been treated as full days. Sometimes a fall of rain interrupted the work, or perhaps, on a traditional " rest day ", a few hours would be spent gathering greens, or digging out tubers for the evening meal.[1] Days spent in the compound, or in visiting friends and kin, have been treated as periods of leisure; while in estimating the amount of time lost for illness I have included not only that of the individual concerned but that devoted to the care of a sick child, another relative or a friend, and to mourning. My records contain several cases of protracted incapacity,[2] but, even when these are excluded, the percentage of days spent at the farm during the whole period still falls below that devoted in theory to farm work. *The percentage of days lost for personal illness has been placed in brackets.*

The results tabulated on pp. 75, 76, 77, 78, and 79 are to a great extent self-explanatory, and my comments merely underline them. There is a significant difference between the amount of time allotted to farmwork in the first and second periods: namely, 48.6%, as compared with 56.9%; or, if cases with over 10% lost for illness are excluded, then 58.8%, as compared with 63.8% (*vide*, Tables VI and VII). In the first period there was only one woman who worked more than 62.5% of the days at the farm; whereas in the second there were twelve, despite the fact that some were incapacitated by illness and took less than 25% of the remaining days for leisure. Again, in the first period it was rare for women to go to the farm for more than two or three consecutive days; while in the second, it was common for them to spend from five to seven, especially when preparing beds for yams and completing the re-weeding of plots for maize. These facts all support my contention that the women work harder during the peak of the dry season than during the rest of the year.

---

[1] From the 21st October to the 9th March, there were showers on only six days.

[2] The individuals concerned were No. 22, who had a bad abscess on her shoulder and who had to go to Bamenda Station Hospital; No. 24, who injured her foot; No. 10 who rested for nearly a month after confinement; No. 14 who went to the mission maternity clinic long before her child was due; Nos. 16 and 25 who suffered from acute bronchial attacks; No. 20 who had a sore eye, and so on.

Adults

TABLE V
DIARY MATERIAL—KIMBAW VILLAGE*

No.	Name; Religion; Marriage; Assistants	Approx. Age	Dependants	Acreage of Farms	Seasons	Per cent Days at Farm	Per cent Days for Leisure	Per cent Days Lost for Illness and Mourning
1	Djingla, P. 3 co-wives.	45	1	1.3 (?)	ii	65.2	26.4	8.4
					i and ii	68.1	25.0	6.9 (1.1)
2	Yadiy, P. 4 co-wives.	35	4	1.4	i	60.5	36.6	2.9
					ii	75.4	23.0	1.6
					i and ii	67.4	30.3	2.3 (0.0)
3	Clara, X. Monog. Assisted by No. 27.	35	6	2.1	i	65.8	30.5	3.7
					ii	61.8	29.0	9.2
					i and ii	64.0	29.8	6.2 (5.5)
4	Yeduda, X. Monog.	35	5	1.8	i	58.0	31.8	10.2
					ii	69.7	26.3	4.0
					i and ii	63.4	29.2	7.4 (3.0)
5	Margaret, X. Monog. Assisted by No. 26.	38	7	2.1	i	54.5	28.4	17.1
					ii	67.1	28.5	4.4
					i and ii	60.1	28.5	11.4 (10.7)
6	Audelia, X. Monog. Assisted by mother.	25	3	3.9	i	56.8	27.2	16.0
					ii	63.1	15.7	21.2
					i and ii	59.7	21.9	18.4 (4.2)

* The data included in the various columns require some explanation. In the second column I have given the name of the individual, and whether she is a Christian (X) or pagan (P); whether divorced, a widow, or an unmarried woman; whether monogamous (monog.) or polygamous (the number of co-wives has been indicated); and whether she is assisted by, or assists, others. In the fourth column, the number of dependants in the household (children and husband) is given. After the percentages of days lost for illness, etc. for the whole period (i and ii) I have placed, in brackets, the percentage of days lost for *personal* illness.

75

TABLE V—Continued

Adults

No.	Name; Religion; Marriage; Assistants	Approx. Age	Dependants	Acreage of Farms	Seasons	Per cent Days at Farm	Per cent Days for Leisure	Per cent Days Lost for Illness and Mourning
7	Shemsum, P. ... ... 3 co-wives.	60	1	1.4	i ii	52.9 67.1	34.1 31.5	13.0 1.4
					i and ii	59.6	32.9	7.5 (7.4)
8	Kibong, P. ... ... Divorced, and living with No. 17.	30	—	1.3 (?)	i ii	59.5 58.6	38.0 36.0	2.5 5.4
					i and ii	59.1	37.1	4.9 (0.6)
9	Dzwndzaiy, P. ... ... Monog.	28	3	1.4	i ii	51.1 64.2	28.4 30.0	20.5 5.8
					i and ii	57.1	29.2	13.7 (0.0)
10	Wanaka, P. ... ... 3 co-wives.	25	2	1.2	i ii	59.0 52.6	31.3 21.0	9.7 26.4
					i and ii	56.0	26.4	17.6 (17.6)
11	Mbaina, P. ... ... Unmarried mother. Assists No. 21 below.	23	—	—	i ii	52.9 59.4	35.2 33.3	11.9 7.3
					i and ii	55.9	34.4	9.7 (7.1)
12	Fhshwaa, P. ... ... 3 co-wives.	60	2	1.3	i ii	48.1 60.5	35.4 30.2	16.5 9.3
					i and ii	54.9	32.2	12.9 (7.7)
13	Vindjan, P. ... ... Assisted by married daughter. 4 co-wives.	45	8	5.2	i ii	43.5 67.6	32.0 25.0	24.5 7.4
					i and ii	54.7	28.7	16.6 (8.2)

76

14	Biy-Djem, P. Monog.	20	2	1.3	i	60.7	28.0	1.3
					ii	42.8	17.1	40.1
					i and ii	52.6	28.5	18.9 (17.5)
15	Melalia, X. Unmarried mother.	35	2	1.3	i	59.0	38.6	2.4
					ii	39.4	43.4	17.2
					i and ii	50.0	40.8	9.2 (3.0)
16	Camilla, X. Widow.	50	—	0.9	i	42.0	34.0	24.0
					ii	52.6	27.6	19.8
					i and ii	46.9	31.0	22.1 (21.3)
17	Yirbongka, P. Divorced.	50	—	1.2	i	43.7	37.5	18.8
					ii	48.0	30.6	21.4
					i and ii	45.8	34.1	20.1 (5.1)
18	Biy-Menggu, P. Monog.	25	2	1.2	i	39.2	32.9	27.9
					ii	52.1	33.8	14.1
					i and ii	45.3	33.3	21.4 (16.6)
19	Yuliy, P. 4 co-wives. Assisted by No. 29, below	55	1	1.9	i	31.3	20.4	48.3
					ii	60.0	31.4	8.6
					i and ii	44.4	25.5	30.1 (24.1)
20	Elizabeth-Kila, X. Monog. Assisted by H. Br. daughter.	45	7	1.7	i	36.4	31.8	31.8
					ii	51.3	40.7	8.0
					i and ii	43.2	35.9	20.9 (18.9)
21	Kengeran, P. 4 co-wives. Assisted by No. 11 and No. 30.	45	7	4.5	i	37.5	28.4	34.1
					ii	49.2	23.1	27.7
					i and ii	42.6	26.1	31.3 (14.0)
22	Elizabeth-Bika, X. Assisted by No. 28 and mother	43	7	4.0	i	55.7	39.8	4.5
					ii	17.1	10.9	72.0
					i and ii	39.4	27.6	33.0 (30.9)

TABLE V—Continued

Adults

No.	Name; Religion; Marriage; Assistants	Approx. Age	Dependants	Acreage of Farms	Seasons	Per cent Days at Farm	Per cent Days for Leisure	Per cent Days Lost for Illness and Mourning
23	Juliana, X. Monog.	25	2	1.4 (?)	i	—	—	—
					ii	59.2	34.2	6.6
					i and ii	38.0	27.0	35.0 (33.5)
24	Sui, P. Widow.	50	1	1.07	i	28.5	38.0	33.5
					ii	40.9	23.6	35.5
					i and ii	33.8	32.4	33.8 (30.9)
25	Bertha, X. Widow, assisted by niece.	45	2	1.7	i	17.4	17.4	65.2
					ii	38.1	21.0	40.9
					i and ii	27.2	19.1	53.7 (53.7)
	Adolescents—							
26	Natasha, X. Assists No. 5.	14	—	—	i	—	—	—
					ii	67.1	32.9	0.0 (0.0)
27	Julia, X. Assists No. 3.	16	—	—	i	—	—	—
					ii	64.8	30.9	4.3 (0.0)
28	Regina, X. Assists No. 22.	17	—	—	i	58.2	40.3	1.5
					ii	62.9	32.2	4.9
					i and ii	60.4	36.4	3.2 (1.5)
29	Wirngoran, P. Assists No. 19.	18	—	—	i	51.3	46.1	2.6
					ii	61.4	37.1	1.5
					i and ii	57.9	40.3	1.8 (0.9)
30	Kisif, P. Assists No. 21.	18	—	—	i	40.5	44.5	15.0
					ii	69.5	29.0	1.5
					i and ii	54.5	37.0	8.5 (1.4)

TABLE VI

AVERAGES—1

Date	No. of Cases	Per cent days at Farm	Per cent days for Leisure	Per cent days lost for Illness, Mourning
i 28th Sept., 1947 to 24th Dec., 1947	26	48.6 max.: 65.8 min.: 17.4	33.3 max.: 46.1 min.: 17.4	18.1 max.: 65.2 min.: 1.3
ii 25th Dec., 1947, to 9th Mar., 1948	30	56.9 max.: 75.4 min.: 17.1	28.5 max.: 43.4 min.: 10.9	14.6 max.: 72.0 min.: 0.0
i and ii 28th Sept., 1947, to 9th Mar., 1948	30	53.1 max.: 68.1 min.: 27.2	30.8 max.: 40.8 min.: 19.1	16.1 (11.5) max.: 53.7 min.: 0.0

TABLE VII

AVERAGES II

(EXCLUSIVE OF CASES IN WHICH OVER 10 PER CENT DAYS WERE LOST FOR ILLNESS, ETC.)

Period	No. of Cases	Per cent Days at Farm	Per cent Days for Leisure
i	9	58.8	36.5
ii	19	63.8	30.9
i and ii	13	60.9	33.4

The figures for the amount of time allotted to leisure also show a corresponding difference in the two periods. In the first period it was not only customary for women (Christians and pagans) to take advantage of the traditional rest days, but on occasion they visited a bride, a newly-born baby, a relative in a distant village, or else attended some dance or festivity on a traditional working day. In my sample there were 68 instances of this, as compared with only 15 for the following period—late December to March. Mention was made earlier of an innovation made by Christians in the rhythm of work. They rested on the sabbath, but the extent to which they availed themselves of the traditional days for leisure depended on the time of the year and the exigencies of agriculture,—as indeed one might expect in dealing with practical farmers. In compounds predominantly Christian, most of the pagans stayed at home on Sundays in order to enjoy the company of the others, since leisure is regarded not only as a cessation of labour but as an occasion for social intercourse and relaxation shared in common. Sometimes the pagans were teased for adhering to one Christian practice and not to others; but, as one old woman put it, " Who would cook food for the children, while their parents are at church, if we did not stay at home ? "

There is a final point to be noted: the high percentage of time lost for illness,—namely 18.1% in the first period, 14.6% in the second, and 16.1% as an all-over average. If records for only personal illness are considered the averages are still high: 12.7% for the first; 10.0% for the second; and

11.5% for September to March. With very few exceptions the difference is accounted for in time devoted to sick children. Coughs, colds, intestinal disorders, and low fever seemed to be particularly prevalent at the change of season (May and again in November), and it was usual to find one or more ailing members in a household. Women were reluctant on such occasions to entrust sickly children to nursemaids, and therefore sacrificed several days' work at the farm to tend them. Some were prepared to pay the twopence at the hospital, which would entitle them to a card for medicine as an out-patient; but many feared that they would have to remain at the hospital, and therefore did not go at all. Their reluctance is understandable. It is easier to look after and prepare food for someone in the compound; moreover, those who place warmth before hygiene find the familiar hut with its hearth fire more comforting than the draughty spaces of the hospital with its cold concrete floors and limited supply of blankets. As for the women who contracted complaints, many attempted to go to the farm if work were pressing; or, after a severe bout of illness, they would try to hoe or to weed, when they should really have been sitting in the compound and "feeling the breeze" (*yu fh/wɛɛr*).

My sample for the activities of the men included only eleven individuals (the husbands of the women whose diaries I kept) but my main impression was that the men, as a group, enjoyed better health. They, on their side, often accused the women of indulging in self-pity, and it is true that the latter have a variety of phrases for describing in some detail their aches, pains, and general feeling of being off-colour on occasion. In fact, such terms are regarded as a feminine monopoly and, when I sometimes employed them, the men laughed and said—"now you are a real Nsaw woman!" But if the men are less often heard complaining it is largely because they rarely engage in sustained labour. When they do so they are not at all stoical about their temporary discomfort, they bewail their weariness and the scratches which they have received in carrying bundles of heavy firewood and thatching grass. When I teased them they said they were not so strong as the women! This male rationalization of what appears to be an inequitable division of labour between the sexes is very typical of most Bamenda tribes. In Ngie I was told that the women could carry heavy loads because they had stronger foreheads; and, on one occasion, I heard the following comment from a group of men who were discussing a neighbour who had no wife and who had to fend for himself: "He works hard. Indeed, he works almost as hard as a woman! It is a wonderful thing!"

Pregnant women usually continued to work at the farm until the eve of delivery. They did not appear to regard this as overtaxing their strength, but reserved their complaints instead for the chore of grinding maize. Where possible they often substituted yams, potatoes, plantains, or beans for the evening meal. Once the child is born a woman enjoys a period of leisure in her com-pound and is visited and assisted by some close relative,—a mother, sister or aunt. In two cases, for which I have records, 25 days elapsed before any farmwork was done; in a third case the period was 22 days. Even then the collecting of firewood, weeding and hoeing were done on plots near the compound so that the mother could return frequently to nurse and feed her child. This period of complete rest appears to be typical of most Bamenda tribes; and there is, furthermore, a general recognition that a nursing mother requires plenty of food and oil, as well as meat and fish when they are procura-ble.[1] After two or three months, women only rarely carry their babies to the

---

[1] In the other tribes which I visited the women remain at home for about a fortnight and sometimes for a month after they have delivered a child. The period may be much longer when twins are born.

farms and then mainly because they have been unable to find a nursemaid. Their attitude is understandable, for a baby is an additional burden over the hills and at the farm it is likely to interrupt the work.

At the risk of boring the reader with a text punctuated by figures, I have discussed my diary material in some detail because it records for nearly 6 months the actual pattern of activity in one tribe and may do something to counterbalance the impression, held by many Europeans, that Bamenda women have " but care and woe ". Most Europeans rarely visit the compound and as often as not this may be on a working day, when the women are away and only children and a few men are to be seen—the latter possibly " putting story " and tippling a little palm wine. From the road Europeans glimpse women bending over their hoes and this picture comes to symbolize a depressed and oppressed Bamenda womanhood. The hardship is over-estimated; the content and pride of many of the women in their work are underestimated. The unfavourable impression, once created, tends to over-shadow and even obliterate the gaity and minor festivity of those three days in the eight-day week when the women idle in the compound, gossip over their pipes, sometimes dance, gather excitedly round a new-born baby, rejoice over a harvest, or conduct a bride to her new home. It is not denied that the women work hard on their days at the farm; that they must sometimes sacrifice a rest day, or several, to make up time lost for illness; and that, in short, they have a right to leisure. What is important is that the very great majority do, in fact, enjoy such leisure for some 30% of the days of the year. And this, I think, is typical of most tribes in Bamenda. The actual rhythm of work varies in different areas but, for reasons which I have already advanced and which I need not repeat here, it is highly probable that the practice of agricul-ture in Nsaw makes more demands on the time, energy, and skill of the women than elsewhere. In so far as this is the case, the amount of leisure taken by the women of Nsaw may be regarded as representing the average, if not the minimum, enjoyed by women in other tribes.

Having pointed out that even the women, who enjoy relatively good health, only spend some 60% of the days in the year at the farm, it is necessary to counteract any impression that I am in agreement with the Fɔn that the women do not work hard enough! If a Nsaw woman has not always her hand to the hoe, she frequently has her nose to the grindstone! And here full weight should be given to the fact that, when a woman goes to the farm, she has a long working day which begins about 7 in the morning and does not finish till about 7 in the evening. As Yeduda explained, when I asked her why she did not attempt to learn English, " I must cook, then I have to go to farm; I come home; I wash my child; and I cook the evening meal. I pass from one job to the other and I would forget." Like the average European house-wife, the Bamenda woman has little respite from household chores and, while these are not always as onerous, they are time-consuming. In order to complete our picture of the women's work we shall consider these other tasks in some detail.

DAILY CHORES

In the forest, and even on the plains where there is a certain amount of timber, firewood may be obtained without much effort and loss of time; but, on the uplands in Nsaw, Nsungli, Kom and much of Fungom, women may have to wander far afield to find sufficient kindling for the evening meal and that on the following morning. Women normally spend an hour or so while at the farm gathering a few sticks; but, if they are not going to the farm they may saunter out at midday for their supply. From September onwards maize-stubble yields about a dozen bundles of kindling; while, later, the men cut and

carry in heavier timber from where tracts of country have been burnt off.[1]
Firewood is only purchased occasionally in the market, since a bundle costs
5*d*. or 7*d*. and lasts only some four or five days for ordinary purposes.   Women,
who require a lot for the brewing of beer for sale, sometimes buy a bundle
though this reduces their profits.   Low shrubs and small trees growing in the
bush or on outlying land under grass fallow are free for all; but saplings on
cultivated plots are jealously guarded by the owner for his own use.   I
encountered one instance where a man had granted his married daughter the
right to use a patch of land previously worked by her mother, but he expressly
stipulated that she was not to cut down the saplings, as he wanted them for
firewood for his own household.   In Mbembe and Mfumte the women said
they took advantage of the slack period of the early dry season to accumulate
stores of wood for the rains.

The water-supply may be as much as $\frac{1}{4}$ mile away from the compound, and
journeys to fill pots and calabashes must be undertaken at least twice a day
unless, as in Bamessi, women have very large containers for keeping a good
supply of water on hand.   As soon as the children are old enough to fetch and
carry, the filling of calabashes becomes one of their daily tasks, along with other
small chores, such as the sweeping of the compound, the washing of younger
brothers and sisters, the peeling of potatoes and shelling of beans.   They are
rarely negligent in performance, as these tasks are done in company and,
furthermore, there is the inducement that their mothers may bring home
some tit-bit from the farm as a reward: a handful of groundnuts or bambarra
nuts, a roasted *rizga*, a stick of sugar cane, or a few beetles or grasshoppers to
roast on the fire!   While failure to carry out these jobs may be strongly
upbraided, performance is not accepted casually.   The child is praised and
gravely thanked.   Indeed, the graciousness and courtesy which pervaded all
social relationships in Nsaw is one of the most delightful characteristics of the
people.

Finally, there is the preparation of food which, while not regarded as particularly onerous in itself, is often nevertheless the last straw to break a woman's
back after a long day's work on the farm and a weary trudge home.   In most
tribes, grain porridge is the preferred food and is cooked at least once a day
while supplies permit.   The maize is rubbed off the cob by hand, pounded in
a mortar for a few minutes and then winnowed.   The grindstone, which is
usually placed in the rear of hut, is some 24 inches long and 16 to 20 inches
broad.   A woman kneels at one end, places a slightly concave basket at the other
to catch the flour, grasps a small tortoise-shaped stone with both hands, and
then grinds.   On several occasions, when I timed the process, it took about
one hour for three pounds of grain.   Generally, one grinding is considered
sufficient unless there is a sickly child or a feast.   Old women are apt to pant
and whistle over the work, and where possible they inveigle a young girl in
the compound into assisting in return for a meal.   On the whole, most adoles-
cents do shoulder this burden and relieve their mothers of at least one task.
But the aged grandmothers, as in other societies, are apt to bewail modern
times, and to accuse the young of doing nothing but visiting.   As one friend
said to me: " A bride's mother makes her child proud.   When the child
grows up she goes to her husband's house, but she does not know how to do
anything at all! "   The complaint has a familiar ring.   However some do
conform to the ideal standard: " Some leap up quickly and grind maize
flour.   The girls of the compound see this and then they do the same."
Whatever the truth, it is perhaps just as well that in most Nsaw villages
maize is grown only once a year.

---

[1] But much of the heavier firewood, collected by a man, is usually sold to augment his
income.

When limited supplies are exhausted by about May, the women and girls enjoy a few months' respite from grinding. One trader in Bali had bought a hand-mill, and for a penny he allowed women to grind a small basket of grain. Apparently a number took advantage of this, more especially those who engaged regularly in petty trade and had a few pennies to spare. Whether men in a group of compounds could be induced to contribute to the purchase of hand-mills for the use of their womenfolk is another matter. It is an innovation which might well be given the support of Progressive Associations which have been formed in Kimbaw and elsewhere in Bamenda. Unfortunately the women, with their negligible monetary resources, can do little. They might resort to their traditional weapon of nagging; but, if they went further and worked " according to rule", their children (along with their husbands) would be deprived of maize porridge, and no Nsaw woman (and probably no Bamenda woman) would view this with equanimity. So far from the child being tied to its mother's apron strings, it is the mother who is tied to the child: a fact of which the men are well aware and, on occasion, willing to exploit.

But to return to the preparation of porridge for the household. While the maize is being ground, water is put on to boil in a pot. Flour is added to this and left to cook for ten or fifteen minutes until it has coagulated into a thick consistency. It is then removed with a calabash ladle in dollops, placed in calabash basins, tossed (if for a guest or a husband), and served with a relish, which is put into a separate clay container (Lamnso, *laŋ*). The relish usually comprises greens such as spinach, cowpea-leaves, pumpkin-leaves, cocoyam-sprouts, elephant-grass shoots or, in an emergency, wild leaves, which have been boiled or heated, and then mixed with about a tablespoon of oil, a teaspoonful of salt, and about the same amount of red pepper. In Esimbi, Mbembe and Ngie the quantity of oil is much larger. Sometimes instead of greens, a sauce (*ntee*) of oil, salt and pepper is used, to which may be added on occasion fungi, pounded *egusi* seeds, groundnuts, okra, dried locust bean, or termites (*ngosi*). Meat, as I have mentioned earlier, is still very much a luxury for the majority of the population; it marks a festive occasion and, while eagerly welcomed in the diet, is not itself regarded as being particularly nourishing: " It is not food; it is something to taste! "

Yams, plantains, potatoes, cocoyams, and cassava may be roasted if a woman is too tired to do more than prepare a scratch meal; but more often they are left to boil slowly in a large pot, and then eaten either in slices, or mashed and consumed with a sauce. Cassava and cocoyam require several hours and are usually cooked on a rest day, or placed on the fire at night and left to simmer in readiness for breakfast. Nowadays, those who have travelled abroad have adopted new foods and recipes to provide variety.

In many of the Widekum tribes cocoyam and plantains are frequently cited as preferred foods, but among the Tikar and Mbembe groups maize or guinea-corn porridge ranks high and is considered as particularly appropriate for an honoured guest or for a feast.[1] In a long discussion on the subject of food, my friend Benedict told me that if he were especially invited to a meal he expected porridge, for it was real " food " and gave strength. If he were served with yams he would be disappointed, for they did not " fill the belly ", and the same applied to roasted plantains, or mashed potatoes unless eked out with beans. He said women liked millet porridge because they had to work so hard to grow the millet! As for relishes, meat was sweet but one tired of it quickly, whereas spinach always tasted good. Groundnuts were also sweet in the mouth, but even if one had chewed a pound of them, the belly would not

---

[1] In Ngie and also, I think, in Ngwo, women boil or roast maize, but do not prepare it in the form of porridge (or *fufu*, as it is known in Pidgin-English).

" refuse " maize porridge! Most men in Nsaw would have agreed with Benedict. Women were less rigid in their preferences, probably because they had the chore of preparing food and, in any case, had to keep a watchful eye on the supply of maize and occasionally substitute other dishes. Nevertheless they too, granted the energy to grind grain, frequently served it for a number of consecutive meals. Bulk is important, and a stuffed belly is equated with an adequate satisfaction of hunger. Early morning visitors to my hut used to view with some dismay and concern my breakfast of orange juice, a slice of toast and coffee, and would demand anxiously: "Does it tighten your belly? Does not hunger clutch you?" During the period of plenty, most adults consume from 2 to 3 lbs. of thick maize porridge, and 2 to 4 ozs. of greens at a meal, or about 2 lbs. of yams, potatoes, cocoyams or plantains. In the period of scarcity, the porridge shrinks to about 1 or ½ lb. for the children, and very often less for the parents. The following menus give some idea of the daily diet for three consecutive days in February and three in May (see Table VIII).

TABLE VIII

February—

Name	Time	First Day	Second Day	Third Day
Elizabeth-Bika ..	a.m.	mashed cocoyam	maize porridge, and spinach	maize porridge and spinach
	p.m.	fried maize and groundnuts	boiled *rizga*	?
Audelia	a.m.	mashed cocoyam and cowpea leaves	maize porridge and *egusi* and fish relish	remains of maize and *egusi* and fish relish
	p.m.	maize porridge and fish and *egusi* relish	maize porridge and *egusi* and fish relish	millet porridge and *egusi* relish
Juliana	a.m.	maize porridge and cowpea leaves	maize porridge and cowpea leaves	maize porridge and cowpea leaves; yams for child
	p.m.	maize porridge and okra relish	maize porridge and cowpea leaves and *egusi*	maize porridge
Bertha	a.m.	remains of boiled yam	maize porridge and spinach	cold remains of boiled yam and sweet potatoes
	p.m.	maize porridge	boiled sweet potatoes and boiled yams	millet porridge and oil sauce
Wanaka	a.m.	boiled cocoyams	maize porridge and okra relish	maize porridge and okra relish
	p.m.	maize porridge and oil sauce	maize porridge and okra relish	boiled beans
Djingla	a.m.	boiled *rizga*	boiled *rizga*	* ?
	p.m.	boiled yams	boiled beans	* ?

* Information not forthcoming because Djingla was in a bad temper; she probably had another meal of yam or *rizga!*

84

Name	Time	First Day	Second Day	Third Day
Djingla	a.m.	maize porridge and oil sauce	remains of maize porridge, oil sauce	maize porridge and egg-plant relish
	p.m.	maize porridge and oil sauce	boiled plantain and oil sauce	fried beans and popcorn
Yeduda	a.m.	mashed cocoyam	maize porridge and meat	maize porridge and meat and egg-plant
	p.m.	remains of cold cocoyam	maize porridge and meat	maize porridge
Fhshwaa	a.m.	boiled plantains and oil sauce	roasted maize and beans	maize porridge and cocoyam leaf
	p.m.	guinea corn porridge	maize porridge and elephant grass shoots	remains of maize porridge and elephant grass shoots
Elizabeth-Kila ..	a.m.	maize porridge and *egusi* relish	maize porridge and spinach relish	maize porridge and pumpkin leaves
	p.m.	mashed cocoyam	maize porridge and spinach	boiled potatoes and oil sauce

The amount of time devoted each day to the preparation of meals varies but, on an average, it is between two and three hours. Once the food is in the pot, the woman is free to idle, gossip with others, nurse her child, or potter about the house—cleaning calabashes with sand and water, or giving the floor a perfunctory sweep.

The brewing of beer is a time-consuming process and in Nsaw is done mainly for some festivity, to reward a working team, or else for trade. In the Plains, in Mbembe, Fungom, and Esimbi where grain is more plentiful, beer is made in larger quantities and often mixed with honey to render it more potent. On the whole, women in Nsaw are stinted of their fair share of liquor. A man occasionally presents his mother-in-law with a small calabash of palm wine, but is more grudging where his own wife is concerned. Often her share is no more than a sip or so from a calabash cup. As one man explained to me: " If I give my wife wine, she will not be able to grind maize for my dinner!" Another informant said that if women wanted a stimulant they could brew beer, but usually they were too lazy. Actually, limited supplies of grain and difficulty in procuring extra firewood are the real reasons. In the forests of Mbembe the women seemed to be better off, for they not only had plenty of beer but, through blandishments or palaver, persuaded their menfolk to share some of the palm wine. In the " dry " season the village has a convivial atmosphere. The men ascend the palm trees with bark slings in the early morning and evening. Sometimes they remain there for half an hour or so, swigging wine and " putting story " before they descend to earth again with a calabash of the residue!

The brewing of beer, and the preparation of foods such as cassava-gruel, bean-balls, gari, and other delicacies by women traders will be discussed in

D

more detail in a later chapter, where we shall be concerned with distribution of food supplies and marketing. But before bringing this section to a close mention should be made of some of the other female occupations. Basket-work and the making of string girdles are usually done when the women are at home on a rest day. Pottery, however, is more time-consuming and, in most villages, is carried on during the dry season. In Bamessi clay is dug out with hoes, matchets, or pointed sticks at a pit some 15 minutes' walk from the centre of the village. It is carried home in bags or baskets and placed in small depressions in the courtyards. The day before pots are to be made, the clay is broken up with a hoe, covered with water and leaves, and then left. Early the next morning it is tempered with sand and mashed with the feet, before being divided into lumps. One of these is put on a sloping board, rolled into a band some 3 feet long, joined at the ends, shaped to form the upper part of a pot and left to stand for awhile. Scraping is done with the fingers, small pebbles, seed-pods and spatulas of raffia midrib some 6 inches long and ½ inch wide. Roulettes of wood or rope are made for the women by the men, and are used for incising a pattern on the outside of the pot. The women work quickly and with fascinating competence, completing a pot in about 30 minutes. The number made during a morning varies: eight if they are half a gallon in capacity; and more if they are only containers for relish. They are left for four or five days to dry, and during this time the women gather bundles of grass, four being required for firing some 30 pots. This last process is carried out at dusk on the eve of market day, and takes about 40 minutes,—a number of women co-operating for the work. In Mbembe and Meta, pots are modelled freely from a lump of clay, but on the whole are con-sidered inferior to those of Bamessi manufacture.

Finally, there is palm oil production. In most of the forest areas this is in the hands of the men, though women sometimes assist in removing kernels from the stem, and later they extract kernel oil for unguents or medicinal purposes. But in Ngie (and also in Mogamaw) women make the pericarp oil. Men look after the palms, cut down the fruit, and carry it to the com-pound; but thenceforth the women are in charge of the process. Half a day may be devoted to removing the kernels and boiling them in large pots. A day or so before market, the bright vermilion kernels are brought in wooden troughs or dark cane baskets to the pits by the streams or in the swamps. Usually about five women work at a pit. One or two pound the kernels with their feet, and the oil runs off the stone ledge into a shallow depression filled with water. From there it is scooped up in handfuls and placed in containers. Several hours may be spent at this task, unless a woman has assistance, in which case she rewards the helper either with a small gift of oil or else permits her to crush the kernels a second time for her own use. Finally, the oil is boiled again and strained into calabashes. Oil production is considered by the women to be one of their heaviest duties but, fortunately for them, it is largely seasonal and does not occupy much of their time during the peak of the rains—that is, from mid-July until mid-October.

THE WORK OF THE MEN

So far the men have remained rather in the background as spectators and commentators on the industry of others; and it remains to consider briefly their contribution to the economy. While keeping the diaries of women I also attempted to record those of their menfolk, but the latter were much more elusive and were rarely engaged in any one task for more than a few hours. If I had missed a woman at the compound, her children or husband could generally tell me to which farm she had gone; but she, on her side, was often ignorant of the whereabouts of her husband, and regarded a display of curiosity as almost unseemly. At most she might say that he was " busy " somewhere in the village. My own impression was that the average Nsaw man (and indeed the average Bamenda man)[1] rather resembled Chaucer's Man of Lawe:

" No-wher so bisy a man as he ther nas,
And yet he semed bisier than he was."

Lineage heads, by virtue of their office, do not stoop to traffic their kolas, wine, or goats in the market place, but arrange for their sons or younger brothers to do this for them. However they look after some of the raffia bush and kola groves; visit the farms occasionally to keep an eye on who is actually working their land; and, if they have the skill, spend part of their leisure making baskets, raffia bins, or caps from raffia bast—all of which are a supplement to their income. House-building and repair are also of importance, and even men of the highest rank do not consider it beneath their dignity to cut raffia poles and peg them into frames for walls and roof.

Men who are not lineage heads, busy themselves with a number of small tasks, in addition to their major occupation,—be it trade, tailoring, bricklaying, carpentry, smithing and so on. From time to time they sweep the compound, clear paths, wash clothes, set small traps for guinea-fowl, hunt, manufacture baskets for kolas or maize, journey to another village to buy wine for a club, take their goats to feed on the hill-slopes or stubble, or sometimes give assistance to a lineage head. A Nsaw man commonly looks after plantains and bananas, —setting, weeding, propping the trunks, and cutting the fruit. Among the Widekum tribes this is almost exclusively a male occupation and prerogative, and a woman may only cut the fruit with the express consent of her husband. The cultivation of tobacco for trade is also in the hands of the men, though women may grow a little for their own use.

It is only in Mbembe, Mbaw, and parts of Befang that the men engage regularly in agriculture. Elsewhere, their contribution is small and probably does not amount to more than about 10 days a year, and even less in some cases. A Nsaw man may devote 21 days at a maximum if, in addition to clearing and the harvest of guinea corn and maize, he also assists with the harvest of finger millet. Thus Mawo and Kibu helped their wives with this task for 7 and 12 days respectively in 1948.

Men entrusted with the care of raffia bush keep it weeded and go once or twice a day to tap wine. This alone, however, does not provide a sufficiently large cash income, and it must be supplemented by the practice of some other craft or by trade. Dealers in kola may headload 1,000 or 1,200 nuts north to Mayo Daga,—a journey which lasts about three weeks and is undertaken three or four times a year, particularly in the periods April to June, October, and again in December to January. It is onerous work and more than one man complained ruefully that he had become " bald " through carrying kolas to Yola, Banyo or Mambila. General traders sometimes take Irish potatoes to sell in Calabar, and return with buckets, cloth, kerosene, and soap after from three to five weeks' absence from the village.

The dry season is probably one in which the men work most consistently and for long hours.[2] The great majority, unless away from home, bring in loads of firewood and thatching grass from the end of November until the beginning of March. For example Mawo, a middle-aged man, carried

---

[1] When I commented on the heaviness of the women's work in Ngie, a Ngie man said " Yes! But the men look after the fowls! "

[2] In the forest areas, near the large streams, the men engage in a certain amount of fishing in the dry season; and, in addition, hunt on a larger scale than men on the uplands.

DI

firewood for 27 days during the period; and his younger brother did the same for 17 days. The latter, together with Vincent Kwangha and Tanye, spent between 17 and 36 days headloading bundles of thatching grass. Two of the men concerned also made sun-dried mud bricks for three or four hours a day several times a week, as they intended building houses within the next year or so. Even the construction of a traditional style of hut is a lengthy process, entailing the gradual collection of poles; the cutting and pegging of these together to form walls, ceiling and roof; and, finally, the mudding of the walls. This last activity calls for the joint labour of about 20 men and is accomplished in a morning and rewarded with a feast of wine and substantial rounds of porridge, with a relish of goat or beef. Of course a man does not build a house for himself every year, but on a number of occasions he gives assistance to kin and neighbours. Children help to carry water for the plastering, while the women prepare the food. In Ngie, as might be expected, women are not even exempt from housebuilding. The men construct the timber walls and palm mats for the roof, and the women throw on the mud. In Aghem, Ngwo, Zhoaw, and Mashi there is a similar division of labour.

Tailors, smiths and tinkers usually ply their craft daily either at home or in the market, and as a rule give less help to their womenfolk in the compound and on the farm. Like most men, however, they have their set days for recreation. Most belong to one or two clubs (Pidgin-English—*djaŋgi*), which meet on specified afternoons to drink wine and arrange financial aid. The organization of these institutions will be described more fully in a later chapter. Lineage heads are apt to lead an even more convivial life; and, if they live in or near Kimbaw, make a point of attending the club at the palace (on a *wailun*) and those held under the auspices of some of the nobility and court officials. In Mbonyaar compound Christian men had formed a club which met on the sabbath unless it happened to be a market day, in which case it was postponed to Monday.

To a very great extent the industry displayed by the men is dependent on their rank, the size of the household for which they must provide, and their temperament. From an early age, boys begin to trade on a small scale in groundnuts, a few kolas, salt or a little game. During adolescence they, like their sisters, visit and attend dances, but are also driven by the necessity of not only earning money for clothes, but also for marriage payments. There is not this latter commitment in Nsaw, and some of the youths lazed about the village except on market day, and gave little assistance to their mothers in clearing of bush or harvest of finger millet. Some of the elderly men complained that the youths did far less now than formerly and that customs were changing. Nevertheless, they said marriage would probably bring a greater sense of responsibility and they would have agreed with Francis Bacon that " Certainly, wife and children are a kind of discipline for humanity ". As my two friends, Vincent and Benedict, explained: " A youth begins to grow; he gets a wife, and then he acquires commonsense. If he has not a wife, he has no sense! If he has a wife and is asked to help (a neighbour) he then goes, because he thinks that later he will be able to send for help in his turn ".

Chapter VI

CONTROL OF CROPS

EARLIER in this book we analysed the claim that lineage heads own the land; but, apart from pointing out that women manage their farms, we left without further comment the categorical statement that "women own the crops or food". We saw that rights over land are never absolute, but are to be defined in terms of social relationship and circumstance. A similar approach is necessary if we are to understand the nature and extent of the control exercised by women over the distribution of foodstuffs: it must, in short, be studied in a range of contexts, such as responsibility for the protection of standing crops, household management, gifts, trade, divorce, and inheritance.

RESPONSIBILITY FOR CROPS ON FARMS

In many parts of Bamenda, fertile land, skill and industry do not necessarily bring the reward of a bumper harvest. Apart from variations in rainfall, losses may also be incurred through the depredations of animals, birds, and human beings. To the first threat reactions vary. The women of the Mbembe forests complained that the birds ate the guinea corn, the wild pigs the cocoyam, and monkeys the maize. Scarecrows, strips of vine or cane stretched across plots, and traps are utilized occasionally; and, in the old days, boys and even the men could be prevailed upon to guard the crops. But, as mentioned earlier, women are finding it increasingly difficult to secure co-operation from the males of the family for this task. Fencing seems an obvious solution for checking some of the pests in those areas where there is plenty of timber; but, on the whole, there is a reluctance to expend the labour and time. In a few of the villages in Mfumte, Nsungli, Ngwo, and Bafut I noticed that kitchen gardens near compounds were sometimes enclosed to keep out fowls and goats; and in Nsaw some farmers, out of sheer desperation and despite the difficulty of obtaining timber, have fenced in outlying farms to protect them against cattle. Goats are often a serious problem, and in most tribes women have the right to kill with impunity those which are found eating their crops. The owners are then called to remove the bodies! Sometimes a woman warns the owner on the first occasion; or, in some of the tribes of the west, she may catch the goat in the presence of witnesses and sue for compensation in court. Complications arise where the owner is a member of the compound, for, in this case, there is a reluctance to create friction, and the aggrieved women often confine themselves to reporting loss and begging him to keep his goats tethered near the compound, or else to graze them on a hillside reserved for that purpose. In most areas men have no right to kill goats or pigs feeding on farms, the correct procedure being to catch the animal and sue in court. In the records of Ngie, there were several cases where men had in anger killed the animal and were compelled to repay its value, though they were permitted to bring an action for compensation for the crops destroyed.

Destruction by cattle is apt to be on a larger scale and is a relatively recent problem, since the Fulani only began to graze their herds after the advent of British administration. Women sometimes appear as plaintiffs, but often they leave it to their husbands or a lineage head believing that the latter may present the case more forcibly and secure adequate compensation. The disadvantage is that, even if the cash value of the crops is obtained, the men are apt to keep the money and to expend only a small portion of it on food for the household. Since 1946, most of the Native Authorities have passed Grazing Rules which give them power to issue permits to Fulani, to limit the size of herds, to stipulate the number of herdsmen, and to enforce rotational grazing. This has led to a reduction of cattle cases and has been welcomed by the women, who are primarily concerned with prevention of destruction, rather than with securing a large monetary compensation.

Stealing is not a problem of serious dimensions, except along some of the main motor roads and in a few of the villages with large stranger communities. Children are at an early age taught not to thieve; and, if they do interfere with the property of others, they are beaten by their parents. Needless to say they occasionally pilfer a few pears, mangoes, sticks of sugar cane, groundnuts, and so on from the farms of their mother, but for this they are usually let off with a reprimand. The adult thief is regarded with contempt by the community, including his own kin. If he is caught in the act and given a beating, his own kin do not come to his assistance. In fact, they may pass by and pretend not to know him. I remember one instance in Kimbaw. The man was detected stealing oil in the market and was thrashed until he wept. His relatives, already cognisant of the incident, asked him somewhat maliciously why he had been crying? He replied that he had been cutting firewood and that a chip had struck him in the eye! When I demanded to know why the lineage head and his brothers did not drive him away from the compound, my friend replied that, although they would not protect him from his due mead of punishment, they could not send him away because the ancestors would be angry and inflict misfortune on his relatives. A similar attitude was adopted by the family of a thief in another compound. Both cases threw considerable light on the kinship system. In Nsaw, the lineage is not bound to assume financial or even moral responsibility for the misdeeds of its members; but, on the other hand, it does not disown a thief unless he steals from his own kin. In the old days, a habitual thief would have been sold into slavery by order of the *Fon*; and the same penalty was at one time in force in many other tribes, including most of the Widekum group.

In general, the chief sanctions are the attitudes inculcated in childhood and the sentiment of shame. On the outlying farms of Nsaw, baskets of guinea corn and finger millet may be left unprotected for days without their owners incurring loss. But, in the time of scarcity and in an exceptionally bad year, individuals are tempted to pluck cobs of corn or to cut cassava. Accusations of theft are bandied about the village; and an owner publicizes his loss and hopes to induce shame by scattering maize stalks by the roadside, or by heaping up a few cocoyams by a raffia pole. Sugar cane is a temptation to the male passerby, and more than one woman complained that the men were worse offenders than the boys! If the thief is caught he or she may escape with a scolding and loss of reputation, or the farmer may take action in the court.[1] But usually detection is difficult, and those who find their crops are being constantly stolen may resort to black magic. In most tribes this is made by a male relative of the woman, but in some cases—e.g. Nsaw, Kom, Mfumte and Ngie—women have their own magical remedies, though these lack the potency of those of male manufacture. The articles used consist of various herbs,

---

[1] Theft from kitchen gardens is rather difficult, since there are normally children about during the day. In some of the Mfumte villages, where there are palm trees, the thief has small hope of privacy since there are often men tapping wine who have an opportunity to survey all that is happening on the earth below. In Nsaw, I was told that the penalty in the old days for a woman or rather a girl caught stealing from the farm of a *Fon's* wife was compulsion to become a bride of the *Fon*, even if she were of *m'tar* status.

inserted into tiny calabashes, cactus leaves, thorn-apples, pods, potsherds painted with red and white clay, land-snail shells, feathers, and so on. The medicine, when placed on the farm, is commanded to seize the thief but not to injure the farmer herself. Different medicines induce different diseases,— all of them of an unpleasant nature and ranging from diarrhoea, gonorrhoea, rheumatism, broken ankle, chest pains, deafness, gastric disorders and boils to leprosy. The culprit who has sickened may be cured by confessing to the owner, who treats him or her with a counter-medicine. Usually repentance and a promise not to offend again are all that is required; but if the owner has incurred a heavy expense in obtaining the preventive magic in the first place, sometimes a payment may be demanded. For example, the *Fɔn* of Bamungo had some Tiko bananas from the sale of which he augmented his income. He had enlisted the services of a medicine man at an outlay of four fowls, and a thief who wished to be cured had to pay, according to the *Fɔn's* information, six goats.

Most women, however, are reluctant to utilize black magic because of the fear that their own relatives may take a little food from the farm and sicken. Christians are of course forbidden to resort to the practice, but do not necessarily disbelieve its efficacy. When I asked one man why he did not protect his crops in this way, he replied that not only would the thief suffer but also any innocent children who partook of the stolen food, and this would be " a bad thing ". Sometimes a person resorts in desperation to subterfuge and places a pod or calabash on a tree or on a farm in the hope that it will be mistaken for magic and deter the would-be-thief from stealing. One woman, whom I knew in Kimbaw, was very much amused because her small daughter had on on her own initiative done this to protect a pepper-tree by the path near the house.

Men may also take magical precautions to safeguard property such as storehouses, raffia poles, kola trees, and bundles of firewood or thatching grass. In Nsaw and Nsungli a small area by the roadside may be cleared, and two or three calabashes containing medicine are placed on the ground "to lock it" against thieves. Individuals may then leave their possessions there in safety, and return to collect them at their own convenience. Not least among the threats to crops are witches, and in most tribes either the chief, village head, or perhaps leader of a particular society brews medicine just before the time of planting and scatters it on the roads leading to farms and also on the farms. On the big finger millet farms of the *Fɔn*, nobility, and lineage heads of Nsaw, rituals are performed to secure a good harvest and to protect it against the ravages of witches. The *ŋwirɔŋ* and *ŋgiri* societies of the Tikar tribes may also be enlisted by owners of raffia and kola trees to erect a specially marked pole (*mbaŋ ŋgiri* or *mbaŋ-ŋwirɔŋ*) in the vicinity. Informants stressed that this was not " magic " (*kifu ke /iib*) but " law " (*nsɐr*). The penalty for theft is not sickness but punishment inflicted by the society—sometimes a fine of several goats. Padlocks on doors are a modern deterrent, but the determined thief may still burrow a hole through the back wall, as happened on two occasions in Kimbaw!

In the preceding discussion we have digressed somewhat from our main theme,—a woman's responsibility for crops on the farm. In general, any woman farmer is justified in taking action to protect them, whether this involve the killing of goats found grazing on a plot, the utilization of black magic, or the sueing of a thief in court. In the case of damage by cattle there is a complicating factor. The monetary compensation may be at least twenty shillings and sometimes as much as £5, and it is the husband who takes it even if he has not appeared as plaintiff, since it is considered unfitting for a woman to handle such a large sum,—a point which also arises in connection with trade. His action in this respect is to some extent sanctioned by custom, in that it is the husband's duty to buy extra food for the household when the harvest has proved inadequate for its needs.

DIVORCE

There is a further crucial question with which we have not yet dealt, namely, a woman's rights to property in the event of divorce or separation. The nature of these rights and the conditions in which they may be exercised will be clearer if we turn for an analogy to our analysis of ownership of land and trees by lineage heads. It will be remembered that if a *fai* consistently neglects his dependants and misuses lineage resources he may be removed from office and deprived of its privileges. He controls the income derived from the produce of kola and raffia; but, while he may utilize some of it for the fulfilment of obligations to his affines, the dispensing of hospitality on a scale appropriate to his status, and the acquisition of a few luxuries, he should see to it that the needs of his dependants are satisfied. This is his primary duty.

Earlier in the book I quoted a statement which was frequently made to me: " a woman owns the crops " (*wiiy kɛr vifa ve yi*). But one of her primary duties as wife and " mother of the house " (*yelaf*) is to grow food. In the performance of this task and in the management of the harvest she has a free hand; it is a " woman's business " and one in which the men do not feel competent to intervene. She is, however, expected to show judgment, to place the needs of her husband and children first, and to ensure that there is sufficient food for them. Granted this, she may give some food away to friends and kin, and sell any small surplus to buy extra delicacies for the house, sweetmeats and trinkets for herself and perhaps for her daughter. But she has not the right to sell the whole crop, any more than a *fai* has the moral right to sell or pledge all the kola trees and raffia which are in his care. In Nsaw this applies particularly to crops grown on plots, which belong to her husband's lineage and which have been allocated to a woman so that she may provide food for her household. If she decides to leave her lawful husband then she forfeits the standing crops, though she has full control over those on land allotted to her by strangers or the head of her own lineage.[1] On the other hand, if she is not a *wiiy-o-nøøne* (a woman given away in marriage by her *fai*), but has been living for many years as a *wiiy-o-tʃɛmin*, her " husband " has no rights to the standing crops which she has cultivated on land of his lineage. She harvests them, but of course would not return to plant the following season.

In Aghem, a woman's duty to feed her husband may be enforced by legal sanctions, as the following cases illustrate. If she leaves him and he has not received a return of the marriage payment from her father or new spouse, he may sue her for the value of the food with which she should have fed him, though the fine may be less if she has not retained the hoe which he bought for her. I found several instances of this principle in the court records. A man brought an action in April 1947 against a wife, who had left him six years previously and who had failed to give him food during the interim. He had presented his mother-in-law with two goats in the hope that she would be able to bring pressure on her daughter to return to him, but in vain. He somewhat optimistically claimed £6 in compensation, but the woman in defence said she had no farm in her husband's section of the village, and that she had returned his hoe to him. The court judgment was that she should pay only

---

[1] When I was in Mbembe, the Village Head of Mbandi told me that he had recently received £2 in compensation for the crops which a runaway wife had taken with her to her new home in another village. In Bamessi a divorced woman has no rights to standing crops on her husband's land, and it is probable that this rule obtains among most Tikar peoples in Bamenda.

ten shillings since she had not kept the hoe.[1] I was told in Kom that, as long as a divorced woman was not using her husband's hoe, she could not be sued for failing to provide him with food; and the same custom obtained in one of the Fungom villages (Mme) and possibly in other villages of that area, though unfortunately I neglected to make inquiries.

DEATH

It is perhaps consistent with the general practice described above that, when a woman dies, her standing crops are inherited by her daughters or, failing them, by her husband.   Some men in Bali pointed out in justification that they owned the land and had helped to clear it; in Bentshan (Fungom N.A.) they said they had given marriage payment; in Esimbi that they had provided the seed; while in Fungom Village one of the senior women, a *Natum*, explained that her husband would have the right because, as she phrased it, " He married me; he suffered for me !"   Tribes which do not follow this rule are few in number, namely, Ngie, Kom, Aghem, Beba, Ngwo and, finally, some villages of the Fungom N.A.—Koshin, Fang and Zhoaw.   But it was stressed that, if the deceased had left any children, her mother, mother's sister, or sister would assume responsibility for feeding them.   Some of these groups have matrilineal descent, but the rest are patrilineal.   Among the matrilineal Aghem, one *Natum* explained that the mother of the dead woman has a claim to the crops because of the care she had lavished on her in childhood, and even during marriage.   When I continued to press for reasons, she answered vigorously and with some heat that, if the dead woman's mother were not permitted to take the crops, it meant that the daughter had been divorced and that relations with the husband were strained.

UTILIZATION OF CROPS FOR HOUSEHOLD

In most parts of Bamenda, a woman's store is her castle; neither her children, nor other relatives, nor co-wives may enter it to take food without permission.   As we pointed out earlier, in some tribes grain is not brought to the compound until November; while in others it is carried immediately to the house, and placed in the loft until dry enough to be transferred to raffia bins.   Root crops in the east and centre of the Province are dug out as required for meals; but in Ngie and the rest of the Widekum group, where cocoyam and yams are important staples, these may be harvested in large quantities and placed in small storehuts in the compound.   With one or two exceptions, which I shall discuss in a moment, it is left to the Bamenda housewife to decide what food stuffs and what quantities are to be used for a meal; and it is she who presides over the cooking pot, serves the family, and takes into account individual preferences in the way of kinds of relish and amounts of salt, pepper and oil.   Though most pagan women seem to favour polygamy, partly because it ensures assistance in providing food for the husband, and also care for children in case of sickness, in most tribes the great majority would resent having to share a hut with co-wife.   They explained that there would be quarrels over food supplies and the use of the hearth, and in this argument the men themselves concurred.   If, however, two or three wives live together in one hut, as so often happens in Nsaw, and also elsewhere in the case of those wives belonging to chiefs, village heads and important lineage heads, they either

---

[1] In another case of April 1947, the plaintiff demanded £4 from his wife because she had not been giving him food for two years.   The defendant said that, two years previously, her husband had sent her back to her father because she had not had children.   He had then gone to prison, and, on his release, she offered to return the hoe which he had given her.   He refused to take it so she kept it at home, and only used on the farm a hoe presented to her by her father.   The Court pointed out that, as she still had the hoe, she must pay 30s.; but one member of the Court explained that the ex-husband had been motivated by spite, so eventually judgment was given for 20s.   She appealed for a review.

have separate bins or take different sections of the attic for their respective crops.

The arrangements among co-wives for preparing meals for their joint spouse follow no consistent pattern in Nsaw; as the men sometimes said, " custom is variable " (*viliŋ–viliŋ*—a word also meaning patchy), and my own observations confirmed this. For example, a *n/ilaf* who has 14 wives has allotted 3 to each house in his compound and from each house cooked food is sent morning and evening to his own hut. In the compounds of minor lineage heads, who may have from 3 to 5 wives, the brunt of the cooking falls sometimes on the youngest, while the older inherited wives only send food from time to time, more especially when they want salt and oil. It is a matter of a *quid pro quo*. If the husband is inclined to be mean in his distribution of those items, the food may be given rather perfunctorily and grudgingly, as happened in one instance when a friend of mine said " I have only given him porridge because the rains have been good and I have had a large harvest! "[1] On another occasion she remarked: " I only give food to the *Fai* when the children have had sufficient." The women draw on their own supplies, but sometimes receive a supplement of grain from their husband's own store.

In the case of Councillors, who may have 12 or more wives, the *Yelaa* appoints 3 or 4 to act as cooks for a certain period. Arrangements in the palace are more elaborate: the *Yelaa* chooses 6 wives to act as *n/ilaf-wiinto* to grind maize; others serve the *Fɔn* with wine or water, and others again fill the calabashes at the *Fɔn*'s own water supply. Finally, there are, according to the *Yelaa*, about 20 wives whom she selects and trains to cook the *Fɔn*'s food and who bear the title of *wiinto-fai* and are highly respected. One *wiinto-fai* is in charge in the morning, one in the evening, and so on through the whole rota. The procedure is for the *n/ilafsi* to obtain grain from the *Fɔn's* storehouse in the inner courtyard of the palace, and to grind it in a special room. They then take it to the *wiinto-fai*, who cooks it and who, in the process, must not touch her body with her hands. · If she wants to scratch herself there are small raffia sticks for the purpose. She carries the food in a calabash to the *Fɔn* and may be present while he eats. Maize for strangers is kept in another store, and is prepared in the quarters of the *Fɔn*'s wives.[2]

However to return to the management of resources in less exalted circles. When a young girl harvests 20 to 50 lbs. of grain from her own little patch of land, she places it in a separate corner of the attic. It is consumed eventually by the household, but her specific contribution is recognized and viewed with pride. When a married woman plants maize or millet in her mother's farms, the harvest is often brought to the latter's compound but always on the understanding that so many *vegati* belong to the daughter and will be removed by her as required.

Throughout most of Bamenda the general practice is for a woman to have control over all the food that she produces; but, as mentioned earlier, there is a deviation in a few tribes. In Mbem and Mfumte, the men give assistance in the cultivation of guinea corn, and the harvest is placed in their own stores or that of senior wives. In either case it is a senior wife who doles out a share

---

[1] My friend was a *wanto*, who was an inherited wife with a large household. Nevertheless, her husband (a *fai*) rarely kept her provided with necessaries. On one occasion, after I had given her salt, her daughter (aged about 9 years) said: " Some people (meaning the *fai*) throw thorn-apples at the *wanto*; but Missus throws salt." The child's older sister was upset by the remark and said " A child should not say these things "; but the mother replied " Let her say it, she has seen well! "

[2] The account I have given was obtained during the reign of the late *Fɔn*, who was simple in his tastes and, apart from a little more meat, had much the same diet as his subjects. In the training of the cooks the Ya-Nkooni (who is a senior wife) assists the *Yelaa*.

to her co-wives. In Mbembe, the men own bulrush millet and guinea corn and women are not allowed access to the granary, without the express consent of the husband. Frequently the young married men store their crop in the granary of the compound head; but, in middle age, they gain more freedom and may contribute only a small portion to him.[1]

Frequent reference has already been made in this book to the fact that, among the Tikar tribes, a number of men plant, weed, and in general tend plantains and bananas and have exclusive rights to dispose of the fruit. On the other hand, if women assume responsibility they are at liberty to cut the fruit and, if they wish, sell it in the market. But in the Widekum group, and also in the Fungom area, cultivation of this crop and, more importantly, its utilization is a male prerogative. The Ngie male householder even takes over its preparation for a meal, presiding over the cooking pot on the verandah of his house, and often surrounded by a group of children, hoping for titbits, while the wives remain in the background until summoned to take away their portion. Tobacco is another cash-producing crop which is largely in the hands of the men, though women in most tribes may grow a little for their own needs.[2]

GIFTS

Granted that a woman not only grows most of the food but also cooks it, there is nothing surprising in the fact that she is considered the most competent person to decide how and when it shall be used for household purposes. But this management of supplies also includes the right to make gifts to relatives and friends. Generally she does not ask her husband's consent for, as both men and women stressed, " food is a woman's thing ". But in some of the Fungom villages and among the more northern Widekum tribes, she would mention the matter beforehand, though there was never any suggestion that he would impose a veto. A husband is, after all, entitled to some knowledge of his wife's activities! He himself, however, has no right to take food from his wife's store and give it to others, though he may on occasion suggest that she make a present to one of his needy kinswomen. But usually the initiative comes from the wife herself and she does not require such marital prompting. This is consistent with the pattern of gift exchange throughout most of Bamenda. Men most appropriately give meat, fish, wine, salt, oil or a little cash to their kin and affines; while the women dispense foodstuffs and beer. The association between the provision of food and women is borne out also in a number of linguistic usages. In Nsaw a man instead of saying he is going to marry may say he is " going to eat porridge ", it being one of the chief duties of a wife to prepare meals for her spouse. Again, the feeding of children is viewed as a function of motherhood, and is reflected in the metaphorical use of the term ' mother ' as addressed to a woman by a man who has received frequent hospitality at her house.

Ties of kinship, then, are expressed not only in assistance in work and care. in case of illness, but also in an interchange of gifts. From time to time a woman hands over a bag of maize cobs, flour or yams to her mother, her sisters,

---

[1] In a great number of tribes a woman, in the first year of her marriage, works on the farm of a senior wife or a husband's mother. Later she is allotted plots of her own and assumes control of the harvest. In Mbembe a woman is not given a store for maize until she has delivered her first child. In Mbem, the senior wife frequently manages the distribution of maize.

[2] In Fungom Village the women told me that they could only smoke in the presence of the husband with his express consent. Often they had to pay for the privilege; or rather they would prevail on a mother's brother to give them about five fowls and some salt to hand over. Occasionally a man may permit his senior wife, *ni'apwi*, to smoke without payment because of her age and status, saying " you are like your sister (*waasu*)." In this area, the tie between brother and sister is close and the former must respect the latter.

her married daughters, husband's sisters and brothers' wives; and, on a later occasion, she receives some return from them. Her husband also remains under an obligation to her kin even when he has completed marriage payment, and he is expected to make contributions of salt, oil, meat, and so on. Beneath the apparent spontaneity of such gifts, however, there is a realistic appreciation of reciprocity on both sides. A *Natum* of Aghem, after she had stressed the generosity of a woman in constantly making gifts of food to her married daughter, then proceeded to point out, of her own accord that the son-in-law " paid " for these eventually, since he had to give her oil, wine, beef and shillings. " Food is not something he obtains for nothing! " If a woman asks her husband to contribute to a feast " he must listen and obey her orders ". She, on her side, " must hear him " and then there is no palaver in the household.

These exchanges are of great importance in strengthening kinship and affinal ties, but, from what has been said, it should not be assumed that the actual quantities involved constitute a drain on the resources of one household, or are a considerable supplement to those of another. The situation varies of course from year to year, and is affected by the frequency of festivals for marriage, childbirth, house-building and, finally, assistance given in case of sickness. A woman who has a long bout of illness is not merely cared for by her mother or sisters but also fed by them. For instance, in my Kimbaw budgets, Kengeran gave to her sick married daughter 2s. 3½d. worth of foodstuffs—an amount which represented a large proportion of the total value of foodstuffs, namely 8s. 4d., given to friends and kin for the period, September 1947 to March 1948. In another budget, the value of food given to a sick relative was 4s. 8½d., as compared with the total value of gifts of foodstuffs and beer—namely 11s. 8½d.—for the whole year.

Nsaw land varies in its fertility and, in a year when rainfall is delayed, certain areas experience more hardship than others. At such times, women or their adolescent daughters go to beg food from their more prosperous kin, including sometimes a lineage head, who may dole out maize from his own store. Again, when purely social visits of two or three day's duration are made to relatives in other villages, the visitor rarely goes empty-handed. Finally, there are the feasts in connection with marriage, childbirth, housebuilding, and certain societies. Whenever possible, most of these are arranged to take place in the dry season when food is plentiful.

At a wedding those who accompany the bride to her new home usually carry from 6d. to 1s. 6d. worth of flour or maize grain; but, it should be stressed, they are wined and dined for two or three days, and are often presented with anything from 3d. to 1s. in cash by the groom or his male kin. Women may attend two or three such ceremonies in the dry season. Gifts at childbirth depend largely on closeness of relationship and whether a journey to a distant village is undertaken. At housebuilding, the women of the compound may prepare from 10 to 20 lbs. of maize porridge or mashed cocoyam, but their work is recognized in that meat, oil, salt, and wine are sent as a reward to them during the feast. In my budgets the value of the gifts of food and beer received and given during the 6 month period (in some cases a full year) varies enormously from a few pence to some twenty shillings. Apart, however, from probable gaps in my records for some individuals, who neglected to mention all transactions, differences are due to the tendency of some persons to visit more frequently than others; secondly, to the size of the household; and, finally, its total income. It is perhaps significant that, in the case of two Christian men who were earning in the vicinity of £20 a year, hospitality was extended on a much more lavish scale than in the lower income pagan households; and the return for such hospitality in kind and in cash was correspondingly large.

Standards of living will be dealt with more fully in the next chapter, but here it may be mentioned that, on an average, a household probably gives away in one year vegetable foods and beer to the value of from 3s. to 6s.

So far we have been considering a woman's right to distribute small quantities of uncooked foodstuffs to others, and also her specific contributions of cooked foods at feasts. But there is also the question of gifts of cooked food to visitors at the house, or to residents of the compound. A woman is expected to provide for her husband's guests as well as her own, and to be ready for any emergency. Generally she prepares extra porridge or mashed cocoyams on market day and on the traditional rest day, when people pass through the village and are likely to call on their friends and kin. Within the compound women, unless they are in the relationship of daughter-in-law and mother-in-law, do not regularly exchange food but, from time to time, those who are particularly friendly invite each other to a meal, or perhaps send a child across the courtyard with a bowl of yams or greens, as the case may be. Needless to say, children pick-up titbits at all doors, and particularly that of the father's mother. In many tribes, husband and wife eat apart; but, even if they sit in the same house, they do not as a rule share the same bowl. If the husband has a hut of his own his food is sent to him there, while the woman remains in the kitchen to tend to her children's needs.

The expert cook receives her due mead of praise: visitors to the house lavish encomiums if the maize has been finely ground and boiled to the right consistency. Conversely one of the greatest insults a woman may suffer is to have her food refused by her husband! The pride which a woman takes in dispensing hospitality, not only at a women's festival but also to her husband's guests, is one of those intangibles most difficult to document; but, again and again, I was struck by the dignity and graciousness of the Bamenda hostess. A senior wife or one of high rank is, furthermore, jealous of her prerogatives and resents any attempts to deprive her of her right to divide the food at feasts. On one occasion the preparation of maize porridge for a ceremony after childbirth was delayed until two senior wives of the lineage head arrived to take over the task; and, whenever I presented meat, salt and oil to the women of a compound, it was carried to the hut of the senior woman for her to divide. Often a favourite wife of high rank and middle age may assist. Such duties are not regarded as menial but rather as a means of acquiring status as well as being a recognition of status. This was brought out very clearly in the case of one of my friends, a woman who was a grand-daughter of the *Fon* and in her late forties. She had been the favourite wife of her late husband but, when he died, his successor neglected her and also failed to provide the household with salt, oil and tools. She said angrily that times had changed. My interpreter, Benedict, pointed out philosophically that everything changed and that she must not grumble. Then she went on to recall with pride how her late husband had always selected her to cook food for his guests and to serve them. They had made gifts to her and they all " knew her ". But her new husband did not bother and none of his friends knew her! This last was an exaggeration of course since her rank as *wanto* secured her respect and deference from those who met her, despite lack of attention on the part of her spouse. But her remarks threw a vivid sidelight on her attitude to her duties,—one moreover which was very typical of most women.

Contributions to Women's Societies

We have already mentioned on several occasions that, during the first part of the dry season when the tempo of farm work slackens and there is plenty of food, the women cook on a more lavish scale and brew quantities of beer. In the tribes of the north-west this is institutionalized, in so far as it may be a means of entering one of the women's societies. Unfortunately, I had only about two months in which to visit different villages and it was moreover during the rains, in June and July. But I was able to obtain some details about the societies; and, in Bentshan, Fungom and Zhoaw, the senior office-holders were good enough to show me the ritual objects of which they had charge. In the last named village, my partial " initiation " was more formal in that palm wine was provided by the chief. We first partook of this with due ceremony, and a little was thrown on the floor of the hut " to make our hearts cold ". This is not the place to discuss these societies in detail but they are relevant to our present problem, namely women's rights to crops, and the means by which they attain prestige through distribution of any surplus.

The areas with which we are principally concerned are Aghem, Kom, and Fungom, though Nsungli, Bamessi, Bum, and Nsaw also have societies.[1] Unfortunately, I spent only a few days in Nsungli where, owing to the insistence and persistence of the women, I had to discuss cattle problems most of the time. But I was told of the *ndju* society whose office-bearers are called *ma-ndju* and *ngaa-ndɔŋ*, the latter being junior in status and responsible for the blowing of a small pipe (*ndɔŋ*) covered with cowries. Usually the *ma-ndju* (mothers of *ndju*) are senior wives of lineage heads, and they are treated with considerable respect by the women. Their role is compared with that of a *nfoomi* in the *mandjɔŋ* club. It is noteworthy that, in the discussion of damage to farms by Fulani cattle, the *mandju* organized the meetings and acted as vehement and voluble spokeswomen.

The Nsaw society of *tʃɔŋ* meets only on a *ngoilum*, and not always every week, possibly because there is little in the way of a farm surplus for feasts. The ritual objects of the society are known as *ʃiib Fɔn* (medicine of the *Fɔn*) and, in Kimbaw, are in the charge of a few of his wives, who have attained the status *Ayinko* (mothers of the society).[2] The *ʃiib* when not in use are kept in one of the *Fɔn's* storehouses. They include a large black stone (*tʃɔŋ*), some 18 inches long and 10 inches wide; small baskets (*nka-ʃiib*), with cowries attached to the rim and parts of the design; calabashes (*bar-ʃiib*), covered with a coarse mesh and also decorated with cowries; a two-foot bamboo with cowries; and a notched stick (*kikwakwar ke ʃiib*), which is scraped in time to the dancing. A woman or adolescent girl must pay for the privilege of seeing these objects (*taŋ tʃɔŋ*) by providing, with the help of her kin and friends, a feast in which wine, oil, fish, *egusi*, and groundnuts are important items, along with the inevitable rounds of porridge and cocoyam. Any woman or girl may take part in the dancing, which is held in the quarters of the *Fɔn's* wives. There is not space here to describe all the details of an initiation, but the high lights of the ceremony may be indicated. A small temporary structure (*laf-ʃiib*), which is made from mats and is some 4 feet in diameter, is erected in the central courtyard, and may be entered only by *ayinko* and the initiate. Dancing goes on most of the afternoon and there is a little feasting. About 6 p.m. the initiate squats in the *laf-ʃiib* and the *ayinko* bring out from a house nearby several baskets, one containing small black stones with which to strike the *tʃɔŋ*. Of particular importance is a farm bag which contains the *tʃcŋ* itself. A *yenko* slowly removes the stone to show it to the initiate, while the women dancing outside the *laf-ʃiib*, shout: " *Tʃɔŋ*! *Tʃɔŋ*! " or " *ʃiib Fɔn*! "[3] Some-

---

[1] With the exception of Beba, where there is a society called *fuŋwɛra*, of which the head is *manfo* (mother of the *Fɔn*), there are no women's organizations in the Widekum group.

[2] Some of the other Nsaw villages also have *tʃɔŋ* stones.

[3] The house, in which the ritual objects are kept for the day of a ceremony, may be entered only by those who are *Ayinko*. In addition to the *tʃɔŋ* stone and calabashes shown to the initiate in the courtyard, there are others in the house which are seen only by *Ayinko*. They bend over (*gvə 'ti*) while standing in their presence, but may sit down to partake of food there. All the other women feast outside in the courtyard.

times *t/ɔŋ* is brought to the compound of a *Fɔn's* son, who is prepared to provide a feast so that his daughters may see it. The *Ayinko*, in describing the purpose of the society, said it was "for rejoicing" (*fɛ /ɛ'ɛri*) and "to give strength for working a farm well " (*fo vitavi a waa lim sum kidjuŋ*), and that the ritual objects were " a thing of the earth " (*kifa ke nsaiy*).[1]

In Fungom, Kom and Aghem most villages have two or three women's societies of varying importance. One, the *Fumbuwɛn* (there are dialectical variations of this term throughout the region), functions mainly for dances at mourning, and the entrance fee is usually a little food and beer,—a contribution which is well within the means of most women. It is the principal society in Koshin and Fang villages, and the fee is larger—food, beer, and two goats in the former case; food, beer, and a fowl in the latter.[2]

N/amte (and variations of this name, e.g. *n/ama, nsama*, etc.) is the society to which most prestige attaches in the villages of Munkap, Mashi, Bentshan, Bidjoon, Mufu, and Ndjan in the Fungom area. Membership is normally attained after marriage, but sometimes a man assists an adolescent daughter by contributing a fowl, one of the items which must be paid in addition to drums of beer and maize. For instance in Bentshan, some 10 drums (or 40 gallons of beer) must be brewed by an ordinary member; the rank of *Natum* or " Mother " in the society necessitates an outlay not only of beer and food, but also two goats, groundnuts, *egusi*, and palm wine.[3] This entails the co-operation of a husband or male kin.

The *fumbuwɛn* is subsidiary to the *afaf* society (variants are *kefa', kefap*) in Aghem, Kom, and the villages of Fungom, Esu, Mme and Zhoaw. Only women who have borne a child may become full members and handle the ritual objects, which are " owned " by the senior women. Payments are graded in Zhoaw, there being four altogether before the status of *natum* is attained. The first is a feast for all members of the society, and the initiate contributes 2 pots of wine or beer, maize porridge, and cocoyams; for the second there is more food and beer, but in addition either a husband or brother gives a bush-cow hide, which is boiled and consumed as a relish with the staple. On the third occasion about 100 lbs. of uncooked cocoyam are distributed; and, lastly, about the same amount of cooked cocoyam and some 50 gallons of beer. Female kin assist, but the first essential is that the intending member herself should have had a series of good harvests. Some never make more than one or two feasts, and so remain associate or ordinary members.

Matrilineal descent obtains in Fungom Village and here (as also in Kom) the brother-sister relationship enters as a factor in the exchanges. A woman, who has a surplus from her harvest, gives some maize and cocoyam to the senior wife (*ni'apwi*), who retains a portion and sends the balance to her husband. He, in his turn, hands this over to his eldest sister, who either divides it among her female siblings or utilizes it as a feast for the *afaf* society. After a woman

---

[1] The daughters and grand-daughters of the *Fɔn* also have a society known as *lalir*, which holds its dances on a *kilooviy*. A *wanto*, who has had a good harvest and who may count on assistance from her matrikin, " cooks *lalir* " (*naa lalir*), and provides a feast which is consumed not only by other *wonto*, but also by women who join in the dance, though their share is very small. A son of the *Fɔn*, assisted by *n/ilafsi*, is put in charge of the proceedings for a year by the *Fɔn*.

[2] In the reign of the previous Village Head, Fang adopted the *n/amte* society from Bentshan and paid 2 goats for the privilege. It should be noted that in Nsaw there is a mourning dance called */induyen* (a term which is obviously a variant of *fumbuwɛn*), but it is not associated with any society.

[3] A Mashi man, who has provided meat, oil, and wine to the value of 5 goats for his wife to become a member of *n/amte*, may, if she leaves him, reclaim the fee from her new husband. If he is unsuccessful, he selects another wife to take her place in the society, and the divorced woman forfeits her membership.

has presented food to the *ni'apwi* about five times (that is, over a period of five years or more), she is informed that she has shown all due respect to her seniors and may now become a member of *afaf*. The husband buys palm wine, oil and salt, while her own brothers and mother's brothers provide wine and fowls. To become a *ni'afaf* (Mother of the society), she must prevail on her husband to contribute a goat, and a very large feast is held. In Kom (which is likewise matrilineal) the father's sister acts as sponsor, and approaches the father to tell him it is time his child should join. He hands over to her about two shillings' worth of salt, and meat to the same value. The girl, with the assistance of her female matrikin, then brews a large pot of beer and cooks five large baskets of maize porridge.[1]

It was noteworthy that many of the office-bearers in both *n/amte* and *afaf* societies were either wives or daughters of Village Heads, Section Heads or important lineage heads. These men, as a rule, possess more sheep and goats than the average villager and so are in a better position to make the contribution which is necessary if a woman is to attain senior status. There is a tendency for a *natum* or *ni'afaf* to designate a daughter as her successor and, in that case, the girl's father (or husband if she is married) is under some obligation, quite apart from reasons of prestige, to provide the more costly items of the feast. A number of women whom I questioned had succeeded their mothers in office.

The " Mother " of a society is treated with respect and often described as " a women who has much food." She is addressed by her title and her personal name is not used. When visiting, she is given the seat of precedence and is served first; and at meetings of the society, she divides the food, beer, and meat and has a right to the largest share. Apart from feasts for new members, the society also assembles irregularly during the dry season to drink beer, women taking it in turns to brew and so acquire prestige. Earlier I mentioned that each society has certain ritual objects. These are hidden in the house of the *natum* and brought forth for special occasions. The Zhoaw *kefa'* has a basket covered with camwood and called a *t/ɔŋ* (note that this is also the name of the Nsaw women's society). A *natum* inserts a pipe (imported from Kom) into the *t/ɔŋ* and blows as she dances. There is also a small iron gong which is kept hidden in a bag called *kefa'* (the name of the society). The *n/amte* of Bentshan has a special basket called *n/amte*, and a pot (*t/ɔŋ*), partly covered with cane, into which a Kom pipe is blown. The *Ni'afaf* of Fungom Village showed me in the privacy of her hut a calabash (*afaf*), bound with cane, and also a pot, partly encased in cane (*itɛn-afafi*), in which a pipe may be inserted.

Besides meetings for recreation or the initiation of a new member, most of the societies have other functions. In Fungom (and also in Zhoaw, Aghem and Kom), the *natum* brews a medicine which makes a woman's body strong and fat. In other villages the medicine is more closely associated with agriculture: just prior to planting it is rubbed on the bodies of members and is believed to bring success in farming. A *natum* of Munkap may also invoke the blessing of the ancestors and of God on the harvest. In all villages the societies dance at the mortuary ceremonies for a dead member; and, at her own death, a *natum* receives a special burial.[2] Finally, the *natum* has a special medicine to give a man who has been unsuccessful in hunting. His failure, in such villages as

---

[1] In Aghem, a husband normally assumes responsibility for providing the goat, fowls, oil, and salt for the entrance fee, but in the case of a Section Head (*Batum*) provision is first made for the membership of a sister and sister's daughter. An exception occurs in the case of the Section Head of *Zɔŋɔkü*, who follows patrilineal descent and assumes in this matter no responsibility for his sisters and their daughters.

[2] If the March rains are late in falling, the *natum* of Mashi goes to the grave of one of her predecessors in the compound of the Village Head, throws water " to cool the ground ", and then dances with the women.

Aghem, Zhoaw, Bidjoon and Mashi, may be attributed to his having inadvertently seen or touched the ritual objects of the society; in Koshin it may be due to a quarrel with a sister, mother, or father's sister, and he then approaches a *natum* for help. She rubs him with medicine and receives in return a fowl and wine. When he next catches game he presents her with a portion, which she shares with other members.[1]

Clearly these societies are of some importance in the economy, in so far as they are one channel through which a part of a surplus at harvest is distributed among a wide group of individuals, who are not necessarily related to one another. Moreover they are an incentive to agricultural production above subsistence level, since feasts must be given for admission, and again later if prestige is to be maintained. They are also a means by which women may attain to a position of authority and responsibility, outside the compound and closed kinship group; for, apart from their other functions, they also settle quarrels among members of their own sex and act as their spokesmen. In Njinikom, a Kom village which lives under the shadow of the Roman Catholic Mission and is largely Christian, the *afaf* society is almost extinct. Elsewhere in the north-west membership of *n/amte* and *afaf* has, according to informants, declined because husbands, with the rise in the cost of living, claim that they can no longer afford to provide oil, salt, fowls, and goats. From the brief inquiries I made in Bentshan, Mashi, Fungom and Zhoaw, it was apparent that in most compounds only one woman might be a member, and in some instances there was none. The fact that women are dependent on co-operation from the men for payment of full fees in most societies brings me to another point, namely that women are not permitted in this region to own fowls or goats. As markets are poorly developed, they lack opportunity for selling produce, pots, or baskets to obtain the necessary cash with which they might make the purchase of oil, salt and fowls. Among the Tikar peoples of the east and centre of the uplands, custom is more flexible. Women occasionally breed fowls and may sell them if their husbands consent. An exception is made in the case of wives of a *Fɔn* or a lineage head who often have to depend on their own resources for many necessaries. And this brings us to the subject of trade or rather to certain aspects, since marketing will be discussed in more detail in Chapter VIII.

TRADE

Throughout most of Bamenda women are free to engage in petty trade of foodstuffs, beer, and so on. Usually they are not obliged to obtain a husband's permission but, in theory, they are expected to hand over earnings to him, or account for purchases. In practice, a man is not concerned with collecting his wife's few pennies and, in so far as she buys utensils, tools, seed, a little salt or oil, his own responsibility for these things is lightened. Nor does he object to her occasionally purchasing a little tobacco, camwood, and trinkets. The wives of polygynists (mainly lineage heads, village heads, and *afɔn*) are subjected to even less supervision: partly because such matters are too trivial for the notice of men of rank; partly because, with the rise in the cost of living, such men are sometimes unable, or else fail, to make adequate provision for all their wives, more especially those who are old and inherited. Some distribute a little salt and oil regularly, but if a woman's household is large this is often insufficient.

---

[1] There is not space here to describe the other societies : the *esɔŋ* of Aghem for which the entrance fee is small; the *ndjan* of Fungom, and also the *t/ain* of the same place. This last belongs to the *At/af* matriclan, which is also that of the Village Head, and only a clanswoman can attain the status of *ni'at/ain*. Women of other clans may become associate-members, but only after they have joined *afaf*. The same custom prevails in Mme, and possibly in the related villages of Kuk and Nyos which I was unable to visit.

In Nsaw and most other tribes, a young girl tells her mother if she has earned anything or has received a present; but she is normally free to expend it on groundnuts or ornaments, or to engage in further trading. A young boy also enjoys a similar freedom in Nsaw; and, if he attends school, he spends part of his holidays trading, in order to assist with the payment of fees and the purchase of clothes and books. Outside Nsaw, boys are expected to hand over earnings to their father or lineage head, since the latter has the responsibility of contributing to the marriage payment for a wife for him later.[1]

The question of a woman's right to handle money is an important one, in view of the development of markets and the demand for a higher standard of living in most areas. Under the traditional system she required little in the way of cash, since the husband assumed responsibility for most articles entailing a relatively large monetary outlay. This attitude has persisted even among many Christians; and, on more than one occasion, men expressed the fear that, if women engaged in large-scale trade and kept their earnings, they would begin to think of nothing but buying clothes and trinkets. This might prove the first step towards looking for another husband who could maintain them in more luxury, or to becoming a prostitute—a somewhat lucrative profession these days. The same reasons were advanced against women joining *djaŋgi* societies. It should be stressed, however, that a few Christian men permit their wives to trade regularly as long as they are kept informed about the extent of their earnings. If the sums are large the husband usually takes them, but on the understanding that he is acting as banker and will eventually buy the woman a dress and head-tie. Women's budgets are discussed more fully in a later section, but we may round off our analysis of women's rights to property by considering inheritance. Contrary to what may be expected, the kin of a deceased woman do not appear to exercise more extensive privileges in the matrilineal tribes than in the patrilineal. In practically all groups, the husband inherits tools, utensils, and ornaments, though if he has daughters they receive a share. Failing daughters, he hands the articles over to his other wives. The exceptions are few: Ngie, Ngwo, Beba, and Esimbi (all patrilineal) as well as Koshin and Aghem. In Nsaw, a husband gives his wife's pots to his daughters or his other wives, but hands over to his wife's father her hoe, farm knife, and beads. Much the same custom obtains in Meta and also in Bafut.[2]

In this chapter we have examined in a number of contexts the control exercised over crops by the women. We have seen that they have the right to take measures to protect their farms, measures which, in some areas, are not available to the men. But when we turn to examine the correlation, if any, between ultimate rights to crops and type of kinship structure we find that in the great majority of tribes, both patrilineal and matrilineal, the husband may claim the harvest in the event of divorce or when his wife dies. This may be associated with the custom in Bamenda of fairly large marriage payments and the inheritance of widows by the lineage of the deceased husband. It should however be borne in mind that the correlation is not absolute, since in both

---

[1] An adolescent girl, whom I questioned in Meta, said she would give her earnings to her father since it was he who would have to find the marriage payment when her brother married. This was exceptional. It is perhaps unnecessary to point out that, while women claim they report the amount of their earnings to their husband, they may on occasion conceal it, especially if he is niggardly.

[2] By the time a girl is ready for marriage she has already received a hoe from her mother or her father, and she takes it with her to her husband's compound. In most of the tribes of the west and north-west, her mother provides her with her first baskets, pots and seed. In Nsaw, a man presents his daughter with a stool (*ntaa-djin*, stool of the bride) and says, " here is your stool. You must sit down in your husband's compound, and not go walking about like a loose woman! "

Kom and Ngie the kin of a dead woman may claim the standing crops which she has cultivated.

We have also seen that, while in theory a husband may veto the distribution of food to individuals who do not belong to his household, in practice it is left to the woman to decide what should be retained for the family and what should be given away to friends, kin or, in some cases, women's societies. The freedom of choice exercised by the women is an important point in considering the relation between formal status and role, and it underlines a contention held by the writer that, while in the formal kinship structure women are subordinate to the authority of the male head of the household, in practice and in meeting the exigencies of day-to-day life it is the women who frequently make decisions in matters pertaining to use of arable land and crops. In other words, an adequate analysis of the economic position of women involves not only a survey of formal rights to property but a comprehensive account of the informal privileges which the great majority of women enjoy. In fact, such privileges are so customary that they may be said to constitute a norm of behaviour; and it is only when, for one reason or another, relationships between husband and wife become strained that such rights are challenged. We are here then faced with a paradox which cannot be resolved by merely asserting that there is always in social life a divergence between the ideal patterns and the observed patterns of behaviour. It is in the abnormal situation—one of conflict or friction—that rights which are structurally determined, in the sense that they derive from the distribution of authority in the kinship structure, may be observed; while in the day-to-day pattern of existence many of the rights enjoyed by the women derive in part from qualities of personality but mainly, I think, from the fact that in the last resort the men are dependent on the competence, goodwill and feeling of moral responsibility of the women for the bulk of the food supply.

Chapter VII

STANDARDS OF LIVING

HARVESTS

WE have traced the agricultural cycle and in so doing have followed the women to their farms, watched them at work, gained some insight into their attitudes to their various tasks; and, finally, made some estimate of the amount of time devoted to agriculture, as compared with that spent in the compound in pursuit of other activities. We have not yet examined the return for their labour in terms of harvest, the extent to which this is adequate for the needs of the household, and the degree to which women engage in trade as a means of supplementing the family income. These matters and their bearing on the standard of living will be discussed in this chapter.

Until recently there was very little information available on farm yields in Bamenda. Earlier Government Reports contained, in most cases, only a very rough estimate of the cash value of crops from an average holding (1.0 to 1.75 acres); and, if quantities were given at all, these were nearly always in terms of baskets of unknown capacity. The lack of precise data is understandable if the conditions in which the surveys were made are taken into account. The Assessing Officer usually spent only a few weeks in each tribe and, even if he were present at the harvest of one or more crops, he had no scales. The cash value assigned was sometimes an arbitrary one, in that some of the foodstuffs were never sold in the market; and, more importantly, in some areas there were no markets at all. Finally, most of the assessments were made between 1926 and 1934, and since then the cost of living has more than doubled. But, apart from this factor, it should also be remembered that the price of foodstuffs in the very large markets near the main roads (Bamenda Station, Kimbaw, and Bali) was and still is higher than in the remoter areas of the Province. Hence the fact that the cash value of crops in Kimbaw is greater than that in Mbembe is not necessarily indicative of a higher standard of living.

In most tribes which I visited I made inquiries about the approximate yields of grain and root-crops, but as I lacked scales I was in the same predicament as my predecessors. I was more fortunate in Kimbaw for I not only witnessed the harvest maize and millet but, in my first tour, I was able to borrow a small pair of scales for weighing small baskets of goods in the market and compound. On the basis of my results, I modified Mr. W. Bridges' original estimate of the weight of a *kegati* of grain from 130 to 110 lbs.[1] In my second tour, when I was lent a large spring balance and could weigh *vegati* of grain, I found that even this had been an over-estimate and that the average weight of millet and fresh maize was about 85 lbs. As I have mentioned earlier, women bring in only very small quantities of root crops as required for the kitchen, and my figures for the harvest of these are more arbitrary. To use a term aptly coined by one Senior Agriculture Officer, they fall into the category of " guestimates ". However in some instances I was present when women were digging out yams, *rizga* and sweet potatoes and was able to measure the area and arrive at some idea of the yield for the whole plot. In nearly all cases this was higher than the estimate made by men and women. Some recent figures were also available for yields of crops produced under local methods of cultivation at

---

[1] *Vide*, W. M. Bridges, *Re-Assessment Report, Banso*, 1934, paras. 188-194; and my own *Preliminary Report on Fieldwork in Bamenda* (*mimeog.*), 1946, p. 6.

Bambui Government Farm and these provided me with some comparative data and a check on my own estimates.

(a) Maize (ŋgwasaŋ). As might be expected, there is considerable variation in the size of the maize harvest in Kimbaw: between 3 and 14 vegati to the acre (or between 255 and 1,190 lbs.) Benedict Somo, a mixed farmer who had an exceptionally fertile strip of alluvial land and who had received some training at the Government Farm, obtained in 1947 some 16 vegati (1,360 lbs.) but even this fell below that of the Demonstration Plot at Bamungo in the Ndop Plain, where 1,500 lbs. were obtained in one year, and 1,885 lbs. in 1947.[1] In most of the villages of the Ndop Plain the yield would be higher than in Nsaw, and in addition there is also that from the smaller dry-season crop. In Laikom (Kom), some of the wives of the Fɔn told me that they filled between 20 and 30 baskets, or an equivalent of some 13 to 20 vegati.

In Kimbaw the average yield per acre for the farms of more than 25 individuals was 7 vegati (or 595 lbs.), but as many cultivated only 0.9 acre or less the amount obtained for the household was about 6 vegati (510 lbs.)[2]. In exceptional cases, where the working team comprised two or three individuals and the area under cultivation was over 2 acres, the harvest was much larger. Thus Elizabeth-Bika in 1945 and 1947 obtained a little over 10 vegati, and Kengeran 20 and 21 vegati. Neither, however, had a surplus for sale, since each had to provide for a household of seven dependants. Most women reserve one kegati of cobs for seed, and from the end of January supplies must be husbanded carefully, a point to which I shall return later.

Those who assist at the reaping of maize on the farm of a lineage head receive a gift of some 8 to 10 cobs or vingaa (rubbish, or leavings) which are either small or have been spoilt by insects. On the 10th September 1945, I witnessed the maize harvest from two adjacent plots belonging to Fai-o-Ndzendzef. The Yelaa first plucked four cobs, the " Maize of God ", from the corners of each plot, tied them together, and placed them in the centre of the farm. Then fifty women and girls worked under her supervision and, by the end of two hours, had reaped 18 vegati from 2.04 acres. Baskets of cobs were tipped on top of the " Maize of God " by the women, who were constantly exhorted by the Yelaa to work quickly and not to steal! A few were caught hiding green cobs in the bush nearby, and the Yelaa not only reprimanded them but threatened they should have no share of the vingaa. However she did not scrutinize their baskets when they left the farm and she gave each her portion. Out of the total harvest of 18 vegati, some 15½ were sent to the storehouse of the fai, the remaining 2½ being divided among the workers, including a man from an adjoining compound who had watched over the standing crops for the last few months and who received about 20 lbs. for his pains.

(b) Finger Millet (saar). My figures for the millet harvest showed a considerable variation, which was not only due to differences in the size of area cultivated but differences in the fertility of the soil. Thus Margaret, who had planted millet on a steep and rocky slope at Ro Kɔŋ, obtained only ¾ kegati for her labour; while Bertha, who had a plot on more level ground at Dzɵɵdzɵŋ, got only one kegati. The crop on a plot close by, belonging to Yirbongka, was so poor that it was not even worth cutting. At the other extreme were Yuliy who obtained 5 vegati from 0.4 acre, and Yeduda with 5¾ vegati from 0.3 acre. The average yield for 0.5 acre was 3 vegati or 225 lbs. of unthreshed grain

[1] Agriculture Department, Bambui: " Planned Land Use and some ' Guestimates ', " No. 585.13; 1946. Also Annual Report, Bambui, 1947.

[2] In my Preliminary Report, op. cit., p. 7, I gave the yield of maize and millet from the farms of one of my informants, Dzɵɵndzɵiy. Later investigations showed that these were higher than the average, as she had very fertile land. Mr. Bridges estimates (op. cit., para. 192) of 6 vegati of maize and 4 vegati of millet are more typical, though he overestimated the total weight.

(510 lbs. to the acre). Most women said that they kept from ⅓ to ⅔ *kegati* of unthreshed grain for seed, but of course not all of that would be required for the purpose.

Most *afai* do not bother to have millet sown on their own farms; but, when they do so, the harvest is an occasion for festivity. Women and girls put on their best ornaments and form the main labour *corps*, though a sprinkling of young men assist spasmodically with the reaping. Male kin and affines of the *fai* bring calabashes of palm wine, and it is consumed on the outskirts of the field by men of rank. At one stage in the proceedings the *fai*, with his guests, parades in slow and dignified procession through the farm, distributing kola nuts to the women, thanking them for their assistance and urging them to work even more rapidly!

(c) Guinea corn (*saŋ*). Guinea corn, as mentioned earlier, is not grown in very large quantity in Kimbaw; elsewhere in the Province it is becoming more and more a minor crop except, perhaps, in Mbembe and Mfumte. One of the N.A. Agriculture Assistants, who measured selected plots at Tabessob and weighed the harvest in 1948, obtained an average of 1,038 lbs. to the acre. As most women cultivated only one-third of an acre their average harvest was 340 lbs. (or 4 *vegati*). In Kimbaw in 1946 only three individuals in my sample planted guinea corn: one obtained nothing because birds destroyed the crop; another reaped about ¼ *kegati*; and a third, Elizabeth-Bika, only one *kegati*. In 1948 the latter reaped 1½ *vegati* from a little under half an acre.

(d) Root Crops. For reasons which I have advanced previously, my figures for root-crops must be treated with considerable reserve. On plots for trifoliate yams (*rɛ*) I watched on several occasions women dig out between 75 and 120 lbs. from 60 square yards, the former weight being a very poor one indeed for Kimbaw. I have assumed the average to be about 100 lbs., and this would give about 8,000 lbs. to the acre. Patches of 24 square yards under *rizga* yielded between 45 and 60 lbs., and I have taken the average here to be about 50 lbs. This gives an exceptionally high yield per acre, namely 10,000 lbs., but it should be noted that Nsaw women prepare the soil very thoroughly before planting. A patch of 60 square yards of sweet potatoes produced an average yield of 65 lbs. (5,040 lbs. to the acre), and some of the women estimated the yield of Irish potatoes would be a little less, or about 60 lbs.[1] Cassava does not thrive in Kimbaw and I have hazarded a " guestimate " of 100 lbs. for the total crop from one woman's farms; while my figures for cocoyams— 800 lbs.—has also been based on estimates given by the women and some records from Bambui.

(e) Plantains and Other Crops. When measuring farms I also counted the number of plantains and bananas, though I regret to say that I did not always distinguish between these two kinds of tree. In general, young men and women have only about 50 trees, while the more elderly, particularly if they have large households, have anything from 150 to 500. But it should be stressed that less than half of these bear in any one year, and that losses are often incurred when torrential rains and gales beat down the trees. Some people sell a little of the fruit, but among those whose budgets I kept the maximum earnings for six months were only five shillings. Dwarf beans and groundnuts do not thrive in Kimbaw, but in the more lowlying areas of Nsaw about 4 *vegati*

---

[1] At Bambui Government Farm various experiments have been carried out with different varieties of potatoes. In 1944, the local " Twenty-Eye " potato did not give as good a yield as " Up-to-Date ", but some 34% of the latter were affected by black-heart disease. A smooth kidney-shaped variety is also grown by Nsaw women, but is often affected by the same disease. *Vide, Annual Report, Bambui,* 1944. Beds prepared as *kinfuuni* gave a yield of 4,772 lbs. Mr. J. Pedder (S.A.O.) suggested, in his " Guestimates " in 1946, a yield of 6,720 lbs. of sweet potatoes per acre on local farms outside Bambui, and a yield of 1,500 lbs. of cocoyam per acre.

(or 120 lbs. shelled) of the latter crop may be harvested in one year.   Gourds
for calabashes are grown in most farms and provide about ten in a good season,
but only about one or two in a bad one.   Large calabashes of more than a
gallon in capacity are bought from Ndop.

On the following page I have tabulated the approximate annual yield of
various crops from a farm-holding of 1.3 acres in Kimbaw and have therefore
omitted guinea corn.[1]   For the more southern and lowlying parts of Nsaw a
guinea corn harvest of approximately 340 lbs. per holding should be included;
and it should also be noted that the yields for groundnuts, beans and cassava
would be higher.   The list of crops is more comprehensive than that given in
the *Report* by Mr. W. Bridges, and the cash value has been based on market
prices in Kimbaw in 1947-48.   Throughout the year the cost of maize and
potatoes varies considerably: at harvest a 35 lb. bag of hulled grain is about
1s. 6d. as compared with 3s. and even 4s. in the period of scarcity;   while a
30 lb. basket of Irish potatoes rises from 3d. at harvest to about 6d. or 9d. later.
Neither finger millet nor guinea corn is ever sold in the market, and the value
given is based on assessments made by the Nsaw Council, when judging cases
in which Fulani cattle had destroyed these crops.

The figures in Table IX have been calculated on the basis of the average
size and yield of plots in one woman's holding given over to the main crops—
maize, millet, yams, *rizga*, sweet potatoes, and so on.   The gross weight from
1.3 acres is about 5,340 lbs. (exclusive of guinea corn), and the approximate
market value at harvest is £5-8-0.   In so far as plantains and bananas are
frequently tended by the men these crops should in most cases be excluded
when estimating a woman's contribution to the household.   The value of the
crops grown by her would then be £4-13-0 in Kimbaw, and a little higher
elsewhere, if guinea corn is planted.   Of course, not all individuals grow the
same amount of cereals, root vegetables and legumes, but the average value of
all crops is fairly constant.   In my sample of all the plots of twenty-one
individuals (excluding those of the *Fɔn*, lineage heads and one mixed farmer)
only nine had total holdings which ranged between 1.0 and 1.4 acres;   the
majority of the others cultivated a little more, since they received assistance.
The average value of the crops harvested by the nine women was £5-9-9;   or,
if plantains and bananas be excluded, then £4-9-3,—figures which approximate
closely to those given in Table IX.

For the reasons adduced previously, a comparison of the figures given above
with those in the Government Reports for other tribes in Bamenda would be
of little value, but there is some justification for regarding them as a maximum
for the Province as a whole.   It is true that, in the fertile Ndop Plain, the yield
of maize and groundnuts is higher than in Nsaw, but there is not the same variety
of crops.

In the seventh column of the Table, I have made a rough estimate of the net
weight of each crop (exclusive of that kept for seed) left for the household.
Maize and guinea corn depreciate about 15% when hulled, and finger millet
about 20%.   The average amount of grain, root vegetable or beans consumed
at a meal by a household, comprising a man, wife and child is given in the
eighth column.   This is based on my observations of quantities cooked, and
also on statements made by various women as to what they used at harvest
and during the period of scarcity.   Children ate as much, if not more than,
adults and, in addition, they had snacks of cooked food at mid-day.   If
supplies were short it was the mother who deprived herself of her due share,
just as in this country it is the woman who frequently surrenders her ration of

---

[1] For comparative data on the estimated size and value of harvest in Nsei (Bamessing),
vide Agathe Schmidt, " Some Notes on the Influence of Religion on Economics in a Tikar
Subtribe, West Africa," *African Studies*, 1951, vol. X, No. 1, p. 22.

TABLE IX

Approximate Harvest etc., from 1.3 Acres in Kimbaw

Crops	No. of *vegati*	Gross weight in lbs.	Amt. kept for seed	Market price at harvest	Total cash value at harvest	Net wght. left for house	Amt. used for 1 meal by woman husband and child	Approx. no. of meals from crop
					£ s. d.		lbs.	
Maize cobs (0.9 acre)	6	510	⅛	35 lbs. husked grain @ 1*s*. 6*d*. ..	18 0	360	3	120
finger millet (0.5 acre)	3	255	⅛	85 lbs. unthreshed grain @ 2*s*. 6*d*.	7 6	194	2	97
trifoliate yams (500 sq. yds.)		830	¼	3 lbs. @ ½*d*.	12 0	625	10	63
long yams		50	¼	3 lbs. @ ½*d*.	0 9	38	10	4
rizga (300 sq. yds.)		625	¼	3 lbs. @ ½*d*.	9 0	470	10	47
sweet potatoes (2 crops—total 800 sq. yds.)		840		3 lbs. @ ½*d*.	11 6	840	10	84
Irish potatoes—(2 crops)		800	¼	30 lbs. @ 3*d*.	6 6	600	10	60
cocoyam		800	?	3 lbs. @ ½*d*.	11 0	800	10	80
cassava		100		2 lbs. @ ½*d*.	2 1	100	10	10
tu'ngam		20	¼	2 lbs. @ ½*d*.	0 5	15	10	2
dwarf beans (2 crops)		30	?	½ lb. @ ½*d*.	2 6	25	1½	15
pumpkins		30		3 lbs. @ ½*d*.	0 5	30	10	3
plantains and bananas (30 bunches)		300		10 lbs. @ 6*d*.	15 0	300	10	30

Crop	Quantity	Rate	£	s.	d.		Meals
cowpeas (2 crops)	6 ⅛	1 lb. @ 3d.		1	6	.5	
bambarra-nuts	8			1	0	8	
egusi	6 ⅛	1 lb. @ 3d.		1	6	5	
spinach (2 crops)	100	1 lb. @ ½d.		4	2	100	
peppers				0	6		
okra				0	3		
egg plant	10	1 lb. @ ½d.		0	5		
groundnuts	20	20 lbs. unshelled @ 1s.		1	0		
sugar cane				0	6		
calabashes (6)		1 @ 1d.		0	6		
Total for Kimbaw	5,340 lbs.		5	8	0		615 meals
guinea corn	340 (4)	85 lbs. unthreshed grain @ 3s.	12	0	252	3	84
Total for farm outside Kimbaw	5,680 lbs.		6	0	0		699 meals

bacon and eggs to child or husband! During the time of plenty about 1½ lbs. of maize grain may be consumed per person not to mention roasted cobs as an hors d'oeuvre or savoury! After April this quantity is reduced to ½ or ¾ lb. per person in most households. For example, in July 1945, Julia of Kingaa Compound used only 3½ lbs. of grain for herself, her husband and child for *two* meals. In May of the same year Elizabeth-Bika had sufficient stored to grind 7 lbs. of maize to feed a family of seven for one meal; two months later she used only 2½ lbs. for the household, and had to eke this out with greens. The year 1945, however, was a very bad one and many men had to spend from ten to twenty shillings on staples from May to the end of July. In normal years expenditure would be considerably less in most families, though there are always a few women who have had a bad harvest, owing to a prolonged bout of illness which has thrown farm work in arrears, or owing to soil depletion in their larger plots.

In the last column of Table IX, I have estimated the approximate number of meals from each crop for a Kimbaw household of three persons. As it is customary whenever possible to take two meals a day, in addition to the child's snack at midday (½ to 1 lb.), and to cook extra quantities for guests on occasion, it is apparent that the amount of food actually available is insufficient to meet these modest requirements. It is still less adequate if it is remembered that some of the crops cannot be stored for long periods, and hence cannot be sparingly used over several months. By the end of February yams and *rizga* have been eaten; and from then, until about the end of May, the family relies on plantains, cocoyams, a few sweet potatoes, and diminished stores of grain. If maize and millet are in short supply the situation is serious. The following figures in Table X give some idea of the contents of the granaries of 21 women at the end of January 1948. I have excluded the amount set aside for seed.

TABLE X

Name	No. of depts.	*Vegati* of maize	*Vegati* of millet	Name	No. of depts.	*Vegati* of maize	*Vegati* of millet
Margaret ..	7	0	¾	Yuliy	1	2½	5
Yirbongka ..	0	0	0	Elizabeth-Kila ..	7	2½	3¾
Camilla	0	0	0	Dzøøndzøiy ..	3	3	6
Biy-Menggu ..	2	0	0	Sui	1	3	2¼
Bertha	2	0	1	Yeduda	5	3	5¾
Clara	6	½	2	Elizabeth-Bika ..	7	3	6¾
Shemsum ..	1	¾	2	Fhshwaa	2	3½	1½
Wanaka	2	1	2	Audelia	3	5½	10½
Melalia	2	1	1½	Kengeran ..	7	10½	7½
Biy-Djem ..	2	2	4	Vindjan	8	10¾	9¾
Yadiy	4	2	3¼				

In Table X, 5 out of the 21 women had no maize left at all, and among these 3 also lacked finger millet while the 2 others had only one *kegati* or less of that crop. Yirbongka was able to draw on her adult daughter's supplies and in any case her son, who was a storeboy in the U.A.C., would see that she never went hungry. Camilla, an elderly widow, received some extra food from Elizabeth-Kila, her brother's wife; but Biy-Menggu and Margaret were in serious straits. Margaret's husband, a tailor, bought 12 bags of hulled maize between November and the 5th March (almost one a week) at a total cost of 23s. 8d.; and Tanye, husband of Biy, purchased between the 9th December and the 19th February 6 bags at a cost of 12s. 9d. As the next season's crop of maize would not be harvested until August at the earliest, the drain on the monetary resources of both men during the period of scarcity would be considerable.[1]

Admittedly the plight of the two women, and one or two others included in the Table, was exceptional; but it should be clear from the preceding discussion and also from a survey of the budgets in the Appendix that there is little in the way of a surplus for sale even from the best of the farms in Nsaw. It is true that a considerable number of women are to be found engaged in petty trade in the Kimbaw market once a week, but many come from surrounding villages as much as 12 miles away; they do not sell regularly; and, in so far as they dispose of small quantities of root vegetables, beans, and greens, they do not earn more than one to four shillings a year. In the Ndop Plain and those Nsaw villages where two crops of maize are planted annually there is more of a surplus, but even so it is doubtful whether more than one or two bags of grain are disposed of in trade by the individual woman farmer each year. A possible source of income in the future may be increased production of tomatoes, cabbages, and onions. From Santa and Bali quantities of cabbages are exported to the coast at a good profit; while in Kimbaw one man made 8s. 8½d. from the sale of tomatoes, and £1-17-2 from onions during the year February 1947 to February 1948.

The contribution of the Nsaw woman and indeed that of the average Bamenda woman to the subsistence of the household is an important one and, in terms of its cash value, it may be as large as that made by a husband, who follows one of the traditional occupations such as small-scale trade in kola nuts, oil, sheep, goats, tobacco, or the manufacture of baskets, mats, bags, or caps. But, if a sense of proportion is to be maintained, it should be pointed out that most men do put in a few days' labour at clearing and harvest; secondly, that a great many assume responsibility for the cultivation of plantains, the yield of which may be worth anything from 7s. 6d. to £3-12-0 (see budgets in Appendix C); and, finally, that they are expected to buy food when necessary during the period of scarcity and even before that if maize and millet have failed. But this merely covers their contribution to the provision of staple foods for the household. In addition they must provide salt, oil, meat or fish— the two former representing a considerable cash outlay for people living on the uplands or in the plains. The extent to which men fulfil these duties adequately and indeed generously varies: it is not without significance that some of the Nsaw women when asked for a definition of a good husband specifically mentioned " one who buys salt and oil "!

THE FAMILY BUDGET

(a) *Oil and Salt.* In Kimbaw, and also the rest of Nsaw, if one may judge from statements made by women from different villages, the most parsimonious husband endeavours to buy at least ¼ pint of palm oil at a cost of 2d. or 3d. each week. But even ½ pint allows of only two tablespoons a day for relish eaten with the staple food. Towards the end of the week the housewife is often reduced to the scrapings of the oil calabash, or she may from the first

---

[1] Needless to say, both women had taken steps to ensure a better harvest in 1948. Biy had obtained the loan of a plot from a distant maternal relative of her husband; and Margaret was lent about ¼ acre, some 4 miles from the compound, by her friend Camilla who was elderly and no longer felt strong enough to make the long journey.

111

merely dab a stick into the calabash and smear the oil over the greens.[1] A man, then, with a small household spends at least 11s. a year on oil, and more if he can afford it.   If he has five or six dependants and his cash earnings are £4 odd, the cost of oil is, at a minimum, 16s.   It is significant that those with an income of £10 and upwards may spend 20s. a year; in the case of Benedict Somo it was 52s. (see Appendix C, No. 2).

Salt is another necessity but, while expensive, it is used in smaller quantities.[2] Some families make do with 5 ozs. a month and, according to their budgets, consumed about 2s. 6d. worth a year.   Vincent Kwangha, with seven in his household, spent 5s. 10d.; Francis Lole, who earned about £20, spent 17s. 6d.

(b) *Meat.*   Meat and fish are luxuries in most of Bamenda and rarely figure in the menu, unless game has been caught in the dry season, or the householder belongs to the higher income bracket and lives near a market village where beef is available.   In general, women probably have less meat than their children and menfolk.   In Nsaw goat-flesh is eaten by few women, and in most of the Western tribes there is a strong taboo on their eating, or even cooking, fowl.   Most people catch a few bush rats (*mbafsi*) in the dry season, and throughout the year flavour their relish with various kinds of insects such as termites (*ngosi*), green beetles (*mɛnsiŋi*), and crickets (*vintʃi*).[3]   The poorest obtain their share of 4 or 5 ozs. of meat at feasts for housebuilding, marriage, and when the newly harvested finger millet is eaten for the first time.   Christians, if they can possibly afford to do so, buy a little for Christmas; but so much beer and wine are consumed at that time that solid fare fills a subsidiary role in the belly!   Indeed, to judge from an account which I received in Ngie, both Christians and pagans regard Christmas as an opportunity for a three-day binge.   However to return to more every-day menus.   Some families may go two months without tasting meat or fish, especially during the rainy season, when a slender purse must be stretched to procure additional staple foods, as well as oil and salt.   Thus Vincent Kwangha who, during the year 1947-1948 spent the sum of 6s. 7d. on beef, did not buy it regularly each week.   From the 8th May to the 27th September he bought none at all.   Some of the other men, whose budgets I recorded for a little over 5 months and who earned under £5 a year, spent sums varying from 6d. to 2s. 10d.   Those earning £10 or more bought larger quantities of meat and fish: as much as £1-7-11½ in the case of Francis Lole, and £3-13-0 in that of Benedict Somo.   In other words, an increase in income is usually reflected in a marked increase in the expenditure on salt, oil, meat, and fish, not to mention additional condiments and relishes, such as *egusi*, okra, *davadava* (imported by Hausa), tomatoes, onions, and cabbages.

(c) *Groundnuts, Tobacco, Beer, etc.*   It is a poor Nsaw father indeed, who cannot afford a halfpenny for some groundnuts for his children; and often his wife spends her tiny profit in the purchase of these and other sweetmeats.   Very few men buy kolas, since these are expensive; they rely instead on the hope of

---

[1] In the forest areas where there is oil palm, an Esimbi woman may use 3 pints of oil a week, and a Ngie woman 1½ to 2 pints.   On the uplands and plains the price varies considerably during the year, falling to a minimum of 8s. for 4 gallons in May and June, and rising to 17s. or 18s. in January and February.   Butter is sold in some markets by Fulani women, but is expensive.   Only one householder in my sample of 16 budgets bought a little.

[2] Very little potash is now made in Bamenda except in the outlying forest areas.   Some is occasionally sold in Kimbaw market, but it is almost as dear as the European salt which is in any case preferred.   However, women sometimes take the ash of certain woods, put it in a sieve, and pour water through it onto the food as a flavouring.

[3] During the dry season the three daughters of Kengeran caught between them only 12 bush rats (*mbafsi*), and 9 tiny fish (*boiy*).   I never saw frogs eaten in Nsaw, but was told that they are caught and dried in November, and used as a relish.   Termites are available, particularly in May, September, and January, and are sometimes fried, for sale in the market.

picking up windfalls, or of receiving some from friends or relatives. Lineage heads who own most of the trees sell the large nuts, but distribute the smaller ones from time to time among guests and dependants, who in turn share their gift with others. This wide-spread re-distribution of nuts among all sections of the population has not, perhaps, been sufficiently stressed in considering the monopoly enjoyed by lineage heads. Tobacco is another commodity which is rarely bought, except by inveterate smokers among the men and women. Vincent Kwangha spent 1s. 1d. during the year, Nicholas Ngee as much as 3s. 3d. The woman, Vindjan, who made 3s. 2d. from the sale of plantains, sugar cane, and pears during a period of 5 months, bought 4½d. worth, in addition to what she received from friends. Tobacco does not grow well in Kimbaw, but in other villages most farmers have small plots devoted to the crop. Beer is made occasionally for household consumption during the dry-season, but most of it is for sale in the market place, or in the hut by the main road, which serves as a miniature pub for the younger married men with a copper or so to spare.

It may be said that a man with a wife and one or two children spends, on an average at least 11s. a year on oil; 2s. 6d. on salt; 3s. on meat; 1s. on ground-nuts; and, in the time of scarcity, 7s. 6d. on staple foods such as maize, plantains, and root vegetables—a total all-told of 25s. In so far as he also assumes responsibility for the care of plantain groves, which yield at least 15s. worth of fruit, his contribution to the food supplies of the household is some £2 in a good harvest year, and at least £3 in a bad year, when his wife's maize and millet crop are inadequate.

(d) *Farm and House Replacements.* As far as the purchase of seed is concerned, most Nsaw women either buy, or ask their husbands to buy, about twopence worth of cowpea-seed in October, and the same amount again in March for sowing with maize. More rarely seed-yams are bought if the previous season's crop has been poor or diseased.[1] The cost of replacing household utensils and farm tools is more difficult to estimate, since there is considerable variation even in the requirements of a single family from year to year. The Nsaw housewife needs a number of pots of different sizes and shapes: about half a dozen relish bowls (*laŋ*) at 1d. or ½d. each; large pots (*kiŋ*) for cooking maize porridge or root vegetables; a large shallow dish (*kikaŋ*) for frying maize before it is pounded; and a smaller, though similar type, for boiling water for washing (*ntɔn*). With care these may last two or three years but the best of bowls may crack or be dropped! Approximately one shilling a year may be spent on these articles over a long period. Calabashes for food, and also for oil, water, and beer, are almost as fragile and must be bought where supplies from the farm are inadequate. On the basis of my budgets, I have estimated an outlay of 6d. for these and the same amount for replacement of baskets. Most Nsaw women buy one woven farm-bag (costing 7d. to 9d.) each year, a small knife (1d.), and a razor blade. Other articles such as sleeping mats, mats for drying cowpea-leaves and millet, hoes, hoe-handles, umbrellas, stools, cutlasses, and raffia store bins are bought every two or three years. All told, about 8s. a year is spent on tools and utensils for house and farm, but in some years the amount is less, in others more. Very few Nsaw have European articles, though they often covet them for their superior workmanship, durability, and also for reasons of prestige. In the houses of the " well-to-do ", one most commonly finds garden seats, enamel food-bowls, basins, spoons, mugs, tumblers and, more occasionally, coffee or tea-pots for serving palm wine! Empty bottles, cigarette tins, and kerosene tins are in great demand as containers, and a steward or houseboy makes a little on the side by selling

---

[1] Some Nsaw men are beginning to buy coffee-seedlings but do not do so annually. In Ngie, in the west of the Province, many women buy a few cobs of maize in April as seed for planting, or barter a little oil for them.

those discarded by his European master, unless the latter happens to be an anthropologist who gives them away as ' dashes ' to friends in the village!

House repairs usually involve no cash outlay, since a man cuts thatching grass during the dry season and sets aside 5 or 10 bundles for that purpose. A Nsaw house lasts at least 10 years, so that the cost entailed in the construction of a new one, when spread over such a long period, is negligible. About 700 to 800 raffia poles are required for walls, ceiling and roof, but these are accumulated gradually over two years and are " begged " from friends and kinsmen. Their cash value is about 25s. Some 35 bundles of thatching grass are needed for the roof which, if purchased, would cost 10s. or 11s. The house owner normally pegs together the framework himself and, for the erection of walls, may count on the assistance of members of his compound. The mudding of the house is carried out by a team of 15 to 20 adult men, plus about the same number of boys and girls who perform odd tasks and bring water. The work is completed in a morning and capped by a feast of beef or goat, seasoned with ¼ lb. salt and ½ pint of oil; maize porridge and root vegetables prepared by women relatives; and, finally, 2 or 3 calabashes of palm wine. The cash outlay is in the vicinity of 10s. If the owner is not skilled in thatching, experts are called in and are given food, wine, and 3s. for three days' labour. When one or two members of the compound assist they are given palm wine. Nowadays, if a contractor is called upon to provide all building materials and labour, the cost of a small house may be in the vicinity of £3, an estimate which also correponds to that given me by men in Ndop and Ngie. A sun-dried mud brick house of somewhat larger dimensions, with plank doors and window frames, costs at least £7.[1]

(c) *Gifts to Affines.* The Nsaw man is apt to grumble about the gifts which he must make to his wife's kin each year; but, if he is fair-minded, he will generally admit that the demands made upon him bear some relation to the size of his family and his income. The newly married man is expected to be lavish, but, if his earnings remain small and he has many children, he is not pressed unduly by his affines. His father-in-law and the head of his wife's lineage may ask him to provide wine, fowls, oil, or salt when a house is to be built, or some such ceremony as a marriage takes place; and his mother-in-law, when visiting, must be treated as an honoured guest and given a parting gift of oil, salt, and perhaps a little meat. But if expenses have been heavy for one year, the considerate man lets his son-in-law " rest " the following year, unless some untoward event such as a death occurs. Often commitments may be met from household-supplies, so that they do not entail an immediate cash outlay, though they represent a loss of potential income. Most men keep a few fowls, while many lineage heads have at least four or five sheep or goats, some of which they sell in the market. They must, however, always keep some in reserve, not only for affines but also for sacrifices carried out on behalf of male and female members of the lineage,—a fact which is not always allowed for in estimating the annual income of such individuals. Again, polygamy is a privilege which must be paid for, as the example given below will illustrate. A Councillor whom I knew kept a record of his expenditure over a long period. In 1947 he gave 3 kerosene tins of palm oil (51s.) to the kin of a new wife; 2 tins (35s.) to those of a wife, who had just borne him a child; and cloth to the value of 25s. to the father of another. The lineage head of a fourth wife had died and, as no successor had been appointed immediately, expenses were light; but the mother-in-law paid a visit and was given 2s. and a fowl. The Councillor had also been betrothed since 1939 to the daughter of the Fon-

---

[1] According to a rough estimate which I made a house, which is 33 ft. × 15 ft. × 9 ft., requires a little over 7,000 bricks. Many men are beginning to make their own bricks and turn out about 50 a day. In 1948, a hundred bricks cost one shilling.

Nkor. In 1948 she still had not reached puberty, and so the marriage had not been consummated; but, from time to time, she had stayed for several months in her fiancé's compound under the guardianship of his senior wife, and each time her kin came to conduct her back to her own village they had to be rewarded lavishly. For example, in 1947, a *Ya* of Nkor who was in the party was given 10s. in cash, and a cloth worth 8s.; the fiancée's brother was presented with 3s.; a sister got 3 yards of cloth, costing 9s.; and 9 wives of the Fon-Nkor each received a fourpenny cooking pot and a shilling in cash. Between 1939 and the beginning of 1947 the Councillor had, in addition, made a series of gifts in goats, oil, cloth, fowls, and cash to the *Fɔn* which amounted to some £22.[1]

These figures are of course astronomical, compared with those in the budget of the average Nsaw man. Thus Vincent Kwangha, whose cash income was about £4-10-0, gave gifts to the value of 6s. 8d. during the year 1947-1948; but it is noteworthy that he received cloth and goods to the value of 7s. 5d. for his family from his mother-in-law. Two other men, whose income was about the same as Vincent's, gave over a period of five months to their respective affinal relatives 3s. worth of goods in one case, and 10s. in the other. The second amount included expenditure on goats and fowls for sacrifices, carried out on behalf of a pregnant wife by the head of her lineage. The demands on this individual's income were thus heavy, and not representative of his normal commitments. Men who earn some £10 a year may give 10s. to 15s. to affines, while those earning £20 or more may distribute anything from £1 to £4. Thus Benedict Somo spent £3-19-8 in one year; but, it should be stressed, he also received from his wife's kin £1-5-0 in cash, as well as clothes and other articles for the use of his family. Clearly, it is difficult to strike an average, but in the low income group marriage gifts probably amount to from 5s. to 7s. a year; and, in the higher income group (£20 and more), about £2.

(d) *Miscellaneous.* Income tax is not levied on earnings below £24 a year, so that most men only have to pay the poll tax of from 5s. to 8s. In addition, a man requires a loin cloth for himself, and a small strip of baft as a pubic covering for his wife,—these items costing about 12s. a year. If both he and his wife are Christians his expenses are heavier, since she will need some sort of wrap for every-day wear, as well as a dress and headtie for Sunday and other festive occasions. If income is small it may take him two years to accumulate the money necessary. Francis Lole, during 1947-1948, spent 16s. on cloth for his wife; while Alphonse Fannso spent 21s. 6d. on dresses for his wife and daughter at Christmas, and Nicholas Ngee, a tailor, used 31s. 6d. worth of cloth for his. Somo, who had a larger income than these men, devoted £3-1-2 to the purchase of clothes and shoes for his wife, Christina, in addition to the amount expended on clothing for himself and his sons (see App. C., No. 2). Roman Catholics must also pay a monthly contribution to the Mission, 6d. in the case of men, and 3d. for women. If they are short of cash they may do a week's work at the mission instead, but not all are able to spare the time. Finally, most men, be they Christian or pagan, endeavour nowadays to provide education for at least one of their sons. Fees in the Infant's Grade are low— some 6s. a year—, but to these must be added the cost of writing materials and clothing.

---

[1] Soon after 1939 the Fon-Nkor died, and the Councillor sent 5 goats for the mourning ceremonies in addition to the 3 goats, which he handed over to some of the late *Fɔn's* kin when they visited Kimbaw. When a new *Fɔn* was appointed, he sent cloth worth 25s., a European chair (18s.) and gunpowder (10s.). Later the *Fɔn* married a Nsungli woman and the Councillor contributed 2 goats (£1) to the marriage payment. On another occasion the *Fɔn* struck his foot against a stone and the Councillor, who was present when the accident occurred, gave a goat worth 12s. to express his regret, and to assist in restoring the dignity of the stricken *Fɔn*! It is worth noting that the Councillor, in giving a list of his expenses, usually mentioned the circumstances in which they had been incurred.

In the preceding discussion I have attempted, on the basis of my observations, budget records, and statements made by individuals, to estimate the *minimum* expenditure incurred by a Nsaw man with a wife and one or two small children. It totals about £3-6-0, if 25s. is allowed for food (staples, salt, oil, meat, ground-nuts, etc.); 8s. for house and farm replacements, 6s. for gifts to affines; 5s. for tax; 12s. for clothes; and 10s. for incidental expenses. If the family is a Christian one, the purchase of clothes for womenfolk brings the budget to about £4. School fees for one child raise it another 10s.

In comparison with estimates given for some regions of Nigeria, the minimum expenditure may seem high,[1] or even in relation to my estimate for Esimbi (*infra*, Ch. II, pp. 25—26). But it should be pointed out that in the forest areas of Bamenda a man saves at least 11s. on oil; he frequently uses potash instead of European salt; he catches more fish and game; and, finally, he does not need to buy most household utensils, since if neither he nor his wife is skilled in manufacture she may obtain them by bartering food or oil. In Nsaw, on the other hand, my estimate of expenditure still leaves the household very short of oil, salt, and meat; and it would not permit of much margin for the purchase of firewood, extra quantities of staples after a very bad harvest, and European household articles and ornaments. The 10s. allowed for incidental expenses are required for soap, matches, medicine, hospital fees, club-fees, contributions to ceremonies, and so forth. The figure which I have calculated for the average minimum expenditure of a small pagan family would, I think, be typical of most of the Tikar tribes of the uplands and plains, with the possible exception of some villages in Fungom and Bum. In some areas, foodstuffs may be more plentiful than in Nsaw during the period of scarcity, and palm oil may be cheaper; but against the saving on these items must be placed the marriage payment which, even if spread over a number of years, probably amounts to more than the total value of marriage gifts handed over to affines during the lifetime of a wife in Nsaw.[2]

In the foregoing discussion I have mentioned only in passing the plight of polygynists. I say plight, because their commitments remain relatively heavy and their income small until their own daughters, and those of male dependants, reach marriageable age. Their wives produce enough food to feed themselves and their children, but not sufficient, as a rule, for sale so that their agricultural activities are not a source of cash income to their joint-husband. He, on his side, if he has three or four wives must spend at least £2 a year on oil, and 25s. on salt, in addition to about £1 on house and farm tools and utensils. Cloth for himself and his sons costs about £2, house repairs entail an outlay of some 10s., and gifts to affines another £3 at least. If he is a *fai* or /e, he normally has kola trees and raffia bush, but he is expected to dispense nuts and wine on a lavish scale, and to assist his dependants with raffia poles when these are required for house-building. Finally, as the intermediary between the living and the ancestors, he must from time to time sacrifice fowls, sheep and goats. From his own sons-in-law, and those of his male dependants, he receives gifts in kind, but often these are an immediate contribution to ceremonies, in which he himself incurs the major expense; while others again, such as salt and oil, are distributed among his wives and children. He thus requires a cash income of at least £10 a year.

---

[1] Professor Forde has estimated that, among the Yakö of the Cross River in Nigeria, a small Umor household has to meet a basic cash outlay of from 50s. to 60s. a year. *Vide*, D. Forde and R. Scott, *The Native Economies of Nigeria*, 1946, pp. 61–62.

[2] It is true that in most tribes a man is assisted by his father or his lineage head in the marriage payment; but, during his adolescence, he has himself handed over his trade earnings to one of these men; and, once his own sons reach puberty, he is expected to assist them in securing wives. A man also incurs expenses in providing a feast and gifts for his wife's kin when she bears him a child.

(a) Ya-Nsolaa, one of the Queen Mothers of Nsaw, leads the women in a dance at Kimbáw. Note the cap, ivory bangles and other regalia associated with her royal status.

(b) *Natums* in their regalia sitting as honoured guests for a feast in Aghem Village.

(*a*) A Christian family of Kimbaw : Benedict Somo (grandson of the late Fon), his wife, Christina Lambiif, and their three children.

(*b*) The marriage of two Christian schoolteachers in Kimbaw. The girls on the left bear the wedding cakes on their heads.

(*a*) East end of Mbonyaar Compound, Kimbaw. The two huts flanking the entrance to the *Fai's* inner courtyard are occupied by his senior wife (left) and his junior wife (right).

(*b*) Section of Akonkaw Village (Mbembe). Note the well-constructed grain stores.

(*a*) Kimbaw man bringing home thatching-grass from the hillside.

(*b*) Tanye cutting up goat flesh at a house-building feast given by Fai-o-Mbonyaar. The bowl on the left contains palm oil, and the two calabashes palm wine. The children also receive their share.

(a) Kimbaw. Looking south-east over farm land held mainly by Fai-o-Mbonyaar and /e-o-Ka. Ro-Kimbaw is in the foreground ; Ro-kong on the lower slope below grove of kola trees ; and Dzøødzøng is above the trees and to the left. See App. D.

(b) Looking east up the Kimbaw valley to Djem Compound. One hut of Kinga Compound is on the extreme right. See App. D.

(a) Kengeran and her two daughters sowing maize in March, 1948, at Kimbaw.

(b) Harvest of finger millet belonging to Elizabeth-Bika of Djem Compound, Kimbaw. Anthropologist on the left.

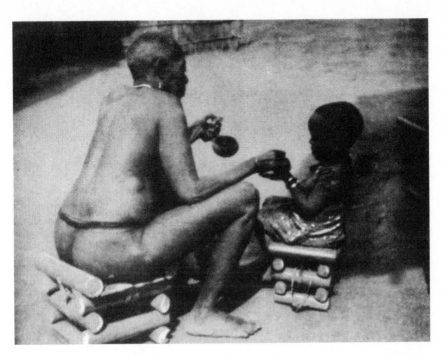

(a) Yirbongka of Mbonyaar feeds her grandchild with porridge and greens.

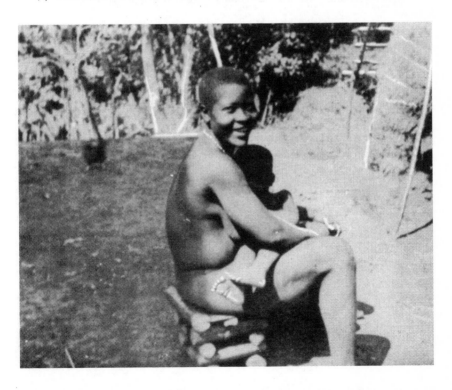

(b) Dzøøndzøiy of Djem Compound nursing her child.

(a) Children of Mbonyaar Compound taking their water calabashes to fill at the stream. The hut of Camilla Labam is in the background.

(b) Margaret Labam of Ka Compound grinding maize outside her hut in the evening.

(*a*) Woman of Ako Village (Mbembe) moulding a pot from a lump of clay.

(*b*) Pagan women selling foodstuffs in the Kimbaw market.

(a) Kengeran, a grand-daughter of the late Fon of Nsaw, and inherited wife of Fai-o-Djem.

(b) Yuliy, co-wife of Kengeran, enjoying a pipe in her compound on a rest-day.

Chapter VIII

KIMBAW BUDGETS—Part I

BUDGET SAMPLE

SO FAR we have been concerned with the value of the harvest contributed by Nsaw women to the subsistence of the household, and the extent to which this has to be supplemented by the purchase of extra food and of such necessaries as salt, oil, meat and so on. We have also outlined in general terms the other commitments which involve a cash outlay and for which a husband assumes, as a rule, responsibility. Here we shall consider some of the main occupations from which the Nsaw derive an income, and we shall analyse for purposes of illustration some of the 16 budgets which are set out in detail in Appendix C.

The amount of quantitative data which I obtained may appear small to the economist, but even so the collection of that data made considerable inroads on the time available to me for a general survey of the life of the women. The budgets were few in number and the sample was not a random one, for the reasons already discussed in an earlier chapter. The alternative would have been to have made a random and larger sample by collecting budgets over a period of two or four weeks. On this basis and with inquiries about general expenditure and income an estimate could have been worked out for a full year. The course which I eventually adopted appeared to me to present definite advantages. In the first place, it enabled me to obtain, as it were, a close-up of the activities of 21 families over a period of $5\frac{1}{2}$ months. Secondly, the selection of the families for intensive study was made only after I had already spent some nine months in Nsaw and was in a position to form an opinion as to what was and what was not typical in terms of size of household, type of marriage (whether Christian or pagan), forms of occupation, and so forth. In some cases the generalizations based on an examination of quantitative data merely confirmed those which I had tentatively formulated on the basis of qualitative material obtained in the first tour.

Unfortunately there are no lineage heads in my sample. Even my friends in that category were reluctant to furnish details of their income and expenditure, lest it should prove a prelude to the imposition of income tax. Actually, from my knowledge of their resources, I knew that at least four of them would not have been held liable; but, as they gave me much valuable information on other matters, I did not want to endanger our friendly relationships by continuing to press inquiries after my first abortive or unsatisfactory attempts.[1] In the case of two of them there was also, I think, another reason for their reticence. They were somewhat apprehensive lest any admission of having bought salt and oil might be repeated by me to their wives, who would then

---

[1] Among the 69 men of Kimbaw, who had the title of *fai* or */e*, only 18 were assessed for income tax in the year 1947-48. Among the 18, only one—a Councillor—had a money income over £40, the rest earning from £26 to £35.

In the same year there were only 235 men of the Nsaw N.A., who were held liable for income tax, as against 9,074 who paid a poll tax of 5s. From both figures I have excluded strangers such as Hausa, Bamum, and men from Ndop. A further analysis of income in relation to occupation will be made later in this chapter, but it should be pointed out that the major source of cash for most *afai* is the sale of kola nuts to local traders. About 1,000 to 2,000 nuts are obtained from a tree in a good year, and these sell at approximately 1s. to 1s. 6d. a hundred. Lineage heads do not headload to Yola, where profits are much larger, since they must remain at home to look after their dependants. In fact, the disinclination of many men to become *afai* springs in part from the limitations which will be imposed on their freedom of movement.

intensify their demands for those commodities. They were aware that the women were particular friends of mine, and that they frequently grumbled to me about the inadequate amounts they received! But while the lack of detailed information about budgets of lineage heads is a matter for regret, it should be stressed that, in the first place, they constitute a small section of the total population of Nsaw;[1] secondly, that their annual income, in so far as it is derived from kolas, raffia and a few livestock, is usually in the vicinity of £10 to £20; and thirdly, that their standard of living, in most instances, does not differ markedly from that of other men who adhere to the traditional way of life. They have a little more meat, wine, oil and firewood but, when they have met the commitments associated with their office, they have very little surplus to spend on European goods.

While, then, the number of occupations represented by my budgets is limited, the earnings derived from them are, it should be stressed, typical of the general level of income in Nsaw and indeed throughout much of the Province. The intensive analysis of budgets in this and the next chapter is intended to bring out clearly the standard of living in many Nsaw households, the small margin of profits on which both men and women work, and the ways in which limited resources are allocated to the purchase of food, tools, utensils, clothes, and to the fulfilment of social obligations. The records cover a whole year for five out of the 16 budgets, but only a little over 5 months for the remaining eleven. In the case of the latter I have made an estimate of the income and expenditure for the whole year. During the period when I myself collected the material I visited my informants on market-days in the evening when sales and purchases had been completed. From time to time during the week I made enquiries about smaller transactions in the tiny Hausa market which functioned daily. During my absence from Kimbaw in the earlier period of 1947 I arranged for two schoolboys to collect some budgets for me. One was the son of Vincent Kwangha who kept his father's budget and also that of Kengeran, an inherited wife of the *fai* of Djem compound. The other lad was Francis Kpuntir who had reached Standard VI at school and who recorded the budgets of his father (Lole) and of Melalia Shikiy, a woman who traded regularly in cooked food. The fifth individual was Benedict Somo, an ex-schoolteacher who kept his own accounts. I coached all three recorders for a fortnight before I left Kimbaw at the end of February 1947, and gave them written instructions. On the whole they did their work well though occasionally they neglected to note the purchase of incidental items such as tobacco and groundnuts, or gifts in kind received from kin and friends.

Particularly interesting, from the point of view of changes in the economic pattern, is the material drawn from the budgets of those Christians, who earn about the same amount of money as *afai* and who spend a considerable proportion on education, clothes for womenfolk, and extra foodstuffs. At the other end of the scale I have some budgetary data for men who follow traditional crafts, such as retailing of kola nuts and thatching grass, and who earn only about 90s. per annum. This is not the minimum, as it was my impression that makers of stools, mats, bags, and baskets earn even less; but it is probably representative of the average cash income in Nsaw and other Tikar tribes. It is less typical of the forest areas where markets are on the whole poorly developed.

SUPPLEMENTARY SOURCES OF INCOME

Except in the case of a few occupations, most Nsaw men find it necessary to eke out their main source of income with the occasional sale of plantains, and

---

[1] Mr. W. M. Bridges in 1934 estimated that there were about 450 *afai* in Nsaw. I am not sure whether he included sub-lineage heads (*a/e*); but, on the basis of my Kimbaw figures, I would hazard a " guestimate " of between 500 and 550 *afai* and *a/e* at present.

also of avocado pears, mangoes, and oranges where these are cultivated. But, as, mentioned earlier, the cash income from this type of farm produce is small, and probably does not amount to more than 10*s.* a year at the outside. Thus Kengeran sold 8*s.* 10*d.* worth of plantains; Vincent Kwangha, 8*s.* 10½*d.* worth of plantains, and pears; and Francis Lole, 8*s.* 9*d.* worth of plantains, pineapples, pears, and oranges. Many men do not make as much as 5*s.* from their plantain groves. Most individuals, however, keep a few fowls and dispose of from four to six in the market during a year for about 6*s.* to 8*s.* Profits from poultry should be larger than this, but very often out of a clutch of twelve only two chicks may survive owing to destruction by hawks.

Many men, if they are energetic and pressed for money, take the opportunity during the dry season to cut bundles of thatching grass and firewood; but it requires a considerable amount of strength to accumulate 50 bundles of the one and 20 of the other, and even then not all may be sold. Few men rely on these occupations as their main source of income nowadays; but, in 1934, about 1.4% of adult taxable males in Nsaw gave grass-cutting as their work, while 6.4% gave the selling of firewood.[1] Small though the pickings from such transactions are, they are not to be despised when the main occupation, such as retailing of kolas locally or a small range of European articles, brings in only £2 or £3 in addition.

Skill in marketing is greatly admired in Nsaw, and men who exercise it are regarded as " clever " or as " having intelligence ". The man who buys without haggling is a fool; but the man who sells at the first offer is an even bigger fool. Thrift is another quality which is esteemed, and it is recognized that not all men are equally provident. A friend of mine said one day: " Some men pick up a penny on the sale of pears; pick up a penny for bananas; they do not despise it. They must work; they must get together money. But some go to the market and do not know how to pick up the odd copper. Then they stay where they are. They are not skilled." He then went on to draw a parallel between the thrifty man who puts something aside for a rainy day and one who plants seed in the ground. " It stays there. If God agrees, then we shall eat." Boys and even girls are encouraged, at an early age, to engage in a little trade, the former with the prompting of their father, the latter with that of their mother. Young girls sell a few vegetables from their plots or brew a little beer. Boys gather windfalls from the kola trees, sell them and gradually accumulate enough to buy groundnuts which they retail (*bin*) at a small profit. In these enterprises they rarely receive financial assistance from their father; still less from their lineage head. But a mother's brother or mother's father often gives a boy sixpence or a shilling to set him up in trade. As far as earnings are concerned, parents expect to be informed but would consider it undignified to commandeer a few coppers, or to ascertain that the truth is always being told! On the other hand if profits are large then a father usually holds them in trust. Schoolboys, once they approach the age of puberty, trade during their holidays and are thus able to make a contribution to school fees.

DJAŊGI

As noted previously, most men work on a very small margin of profit and have, as a rule, very little ready cash in hand. But the problem of purchasing relatively expensive equipment or trade goods is met to some extent by an institution, which is called *djaŋgi* in Pidgin-English and which is an adaptation of the traditional custom whereby, in most tribes, groups of men assembled

---

[1] *Vide*, W. M. Bridges, *op. cit.*, Schedule ' F '. Only the actual number of men engaged in various occupations is given in the *Report*, so I have worked out the percentages myself. For the percentage of men engaged in 1934 in occupations, other than grass-cutting and firewood, see Appendix B.

from time to time to drink palm wine or mead. This convivial element has been retained; indeed, it is difficult to conceive of two Bamenda men meeting together without partaking of wine! But nowadays members of a group may also make weekly, fortnightly or monthly payments, ranging from sixpence to five and even ten shillings according to their means. Each member in turn " cooks *djaŋgi* " (*naa ngwa*), that is, he takes the total contribution made at a meeting, at the same time providing refreshment for the others. He pays no interest, and he uses the money for his more pressing commitments, such as housebuilding, marriage payment, the settlement of debts, and especially the purchase of trade goods such as cloth, kerosene, kola nuts, and so on. At the following meetings he is under an obligation to repay to each " cook " whatever he received from him. The number of members varies from ten to fifty and the nucleus is, almost always, men of a compound who are kin, together with other close neighbours and friends. The head or " Father " of the *djaŋgi* (*ta-ngwa*) is a man who is respected and trusted, and is not always a *fai*. Accounts may be kept if one member is literate. There is still a considerable prejudice against women participating in this institution, on the grounds that it is unseemly for them to foregather with men to drink, and, more particularly, that they may be tempted to devote too much time to trade and recreation, and neglect their farms and home responsibilities, not least the feeding of a husband! Even Christians share these fears but there are exceptions. For example, there was a large *djaŋgi* at Mbonyaar, which met on Sundays and which admitted women, though the latter were not allowed to drink inside the house with the men, but had to be content with the small measure of wine sent to them in the courtyard. It was a very small measure indeed, and the women laughingly complained that the men "cheated" (*boti*) them! However, they paid their contributions, took their turn in "cooking *djaŋgi*," and provided beer for the occasion. Usually they left it to their menfolk to look after the money or to buy cloth, since men were said to be the most competent judges in such matters.

Besides the *djaŋgi* proper there is also a type of thrift society or " bank ", which is gaining in popularity. Men pay in a set sum at the beginning of each year, and this is allowed to accumulate as a reserve against emergencies. For instance, in Mbonyaar, a group of members each paid 5s. in 1945, 10s. 5d. in 1946, and 16s. in 1947.[1] About four times a year most of them drew out sums, ranging from ten to thirty shillings, but were under an obligation to repay each amount at the end of two months, in addition to interest at a rate of a penny in the shilling. A fine was imposed if repayment was delayed. The club also bought each month or fortnight either a 40 lb. bag of salt or a 4 gallon tin of palm oil which was retailed in small quantities to members at less than the market price.

THE MARKET-PLACE

Before we discuss in detail the budgets of some of the men traders, something must be said about the layout of the market and the general pattern of buying and selling. From early morning on market-day there is a steady stream of people along the roads and paths leading to the village. Youths bear on their heads long cradles containing kola nuts, or bundles of firewood; others have baskets of fowls slung over their shoulders, or tug or drive a recalcitrant sheep or goat; women from the northern areas carry on their backs conical baskets filled with potatoes, or support on a walking stick a woven bag packed with

---

[1] Records of amounts banked by members and of the price of salt and oil purchased were kept by one of the literate men of the compound. In the preamble to these accounts he stated that the purpose of the society was " for the protection of orphans, because all may be orphans some day!"

potatoes, cassava or greens. From midday until about 3 p.m. attendance reaches its peak, and the crowds are so dense that it is difficult to see the goods, although some of the more odiferous foodstuffs may be smelt from far away! As a rule, certain commodities are sold in certain parts of the market: in Kimbaw, vendors of kola nuts tend to congregate along the north-west side, while below them men from Nsungli ladle out palm oil into calabashes for a steady stream of customers. In the north-east corner, the N.A. has constructed a meat stall where beef is examined by the Sanitary Inspector before it is sold. Behind it ten to twenty Fulani women sit with their bright yellow calabashes of butter pats and milk; while, further down the market, women of Nsaw lay out their cooked foodstuffs on plantain leaves, or keep them in baskets. Men from Ndop display their pots in another part of the market, and livestock is tethered on the outskirts by the main road. Along the sides of the market rough shelters have been erected and here squat Hausa who trade in cloth and leatherwork, tailors who treadle their machines, and vendors of tobacco or of herbs and medicines. A vast miscellany of articles is to be seen in the centre of the market: salt and groundnuts; fried termites and bush rats; sandals made from discarded rubber tyres, and lamps ingeniously contrived from milk tins and beer-bottle tops; stools and umbrellas, pipes and knives, kittens and fowls,—the catalogue is diverse and almost endless!

As might be expected, market-prices fluctuate not only during the year but even during the day. In the early morning there are always a few traders, who are anxious to be rid of their wares and who sell at a lower price in order to be free for the rest of the day. Between midday and about 4 p.m. profits are higher, and towards evening they fall again. The variation depends of course on the type of article and quantity. A bag of maize, for which 1s. 6d. is demanded at 2 p.m., may be disposed of thankfully for 1s. 2d. at 5.30 p.m.; while during the same period, 12 ozs. of cassava gruel for $\frac{1}{2}d.$ may be increased to 16 ozs. Some purchasers, eager to save a little, may postpone their transaction until the late evening, although they run the risk of obtaining poorer quality or nothing at all. The vendors, on their side, are influenced by the fact of whether their goods are perishable; or, if not, whether it is worth waiting until the next market day. Some women hesitate to go to the trouble of carrying 30 lbs. of potatoes back to their village, which may be 12 miles away, and are therefore prepared to sell for less than they hoped; others, who wish to obtain a certain amount of money for a specific purpose, shoulder their loads and return the following week. Women, who deal in perishable cooked foodstuffs, are at a disadvantage, although their children give them a joyous welcome and pounce on what is left of the bean-balls or cassava-gruel when they return to the compound in the evening.

Again, there are periods of the year when attendance falls off at the market and results in a slight lowering of prices. During the dry season many men may be away hunting, cutting thatching grass, or clearing farms. When the first spring rains come, many go to plant maize since this must be done quickly; while, at the harvest of maize and millet, the help of most members of the household is enlisted. It is on this last occasion that there is a noticeable increase in the cost of baskets which are used to bring in the grain from the fields.[1] Lastly, there is the variation associated with availability; for example, on the 26th June 1945, 6 ozs. of maize flour cost one penny, and a 30 lb. bag of hulled grain cost 4s.; on the 24th October, 9 ozs. of flour were sold for a $\frac{1}{2}d.$, and 30 lbs. of grain for 1s. 6d. or 1s. 9d. Potatoes showed a similar fluctuation : in June, $1\frac{1}{2}$ lbs. cost $\frac{1}{2}d.$, and a bag weighing 25 lbs. cost 6d. In October, when they were more plentiful and the demand for them was less

---

[1] The cylindrical baskets (*vegati*), which are used for millet, normally cost 3d. or 4d. but, just before and during the harvest, they may rise to 5d. and 6d.

owing to harvest of maize, 2 lbs. 14 ozs. went for ½d., and a large bag for 4d. In the earlier part of this book reference has frequently been made to changes in the price of palm oil during the year. At its cheapest it cost 2d. a cigarette-cup (about ¼ pint) in Kimbaw, at its dearest 6d.; while, for the larger quantities (4 gallons), prices ranged between 8s. and 17s. It is pointless to extend the list further; and perhaps even more unnecessary to say that the greatest change is the rise in the cost of living, which has occurred over the last ten years and which has affected the price of most commodities. Table XI below, which is based on information in a short report by the S.D.O. in 1938 and on my own data, gives some idea of the situation:

TABLE XI

Items	Quantity & price, Feb. 1938	Quantity & price, Feb. 1948
kolas	1,000 for 4s. to 5s.	1,000 for 15s. to 20s.
plantains	20 to 24 for 1d.	10 to 14 for 1d.
tobacco	3 bundles for ½d.	3 bundles for ½d.
goat	small for 2s.; large gelt for 6s.	small for 4s. 6d. to 5s.; large gelt for 12s. to 15s.
sheep	ditto	ditto
fowl	4d. to 10d.	9d. to 2s. 6d.
maize	5 lbs. for 1½d.	5lbs. for 4d. to 5d.
maize flour	1 lb. for ½d.	½ lb. for ½d.
sweet potato	5 lbs. for ½d.	5 lbs. for 2d.
cassava	4½ lbs. for ½d.	4½ lbs. for 1½d.
cooked yams	6 lbs. for ½d.	6 lbs. for 3d.
potatoes	26 lbs. for 3d.	26 lbs. for 6d.
palm oil	1 gallon—1s. 3d.	1 gallon—3s. 3d.
salt	bag (40 lbs.) 5s. 6d.	bag 14s. (U.A.C.—8s.)

MEN'S BUDGETS

KOLA TRADE

One of the most important sources of income in Nsaw is the production and sale of kola nuts. In the 1934 *Re-Assessment Report*, Mr. W. Bridges estimated that, out of 6,728 adult taxable males, 2,339 or 34.7% were engaged in this occupation. In villages where there were many trees the percentage was even higher: 49% in Kimbaw, 58% in Mufu, 69% in Kiyan, and 73% in Meluf.[1]

[1] *Op. cit.*, Schedule F.

The next two most popular occupations in Kimbaw in 1934 were the retailing of tobacco and the production of palm wine, each engaging some 15% of the adult taxable males. It is noteworthy that the census of 1934 revealed a tendency for the men of certain villages to specialize in certain types of work. In both Ngondzen and Ketiwum, a little over 54% produced and sold tobacco; in Nkor, Lassin, and Dom, between 55% and 68% dealt in palm wine; in Din, 56% in woven bags. Bags, mats and stools are made from the midribs of raffia, and hence are often associated with the production of wine. For example, in Djottin-Vitum, 32% of the men sold wine, 33% bags, 24% mats, and a small percentage baskets and stools.

Many of the young unmarried men and those with small families headload a thousand nuts from two to four times a year to Mayo Daga in Mambila or to Yola, and make about 100% profit. They buy small quantities in Nsaw and sometimes the French Cameroons at 1s. 6d. a hundred, and retail them at 3s. The journey is a long one, involving some three weeks' absence if to Mambila, and as much as six or seven weeks to Yola. Despite the profits there are, however, disadvantages for the married man for he must make provision for his wife and children during his absence, and also arrange his journeys so that he is at home when she needs help for farm clearing and the harvest of cereals. Kibu (see No. 4 in App. C) made, as a rule, three trips a year, his net profits being about 40s. on the kolas. While in Mambila he bought rock salt or blankets, and from their sale made another 10s. These earnings were inadequate to meet all his commitments and were supplemented by the sale of small quantities of kolas in Kimbaw, and the disposal of bundles of firewood and thatching grass collected in the dry season. He had only a few plantain trees, and made, at most, about 6s. on his fowls. All told, his cash income for a year was about £4-6-0. His expenses for the household were lower than most other men, being about £3-8-0, but the margin for saving was still narrow.[1]

Many men, however, when they reach their late thirties find the occupation too strenuous; and more than one said to me: " I became bald through carrying kolas to Yola!" If a man has a number of children there are further ties which keep him to his homestead. And, finally, there is always the possibility that his wife may go off with another man in his absence. This is the more likely to happen if the marriage has never been recognized by the head of the woman's lineage. Left alone for long periods, she is in a particularly vulnerable position in so far as her kin may seize the opportunity to persuade her to leave her husband. I recorded four such cases in one year in Veka'akwi area alone. But, even when a man is reasonably certain of his wife's affection and fidelity, there are the drawbacks which I have mentioned above. The solution is either to adopt another trade such as tailoring; or to combine the retailing of kolas locally with subsidiary occupations such as grass-cutting or the rearing of a few goats. For example, Mawo (see No. 5 in App. C) was a middle-aged man with one wife and a son. He sold about 4 goats annually at 5s. to 7s. each; about 28 bundles of heavy firewood at 14s., plantains at 10s., and 4 fowls at 6s. He occasionally trafficked in kolas locally; but, on the basis of his budget kept for five months, I doubt if he made more than 12s. a year. This brought his cash income to just under 66s., out of which he had to meet household and personal requirements at an outlay of some 60s.

Mawo's earnings were small as he did not deal regularly in kolas in the local market; but, for a full year, I recorded the transactions of another individual, who retailed kolas each week, in Kimbaw. Vincent Kwangha was in his fifties and lived in Djem compound. He was a gentle and a wise man, whom I trusted completely and who became my very good friend. As a youth, he had headloaded nuts to Banyo in the French Cameroons; but, after marriage, he was reluctant to leave wife and children for long periods, and thenceforth he confined his activities to the local market where he had some excellent business contacts among the Hausa. He bought, on an average, 600 nuts on market day, sometimes disposing of them immediately, sometimes waiting until the following week. His profits were small,—ranging from sixpence to a maximum of three shillings; over a full year they averaged a shilling a week.

[1] W. M. Bridges estimated that about 75% of the men in the kola trade made journeys to Ibi and Yola two or three times a year (see para. 197). At that time, 500 nuts fetched a mean price locally in Nsaw of 2s. In 1947, they varied between 5s. and 10s. In the records for 1947-1948, only one kola trader was assessed for income tax. His earnings were £28, and he loaded 4 asses six times a year with nuts and took them to Yola. The use of such transport obviously has possibilities for an expansion of the trade.

The smallest quantity of nuts he ever bought on a market day was 200; the largest 1,000. During the year he handled, all told, some 22,000, at a total outlay of £17-18-6. His sales amounted to £19-13-9, or a clear profit of £1-15-3 (see budget No. 1, App. C). On four occasions he sold at a loss; on three he broke even; and, during seven weeks, he bought nothing either because the market was bad or because he had work on the farm. In a very good year he might make 45s. to 50s. In addition to retailing, Vincent occasionally received a small commission for negotiating a sale for others, and particularly for the *fai* whose trees he tended. He also received from the latter about 400 small nuts and these, with windfalls, brought him in another 4s. 11d.[1]

Clearly, his earnings from his major occupation were inadequate for a bare subsistence, and he looked therefore to other means of supplementing his income: thatching-grass and firewood, which yielded him about 12s. a year; and the sale of eggs and fowls which accounted for another 7s. 1d. For many years he had cultivated pear and mango trees near his compound and on one of his large farms. From their produce he gained 8s. 10½d. He had started as a sideline a diminutive nursery for coffee, and made 2s. 6d. on the sale of seedlings. Finally, from his kin and friends, he received 20s. in cash, so that all told his income for the year was £4-12-10. The weekly margin of profit on which Vincent worked was small and was not infrequently swallowed up in the purchase of necessaries. Having bought a little salt, oil, groundnuts for the children, and some tobacco for himself, he very often, as he phrased it, had "nothing to bring home but his body"! His household was large, comprising his wife (Elizabeth-Bika), two daughters, three sons, and a grand-daughter. Another adult daughter had married a man of Kimbaw, but her husband rarely gave anything to Vincent.[2] Finally, there was an adult son who was a teacher in a mission school in a distant village. He was a good lad who sometimes sent calabashes of oil to his parents, receiving in return bags of maize flour and plantains. From time to time he made cash gifts to his father, and assisted his two younger brothers in the payment of part of their school fees, so that Vincent himself had only to meet an outlay of 12s. 3d. on that score. Vincent's wife and adolescent daughter, with occasional help from his mother-in-law, farmed a large area and had no time to engage in petty trade. The year 1947 was a good one so that Vincent did not have to buy any staple foods; but his expenditure on meat, groundnuts, oil, salt, and pepper amounted to £1-9-4, with an extra 1s. 5d. for tobacco and beer. Replacement of tools and utensils cost him 6s. 4d.; and he also paid 4s. 6d. to the Mission for " contribution cards " for himself and his wife for half the year. To obtain the money for the remaining six months he made 300 mud-bricks during the course of a week for the Mission, while his wife did other work for her contribution. The provision of clothes was something of an acute problem in a large female Christian family! At Christmas, in 1945 and 1946, Vincent had bought wraps and headties for his wife and daughter; during 1947 he had to replenish his own scanty wardrobe and garb his sons. He spent, during the year for which the budget was kept, 51s., part of which went towards the purchase of a second-hand military overcoat. Vincent was not a particularly

---

[1] Mr. Bridges, in discussing the kola trade, mentioned that a man, who confined his transactions to the local market, handled only about 500 nuts a year. His figure is very low, and is undoubtedly an underestimate. *Op. cit.*, para. 197. In my *Preliminary Report* of 1945, where I made a rough calculation of Vincent's income, I suggested 35s. for the retailing of nuts—a figure which is the same as that obtained later from detailed weekly records. However I overestimated by a large amount the value of the perquisities from tending kola trees. The kola nuts in Vincent's storehouse, on which I had based my earlier assessment, belonged not to him but to the *fai*.

[2] Vincent's adult daughter was his first-born child, and hence came under the authority of the head of her mother's lineage in so far as her marriage was concerned.

vain person, as Nsaw men go; but, as head of a large family, he had a certain status to maintain when visiting and when selling in the market. At home he went about in a shabby loincloth and, on more than one occasion, apologized to me for his rags; but, he explained, " better I go naked for skin than my pikin be shamed!" That is, he preferred to be shabby himself rather than his children should be inadequately clothed. Finally, Vincent had saved 25s. from the previous year and, with this, he just about balanced his budget.

I have discussed Vincent's transactions in some detail firstly, because I had weekly records made over a full year; secondly, I could place complete reliance on his statements; and, thirdly, he was a man skilled in an occupation which is still the mainstay of a considerable percentage of the men in Nsaw. He possessed a keen sense of responsibility towards his wife and children, as well as a strong affection for them; he scorned no means of augmenting his slender income; and, at the same time, he managed to clear outlying farms and to tend the kitchen garden by the compound. Even so, his income was larger than that of men engaged in some of the traditional Nsaw crafts,—if general statements might be accepted at their face value. Those men who made bags, caps, or mats earned about 30s. per annum, while those, who specialized in stools, matchet-scabbards, baskets, umbrellas, or raffia bins, earned from 20s. to 25s.[1]

GENERAL TRADE

A more lucrative occupation was general trade which, even in 1934, engaged some 12.6% of the adult taxable males. The number is probably larger now with the increased demand for European goods and greater mobility of population. Income varies, of course, with the type of articles handled and according to whether they are bought in Bamenda or in Nigeria. Among some of the " plutocrats " of Nsaw were tailors who went, with their own carriers, two or three times a year to Calabar or Northern Nigeria to buy cloth, haberdashery, buckets, basins, and blankets. In the records for income tax there were 15 of these individuals who made between £28 and £38 a year. Others, who had no assistants, made less and their profits were in the vicinity of £10. Finally, there were those who confined their activities to Bamenda, sometimes buying fish, calabashes and matchets from the Ndop Plain and retailing them in Kimbaw, Mbiami, and other markets in Nsaw.[2]

Among the small-scale traders was Tanye, whose budget I recorded weekly for a little over five months. He had no licence to buy salt (which was rationed during the war and afterwards) and had, perforce, to obtain it in the market at anything from 10s. to 14s. a bag, as against 8s. in the U.A.C. canteen. He retailed it in small quantities and sometimes his only profit was derived from the sale of the cotton bag at two shillings. He also trafficked in kerosene but, having no friends in the U.A.C., he had to buy it in the open African market at 28s. or 30s. a tin, as against the canteen price of 16s. 5d. On one occasion I sold him at cost a spare tin that I had and, by retailing the kerosene by the pint-bottle, he made 17s. 7d. on the deal. In his jubilation he bought

---

[1] From a number of men I received statements about the amount of time required to manufacture various articles, and the average output per week. These corresponded very closely to those given to Mr. W. M. Bridges in his *Report* (*paras*. 198–230). Prices have increased since 1934, as the following figures show. I have placed the 1934 value *in brackets* for comparison: mat– 9d. to 1s. 3d. (6d.); stool– 2d. to 4d. (1d.); umbrella– 4d. (½d.); hoe-handle– 1d. (½d.); matchet-scabbard– 1s. to 1s 6d. (3d. to 6d.); cap– 1s. 6d. to 3s. (1s. 6d.); basket– ½d. to 9d. (3d. to 4d.); bag– 7d. to 9d. (2d.).

[2] One trader of this type was a Christian who, finding the profits small and fired by the example of his friend who was a mixed farmer, abandoned his occupation and took to farming in earnest. His father, commenting on the change, said to me in some astonishment: " My son works harder than his own wife on the farm! "

a fowl for the evening meal, and a khaki shirt for himself! He made on an average 1s. 3d. a week on the sale of kerosene and salt, or an annual income of £2-16-0.[1]

He had three bee hives and, during the five months, obtained 4s. 6d. for the honey (or about 10s. per annum). He sold only 1s. 6½d. worth of plantains, but he had an extremely large grove and would normally make 10s. from their produce. His fowls brought him in another 6s., and the sale of raffia poles about 8s. Finally, he had cut 59 bundles of thatching-grass during the dry season and, with most of this and a little firewood, would earn another 15s. I estimated that his total annual income was £6-2-3, but, although he had only one pagan wife and a small child for whom to provide, he required every penny. In the previous year he had been deprived of some good farm land, and the harvest from the remaining plots was negligible. Already, by the beginning of March 1948, he had spent 12s. 9d. on maize, and ahead of him lay the long period of scarcity until August. All told, his expenditure amounted to about £5-12-0. It should be stressed, however, that this was an exceptionally bad year for him. His wife, in the dry season in 1948, had managed to secure the loan of some good land and, if her crops were successful, his expenses would have been reduced to about £3-14-0. His savings on this basis would be considerable by Nsaw standards; but they still seem small when one takes into account the multiplicity of his activities,—trade in kerosene, salt, honey, plantains, fowls, raffia poles, thatching-grass, firewood, and a little hunting. In addition, he had started a tiny coffee plantation and in his spare time he was making sun-dried mud bricks for a new house![2] (See No. 6 in App. C). One hears much of the improvidence and laziness of the Bamenda male, but the budgets of the pagan Tanye and his small family, and of the Christian, Vincent, with his large one should do something to explode that myth.

TAILORING

Living in Mbonyaar and the adjoining compound of Ka were two Christian tailors, both with large families. Nicholas Ngee in his youth and early marriage had headloaded kolas to Yola, and with his earnings had bought rocksalt there to sell later to Fulani. As a rule, the profits were good; but if the market were bad it meant that almost two months had been wasted on a tiring and fruitless journey. Nicholas therefore looked round for a more sedentary and steady occupation. His brother was a tailor who, over a period of two years, taught him to sew a variety of garments, including the Fulani type. In 1941 Nicholas bought a second-hand machine for £5 from a Hausa, and set up as a tailor in a stall in the small Hausa market which functioned daily. He told me that he enjoyed the work, but at the time at which he is speaking (February) he was losing heart because profits were small. Men were hunting, cutting grass, burning off, clearing, and housebuilding, and attendance had fallen off in the market. He was longing for the advent of the rains which would herald a period of better trade. Even when he went to the Mbiami market (some five hours' walk distant), where competition was less severe, he often made only a few coppers. As at that time there was a shortage of cotton goods, he was unable to get cloth in the U.A.C. canteen, and so had to buy in the market. Sometimes more affluent friends gave him 6 yards of cloth on credit, and he made it up into garments. For his sewing for other people Nicholas earned about 1s. 9d. a week, or £3-18-0 a year. On clothes made up from cloth, which he himself had bought or borrowed, he made roughly 3s. a week or £6-15-0 a year. His major craft, therefore, brought him in approximately

---

[1] In estimating annual income I have calculated on a basis of 45½ Nsaw weeks to a year.

[2] Tanye belonged to Mbonyaar *ngwa*, which he " cooked " for £3; and also to another *ngwa*, from which he obtained £2. He had 31 5d. in the Mbonyaar " bank ".

£10-13-0 a year. During the five months in 1947-1948, he sold neither fowls nor plantains; but his wife occasionally disposed of small quantities of cooked foods at a profit of 2s. 10d. for the period (see No. 7 in App. C).

Compared with the budgets which we have been discussing, that of Nicholas seems a large one. But his position was, in some respects, much more insecure than that of Vincent who possessed good farm land, whereas he had rather poor plots and a large family of children for whom to provide. The harvest of maize and millet had failed in 1947 and, as mentioned earlier, he had spent by the beginning of March 21s. 5d. on bags of maize. Like Biy-Menggu, Nicholas' wife had managed to obtain some better land about 4½ miles away from the compound; but, even with a good crop of potatoes to supplement the larder in May and June, about another 30s. would be spent on maize during the period of scarcity. Margaret, his wife, farmed about 2.1 acres with the assistance of her energetic daughter, Natasha, aged about 14 years, whom the women of the neighbourhood already regarded as " a great little worker of *rizga* plots (*ngaa-kin/ɛf feyi*)." Nicholas himself was sickly, had a bad goitre, and rarely gave any help on the farm, or even with the weeding of the small plantation of coffee which he had started about 2 years previously.

During the period in which I recorded his budget, Nicholas spent £1-5-5 in five months on salt, oil, and meat, which was not much for a household of nine. He sent a portion of these commodities to his wife's kin. House and farm replacements cost him 3s. 2d., and firewood another 3s. 2½d. The last item requires some comment. Nicholas had built for his family a large mud-brick house which, by Nsaw standards of comfort, was cold and far too well-ventilated! The kindling brought in by his wife and daughter was only sufficient for cooking; and, as Nicholas was too sickly and also too busy to gather firewood himself, he had to buy it. Even so coughs and colds seemed to be endemic in the household.[1] Clothes were also a problem and, during the period when I was in Kimbaw, he provided cloth to the value of 38s. 6d. for wraps for his wife and daughter, and shorts and shirts for his school-boy son. The cloth had been bought early in 1947 and so does not appear as an item in the recorded budget. I estimated that he spent about £3 per annum on clothes for himself and his household. He had one adolescent son at school and paid 12s. a year for fees, plus another 3s. 6d. for books and pencils. Both he and Margaret worked at the Mission in order to pay for their contribution cards. Granted a better harvest, Nicholas would in normal years have to meet an expenditure of about £9-15-6. But in the year under review—March 1947 to March 1948—I estimated that his outlay was in the vicinity of £11-6-2, a sum which just balances my estimate for his income (plus a little from his wife's trading profits), namely £11-6-2½. He had " cooked " the Mbonyaar *djaŋgi* for £4, and the one in his own compound for £1-9-0. He also had 31s. 5d. in the Mbonyaar " bank " as a reserve against emergency. In June and October 1947, and again January 1948, he had on each occasion borrowed 30s., but had repaid these sums with 2s. 6d. interest after a lapse of two months.

As this chapter is already somewhat long I do not wish to devote much space to the affairs of three other men, whose incomes were about the same as that of Nicholas. Thomas Kintarir had traded kolas in his youth, but had later been trained by his father's brother to be a tailor. He bought a second-hand machine for £4, and devoted much of his time to sewing in his hut in the compound, except on market days. He had four children (one at school), and his wife farmed 1.8 acres unaided. She had a pleasant placid disposition,

---

[1] It is worth noting that two members of the nobility, who had built large mud-brick houses, normally slept in smaller huts because these were warmer. Until the people have more fuel or can buy large supplies of blankets, better housing has definite disadvantages from the point of view of comfort and even health!

was almost completely absorbed in her household affairs, and was regarded as somewhat of a field-drudge by the women of the compound. During the dry season she devoted nearly 70% of her days to her farms. Her harvest of maize and millet was good by Nsaw standards; and, in addition, Thomas augmented supplies by spending 15s. in five months on maize and potatoes (see budget 8 in App. C.). Another man of Ka was Alphonse Fannso who repaired pots, pans and guns, and sold gunpowder as a sideline. He was a somewhat elusive person and, when caught, was apt to be reticent about his earnings; but from my records I estimated that he made about £1 on the sale of gunpowder, and about £9 per annum from his craft. With the sale of pineapples and fowls, as well as the petty earnings of his wife from trade (about 8s.), he probably had an annual income £10-15-0. He had five children one of whom, an adolescent daughter, helped her mother to cultivate 2.1 acres. But the crops had been poor in 1947 and by March 1948 he had already bought 12s. 9d. worth of maize (see No. 9 in App. C.). As in the case of Nicholas, this additional drain on his resources would have left him very little in the way of savings for the current year.

The third individual had secured employment as a handyman at the Government Resthouse at a wage of 26s. a month. In addition he got 30 lbs. of coffee from a small plantation, which brought him in another 10s. a year. He had only two young children; his wife was a young and energetic farmer, who cultivated 3.9 acres of good land with the help of her mother; and his standard of living in the matter of food and clothes was higher than that of most other members of the compound. (See No. 10 in App. C.)

BRICKMAKING AND HOUSE-BUILDING

Francis Lole of Mbonyaar was a man in his fifties who, in his youth, became a Christian and married his Christian wife against the wishes of her kin,—an event eternally commemorated in the names which he had bestowed on his first-born children. With the passing years, however, a reconciliation was effected, one which without doubt was facilitated by the fact that he was related, through his mother, to a senior councillor, and through his father to one of the Aya. Francis was a wiry, indefatigable little man of exceptional tenacity and initiative. He was devoted to his own wife and family, and had a keen sense of responsibility towards the children of his deceased brothers,— providing them with food, sending some to school, and training others in his craft of brickmaking. His two eldest daughters had passed standard VI, in 1943 or 1944, at the Mission School and, as there seemed to be no opening for them as teachers, he got them to apply for government scholarships for training in midwifery. In September 1947 they returned from Nigeria, one being appointed a health visitor in Bamenda Station, and the other in Kimbaw. Just before I left in 1948, his eldest son, who had kept his father's budget for me during my absence in the west of the Province, secured a scholarship to a secondary school at Sasse in Victoria.

Francis, as a skilled bricklayer, had built a relatively large four-roomed house as sleeping quarters for his family; a store and a kitchen for his wife; and a small room adjoining for his widowed sister, Camilla. During the year under survey, 4th March 1947 to 5th March 1948, Francis made £5-10-8 from brickmaking and supervision of housebuilding for people of Kimbaw, in addition to the £9-15-0 which he secured for a contract to provide bricks and bricklayers for the new Domestic Science Centre. Finally, he had earlier signed an agreement to take on an apprentice in consideration for a payment of £3; but although the training was completed in 1947 he had received only 30s. Typically, he had not pressed his debtor for the money. His earnings from his major craft for the year were thus £18—5—0; but, as the government work was in the nature of a windfall, his normal earnings would be £10 or £12. Besides his main job, Francis found time to give some assistance to his wife on the farm; to tend some raffia he had planted 5 miles away, to weed a coffee plantation from which he obtained 38s.; to traffic a little in such commodities as soap, shirts, fish, and groundnuts; to participate in two *djaŋgis*, and to attend church frequently! His total income for the year was £19-18-0½, in addition to which his wife made a profit of £3-0-9½, from the brewing of beer.

With eight in the household, his expenses were considerable although his wife farmed 1.7 acres with occasional assistance from his adolescent niece who lived with them. On foodstuffs alone (staples and relishes) Francis spent £4-3-9½; on meat, fish and eggs—£1-8-2½; and on salt and oil—£2-7-11 (see No. 3 in App. C). Additional fuel was required, not only to warm his large house, but also for the brewing of beer and entailed an annual outlay of £1-4-7. Besides locally made tools and utensils, Francis also purchased an enamel basin, a blanket, and an alarm clock—the last to ensure an early rising for his work at the Domestic Science Centre! Clothes accounted for another £3 odd; and school fees for another £2-9-0 for his own daughter, a brother's son and a sister's daughter's son. Both he and his wife paid for their " contribution cards ", plus an extra shilling or so for the church collection. Finally, there were miscellaneous expenses for gunpowder to celebrate his daughters' return from Nigeria; for medicine and hospital treatment; for tax; for wine and beer to the four *djaŋgis* to which he belonged, and interest on his withdrawals from the " bank ". He and his wife had many visitors and, during the year, Francis gave away £1-19-0 in cash to needy friends and relatives.

COFFEE-PLANTING AND MIXED FARMING

The last budget, which I wish to discuss in detail, is that of Benedict Somo. In his early married life he had been a teacher at the Mission School; but, finding wages small and prospects limited and also being interested in farming, he resigned. When I arrived in Kimbaw in 1945, he already had 3.2 acres of coffee under cultivation, some castor plants, and an acre of Irish potatoes at Meluf which he hoped to sell to the Government. The last proved a disappointment, since the cost of motor transport at 2s. 6d. a mile over a distance of 65 miles made the enterprise uneconomic. Towards the end of 1945, the S.A.O. suggested that Somo take two months' training at Bambui Government Farm in mixed farming and that he should then, with financial and other assistance, build his own styes on a strip of good alluvial land, where he could grow food to feed his pigs. Somo and his wife, Christina Lambiif (who also traded in starch, gari, and other foods), worked very hard and in the face of considerable setbacks and a small amount of capital. The first styes, constructed mainly from local materials, were not strong enough and their cost represented almost a total loss. The second lot entailed the use of cement which, with timber, etc., ran him into an outlay of £3 odd, plus a debt to Bambui for some £17. Moreover, during the first year, the farm did not produce enough to feed the pigs and Somo had to spend £5-8-6 on that item alone, not to mention overhead for labour (budget No. 2). His sale of pork in the local market in the 12 months under review amounted to £10-17-3. When I left Kimbaw in March 1948, Somo had his styes built, his pigs breeding, and his farm under cultivation. But he faced a debt of £28 for pigs and cement to the Government Farm, another to a soldier who had lent him £5 earlier in the year. A year previously the N.A. Treasury had lent him £15 of which he had still to pay off £1. It was not without a touch of irony, mingled with some hope for the future, that Somo had named his last-born son, Christopher *Bɛrdu*, the Lamnso meaning " it remains to go forward! " Fortunately, he had in February 1948 sold £18 worth of coffee berries; and, in case of necessity, he could sell his horse which he had bought for £6.

Before discussing the rest of Somo's budget it is relevant to point out at this stage that his experiences with pig-raising do not augur well for any development of this industry in Nsaw.[1] He was industrious and had a certain amount of working capital from his coffee. But it was inadequate in the initial stages. More importantly, he could not produce enough food to feed the pigs, although he had good land and had terraced the slopes. In view of the period of seasonal scarcity for many farmers of Nsaw, the question might well be raised whether it would not be better to reserve any surplus food for supplementing the diet of human beings rather than of pigs! In a letter recently received (1950) from a friend in Kimbaw, I was told that Somo had decided to kill off his pigs and start raising cattle. But, if he is to make a success of this, he would have to leave his compound in Kimbaw and go farther afield. Cattle trading would be an alternative but would entail journeys to Victoria or Northern Nigeria. The profits are good. In the income tax assessments for 1947-1948, there were 44 Nsaw men engaged in this occupation, of whom 33% had 10 to 19 head of cattle, and another 33% had 20 to 39 head. A few individuals had as many as 68 to 106, and one had 176. It was estimated that £3 profit was made on each animal.

Somo was very successful with his Arabica coffee plantation. In 1948 he sold £18 worth at 5d. a lb., less transport, to the U.A.C. in Bamenda Station, and he disposed of small quantities of ground coffee in Kimbaw for £3-7-2. As the price of coffee has now risen to 9d. a *lb.*, his plantation should bring him in a tidy income and this may have been one factor in his reported decision to give up pig-breeding. Somo also obtained 12s. from the sale of castor seed, and another £2-11-5½ from onions, tomatoes, cabbages, beans, peas, and potatoes. In his spare time he occasionally did a little tailoring and during the year earned £1-17-9. His total cash income was about £37-17-0. His wife was of considerable assistance to him not only on the farm but also by her enterprise in making starch and gari for sale, and in knitting sweaters and caps. She obtained from these activities a little under £4, most of which she spent on relishes and luxury foods for the household.

Despite his debts and his difficulties Somo and his family enjoyed, by Nsaw standards, a relatively high standard of living. With his wife, three children (a fourth stayed for long periods with the mother-in-law in Bamenda Station), a brother's child, and a labourer, he lived in the compound which he had built in Banka area. There was a traditional type of kitchen for his wife; a large two-roomed dwelling which provided bedroom and living room; and a third house consisting of two small rooms,—one for sewing and business conferences, and the other for a small store. Over a number of years he had accumulated a certain amount of European furniture—chairs, tables, iron bedstead and mattress, pots and pans, not to mention the inevitable Victorian array of photographs for the walls! He and his wife possessed a fairly extensive wardrobe, which also included shoes and hats; and, finally, they kept open house and entertained lavishly. From their guests, some of whom stayed a few days and even weeks, they received gifts of food, as well as cash; but, on the other hand, Somo and Christina were generous to their own kin and friends.

On salt, oil, butter (a luxury for most people), meat, fish and eggs, Somo spent £7-7-1 during the year; on staples, relishes and honey (the last as a sweetening for coffee), another £5-2-0. Clothes cost him £5 odd, and in addition his wife's sister, who was a teacher, frequently presented members

---

[1] This does not apply, however, to the more fertile parts of Nsaw. According to the Colonial Office Report for 1950, paras. 303 and 348, there are now eleven mixed farmers in the Province who have received training at Bambui. The Headmaster of Bambui N.A. School and the Fon of Bali have both received loans for the improvement of piggeries.

of the family with frocks, shirts, shoes, and ornaments.[1] I do not wish to enumerate here all the items, which have been set out in his budget and which I have placed on the pages following that of Vincent Kwangha. These two men represent in my sample two extremes in income for large Christian families. In the case of Vincent, we have a middle-aged, skilled and thrifty man following a traditional Nsaw occupation. His wife is in her late forties and much of her time is absorbed by farming. In the case of Somo, we have a much younger man who, in his youth, had gained some experience working for Europeans in Victoria and who later became a school teacher. With good health, intelligence, and ambition and, not least, a young, energetic and co-operative wife, he could afford to take some risks in launching out into occupations which represented a break with tradition, and even with the traditional division of labour between the sexes.

---

[1] A Nsaw man, who was a Government employee and earned just under £40 a year, showed me a budget which he had kept for 2 months in 1946. I calculated from it his annual expenditure on various items, and it is worth noting that it is similar to that of Somo who had about the same income, though many more debts! Oil cost approximately 56s., salt, 22s.; meat and fish, 71s. 3d.; staples and relishes about 82s. 6d.; groundnuts for the children 20s.; and honey for coffee 20s. Kerosene was bought in relatively large quantities, since he used to read at night, and cost 45s.; firewood accounted for another 40s.; and clothes about 80s. His wife worked on the farm but also traded regularly in gari and starch and made, according to him about 6s. a week. This last was probably an overestimate.

Chapter IX

KIMBAW BUDGETS—Part 2

WOMAN TRADERS

The men have so far dominated the scene in this discussion of trade but they should not be regarded as intruders, still less as usurping the interest in a book devoted otherwise to the activities of the women. My aim throughout has been to preserve some sense of proportion by examining the role of the women within the wide context of the economic life of the community, by comparing it with that of the men, and by revealing its complementary function. Women still play a relatively small part in the total system of trade, and therefore any account of their participation would result in distortion if due weight were not also given to that of the men. This point rises again in a discussion of their standard of living. Any attempt to assess it, without reference to that of the members of the opposite sex, who are their co-partners and dependants, would be meaningless. The unit of study must be the household which, in Bamenda, is generally the elementary family. Within this group, one may analyze the contribution made by each individual.

In the traditional economic organization, the principal responsibility of women was farming. In so far as they traded at all (and it should be remembered that many villages in Bamenda do not lie within easy access of markets) they dealt in small quantities of foodstuffs, beer, or articles such as pots and baskets which they manufactured. Their object, usually, was not to acquire capital on which to support a family, but to obtain a few coppers for the purchase of something needed immediately in the house or for the farm,—utensils, seed, perhaps a little tobacco, or an ornament. Even today many women never sell anything from one year to another. In the compounds with which we have been chiefly concerned, there were six out of eleven adult women at Djem who never trafficked in the market; and six out of thirteen at Mbonyaar. Elizabeth-Bika was middle-aged, frequently busy on the farm, and relied on her husband to supply all her needs. Djo'kem, a pagan woman of about the same age who was rather sickly, was also content to remain at home on market day. The young and favourite wife of the *fai* received sufficient salt, oil, and trinkets from her complacent husband; while Semtur, an elderly, mournful woman married to an even more elderly husband, did nothing to remedy the chronic shortage of salt and oil in the household. There were also at Djem two young married pagan women—one with two children, the other with none. These, with Biy-Menggu and Wanaka of Mbonyaar, either remained at home on market-day, or pottered about on the farm, or visited friends and kin. They were typical of other women of their age and status in this matter. For, although many adolescent girls go to market to sell pounded orchid root (*nyanguf*—a relish), a few potatoes, pears, or greens in order to buy groundnuts, beads, ear-rings, or perhaps something for their mother, the young matron is, as a rule, reluctant to mingle with the crowd. Quite apart from the fact that her husband is generally assiduous in supplying requirements for house and farm, she is apt, in the first years of marriage, to be shy and retiring. During her first pregnancy she would, in any case, shun the market-place on pain of being regarded as brazen; and, finally, until her

132

child is weaned she is fearful of the evil eye.[1] Biy-Menggu had a child, who was about three years old, and she was free to visit the market; but, it was not until just before I left Kimbaw, that she attempted to sell a little prepared foodstuffs. Lacking experience, she was unmercifully cheated by the urchins who frequent the stalls. They took more than they should, profferred bad coins and, as she put it, "were very happy about it all *(awinni /ɛ'ɛri feyi)*!" She made a penny profit on the transaction.

At the other extreme in age are some of the old women, who either have no dependants, or only a grand-child as companion and diminutive helpmeet. They have no surplus on their farms, and no spare cash with which to buy food-stuffs which they might cook and retail. Even if they have an odd copper presented to them, they are reluctant to change their ways and contend with the bustle and sharp practice of the market. Shemsum, the *Yelaa* of Mbonyaar, had no children of her own and received very little salt and oil from her husband, who had inherited her when he was appointed *fai*. But when I used to inquire, somewhat tactlessly, at the close of a market-day whether she had been to market she would reply caustically: " Have I so many things to sell?", or: "Why should I go to market?   In a little while I shall go to earth (I shall die)!" An elderly co-wife of hers, Fhshwaa, adopted much the same attitude, but was more fortunately placed in that her two adult sons kept her supplied with salt, oil, and other necessaries.

However it not infrequently happens that the wives of polygynists, and particularly inherited wives, either send their daughters to sell any small surplus of plantains and vegetables, or go themselves for this purpose. Yuliy of Djem (see No. 13 in App. C), during the course of five months, made 4s. 11d. from bananas and sugar cane, and with this bought at different times and in small quantities 2s. worth of oil, 3d. of meat, 3d. of groundnuts, ½d. of tobacco, and 2d. of cowpea-seed. Her co-wife, Vindjan, who was also inherited and had three children, earned 3s. 2d. from the sale of bananas, sugar cane, and pears (see No. 14 in App. C). Most of this was spent on items for the house and farm: cowpea-seed, pots, and baskets. In addition she bought, all told, 4½d. worth of tobacco, a few groundnuts, bead-thread for her little daughter, and a pencil for her schoolboy son. Yadiy, the third and younger co-wife had an even more miniature budget (No. 15): in five months she disposed of bunches of bananas for 3½d. and sold 6d. worth of beer, brewed from her own maize. With the proceeds she bought cowpea-seed, a knife, a bag, a basket, and a little thread for beads. She depended for her other requirements on her husband. The fourth wife, Kengeran, who was inherited and had a large household comprising her own three daughters and three grand-children, never received sufficient salt or oil from her husband. Worse still, he failed to buy the more costly tools and utensils, such as raffia storebins and hoes. Fortunately, she had a large farm and good harvests, and was able to dispose of much of the fruit from her extensive plantain groves. Over a full year (6th March 1947 to 5th March 1948), she and her daughters sold plantains for 8s. 10d., beans for 9d., and sweet potatoes for 1d.: a total cash income of 9s. 8d. In addition to this she received 11s. 1d. from friends and kin. Out of this income she spent 8s. 6½d. on house and farm replacements, 7s. 7d. on oil, 2s. 5d. on meat, and 11½d. on groundnuts for her children. A necklace, cam-wood, medicine, and a razor blade accounted for another 9d., while a tiny shirt for her grandson, to whom she was passionately devoted, cost 3s. (see No. 11 in App. C). I should stress that her plight was exceptional, for even when

---

[1] In Nsaw, Kom, and many other Tikar groups, the wives of a *Fon* are not permitted to enter the market-place, although they sometimes buy and sell on the outskirts, or send their children to make tiny purchases and sales. Among the Widekum people there is no such taboo.

polygynists tend to be neglectful of elderly wives who have no dependants, they usually fulfil their obligations more adequately when there are children in the household.

Vindjan, Kengeran, and Yuliy were all typical of women who only engaged in petty trade occasionally, and who were fortunate in possessing a surplus of plantains. There was another woman, Audelia-Kilar, who was much better off butwho liked to buy extra relishes and ornaments. She disposed of bananas, pears, oranges, and sugar cane at a profit of 7s. 5½d. during five months. (See No. 10 in App. C.) She was young and lived in a compound where some of the women traded regularly in cooked foodstuffs. When I asked her why she did not do likewise, she replied that she preferred to sell bananas and pineapples, since no additional work was entailed. Moreover she had a friend in the Hausa Market with whom she could leave her produce, and this left her free to go on to her farm and stay there for the rest of the day.

Women, who have no farm produce to sell but who require something for the house, must save up the odd coppers received at festivals or from friends, buy vegetables, cook and retail them in the market. For example, Yeduda occasionally bought beans which she boiled, ground, mixed with salt, pepper and oil, shaped into balls, and sold at 2 to 5 a penny according to size. Even when she had only 4d. worth to sell she might be left with a few on her hands at the end of the day; or, sometimes before she had even reached the market, her husband would appear in the kitchen, snatch a few and, as she pointed out more in resignation than in anger, " eat her profit "! (See No. 8 in App. C.) When I asked her why she did not trade in gari or cassava gruel, she said that the first was very hard work (lim ye tavine feyi), and that the latter was a trouble (mɛ dzə ngɛɛ) since it entailed the cutting up of banana leaves to serve as wrappers for the paste. In any case, she had tried several times but she kept cracking pots and grew tired. The easiest thing to prepare was beans, though the profit was small (kifa ke fɛtɛr ki dzə kuni. Abei sɛɛ yi dzə ſiſar). It was indeed! On a total outlay of one shilling she made only 2d. Margaret Labam, whose husband was the tailor Nicholas of Ka, also traded occasionally and she too obtained only 3d. profit on 18d. worth of beans. But she was more enterprising than Yeduda, and went to the trouble of cooking cassava gruel,— buying 3d. to 7d. worth of raw vegetable at a time for the purpose. Over the period of five months she earned 2s. 6d. on an outlay of 4s. Clara, who lived in the same compound and was the wife of Alphonse Fannso, also sought to augment the family income in the same way, and she made 1s. 1½d. on 2s. 0½d. worth of cassava. Just before I left Kimbaw, she had persuaded her husband to buy her two bags of maize for beer-brewing, and hoped to be as successful as her friend, Elizabeth-Kila who dealt regularly in that commodity. (See Nos. 7 and 9 in App. C.)

And this brings us to the category of women who sell something every week in the market. In the minority, but a minority which is increasing in number, are those Christians whose husbands already earn more than the average householder in Nsaw, but who desire a better standard of living for themselves and their dependants: better food, clothes, house comforts and also schooling. Elizabeth-Kila was the wife of Francis Lole, whose activities we have already discussed above (see No. 3 in App. C). Throughout practically the whole year she brewed beer, which she sold to one djaŋgi which met at Mbonyaar every Sunday, and to another at Banka. Her profits varied; but she made from 2s. to 4s. on 4s. worth of maize. She was exceptionally fortunate in possessing " a corner " in beer, and so could afford to risk a bigger outlay than most women. During the year she spent, all told, £7-2-4½ on bags of grain which she sold as beer for £10-3-2,—a profit of £3-0-9½, less the cost of fire-wood used in the brewing (about 5s.). She was a member of the Mbonyaar

134

djaŋgi, contributing a shilling a week; and she gave the rest of her earnings to her husband, saying that later he would buy her a dress. He was the best judge in such matters! Another regular trader, to whom reference has already been made, was Christina Lambiif, wife of Benedict Somo. She was younger and more " modern " than Elizabeth, having had a little schooling and having travelled more extensively in Bamenda. She made gari and starch regularly, though she frequently complained of the hard work entailed and the inroads on her leisure.[1] She would buy anything from 1*s*. 5*d*. to 7*s*. worth of raw cassava on market-day, process it and dispose of it during the following week. Her earnings were her own, but were mostly spent on luxury foods for the household, and ornaments for herself and her children. During a full year she bought cassava at £3–18–8; she sold part of it as gari at £5–15–10½, and part of it as starch at £1–1–8: a total profit of £2–18–10½, and one which was proportionately higher than that obtained by Elizabeth from beer. Christina sometimes sold bean-balls as a sideline, a transaction on which she gained 1*s*. 5*d*. profit from an outlay of 3*s*. 10*d*. Finally, she had learnt to knit: she purchased some wool for 12*s*., which she made into a sweater and a cap and sold for 24*s*. 6*d*. (See No. 2 in App. C.)[2]

Most women, when questioned, were in agreement that gari was the best foodstuff in which to deal in the market, since the demand for it was fairly constant, the profits good, and any remainder would keep for a week, whereas other things such as bean-balls, cassava gruel, or maize porridge would not. Against these advantages, however, was the fact that its preparation entailed time, labour, patience, and a resignation to having ones legs scorched while frying it over a fire in the house. For this reason and also because, unlike Christina, she had no assistance on the farm Melalia of Mbonyaar preferred to sell maize porridge and relish. In the early morning she would go to the market to buy 1*s*. to 2*s*. worth of maize flour, return with it to the house, cook it into rounds weighing ¾ lb. to 1½ lbs., which she sold at her stall for ½*d*. or 1*d*. each. Usually she concocted a relish of cassava leaves, salt, and oil, contriving where she could get away with it to give more liquid than substance! But she was a good cook, was popular, and had her regular customers, who were mainly boys or men who came from other villages. Her takings for the day ranged from 4*d*. to 1*s*. 6*d*., or an average of 8*d*. Unfortunately, during the year under review, the new *Fɔn* closed the market to women from the 18th July to the end of September, that is, for 10 market days. In May 1947, and again in February 1948, Melalia made two long journeys,—one to Fumban and the other to Bamenda Station. On Christmas Day 1947 she was celebrating in her compound, and on five other occasions she was either ill or did not buy flour because it was too dear. All told, then, she engaged in trade for only 28 weeks out of a possible 46. During that period she spent £1–9–4½ on flour, and sold porridge for £2–4–0,—a profit of 14*s*. 7½*d*., or nearly 50% on her outlay. Sometimes she cooked bean-balls or cassava gruel, but her earnings from these were only 5*s*. 5*d*., bringing her total income from trade to £1–0–0½. In normal years it would be in the vicinity of 30*s*. (see No. 12 in App. C).

---

[1] Gari-making is a tedious process. The cassava must be peeled, cut into slices, washed, grated, tied tightly in a bag, and left for four days. It is then re-grated and fried in oil in a shallow pot (*kikaŋ*), an activity which demands constant attention. To make cassava gruel, a woman peels the cassava, washes and pounds it, and leaves it to soak in water for 3 to 5 days. The water is drained off, and the pulp is left for a while in the sun on banana leaves. It is tied up in small bundles in the leaves, boiled, and sold at about 9 ozs. a halfpenny.

[2] In Appendix C, the earnings of some of the women have been listed in the budgets of their husbands, cf. those of Elizabeth-Kila, Christina-Lambiif, Clara-Yaya, Yeduda, Audelia-Kilar and Biy-Menggu. Those of Sui, Melalia, Vindjan, Yadiy, Yuliy, and Kengeran have been tabulated separately.

Melalia had to feed two sons, both of whom were at school, and to provide herself with tools and utensils. One son, however, earned sufficient from trade and from the sale of straw hats for his fees and his clothes, and to pay her contribution to the *djaŋgi* when she lacked the means. The other son was assisted by a man of the compound, who was related to Melalia and who also, together with her brother, made her gifts of salt and oil from time to time. From other kin and friends she received 14s. during the year; and when she went to Fumban somebody gave her a dress and headtie. She was thus able to maintain her small household as far as its basic needs were concerned. She was an energetic farmer and had plots at Kimbaw, near the Mission at Shisong, and also at Meluf where her mother lived. Unfortunately the house, in which she was living and which had been lent to her by Francis, was in bad repair and was sagging dangerously. She had requested permission from the *fai* to pull it down and have another built, but he had refused on the grounds that he needed the space for his own dependants. Melalia was not a member of his lineage, and had therefore no moral claim to a residential site. When I asked her why she did not return to Meluf she objected that she had her plantain groves in Kimbàw, trade contacts and, finally, her intimate friends. She therefore continued her efforts to find a vacant house nearby.

Melalia had no husband and was a member of that group of women, comprised of unmarried mothers, widows, divorcées and prostitutes, which is almost entirely dependent on its own efforts to secure food and other necessaries although relatives do what they can to help. Lacking, as a rule, assistance on the farm, they have no surplus to sell except for plantains, and they therefore buy small quantities of raw vegetables, greens or flour, to cook and retail in the market. Prostitutes often supplement their main source of income by brewing beer, and enjoy a relatively high standard of living. Several had houses lined with pith-matting and furnished with tables, chairs, and a variety of ornaments. As might be expected they had good clothes, and, almost inevitably, umbrellas of European manufacture![1] Quite a number of Christian widows and divorcées sell porridge, flour or gruel; but elderly pagan women in this group, either because they are more conservative or more probably because they are fearful of taking risks with their slender savings, cultivate plantains, are sedulous in picking up windfalls from kola trees, and from time to time buy small quantities of groundnuts or vegetables for retailing. Sui was a typical example and was noted for her skill in squeezing a profit from diminutive resources. Some of the men said she could drive as hard a bargain as any male trader; and often women, who could not afford the time to stay in the market or were inexperienced in haggling, would entrust their foodstuffs to Sui and give her a small commission. She was regarded as somewhat mean and was sometimes ridiculed by the other members of the compound. Like most Nsaw women, she had a caustic tongue for the parsimonious host at a marriage or festival; unlike the others, she made no bones about openly balancing accounts! She would point out that she had contributed two shillings' worth of flour to a marriage and had received in return " a little meat (*ʃinyam*), a little wine (*ʃilu*), and a little threepence (*ʃitoro*)! Her habit of prefixing most words with the diminutive, *ʃi*, was mimicked by the others: " I sold a little groundnut and ate a little profit; I picked a little plantain and sold it for a little halfpenny ". When others were paying at least one

---

[1] Many of the prostitutes were attractive and appeared to me to have intelligence above the ordinary. One of them was known as the *wiisaki sardjin*, the Sergeant of the Prostitutes, because she was prosperous and had a fine house. Although she was not shunned by most of the women, she had few intimate friends among them because their respective husbands (whatever their own morals) were fearful that their wives would be tempted " to go walka " if they associated with her. Some of the prostitutes were Christians who had refused to marry the men chosen for them by their respective lineage heads.

shilling for a raffia storebin, Sui was aggrieved because she could not obtain one for sixpence! Nevertheless, her reluctance to part with her little half-pennies was understandable, since she had to keep herself in all necessaries. Unfortunately the records of her transactions from September to March were not typical, and gave no index of her skill as a trader. She had injured her foot and was confined to the house for weeks. But, from accounts which I received from her in my first tour, I estimated she made about 3d a week and earned about 10s. to 12s. a year (see No. 16 in App. C). Incidentally, it should be noted that when she had her accident the women in the compound were the first to come to her assistance by visiting her, cooking food, and contributing firewood, and one of them harvested her finger millet for her.

CHANGES IN TRADE

I collected only 12 budgets among the women for the simple reason that the others in the compounds, which I visited regularly, never traded at all. But, despite the smallness of my sample, it serves to illustrate the diversity and extent of market transactions and their relation to the status and conditions of life of the women concerned. It is perhaps unnecessary to point out that the generalizations made in this chapter are based not merely on the slender budgetary material discussed, but also on observations and information gained from many individuals during the course of my tour; and in particular from data obtained in the market, which I attended weekly and where I recorded variations in the price of the principal commodities sold.

Several points require emphasis. In the first place, there are still many women in Nsaw who, although they visit the market to sight-see or perhaps to buy something with money given them by their husbands, rarely have anything to sell themselves. At most they may make one or two shillings a year from a few plantains, sticks of sugar cane, beans, cassava, or potatoes. Secondly, the earnings of those who trade regularly represent but a small fraction of that gained by their husbands in their occupations. This is understandable, in so far as women must still spend most of their time on the farm. But there are changes occurring in the pattern of trade which affect the standard of living in the household, and which may well modify not only the existing division of labour between the sexes but also the status of women in marriage. There are indications that the number of women who trade regularly is steadily increasing. This includes not only the category of husbandless women, in particular Christian widows and divorcées, but also the wives of Christian men who are already earning considerable incomes by traditional Nsaw standards. Christina Lambiif is a case in point, Elizabeth-Kila another; while both Margaret and Clara were attempting to sell a little weekly for two or three months before I left Kimbaw.

It is true that even among the Christian men, and more especially the middle-aged, who themselves follow a traditional craft or profession, the old prejudice against women trafficking frequently in the market-place and handling relatively large sums of money dies hard. Somo, on more than one occasion, expressed the fear that his wife was spending too much time on the making of gari to obtain little luxuries, instead of concentrating most of her energies on farming. Nevertheless, attitudes are changing under the pressure of economic necessity. A cash contribution from a wife to the running expenses of the household is welcome, providing she does not neglect her duties and is not secretive about her earnings. Moreover, entertainment may be carried out on a more lavish scale and gifts made more often to kin, affines and friends. To a hospitable people like the Nsaw generosity in such matters is both a pleasure and a source of prestige: the man or woman whose hand is always open to bestow freely is admired; while he, who keeps his closed for his own benefit, is disliked and despised.[1] Finally, Nsaw women—young and old, Christian and pagan,—have their due share of vanity. Once they have acquired the habit of wearing clothes they want more than a modest covering. They delight in fine materials, brightly coloured headties, beads, ear-rings, and even henna for their nails.[2] But the average family purse does not stretch to cover all these items, and a woman must find the additional means herself.

Besides this change in the category of women who engage in petty trade, there is also one in the type of goods which they handle. This is not very noticeable in Nsaw and the markets to the north, where it is still almost inconceivable that a woman should be entrusted by her husband with the sale of kolas, salt, kerosene, bags of grain, cloth and livestock; still less that she should traffic in these things on her own account. But in Bali, and especially in Nyen (Meta), I was struck by the number of women who did so. There were even a few who had learnt to use sewing machines and who made a small turnover from tailoring.[3] As yet, the numbers concerned are very small but any increase will pose problems in the future, for it will not only bring the women into competition with the men, but may well tempt them to spend less and less time on their farms. Of course, in so far as the best profits can only be obtained by buying cloth and other European articles in the larger centres of distribution near the ports, the men have the advantage because there are difficulties in married women, who have children, travelling so far afield.

While noting the desire of the women to engage in petty trade on a larger scale, or more frequently, than formerly in order to obtain extra articles for the household or pin-money for themselves, one should also emphasize the general expansion of trade which has occurred over the last decade and, with that, the enlargement of old markets and the establishment of new ones. This has created a greater demand for the products (food and beer) sold by the women, and has provided centres where they may easily dispose of any small surplus.[4] The factors which have contributed to this extension of trade are multiple, and reference has already been made to some of them. The spread of Christianity and, with that, a demand for a higher standard of living is one; the development of new and more lucrative occupations is another. These have led to the emergence of a class of individuals, some literate, who have a bigger income and can afford more money not only for European articles, but also for additional quantities of food, oil, salt, and meat.

Again, better roads and greater mobility of population have increased attendance at markets.[5] The transients, particularly among the men and boys, require a meal during the day, while those who live in the village are tempted to have a snack from the array of cooked foods which quicken and tantalize the appetite. Strangers resident in the community or near it are also another

---

[1] The Nsaw phrase—*kiwo ke tsteer*—means literally outstretched or flat hand, and is used for the generous person. *Kiwo ke kfaftin,* or the clenched hand, is applied to the stingy and the grasping. These attitudes to generosity are not of course confined to Nsaw, but are very typical of Bamenda as a whole. I was told in Esimbi that a woman who grows much food and calls in the passers-by for a meal acquires a good reputation, and "name i go up!"

[2] Some of the young women spend a considerable amount of time trying out different styles of coiffure. Those from Southern Nigeria are particularly popular.

[3] In the forest areas women occasionally sell oil and palm kernels for their menfolk, more especially when it is a matter of buying extra food, pots, or pans for the household.

[4] As mentioned previously, some foodstuffs grow better in some villages than in others, and the existence of a market provides, therefore, a means for their distribution over a wider area. It is noteworthy that new markets have developed, often with the encouragement of the Mission, in centres where there is a large Christian population or a school, e.g. Njinikom.

[5] Even the stay-at-home Ngie have recognized the importance of roads in stimulating trade, and have advanced this as an argument in their request for the construction of a motor road through their territory.

potential source of custom: the Hausa women, who do no farming and who must buy food; the Fulani women who come in from the hill tops to sell their butter and milk, and to purchase flour, grain, and other vegetables; men and women from other parts of the Province and the French Cameroons who may have insufficient land to produce all that they require.

Finally, the wide range of articles displayed in the larger markets attracts many sight-seers, not least the women and young girls who may come from several miles away dressed in their finery, frocks and headties if they are Christians, or liberally besmeared with camwood if they are pagans. They wander arm-in-arm about the stalls content to watch, chat and if possible pick up the odd halfpenny. I remember one who had crowned her graceful nudity with a strawboater made by her schoolboy-brother; two others, who had strung halfpennies together to make anklets, which they jingled provocatively to induce some admiring males to make a further contribution to their collection! More and more, the women are coming to regard market-day as a day of leisure and pleasure. Money, news, and views circulate in the market-place; new friends are acquired, and assignations made.

WOMEN'S CONTRIBUTION TO HOUSEHOLD PRODUCTION

Throughout this book we have described in some detail the activities of women on the farm, in the home and, lastly, in the market-place. But, while distinctions have been drawn between the work of men and women and their respective rôles in the economic system, we have been mainly concerned with the differential roles of members of the family and have taken this group as the unit of study. For certain purposes it is profitable to discuss the nature of the particular contribution made by women to the functioning of the economy as a whole; but, in analyzing processes of change and in considering measures for the improvement of the standard of living and especially that of the women, a primary question is not merely how and when the women work, but for whom they work. We have seen that in the economic sphere the focal point of a woman's interests is the family, and it is in relation to this group that her chief responsibilities may be defined,—as a daughter in her youth; and as a wife, and normally as wife and mother, after marriage.

I have set out in Table XII below some figures on the relation of cash to gross income and the proportional value of the wife's contribution to household production. Before we look at them in detail one or two points require comment. In the case of Budget No. 12, Melalia Shikiy was the head of the household as she had no husband. Her budget was recorded for a year but during my absence from Kimbaw no details of her son's contribution were noted. Through petty trade in groundnuts and soap, as well as the sale of straw hats, he was able to pay for his school fees and books (about 15s. a year) and provide clothes, the sewing being done for him as a gift by a tailor in the compound. On occasion he contributed a shilling or sixpence on behalf of his mother to the djaŋgi to which she belonged. A relative paid the school fees and bought some clothing for the other son. The contribution made by the sons, or on their behalf by relatives, has been included in the figures placed in brackets in the Table.

In Budget No. 6 I have also set out in brackets a second lot of figures which are inclusive of the wife's production in a normal year. As mentioned previously she usually farmed 1.2 acres but during 1947 she was deprived of land and cultivated only 0.46 acre. Finally, in Budget No. 11, I have worked out an approximate estimate of the income of Fai-o-Djem on the basis of some data I collected on the number of kola trees, raffia stands, livestock and maize harvest owned by him. I have regarded him as the male head of Kengeran's household and in calculating his gross income have included only the value

139

of the crops produced by Kengeran, and not that produced by his other wives, and from which, in any case, Kengeran derived no benefit. Kengeran's household was almost entirely self-supporting in that the only source of income from the husband was about 7s. 2d. worth of salt, oil and meat during the year. If, then, Kengeran is considered the head of the household, she and her daughters produce 98% of the gross income. Her earnings from trade and cash gifts constitute 6% of the total income. I have excluded from the Table the budgets of four women (Nos. 13–16) since their earnings from petty trade were diminutive, ranging from 9d. to a maximum of 5s. 6d.

The budgets of Mawo, Kibu, Vincent and Tanye may be regarded as typical of those of Nsaw men who engage in one of the traditional occupations on a traditional scale. Cash income ranges from a little over £3 to just over £6, and gross income from £12 odd to nearly £22. The last figure is large since the man's wife farmed, with the help of her daughter and her mother, 4.0 acres, as compared with 1.3 acres by the respective wives of the other men. In my opinion, the average gross income for the adult married man in Nsaw varies between £11 and £15.[1] The proportional value of cash to gross income ranges between 22% and 33% for those men who earn 92s. in cash or less; but it is worth noting that in the case of the female household head, Melalia, it falls to 17%. In the remaining budgets listed in the Table (see next page) the proportion of cash income to gross income increases to over 50%, and is as much as 62% and 63% in the case of Francis and Benedict. All these men followed occupations which were either of comparatively recent introduction in Nsaw or else, under present conditions, offered a more lucrative source of income than formerly, as for instance smithing and the repair of dane-guns and sale of gunpowder. Fai-o-Djem alone, in this higher income bracket, depended on traditional sources of income; but, by virtue of his office as lineage head, he had control of the products of kola trees and stands of raffia.

In the sixth column of the Table I have estimated the value of the contribution of the wife (in some cases wife and daughters) to the household and included the crops produced and the kindling collected by her. The last item has been assessed at about 25s. a year. Even so, the woman's contribution does not rise above 48% in the lowest income group, and I am confident that this represents a maximum, not only in Nsaw but also in the other upland areas of Bamenda,—namely Nsungli, Oku, and parts of Kom and Fungom. In the higher income group her contribution falls to 40% or less, but of course such an estimate does not reveal its material importance for the maintenance of the family. Under present conditions the woman is still the economic mainstay of the household. The percentages which have been tabulated reveal certain tendencies of change: the increasing value of the husband's production; they do not indicate those bearing on the economic role of women. For example, Elizabeth-Kila produced only 33% of the gross income of the household, while Elizabeth-Bika in a household of a similar size produced 48%. On the surface the difference might be attributed merely to the larger cash income of the husband of the former. But, in actual fact, Elizabeth-Kila in addition to harvesting crops at an estimated value of £7–5–0 also earned £3 odd from the brewing of beer.

[1] Mr. W. Bridges, in his Report for 1934 (op. cit., paras. 195–231), estimated that the average gross income of a Nsaw adult male was £5–9–10; but he suggested that many commodities at that time were fetching only half their normal value and that the income would have about double the value in normal times. In estimating the gross income for Nsaw as a whole, he included only half the value (£14,823) of the farm produce instead of the full value (£29,647). If the latter figure is used, the average gross income per adult able-bodied male is £7–13–8; and the proportional value of farm products to the gross income is 57%. On the basis of my own data I would suggest a lower figure, since Mr. Bridges did not include the value of kindling collected by the women, nor the earnings of men in occupations subsidary to their main one.

TABLE XII

Household-head	Budget No.	Gross Income £ s. d.	Cash Income £ s. d.	% of Cash Income to gross income	% of wife's production to gross income	Remarks
Melalia Shikiy	12	8 15 9½ (11 10 0)	1 14 0½ (2 0 0)	19 (17)	(76)	Melalia has no husband. Figures in brackets are inclusive of son's contribution.
Mawo	5	13 16 7½	3 5 10½	24	39	
Kibu	4	12 16 10	4 6 1	33	48	
Vincent Kwangha	1	20 19 0½	4 12 10	22	48	Cash income exclusive of savings.
Tanye	6	12 15 8½ (15 15 8)	6 2 3½	48 (39)	24 (38)	Wife deprived of some land. Figures in brackets represent a typical year.
Alphonse Fannso	9	19 4 5½	10 15 2½	56	43	
Nicholas Ngee	7	20 6 0	11 6 2½	55	39	
Thomas Kintarir	8	22 5 1½	11 15 8½	52	44	
(Fai-o-Djem) .. .. Kengeran	(11) 11	(44 2 0) 18 2 5½	(16 16 0) 1 5 9	(38) 6	(40) 98	(An estimate based on budget of woman Kengeran, No. 11.)
Maurice Nyingka	10	28 17 11½	17 3 7½	59	39	
Francis Lole	3	36 5 11½	22 18 10	63	33	
Benedict Somo	2	79 9 9	49 11 3	62	44	Cash income is exclusive of loans and savings.

The question arises how far the figures for Nsaw provide a norm for the rest of the Province. It is possible that in the Ndop Plain, Bali and Nyen (Meta) the woman's production may be a little higher than 48% in those households where the man engages in a traditional occupation. Firewood has not the scarcity value that it possesses on the uplands; it is doubtful whether the same variety of crops is grown; but in the last two villages and at Bamessi in Ndop the women manufacture pots during the dry season. Some are for household use, some for gifts for friends and kin, some for sale in the local markets, and others again are headloaded by men to more distant villages. The processes involved in manufacture have been described in Ch. V, p. 86 ; output per week depends on size, and value varies between 8d. and 2s. On an average, production of pottery at local market prices per married woman may be assessed at a figure ranging from 15s. to 30s. per annum.

In the forest areas of Esimbi, Ngwo, Befang and Beba the value of the woman's contribution to the household may be somewhat lower than in Nsaw since firewood is not a problem and there is little in the way of female handicrafts, apart from the pottery produced mainly for home consumption.

In Mbembe and Mfumte in the north of the Province, the figure would, I think, be much lower—perhaps a little under 40%. Firstly, apart from cereals there is only a small range of subsidiary crops, as compared with Nsaw; secondly, firewood is accessible to the compounds and available in large quantities so that the kindling collected by a woman has less value than in Nsaw; thirdly, the men give considerable assistance with the cultivation of guinea-corn and bulrush millet; and, finally, the men in addition to expressing oil, tapping wine, and tending livestock also catch quantities of game and fish during the dry season. It is, I think, only in the forest area of Ngie (and possibly Mogamaw, which I did not visit) that the woman's contribution to the household within the traditional economic system exceeds in terms of cash value that made by the man. Only a little maize is grown in villages such as Teze and the value of the crops produced by a woman would be about 55s. per annum, the husband being responsible for the cultivation of plantains worth about 20s. per year. A woman collects firewood (10s.); expresses about 30 gallons of palm oil (2s. a gallon) during the course of a year; and disposes of about 10s. worth of palm kernels. But, as her husband tends the palm trees, taps some wine, and cuts down the heads of fruit, his contribution might be assessed at 10s. He aslo takes care of livestock (fowls and goats or pigs) which probably bring him in about 40s., catches some game and fish (10s.), and manufactures palm mats for the repair of the roofs of the huts in the compound. The gross income of a small household is in the vicinity of £10–10–0 a year, to which the woman contributes about £6–5–0 (or 60%) and the men about £4–0–0 (or 40%). It is clear that the average man of Ngie does less work than a man of the upland villages, even when allowance is made for differences in economy and climate. Whether the average Ngie woman is overworked is another matter. My impression was that the Ngie women, on the whole, were not only more energetic than the men, indeed necessarily so, but were also more vivacious, high-spirited and independent in their bearing. In Chapter V I have already discussed my reasons for believing that it is the Nsaw women who have the harder row to hoe.

So far we have been mainly concerned with the position of women in the traditional economy, with describing a standard of living and a way of life which is still typical for the vast majority living in Bamenda, more especially in the areas to the north and west, as well as in the villages at some distance from the main motor roads which encircle the south and east of the Province. The number of men who, apart from Government employees and a sprinkling of Mission teachers, pay income tax is still negligible. The more prosperous pagan trader who earns from £10 to £15 in cash a year may be able to provide his wife (or wives) with a little more salt, oil and meat, but he is still, as a rule, reluctant to clothe her in wrap and headtie. It is mainly in the Christian households, where the husband earns about the same income or even less, that there are changes in the standard of living of the wife. But as yet only·about 14% of the total population of Bamenda is converted to Christianity and this figure includes children so that the proportion of adults is probably 10% or less.[1] As might be expected, adherents to Christianity are not evenly distributed over Bamenda but tend to be concentrated, at present, in the southern part of the Province, near the main motor roads and where there are mission stations with Europeans in charge. As early as 1913 the Roman Catholic Mission began its work in Nsaw and, by 1937, it was estimated that it had 21% of the population as converts and catechumens.[2] In the same year it was estimated that some 4½% of the population were adherents of the Basel Mission. I myself made a census of Kimbaw village in 1945 and calculated that about 25% of its population were members of either the Roman Catholic or the Basel Mission. In the outlying villages the percentage would be considerably less.

Most of the differences in the standard of living in the Christian household, as compared with the pagan household, have already been discussed in the preceding chapters and require but a brief recapitulation here. Where the cash income of the husband is from £4 to £5 there is little margin for saving and little for the purchase of extra quantities of salt, oil, and other necessaries. But the woman and her daughters are clothed and, as a rule, the man is more willing than the pagan husband to take advantage of the services of maternity clinic and hospital for his wife and children. Nowadays he is also likely to construct a larger and more substantial house of mudbrick as sleeping quarters, though the traditional style of hut still serves as kitchen. With an increase in income the household enjoys a better standard of nutrition; the wife usually receives better clothes; and, finally, small quantities of firewood may be purchased to provide additional warmth at night and to lighten one of the wife's burdens—the daily collection of kindling.[3]

Perhaps the most radical change, however, is the increasing tendency for the women to participate regularly in trade and to handle larger sums of cash than formerly. And in this category I would include not only married women among the Christians but also among the pagans, particularly when they have a large number of children. This applies also to the inherited wives of polygynists, but as a group they are a small one and probably decreasing in numbers.[4] As yet, the expansion of trade carried on by the women has not altered the pattern of traditional division of labour between the sexes: that is, the women

---

[1] *Vide, Annual Report . : . . . on the Administration of the Cameroons*, Col. No. 244, 1949, pp. 100–101. The number of converts claimed by the R.C.M. for 1948 was 19,120 (or 6.3% of the population); the number by the Basel Mission was 17,823 (or 5.9%); and by the Baptist Mission 5,476 (or 1.8%).

[2] *Vide*, H. N. Harcourt, *op. cit.* paras. 117–123.

[3] It is perhaps unnecessary to point out that the clothes worn by the women on the uplands are sometimes decorative, confer prestige, but are rarely a source of warmth and bodily comfort. Warm woollen sweaters and jackets are sometimes knitted by young girls and women but are almost invariably bought and worn by the men, though it is the women who, in their work on the farms, are far more often exposed to an inclement climate, especially during the season of heavy rains and mists.

[4] In the census carried out in 1934 (*vide*, W. Bridges, *op. cit.*, para. 146) it was estimated that some 64.9% of the total male population of Nsaw were married. Of these 74.5% had only one wife; 18.1% had two wives; 6.3% had 3 to 5 wives; and 0.8% had over 5 but under 11. It is highly probable that the number of polygynists is less now, if, as may be assumed, the number of Christians has increased.

continue to do most of the farming even when they are married to men in the higher income bracket—to teachers, clerks, messengers, and other government employees. In other words, the trend is towards increased production by the women rather than a diminution. And this brings us to a point made in an earlier chapter, where an analysis of some 30 diaries showed that, on an average, a Nsaw woman devoted only about 53.1% of the days of the year to farm work, enjoyed some 30.8% in leisure, and lost about 16.1% through personal illness or the care of sick relatives (see p. 79). Even when a lower standard of health and diet is given full weight she is not, I think, overworked; while the large proportion of days when she does not go to the farm do, and will, permit her to engage in other activities such as trade and the processing or manufacture of goods for trade, not to mention sewing, knitting, and attendance (perhaps somewhat spasmodic) at maternity clinics, domestic science centres, and mass literacy classes.

Chapter X

CONCLUSIONS

s o far we have confined our generalizations to the role of women in the economy of Bamenda. There remain, however, a number of issues which are relevant for a comparative survey of the position of women in society. One is the degree to which the importance of their work is overtly recognized by the community and embodied in its value system, more especially in the fields of ritual, kinship and political organization. There is also the problem whether economic indispensability is, in fact, associated with economic independence, and whether the women individually or corporately resort to economic sanctions for the preservation of their rights, the ensuring of good treatment, and the redressing of wrongs. Again, it is necessary to examine the nature of the control exercised by women over forms or property, more particularly the products of their labour and any income which may accrue therefrom. And lastly there is the relation between efficient performance of agricultural role and the assessment of reputation by male and female members of the community, as well as the extent to which differential skill is made the basis of a prestige system among the women and given institutionalized expression in membership and authoritative status in societies, work teams, age-sets and so forth. These questions have been framed in the light of conditions in Bamenda but, with some reformulation, they are relevant for an analysis of the economic and other social concomitants of the division of labour in other societies. They are not exhaustive, but they enable us to survey a wide range of institutions from an economic base-line. They do not start from the assumption that the responsibility shouldered by women for the maintenance of subsistence is invariably an index of low status. Rather the problem is phrased in more positive terms: granted economic indispensability, how far is this reflected in the value system, and how far is it associated with economic and other social advantages.

As the rights of women to the products of their labour have already been discussed in an earlier chapter they require but brief recapitulation here. If a woman is a widow or if she has been divorced and has taken up residence in the parental compound or with other relatives or friends, she has full control over all that she produces and any profits from trade. On the other hand, if she deserts her husband she forfeits any claim to harvest standing crops on his land or land of his lineage, but she is left in possession of those elsewhere. It is only in Aghem that a husband may continue to claim food for subsistence until marriage payments have been refunded.

A woman living with her husband is mistress of the *ménage* and has the privilege and responsibility of utilizing and distributing those foodstuffs which she herself has cultivated or received from others in the form of gifts. Her primary duty is to her husband and children, just as he is under an obligation to provide certain necessaries for the home. But she is free to make informal gifts to kin and friends, to contribute to ceremonies, to barter, to reward others for assistance, and to become a member of a woman's society in which it is customary to brew beer and give feasts when food supplies permit.

It is when we examine rights to cash obtained from the sale of foodstuffs or manufactured articles, such as pots and baskets, that we find she is expected to inform her husband of the extent of her earnings or any purchases which she may have made with them. This is a convention and one largely ignored in practice where only a few pence are involved. The question of rights to money becomes crucial when larger sums are at stake, as may happen nowadays with the expansion of markets and the opportunities afforded to women to trade on a larger scale than formerly. It is this situation which the Bamenda men have in mind when they insist on the husband's rights to cash earnings. The attitudes are complex and needless to say they vary from individual to individual. Implicitly they reveal the large measure of economic independence within reach of the women under the traditional system, and they throw light on the institution of marriage as a balanced relationship of reciprocal rights and duties. In contrast with other parts of Nigeria, more especially the south-east and among the Nupe, trade in Bamenda was largely a male occupation. Women provided food from the farms, men the necessaries requiring a cash outlay. Husband and wife made complementary contributions to the maintenance of the household. The reluctance of the men to countenance the entry of the women into commerce springs in part from conservatism and distrust of the competence of the women to handle large sums of money wisely. But there is also a genuine fear that it may disturb the mutual dependence of husband and wife, and so undermine the stability of marriage and threaten the welfare of children. There is a fear that women will become money-makers rather than home-makers, and that they will skimp their duties and devote their efforts to accumulating savings for the purchase of clothes and other European or costly goods. That there is some foundation for male apprehensiveness on this score should not be overlooked. On the other hand, it cannot be denied that some men see in the dependence of women on their husbands for articles requiring a cash outlay a means of male control, of maintaining dominance in the household, and of setting a limit to economic freedom. There is, in short, a realization that the women are already in a position to support themselves as far as food is concerned, and that they require only a little money to secure the other necessaries and so attain complete economic independence.

I have stressed attitudes still prevailing among the great majority of men in Bamenda, nevertheless it is clear from discussions earlier in this book that not only are more women engaged in trade, but that some of them do so with the consent and approbation of their husbands, especially when the latter are Christians earning an income above the average. It is my impression that male prejudices will gradually weaken and that, furthermore, the additional economic contribution made by the women is likely to affect their status in the home as well as encouraging them to play a more active part in community affairs. In the market-place where men and women mix to some extent on equal terms and have opportunity for discussion of news and views the dichotomy between the sexes, which characterizes so many economic and other social activities, is broken down. In respect to this question of participation of women in trade some of the data from other areas of West Africa are of interest. Among the Ibo of Owerri Province women are responsible for the cultivation of some of the crops and, with a portion of these, are under an obligation to feed the household for a part of the year. But, in the event of a quarrel with her husband, an Ozuitem woman cuts off food supplies.[1] According to research

[1] J. Harris, " The Position of Women in a Nigerian Society ", *Trans. N.Y. Ac. Sces.*, Series ii, Vol. 2, No. 5, 1940, p. 4. In theory the Ozuitem woman has no absolute rights to property, but in the event of divorce she takes a number of things with her, including a few head of sheep. In only a few cases does a woman leave with no property (p. 6). The distinction between the nominal rights of the husband and the *de facto* rights of a wife may also be drawn in other West African societies. *Vide*, K.L. Little, " The Changing Position of Women in the Sierra Leone Protectorate ", *Africa*, vol. xviii, 1948, pp. 7–8; and also Meyer Fortes, *The Web of Kinship*, O.U.P., 1949, pp. 102–104.

in other villages women retain profits from trade and enjoy considerable freedom. Some dispose of small farm surpluses or sell processed foods; many purchase yams, cassava, palm kernels, pots, mats, or even European goods such as cloth, salt, tobacco, soap, matches and so on and retail them in the various markets. Others derive an income from dressmaking, and there are even a few licensed pawnbrokers. In short, many Ibo women combine money-making with home-making. Marriage is, among other things, a business partnership, the husband having an appreciation of his wife's powers and the expectation that she will contribute to the family exchequer. On her side, her own sentiment of self-respect demands that she does so.[1]

In drawing attention to the considerable measure of economic independence enjoyed by the Ibo women it is also worth noting that, in addition to their councils, courts and clubs, they may on occasion resort to corporate economic sanctions against the men to secure redressal of wrongs. Dr. Harris, in the article already cited,[2] gives several examples. In one case the men of a clan were angry because their wives were openly having relations with lovers. They met and passed a resolution that every woman should renounce her lover and present a goat to her husband in token of repentance. At first the older women were excluded from the penalty but they ridiculed the men and so were included! The women held meetings and a little later went to a neighbouring group, leaving all but suckling children behind them. The men had to care for crying children, carry water, bring in firewood, and do the women's work. They endured this for a day and a half, then went to the women and begged them to return. They gave them a goat and apologized formally and informally. The women returned! On another occasion the women repeatedly asked the men to arrange for the men of an age-grade to clean farm paths for them and repair a bridge. The men neglected to do so and the women thereupon refused to cook food for their husbands until the order was carried out.[3]

In Bamenda I did not witness such organized economic sanctions by the women. Either the Bamenda men are better behaved than the Ibo or, as seems more likely, the women have not yet realized the effectiveness of such joint action. The women told me that if men interfered with the women's societies penalties would be inflicted; and, in general conversation, they were aware of the inconvenience created by the departure of an aggrieved wife from the house. More than one deserted husband complained bitterly to me of the troubles attendant on a wife's absence: the bother of cooking, of fetching firewood, and bringing in water, not to mention arrears in weeding and its possible effects on the size of the harvest. In Ngie it was pointed out by the men that one of the reasons for a husband consulting his wife about his intention to pledge or sell farm land was the fear that if he did so without her approval she would go away.

It is, however, important to draw a clear distinction between on the one hand the economic consequences of a wife's desertion and their influence in inducing a husband to make his peace and, on the other hand, a deliberate resort to an economic sanction by the wife herself. The last is particularly difficult to document. In the event of a quarrel her dominant motive is likely to be a desire to remove herself from the scene and to seek the protection and

[1] Sylvia Leith-Ross, *African Women*, Faber and Faber, 1939, Ch. XIX.

[2] J. Harris, *op. cit.* pp. 6–7. The women sometimes employ the sanctions of ridicule or the invoking of a curse of the female ancestors on the men who have wronged them.

[3] Among the Tallensi of the Gold Coast if a husband annoys his wife she can make a point of being too busy to attend to some want of his or too tired to cook the evening meal. This, the men say frankly, is one of the strongest arguments in favour of keeping on good terms with one's wife. *Vide*, M. Fortes, *op. cit.*, p. 105.

sympathy of her kin. It is only later that she may reflect with satisfaction on the dislocation of the *ménage* which her absence has caused.[1]

So far we have been examining the nature of women's rights to special forms of property—cash, food and other movable goods—and the way in which these affect marital relationships. There is, however, one further point which is relevant for a consideration of those factors that set limits to the independence which women, as farmers, may achieve, and that is availability of land. In so far as formal titles to land are vested in the men, irrespective of whether descent and inheritance are matrilineal or patrilineal, the men would appear to be in a strategic position to deny the women access to farm plots. I do not propose to summarize here the principles of land tenure already discussed at some length in an earlier chapter, but as we have stressed again and again ownership is inseparable from moral responsibilities. The system of land tenure forms part of a wider network of rights and obligations within the kinship and political organization. It is only in two or three tribes in the south-west of the Province that land is ever sold or pledged. Elsewhere arable tracts are held in trust, administered and allocated by lineage heads (more rarely by ward or village heads) for the benefit of their dependants. Women are not eligible for the headship of kin or political groups, but they nevertheless enjoy rights of usufruct as members of such groups, and in most tribes their needs are not subordinated to those of male dependants.[2] It should also be emphasized that once a woman has been allocated a plot by a kinsman she has security of tenure, providing she cultivates it and fulfils obligations. If, for exceptional reasons, she is deprived of the plot she has a moral claim to another in exchange. Finally, we have seen that she decides when and what to plant and the period of grass fallow. In Nsaw and most of the other Tikar groups she is free to lend plots to kin or friends, and she may even have a voice in selecting her successor once she has reached a decision to abandon permanently a tract of farm land.

With the exception of Ngie (and even there the women have certain safeguards), the indigeneous system of land tenure in Bamenda does not, then, place the women at an economic disadvantage. If a woman quarrels with one landholder she has, as a rule, no difficulty in securing plots from someone else. But, if pressure on land were to increase to the extent of creating shortage or if rental and sale of land were introduced then, in my opinion, the tradition that women cannot ' own ' land might well constitute a threat to their economic welfare. In such circumstances there would be a strong case for making provision for women to acquire plots on equal terms with the men.

We have indicated what appears to be a series of correlations between economic role, rights to property, and economic independence in Bamenda. There remains the important question of attitudes to the women's work and the extent to which skilled performance confers prestige or provides the means for the attainment of prestige.

In Nsaw and probably elsewhere in the Province the industrious and expert farmer receives the encomiums of members of her own sex and also of the men. On certain occasions, such as the preparation of *rizga* plots or the clearing of

---

[1] When the *Fɔn* of Nsaw closed the market to women there was a considerable amount of criticism and grumbling. But when I asked why they did not down tools and refuse to do any work they said that they feared the *Fɔn*, and that in any case they doubted whether all women would co-operate. But their main argument was that the children might suffer. They did not mention the men!

[2] In Ozuitem in Owerri Province Ibo women likewise have no rights to ' own ' land but, as is the case among the Nsaw, they have considerable freedom in practice. If a woman requires extra plots she is usually able to buy or receive them in pledge through a male proxy—husband, kinsman or lover. *Vide*, J. Harris, *op. cit.*, p. 5.

land for a bride, an adolescent girl who is generally acknowledged to be a keen worker is selected to make the first cut with her hoe and lead the others. Apart, however, from such informal ranking in relation to skill, prestige is enhanced and indeed validated when associated with a generous dispersal of gifts to kin and friends and lavish contributions to ceremonies. Finally, women's societies in addition to their other functions constitute a prestige system among the women for the measurement of status. A woman with a surplus of grain and root vegetables may provide a feast to become a member or, if she has already achieved this, she may do so to strengthen her claims to leadership and eligibility for the rank of " Mother ". As such she attains to a position of respect and authority among the women, settling their minor disputes and organizing the activities of the society.

Unfortunately my visit to the Widekum group, where women's societies do not occur, was too brief for me to investigate the existence of any informal ranking in relation to economic productivity, although I was told in Esimbi that ' important women ' were those who distributed plenty of food. But it is highly probable that contributions to ceremonies connected with childbirth, puberty, and possibly marriage and even death provide opportunities for display and enhancement of reputation. The problem of the way in which women utilize those resources over which they exercise some control for " maximizing " their own personal satisfactions, and the nature of those satisfactions, has to some extent been neglected in anthropological studies both in Africa, Oceania, and other parts of the world. There is obviously scope for a comparative survey along such lines in those communities where women play an important part in food gathering, horticulture, fishing, trade or the manufacture of certain handicrafts. Where voluntary associations are not a feature of the social life any surplus of goods may be absorbed in the fulfilment of kinship obligations, ceremonial distribution, and in exchanges associated with prestige rather than utilitarian values. In some cases a woman may act as an independent agent, as the co-partner of some male kinsman or spouse, as a member of kinship or local group, or as economic entrepreneur of projects in which the men have a major concern.[1] In stressing the need to examine those social mechanisms by which women secure some recognition of their own importance it should not be assumed, however, that they are always intent on pressing their economic advantage or capitalizing their assets for enhancement of their reputation. A sense of responsibility for the welfare of husband, children and other kin, the sharing of common interests, and the merging of personal ambitions with those of others all enter as factors in the complex relationships between men and women.

Our discussion of the prestige linked with skill in agriculture has already revealed something of the attitude of the women towards their work. The question may be raised how far the men regard agricultural activities as indispensable but menial, or as important and worthy of respect. The traditional division of labour between the sexes is still a matter about which the people of Bamenda tend to be conservative for it is associated with certain fundamental values in connection with marriage and parenthood. But the reluctance of the men to wield a hoe in most parts of Bamenda should not automatically be interpreted as contempt for the occupation *when* it is engaged in by women. A parallel might be sought in our own community where, until recently, home management and the care and rearing of children were considered a sphere in which women might most effectively exercise their abilities. These were

---

[1] It lies outside the compass of this book to make a comparative survey of the role of women in transactions involving the distribution of goods, and the prestige deriving therefrom, but it is worthwhile drawing attention to the material already collected in connection with such different economies as those in N.W. Australia, New Guinea and Malaya.

F

women's duties and commanded respect. But when they were carried out by a member of the opposite sex they were regarded with some contempt and were apt to provoke ridicule among spectators and embarrassment in the performer. Much the same situation obtains in Bamenda. Agriculture is basic to existence but it is most appropriately carried out by the women. Men have their own appropriate tasks which are complementary to those of the women.

We have already pointed out that in Nsaw and elsewhere in the Province the women take a pride in their own skill and competence as farmers, in their responsibility for the feeding and care of the household, and in their knowledge that they are, in some respects, the backbone of the country. It is especially significant for a discussion of the position of women that they not only play an indispensable role in the economy and exercise considerable freedom in the management of land and the crops which they produce, but that the importance of that role is explicitly recognized by the rest of the community. In the *Introduction* to this book two statements were quoted which threw some light on the attitudes of the women toward their duties, and also on the attitudes of the men towards the women. They will bear repetition. Significantly they were answers to inquiries which I made about the custom of having a " cry-die " (*di kpu*) of four days for a woman and only three for a man; of planting four cocoyams at the birth of a girl and only three for that of a boy. They were as follows :

1. Yadiy, Djo'kem, Yuliy, Kengeran and other women:—

> " A woman is an important thing. A man is a worthless thing indeed, because a woman gives birth to the people of the country. What work can a man do ? A woman bears a child, then takes a hoe, goes to the field, and is working there; she feeds the child (with the work) there. A man only buys palm oil. Men only build houses." (*Wiiy dzə kifa ke ku'un ki. Lumɛn dzə kifa ke kisaŋ ki feyi, bifɛ wiiy dzøø wiri e wɔŋ Adzə lumɛn yi lim ɣa ? Wiiy dzøø wan, wu nɛna li kisoo, du fɛ kwa, lim lim ʃo; yir wan ʃo. Lumɛn yun mɛŋgvər tʃatʃa. Vilum bari laf tʃatʃa.*)

2. Kengeran:—

> " Important things are women. Men are little. The things of women are important. What are the things of men ? Men are indeed worthless. Women are indeed God. Men are nothing. Have you not seen ?" (*Vinyu ve ku'un vi dzə viki. Vilum dzə ʃiʃar. Vifa ve viki vi dzə vi ku'un. Vifa ve vilum dzə ka ? Vilum dzə kisaŋ feyi. Viki adzə nyooiy feyi. Vilum adzə kisaŋ. B' ai yone yɛn a ?*)

3. Yuliy, when asked why there were four days' mourning for a woman, replied:—

> " Because a woman is an important thing, a thing of God, a thing of the earth. All people emerge from her." (*Bifə wiiy dzə kifa ke ku'un ki, kifa ke nyooiy, kifa ke nsaiy. Wiri adzəm fər fɛ win.*)

4. The *Fɔn* and Council, when asked the same question, answered:—

> " A woman is a person who gives birth to a person. Women are very important people. Women are like God because they give birth to the people." (*Wiiy dzə wir o dzøø wir. Viki dzə wiri ku'uni feyi. Viki dzə m'aa nyooiy bif'aa dzøø wiri.*)

There were other statements to the same effect, but those quoted serve to indicate the overt emphasis on the importance of women as childbearers and food producers and the way in which certain ritual practices are rationalized in terms of that importance.

This brings us to the problem of the relation between agricultural role and fertility rites. In general, the annual ceremonies performed for the welfare of the whole community, be it tribe or village, are in the hands of the men or under their direction. Specific rituals are, however, carried out by the women but they tend to be regarded as subsidiary and limited to the well-being of a smaller group. In Ngie some of the senior women offer sacrifices at the altar of the farm god at planting and harvest. In those Tikar groups, where women's societies still function, the " Mothers" invoke the blessing of God and the ancestors and brew magical herbs to endow the women with health and ensure an abundance of crops. It will be recalled that a *Yelaa* of Nsaw in describing the purpose of *Tʃɔŋ* said it was to give strength to the women to work their farms well, and that the ritual objects were " things of the earth."

The association between the fertility of women as childbearers, their agricultural role and the fertility of the land would seem to be implicit in much of the ritual. In Nsaw the *Yesum* or " Mother of the Farm " assists the lineage head in the sacrifices to God after the harvest of finger millet. Again, one of the Queen Mothers bears the special title of *Yewɔŋ*, Mother of the Country, and acts as High Priestess. In the annual sacrifices performed at Kovifem she carries the " Basket of the Country " and the " Hoe of the Country " and assists the *Fɔn*, the High Priest, and Ndzendzef in the rites believed to ensure the fertility of the land and women, and the well-being of all Nsaw. The Queen Mothers in the other Tikar groups of Bamenda also have their ritual functions; while in Ngie women are believed to have the power to render a farm plot barren, and they may employ such power as a ritual sanction if they feel that they are being deprived by their menfolk of land required for the subsistence of their households. Throughout Bamenda, as far as I am aware, the blessing of both male *and* female ancestors is invoked on the crops; and, in the Tikar communities, sacrifices are made to the deceased mother and mother's mother of lineage heads. When I asked one *Tiɛnda* (Compound Head) in Bamessi why he did so he retorted: " If the mother is not, where will the *Tiɛnda* be ? The mother is important." In so far as lineage heads are the main and indeed official intermediaries between the living and the dead they perform most of the sacrifices; but on occasion a woman working on her farm will ask for the blessing of her female ancestors on the crops, and pour a libation of water or of palm wine if available on the ground.

In much that has been said it is clear that the functions of a woman as ᴜᴜother and giver of food tend to be so identified or so fused in African thought that it is difficult to separate them in analysis. A mother will always provide her children with food, and a woman who feeds a non-relative may be addressed as ' mother '. And this brings me to another point: family relationships, especially those of parenthood and siblingship, serve as a paradigm for a wide range of relatic oships in the fields of kinship, economics and political organization. Both mother and father occupy positions associated with respect, authority and privilege on the one hand, and with an active sense of responsibility towards dependants on the other. The identification of authority and responsibility with parenthood occurs again and again in Nsaw values. I have already cited the titles for High Priest and Priestess,—Father of the Country and Mother of the Country. A lineage head is addressed as " Father of the Compound ", and his most senior wife as " Mother of the Compound." On the farms of the nobility there are always a " Father of the Farm " and a " Mother of the Farm "; while in such an exclusively male society as *ŋwirɔŋ* the ruling clique is referred to as " Mother of *ŋwirɔŋ* ". Such a metaphorical use of the kinship term of ' mother ' reveals the respect in which women as childbearers and food-producers are held, and it furthermore indicates that such statuses are acknowledged to be associated with the exercise of authority and responsibility in certain defined spheres such as the home, the farm and women's organizations. The question might well be raised here whether it is also conceded that the women are competent to assume the responsibilities of political offices ?

Most Bamenda men and, I think, most Bamenda women would answer this query with a somewhat emphatic denial, pointing out that a woman's work is on the farm and that she has not time to rule the country. As one *fai* explained to me: " Ruling is for the man. If you catch trouble, will you send for a man or a woman? A woman has farm work. You call her the mother of the farm." In addition to this argument others were frequently cited, more especially the alleged temperamental differences between the sexes. It is believed in Nsaw that women are more sensitive, quicktempered and capricious than men, and hence less capable of adopting the dispassionate attitude necessary for the judgment of cases. Women change their minds! One of the Queen Mothers was discussing the question with me in connection with a decision which had been made by the *Fɔn* and Council and in which the women were interested. With, I think, her tongue in her cheek she concluded her remarks by saying: " Women are like children. A child gives a grasshopper to another child. In a short time it cries to have it back again. Women are not sure what they want!" On another occasion Kengeran, whom I have already quoted frequently, said that although women were important and like God this did not mean that they were fit to rule the country. " If you give the country to women, some women will spoil the country. They have not intelligence like men. Anger burns women greatly and they have grieving hearts indeed. If you say something, a man hears it with indifference. If you say it to a woman then she is deeply pained. All troubles come to women. If food is prepared, the husband will eat and then curse you." Kengeran had, in the course of this statement, reverted to her own particular grievances but her opinion was to a great extent that of the men. After the *Fɔn* and Council had explained to me why they regarded women as important, I asked them why women did not play a more prominent part in the government of the country. I was told that " Women can't rule because they can't control themselves. They vex easily, they lose their heads." When I pointed out that I had seen men lose their tempers, the *Fɔn* replied that if a man lost his temper quickly he was reproved and chided for " behaving like a woman " (*wu fh/wi kilɔŋ t/ɛrt/ɛr, wu nɛna adzə mo wiiy*). It is worth noting here that later in this discussion with the Council, when some of the members were bemoaning the fact that women are beginning to claim a voice in the selection of husbands for their daughters, I asked—" why not, if women are like God as you have said ? " The men retorted: Yes a woman is like God, and like God she cannot speak. She must sit silently. It is good that she should only accept!

The subject of the alleged temperamental differences between men and women is an interesting one but it must be postponed for another publication. It was, however, my impression that the women did, on the whole, feel their responsibilities more keenly than the men and were subject to more stress, strain and ill-health. More than one man made the comment that women like to " foregather to indulge in self pity (*awinni tati fɛ ki/am wun*)," and it was true that the word ' trouble ' was often on a woman's lips and that I heard more about the " troubles of women " than those of the men. One *fai*, when asked to give his idea of a good wife, defined her as one " who cooks porridge quickly. Then her lineage head (her husband) tells her to go and sweep the courtyard and she sweeps it. If she is ordered to go to a place, she goes quickly. A bad wife complains about sickness always; she is constantly saying ' my body is aching '. This is a bad thing!" But it is on the woman that the chief responsibility for providing food for the husband and, more especially, the children falls. Even if the season is a good one her own health may be weakened by coughs and colds and then work becomes a burden and weeds a menace to the harvest. This anxiety about her own health is largely a reflex of her concern for her children, and it was expressed again and again by the women when fever or ' flu ' prevented them going to the farms for several consecutive days. Vindjan, when asked to give her idea of a good life, replied: "First of all strength so that I do not sicken. If I am strong then I am working well to get food. The children are well and have food. That indeed is a good life!" Another woman made a similar answer: "First of all strength because if I am not well I cannot work at all." On another occasion she said: "A good life for me is to sleep well, to have food. If I have food, I grind flour with it and feed the child with it. When the child has eaten the belly is tight. Then I am well." Most women included a husband among the good things of life providing he bought salt and oil and did not nag or curse! As one Christian woman explained to me: "It is a good life to have a husband. Then he will buy palm oil for me; he will buy salt. When hunger clutches me, then he buys maize. He buys clothes for me. That is all. If I don't have these things then my heart aches!" Some Vekovi Village women were unanimous on the point that "if a man gave a little oil, gave salt, then indeed all women would regard him as a good man. If he does these things what reason have they to hate him?" For his part a man desires much the same things. He dreads the prospect of living with a wife who bickers, who waxes sarcastic when asked to bring water and acidly retorts: "Do you only want cold water? Are you sure you don't want me to boil it for you?" If he has "health, children who are well, food and a wife with a good heart, then indeed there is happiness."

Here in these statements we have nothing so elaborate as a blueprint for the future or the envisaging of a remote Utopia. Again and again the women and the men stress a few, simple, basic needs. The problems involved in the satisfaction of such needs are common to most undeveloped parts of the world; they are problems with which the Administration has been and is still grappling. They include an extension of medical services, a reduction of infant mortality, conservation of land, improved agricultural techniques, and a better diet. Marital relationships alone are not amenable to legislation either in Africa or anywhere else! But it would be wrong to assume from the statements which I have quoted that there is an atmosphere of perpetual marital discord in the compounds of Bamenda. On the contrary I heard few arguments and disputes between husbands and wives in Kimbaw, where I had ample opportunity to observe relationships among my Nsaw neighbours. Moreover, within the last 25 years, the legal disabilities to which the women were subject in some tribes under the traditional system have been removed by the Administration, and there is now much greater freedom of choice in marriage for the women, facility in obtaining divorce, and the possibility of securing custodianship of children where the Court decides that it is in the interests of their welfare. Polygyny is limited to a very small section of the population and it still is associated with certain economic advantages for the women under the traditional system. There is little to be gained from an attempt to make it illegal. Such a step would not of itself raise the status of women, and it would create misunderstanding, resentment and even hardship for the women in some cases, as well as dislocating kinship and political organization. The changes will come from within the society and are already taking place. Quite apart from the influence of Christianity, the average man is unable to afford a plurality of wives once they begin to demand clothes, better housing, European "luxuries" and a higher standard of living in general.

The main theme of this book has been the role of women in the economy: an analysis of the conditions under which they work, their methods, their attitudes to their occupation, their rights to property and the bearing of these factors on their formal status and standing in kinship groups and the community in general. As yet the vast majority of women do not envisage a future in which they will not farm. Even in the households of salaried teachers and government employees women continue to cultivate plots, though they may also engage in trade to earn pin-money and ease the husband's burden in meeting day to day expenses. How far agricultural production can be raised above subsistence level without the participation of the men and the introduction of mixed farming is a problem for the technical experts. Clearly every effort should be made, and indeed is being made, to encourage the men to adopt farming as their main occupation. Already some individuals are planting cash crops such as coffee and castor, as well as potatoes and cabbages for export to the coast. But in the meantime any plans for economic development must take into account the fact that the women will most probably continue to assume the major responsibility for subsistence crops, and that the immediate problem is to improve their techniques and possibly organization of labour.

In Bamenda steps have been taken in this direction. Both girls and boys now spend some time in the gardens attached to schools, but since the percentage of girls attending school is still very small this policy leaves untouched the needs of the vast majority of women, old and young. To meet their requirements Women's Centres have now been established in many of the Native Authority Areas. Demonstration plots have been laid out by the Agriculture Department, and in addition courses are given in cooking, needlework, hygiene and infant welfare. In enlisting the interest of the women efforts might well be made to secure the co-operation of the heads of the women's societies, Queen Mothers and, finally, the senior wives of compound heads. Something might also be done to carry on propaganda through such women for the organization of working teams to assist women who are attempting to farm when in a stage of advanced pregnancy or are convalescing from a bout of illness. Finally there should, I think, be some attempt to provide careers for African women in the Department of Agriculture. I am of course aware that there is a pressing demand for teachers, midwives and nurses; but the problem of improving the standard of living is so closely bound up with the improvement of agriculture that there is a strong case for training some Bamenda women either as agricultural instructors in the Department of Education or as Assistants in the Department of Agriculture.

APPENDIX A

BAMENDA ITINERARY: APRIL 1945—APRIL 1948

A. FIRST TOUR

4th April to 1st November, 1945	Kimbaw (Nsaw N.A. area)
2nd November to 11th November, 1945	Nsungli area
12th November to 13th November, 1945	Misaje N.A. area
14th November to 30th November, 1945	Mbembe N.A. area
1st December to 7th December, 1945	Mfumte N.A. area
8th December to 17th December, 1945	Mbem N.A. area
18th December to 19th December, 1945	Nsungli area
20th December, 1945	Kimbaw (Nsaw N.A. area)
21st December to 26th December, 1945	Bamenda Station
27th December to 28th March, 1946	Kimbaw, Vekovi, Nkar, Djottin-Vitum (Nsaw N.A.)
29th March to 31st March, 1946	Laa-Oku (Ndop N.A. area)
1st April to 13th April, 1946	Laikom (Kom N.A. area)
14th April to 16th April, 1946	Bamenda Station
17th April to 24th April, 1946	Bafut (Bafut N.A. area)
24th April to 26th April, 1946	Bamunka (Ndop N.A. area)
27th April to 1st July, 1946	Kimbaw (Nsaw N.A. area)

B. SECOND TOUR

29th January to 22nd February, 1947	Kimbaw (Nsaw N.A. area)
23rd February to 7th March, 1947	Bamessi, Bamungo and Bamunka (Ndop N.A. area)
7th March to 9th March, 1947	Bamunka to Bamenda Station
11th March to 25th March, 1947	Nyen (Meta N.A. area)
26th March to 22nd April, 1947	Teze (Ngie N.A. area)
23rd April to 1st May, 1947	Asarabiri (Ngwo N.A. area)
1st May to 6th May, 1947	Trek from Ngwo via Beba-Befang to Esimbi
6th May to 15th May, 1947	Benakamø (Esimbi N.A. area)
16th May to 23rd May, 1947	Befang (Befang N.A. area)
23rd May to 28th June, 1947	Trek through Fungom N.A. area with protracted visits to Fungom and Zhoaw villages
29th June to 26th July, 1947	Aghem (Wum N.A. area)
27th July to 6th August, 1947	Fundong and Njinikom (Kom N.A. area)
6th August to 7th September, 1947	Bamenda Station
8th September to 14th September, 1947	Bali (Bali N.A. area)
16th September, 1947 to 16th March, 1948	Kimbaw (Nsaw N.A. area)
17th March to 25th March, 1948	Bambui and Bamenda Station (in Bafut N.A. area)
25th March to 31st March, 1948	Kimbaw (Nsaw N.A. area)
1st April to 8th April, 1948	Bamenda Station

Number of men engaged in various occupations in Nsaw, 1934. Information included in the Table below is based on Schedule F : Form 3, in the *Banso-Re-Assessment Report*, by Mr. W. M. Bridges. The total number of adult taxable males in Nsaw in 1934 was 6728.

Occupation	Number of men	Percentage of adult taxable males
kola trade	2,339	34.7
tobacco	1,357	20.7
palm wine	1,082	16.0
bags	860	12.7
general trade	849	12.6
honey	700	10.4
hunting	611	9.0
baskets	579	8.6
firewood	446	6.4
miscellaneous	400	5.9
cotton and caps	236	3.5
mats	176	2.6
stools	109	1.6
grass cutting	100	1.4
traps	72	1.0
thatching	69	1.0
doctors	66	0.9
butchers	64	less than 0.9
chief's messengers	62	
laaf and hunting nets	53	
hoe handles	37	
catechists	35	
ironworkers (tinkers)	34	
tailors	30	
carpenters	29	
matchet-scabbards	25	
umbrellas	19	
drums	15	
bricklaying	4	
sawyers	4	
carving	2	∨

APPENDIX C

BUDGET 1

(February 1947 to February 1948)

A.—EXPENDITURE AND INCOME IN CASH

EXPENDITURE	£	s.	d.	£	s.	d.
Food—						
meat		6	7			
groundnuts			8			
oil		16	1			
salt		5	10			
pepper			2			
				1	9	4
Stimulants—						
beer			4			
tobacco		1	1			
				1	5	
House & Farm Replacements—						
stool			6			
hoe for wife		4	0			
3 pots			6			
farm bag			7			
calabash			½			
cowpea-seed			3			
soap (a)			2½			
kerosene (b)			3			
					6	4
Clothes—						
cloth for husband (c)	1	0	0			
sweater for husband (c)		17	0			
khaki trousers for husband (c)		14	0			
				2	11	0
Church dues—						
contribution cards for husb. & wife (d)		4	6			
collection (e)		1	9			
					6	3
School fees—						
two sons (f)		10	0			
books, etc.		2	3			
					12	3
Miscellaneous—						
tax		5	0			
hospital card			2			
wine for son's *djaŋgi* (g)			9			
					5	11
Gifts—						
to wife's kin (h)			6			
to husband's kin (i)			2½			
to friends (j)		1	7½			
					2	4
Expenditure for one year:				**£5**	**14**	**10**

INCOME	£	s.	d.	£	s.	d.
Cash in hand at January 1947 (s)				1	5	0
Sales of—						
plantains		4	1½			
pears		4	9			
coffee-plants (k)		2	6			
cocoyams, etc. (l)			2½			
					11	7
eggs (m)		1	1			
fowls (n)		6	0			
					7	1
10 bundles of firewood		5	0			
24 bundles of thatching grass		7	0			
palmwine (o)		2	0			
					14	0
Profits from—						
kolas retailed (p)	1	15	3			
other kolas (q)		4	2			
commissions (r)			9			
				2	0	2
Gifts—						
from wife's kin (h)		1	0			
from husb.'s kin (i)		15	0			
from friends (j)		4	0			
				1	0	0
Income for one year:				£5	17	10

157

BUDGET 1

(February 1947 to February 1948)

B.—ESTIMATED VALUE OF OUTLAY (INCLUDING CONSUMPTION) AND INCOME IN KIND FOR ONE YEAR

OUTLAY ETC.. IN KIND	£ s. d.	£ s. d.	INCOME IN KIND	£ s. d.	£ s. d.
Gifts—			*Gifts—*		
to wife's kin (*t*) ..	6 2½		from wife's kin (*t*) ..	6 5	
to other affines (*u*) ..	3 2		from husb.'s kin (*v*)..	12 0	
to husb.'s kin (*v*) ..	1 4		from friends (*w*) ..	1 2½	
to friends (*w*) ..	10½				19 7½
		11 7	soap from Hausa (*x*) ..	2 0	
			kindling collected:		
soap and kindling used by household ..		1 17 0	by wife and daughter	1 10 0	
			by husband (*y*) ..	5 0	
					1 17 0
payment of " contribution cards " by work, and grass to mission		5 2	work at mission (*z*) and gifts of thatching grass		5 2
fowls and kittens ..		10 0	fowls	6 0	
			kittens (*aa*)	4 0	
					10 0
wine, poles, grass, bricks, kept for household		1 6 11	Perquisites from tending raffia (*bb*):		
			wine	3 5	
			raffia poles	7	
					4 0
value of crops kept for house		11 7 6	thatching grass kept for roof repairs	2 11	
			2,000 sun-dried mud bricks (*cc*)	1 0 0	
					1 2 11
			Market value at harvest of crops (exclusive of sales) produced by wife and daughter:		
			1,529 lbs. grain (*dd*)	2 12 3	
			7,125 lbs. roots (*ee*) ..	4 17 7	
			66 lbs. beans & cucurbits ..	4 5	
			greens & other relishes (*ff*)	11 1½	
					8 5 4½
			produced by husband:		
			1,115 lbs. plantains (*gg*)	2 15 10½	
			pears	1 3	
			coffee-seedlings ..	5 0	
					3 2 1½
		£15 18 2			£16 6 2½

Estimated expenditure, etc., for one year—		£ s. d.	£ s. d.	Estimated income for one year—		£ s. d.	£ s. d.
in cash	..	.. 5 14 10		in cash	..	.. 5 17 10	
in kind	..	..15 18 2		in kind	..	..16 6 2½	
			£21 13 0				£22 4 0½

Cash income is 22% of gross income.
Value of wife's contribution is 48% of gross income.

BUDGET 1

Vincent Kwangha and Elizabeth-Bika

Vincent Kwangha of Djem Compound is in his fifties. He and his wife, Elizabeth-Bika, have been Roman Catholics for 25 years. His eldest son, Maurice, is a teacher in a mission school some 15 miles away. Maurice occasionally assists his parents with gifts of oil and meat, as well as paying part of the school fees for his two younger brothers, and making presents in cash to his father. The boys who attend school are Felix and Laurence. They return home for weekends, and food is sent to them at the school during the week. Felix trades in his holidays and pays for half his own fees and clothes, besides making an occasional gift to his brothers and sisters. During my absence from Kimbaw, from 28th February to 17th September, he kept the budgets of his father and of Kengeran, a wife of the *Fai*. Elizabeth-Bika never trades and, if she requires anything, asks her husband for the money. With the help of her mother, Diy (who lives in a compound about one mile away), and of her adolescent daughter, Regina, she cultivates 4 acres. Regina only sold very small quantities of farm produce, but during the period she frequently disposed of pears and plantains for her father, and sometimes groundnuts for her brother, Felix. In addition to the members of the household already mentioned there are a young daughter (who occasionally stays with her married sister and acts as nursemaid), a small boy aged about 4 years, and a grand daughter of about the same age.

Vincent Kwangha trades locally in kolas, but ekes out his income by the sale of thatching-grass, firewood, fowls and coffee-seedlings. The budget set out above was recorded over a full year.

NOTES

(*a*) Vincent, like many people in Kimbaw, rarely bought soap of European manufacture. His wife gave ashes regularly to a Hausa woman, who gave her in return about ½*d*. worth of Hausa soap (*sabulu*) every 8 days.

(*b*) Vincent's son, Maurice, had a bush lamp and occasionally Vincent bought very small quantities of kerosene for it.

(*c*) At Christmas in 1946 Vincent had bought his wife a dress and headtie from his accumulated savings, and so did not buy her anything else during the year under review. In February he bought cloth for himself, and in July he bought a sweater for 17*s*. and khaki trousers for 14*s*., but actually could only afford 10*s*. from his own savings. His son, Maurice, had cooked *djaŋgi* (for which Vincent himself provided 9*d*. worth of wine) and he said his father could use some of the money to pay the balance on the clothes. Vincent, being a scrupulous man, refrained from wearing them until he had repaid his debt to his son. This was not until about the 17th January 1948. The budget tabulated above is only until the 10th February, but I have records until the 27th. It is worth noting that, on the 27th February 1948, Vincent sold his two sweaters (one for 17*s*. and the other for 16*s*.). He bought a Munshi cloth for 8*s*. for his daughter, Regina, and used the balance or rather 22*s*. as a part-payment on a secondhand military overcoat. During the year some of his other children received gifts from their mother's mother and brothers (see notes (*t*) and (*v*) below).

(*d*) For six months of the year under review Vincent paid in cash for the contribution cards o himself and Elizabeth. In the other six months both he and Elizabeth worked at the Mission in order to meet their commitment.

(*e*) In addition to the odd copper and halfpenny Vincent also gave 6*d*. to the collection on the occasion of the Bishop's visit to Shisong.

(*f*) The sum of 10*s*. represents only half the annual fees for the two sons—that is 4*s*. and 6*s*. The balance was met by one of the sons from his own trade earnings, also from a gift by Maurice. Felix paid for his own clothes.

(*g*) Vincent did not belong to a *djaŋgi*, but he contributed 9*d*. worth of palm wine when his son, Maurice, cooked *djaŋgi*. Note also that Maurice lent him money.

(*h*) Most of the gifts made to Elizabeth's kin were in kind (see footnote (*t*) below). As Vincent had a large household his affines did not press him unduly for marriage gifts. During the year under review, he spent 3d. on salt and 3d. on meat for his mother-in-law. In January 1948, Elizabeth had to go to the hospital in Bamenda Station and her ' father ', Fai-o-Dzem, gave her one shilling.

(i) On one occasion Vincent bought 2d. worth of salt to give to his ' brother ' at Ketiwum; and on another he spent ½d. on tobacco for a deceased brother's wife who lived in the compound. Vincent, during the year, received 15s. in cash from his son, Maurice.

(j) Vincent looked after some raffia and kola trees for Fai-o-Bafhshwin, who was a high-ranking duiy in Kimbaw. They were close friends and Vincent frequently bought salt for the Fai. During the year he spent 1s. 4½d. on that item and also 3d. for tobacco. From his friends Vincent received 1s. in cash when his child was ill; and another 3s. when his wife was ill.

(k) Vincent had a number of young coffee-plants and he sometimes sold seedlings to men in Kimbaw, notably to two men living in Mbonyaar.

(l) Regina sold 2d. worth of cocoyams from her own plot, and ½d. worth of egg-plant.

(m) Vincent normally did not sell eggs, but during my stay in Kimbaw he disposed of some to me

(n) In addition to sales of his own fowls, Vincent sold two fowls belonging to his two sons and one fowl belonging to his little grand-daughter. He was scrupulous in pointing out that the money belonged to them although for the time being he was looking after it.

(o) On an average Vincent obtained 1½ to 2 quarts of palm wine a week as a perquisite for looking after raffia belonging to the fai. He used most of it for hospitality and for gifts to his affines, but he sold a little. The figure in the budget is an estimate.

(p) During the year under review Vincent bought a few hundred kola nuts every market-day usually disposing of them immediately or the following week. The total value of nuts bought during the year was £17.18.6. He disposed of them in small quantities at a total value of £19.13.9. He made, on an average, 1s. a week profit. His largest profit for one week during the period was only 3s.

(q) Vincent was given 400 kolas by the owner of a tree, which he tended. He sold them for 4s. He also collected 2d. worth of windfalls.

(r) On one occasion Vincent was given 9d. commission for selling some kolas for the fai.

(s) In February 1947, Vincent had 25s. cash in hand from the previous year. With this he was able to balance his budget.

(t) Vincent was able to meet most of his commitments to his affines from his own stores. I cite them in detail here since they throw some light on the nature and magnitude of marriage gifts. Elizabeth was a wir duiy, i.e. a relative of the Fɔn. When the Fɔn died in April 1947, she gave 1½d. worth of porridge and greens to the vikinto and also 2d. worth of palm wine, which Vincent had handed over to her for the purpose. Vincent also gave her mother 4d. worth of wine to pass on to the vikinto. He himself sent firewood worth 3d.

When Fai-o-Dzem, head of Elizabeth's patrilineage, " cooked " mfu (i.e. provided over 50 calabashes of wine for the mfu society) Vincent sent one of his own fowls (1s. 6d.) and 1s. worth of palm wine. Elizabeth herself gave 1s. worth of flour and 4d. worth of eggplant to her mother for the feast. When her sister died at Memfu village, Elizabeth went to the " cry-die " and took about 1s. worth of flour, ground from her own maize. It should be noted that these are all ceremonial occasions when both affines and kin are expected to make some contributions. But, during the year under review, Vincent gave his mother-in-law palm wine at a recorded value of 6d. The amount was most probably greater as Felix did not always make a note of such gifts during the period when he kept his father's budget for me. Vincent's mother-in-law often gave assistance to, and received help from, Elizabeth on the farms and was a frequent visitor at the house. She partook of many meals there and if there were any meat she received a portion. It is extremely difficult to arrive at any estimate of the cash value of such food, but it should be borne in mind in considering marriage gifts to affines.

It should be stressed that Vincent and his family also received gifts from Elizabeth's kin. At Christmas 1947, Elizabeth's mother gave Regina a Munshi cloth worth 2s. 6d., and the youngest boy a shirt worth 3s. She also presented 3d. worth of meat to Elizabeth and the children. The recorded value of her gifts for the year totalled 5s. 9d. It is probable that Elizabeth received food from her other kin but again the only entry is one for cocoyams worth 8d. from a sister.

(u) So far I have been discussing relations between Vincent and his wife's kin. But he also had other affinal obligations. His deceased brother had been married to a woman of Ka compound. When a man was appointed to be ʃe of Ka in November 1947, Vincent presented him with three long sticks (viseeʃ) of firewood worth 3s., and also kolas and wine worth 2d. He also accompanied the ʃe on a visit to Memfu village.

160

(*v*) The sum of 1s. 4d. refers to the value of gifts to Vincent's own kin for which there are entries. There were probably others. When Maurice sent palm oil from Memfu to his mother, she reciprocated later with about 9d. worth of maize flour, while Vincent sent about 1½d. worth of kolas. Early in the year Vincent gave Fai-o-Djem a bundle of thatching grass.

From his kin and women in the compound, Vincent and Elizabeth received a number of small gifts of beer, potatoes and bowls of porridge at a total recorded value of 11d. The largest contribution was from Maurice who sent, all told, 3s. worth of oil and 6d. worth of meat to his mother. At Christmas he bought 2 little shirts (worth 3s.) for his youngest brother and his sister's child, as well as small cloth (2s.) for his youngest sister. Felix bought his brother Laurence a pair of shorts for 2s. 6d.

(*w*) Again, the value of gifts in kind to friends is probably an under-estimate but it represents the total of actual entries. Fai-o-Bafhshwin (see footnote (*j*) above) was given 3d. worth of avocado pears, and another friend was given about 3d. worth of kolas. From his friends, Vincent received 2½d. worth of tobacco, salt worth 7d., beer worth 3d., and bananas and porridge worth 2d.

(*x*) See footnote (*a*).

(*y*) The value of kindling collected by a woman each week (i.e. 8 days) is about 6d., since she brings in bundles about six days out of eight. On the basis of 45½ Nsaw weeks this gives a total value of some 23s. to 25s. a year. In the budget under consideration both Elizabeth and her daughter, Regina, brought in firewood, so I have allowed a value of 30s. for the year. Vincent also carried some heavy wood, but he sold the greater part of it.

(*z*) Vincent did not always have cash in hand to pay for his monthly contribution card at the Mission. During the latter part of the year he spent one week at the mission making 300 sun-dried mud bricks at a value of 3s. He also presented the Mission with 2 bundles of thatching grass. Elizabeth worked to pay for her contribution card.

(*aa*) Cats are in great demand in Nsaw as they do something to check the depredations of rats on the grain stores. Kittens sell at anything from 9d. to 2s. in the market. Vincent had 4 and told me that he might sell them later at 1s. each.

(*bb*) On an average Vincent obtained 1½ to 2 quarts of wine a week for his own use in addition to what he gave to the owners of the raffia stands. The annual value of the wine to him would be about 7s. 6d., but he sold about 2s. worth and gave away about 2s. 1d. worth to affines. The balance was dispensed in hospitality to friends and kin visiting the compound. Vincent was permitted to keep the midribs which he had to cut away when preparing to tap wine.

(*cc*) Vincent's houses were set a little apart from the rest of Djem compound. He had a hut for himself and a small storehouse where he kept kolas and clothes. His wife had a kitchen and, early in February 1947, Vincent built a small hut for his son Maurice. He provided 11 bundles of thatching grass for the roof, and wine and meat to the value of 2s. for the members of the compound who assisted with the thatching. Maurice met the other expenses. During the latter part of the rains and the dry season (1947 to 1948) Vincent made nearly 2,000 sun-dried mud bricks with the assistance of his sons and also his daughters, who carried water. He intended building a large hut for himself, leaving the old hut for the use of his son, Felix.

(*dd*) Elizabeth farmed 4 acres with the help of Regina and frequent assistance from her own mother, Diy. Most of the plots (of which there were altogether 15) were located on land belonging to Djem lineage; but she had two at Shisong and two at Kingomen which she had 'begged' from strangers. In September 1947 she harvested 10¼ *vegati* of maize from all her farms. In January 1948 she obtained 6¾ *vegati* of finger millet, and 1½ *vegati* of guinea-corn. It is noteworthy that she had good land and that, during the period when the budget was recorded, Vincent did not spend anything on extra staple foods for the household.

(*ee*) The root crops were used for the household with the exception of 2d. worth of cocoyam which Regina sold.

(*ff*) Regina sold ½d. worth of eggplant, as she wanted to buy a small calabash.

(*gg*) Vincent had exceptionally large groves of plantains and bananas: 390 trees near the compound, 9 at the Ro-Ngang farm, 84 at Ro-Kimbaw, and 3 at Shisong. Total 486. But he said that during a full year less than half of these would bear fruit. Of the remainder some would be beaten down by gales, heavy rains and hail even when propped up with poles; others would be spoilt by insects, and others again would not bear. The value of plantains given here represents an estimate of those kept for household use. I estimated, on the basis of his cash earnings, that he sold about 95 lbs.

BUDGET 2

(February 1947 to February 1948)

A.—EXPENDITURE AND INCOME IN CASH

EXPENDITURE

	£	s.	d.	£	s.	d.
Food—						
hulled maize		9	9			
maize flour (*a*) ..		18	11½			
root vegetables ..		13	11			
cooked foods (*b*) ..		13	4			
plantains		2	10			
beans & cow-peas ..		4	2			
greens, *egusi* & other relishes (*c*) ..		18	8			
groundnuts		14	9			
coconuts		1	0			
honey (*d*)		3	5			
pears & oranges (*e*) ..		1	2½	5	2	0
salt (*f*)		18	6			
oil	2	12	10			
butter			10			
meat	2	16	3½			
fried termites ..			8½			
fish		16	2			
eggs		1	9	7	7	1
Stimulants—						
kolas (*g*)		1	8			
wine & beer ..		9	1½			
cigarettes		1	0		11	9½
House & Farm Replacements—						
calabash ..			1			
10 farm knives ..			11½			
sleeping mat ..		2	9			
5 razor blades ..			6			
enamel basin ..		2	2			
jug & basin ..		8	2			
9 baskets		2	2½		16	10
seed-yams		2	6			
cow-pea seed ..		1	6½			
bean seed		3	9			
coffee-plants ..		8	0		15	9½
firewood & charcoal (*h*)		14	0			
kerosene for lamp ..		13	9½			
matches		1	6			
soap		5	6½	1	14	10
Clothes—						
cloth, shoes & trinkets for wife (*i*) ..	3	1	2			
cloth, shoes etc. for husband (*j*) ..		18	6			
shirts for two sons ..		5	6			
shirt for brother's son (*k*)		15	0	5	0	2
Church dues—						
contribution cards for wife & husband ..		9	0			
collection		1	4½		10	4½
Carried forward:				£21	18	10½

INCOME

	£	s.	d.	£	s.	d.
Cash in hand at February 1947				18	18	9½
Sales of—						
onions	1	17	2			
tomatoes		8	8½			
cabbages		1	0			
peas			4			
beans			3			
potatoes		2	0			
pears			2			
plantains		1	10	2	11	5½
castor seed to U.A.C.					12	0
ground coffee in Kimbaw (*aa*) ..	3	7	2			
cases of coffee berries in Bamenda (*bb*) ..	18	0	0	21	7	2
eggs			10½			
fowl		1	6		2	4½
pork in Kimbaw (*cc*)				10	17	3
Earnings from sewing ..				1	17	9
Profits from retailing—						
kolas (*dd*)		1	8			
soap (*ee*)		5	3			
salt (*ff*)		1	10			
bananas (*gg*) ..			1½		8	10½
Profits from trade by wife—						
gari & starch (*hh*) ..	2	18	10½			
bean-balls (*ii*) ..		1	5			
beer (*jj*)		7	1			
sweater & cap (*kk*) ..		12	6	3	19	10½
Gifts—						
from wife's kin:						
wife's mother (*u*) ..			2½			
wife's sister, Angela (*v*)		13	4			
other kin of wife (*w*)		11	5½	1	5	0
from husband's kin (*x*)					11	7
from friends (*y*) ..				5	17	11
Carried forward:				£68	10	0½

EXPENDITURE	£	s.	d.	£	s.	d.
Brought forward..				21	18	10½
School fees—						
for son & brother's son (*l*)		12	0			
books, etc. . ..		1	10			
					13	10
Purchase of live-stock—						
horse (*m*)	6	0	0			
saddle & bit ..	1	10	0			
2 rabbits [but they died] (*n*)		15	0			
				8	5	0
Expenditure for coffee farm—						
part-time labour ..	1	9	0			
transport of coffee to Bamenda ..		10	0			
cash to storeboy ..		1	0			
				2	0	0
Piggery—						
cement, wood etc. for styes (*o*)	3	4	9			
food bought for pigs (*p*)	5	8	6			
part-time labour ..	1	7	5½			
rock salt for pigs & horse		3	6			
				10	4	2½
Miscellaneous—						
tax for husband & husb.'s brother's son		10	0			
wine & meat for *djaŋgis*	1	0	3			
sums lost (*q*) ..	1	2	0			
repair of sewing machine ..		3	0			
sewing thread ..		9	0			
machine needle ..		1	0			
				3	5	3
Gifts—						
to wife's kin:						
wife's mother (*u*)..	3	3	2			
wife's sister Angela (*v*)		7	8			
other kin of wife (*w*)		8	10			
				3	19	8
to husband's kin (*x*)				1	1	1
to friends (*y*) ..				1	14	1½
Expenditure for one year:				£53	2	0½

INCOME	£	s.	d.	£	s.	d.
Brought forward..				68	10	0½
Income for one year:				£68	10	0½

Financial position end of February 1948

	£	s.	d.
Debts outstanding:			
Balance of loan from N.A.T. (*r*)	1	0	0
Soldier friend (*t*)	5	0	0
Debts to Bambui Govt. Farm for:			
Pigs	11	0	0
Cement used for styes ..	17	0	0
Total debts c/f to foll. yr.	£34	0	0

BUDGET 2

(February 1947 to February 1948)

B.—ESTIMATED VALUE OF OUTLAY (INCLUDING CONSUMPTION) AND INCOME *IN KIND* FOR ONE YEAR

OUTLAY ETC. IN KIND

	£ s. d.	£ s. d.
Gifts from own supplies:		
to wife's mother (*ll*)	8 6½	
to wife's sister, Angela (*mm*)	17 1	
to other kin of wife (*nn*)	4 9½	
		1 10 5
to husband's kin (*oo*)	19 7½	
to friends (*pp*) ..	1 14 2½	
soap and kindling used by household ..		1 7 0
fowls kept for household		6 0
value of crops kept for household		17 13 9
		£23 11 0

INCOME IN KIND

	£ s. d.	£ s. d.
Gifts received:		
from wife's mother (*ll*)	8 10	
from wife's sister, Angela (*mm*) ..	4 6 8	
from other kin of wife (*nn*)	14 0½	
		5 9 6½
from husband's kin (*oo*)	11 8½	
from friends (*pp*) ..	4 10 6	
Soap from Hausa ..	2 0	
Kindling collected by wife	1 5 0	
		1 7 0
Fowls		6 0
Market value at harvest of crops (exclusive of sales) kept for household and produced by husband and wife:		
2,677 lbs. cereals (*qq*)	4 14 3	
19,725 lbs. roots (*rr*)	9 13 4	
102 lbs. beans & cucurbits (*ss*) ..	8 8	
greens & other relishes	14 8	
420 lbs. plantains (*tt*)	1 1 0	
pears	10	
tomatoes & other vegetables (*uu*) ..	16 0	
12 lbs. coffee ..	5 0	
		17 13 9
		£29 18 6

	£ s. d.	£ s. d.
Estimated expenditure etc. for one year—		
in cash ..	..53 2 0½	
in kind ..	..23 11 0	
		£76 13 0½

	£ s. d.	£ s. d.
Estimated income for one year—		
in cash ..	..68 10 0½	
in kind ..	..29 18 6	
		£98 8 6½

Cash income is 62% of gross income.

Value of wife's contribution is 44% of gross income.

BUDGET 2

Benedict Somo and Christina Lambiif

Benedict Somo lives in the Banka area of Kimbaw and is in his late thirties; his wife, Christina Lambiif, is probably a little younger. Both were Roman Catholics when they married. Somo is the son of a deceased Fai-Tawong, and a grandson of the late *Fɔn*. He has four children—three boys and a girl. The eldest son attends the Mission school and is in the Infant's Grade; the younger stays frequently with his mother's mother in Bamenda Station, while the youngest son is about 2 years old. The number in the household fluctuated during the year under review. In addition to Somo, his wife, and the three children, there was Somo's brother's son, Bunila, for whom Somo paid school fees, and who gave some help in his leisure. For part of the year there was a labourer, but when he left his place was taken by another of Somo's relatives, Mburong, who gave assistance to Somo and received in return food, clothing, and the payment of his tax. There were thus seven permanently resident in the compound, but Somo and his wife had many visitors who sometimes stayed the night or a few days. They were given hospitality, but made some return in gifts of money and food. Somo and his wife occasionally went to Bamenda Station: Somo.twice, and Christina twice.

Somo was at one time a vernacular teacher in the R.C.M. school, but he retired and decided to take up coffee-planting and general farming. He also learnt to be a tailor and bought a sewing machine. Towards the close of 1945 he received two month's training in mixed farming at Bambui and, on his return to Kimbaw, was granted by the Fon 3.1 acres of good alluvial land. He built pig styes and began to breed pigs, but he continued to cultivate his coffee farms (some 3.2 acres). He belonged to two *djaŋgis* (one of which met weekly and the other monthly), and also to a " bank " in Tabessob, where he had maternal relatives. His budget was recorded weekly over a full year, but for the first seven months Somo kept all the entries as I was away from Kimbaw. After September 1947, he continued to note expenditure and income, but brought the accounts to me at the end of each week. \His wife, in addition to her work on the farms, traded in gari, starch and other commodities. Her earnings are included in the budget. She spent much on relishes and cooked food, Somo assuming responsibility for large quantities of staple foods, such as maize, as well as oil, salt, meat, and so on. Christina bought a few trinkets, and was generous in making small gifts of cash to her own kin and friends.

NOTES

(a) Christina bought a considerable amount of flour, roots, beans, etc. to save herself the trouble of grinding grain. The hulled maize was bought to augment household supplies, as the harvest in 1946 was not sufficient.

(b) Christina, with her earnings from trade, often bought prepared foods, some to save trouble of grinding grain, and to provide variety—e.g. gari (9s. 9d.), and others as snacks.

(c) I have not tabulated in detail expenditure on relishes, but out of the amount entered in the budget 6s. 11½d. was spent on *egusi*, 1s. 11d. on dried locust bean (*davadava*), 4s. 6d. on spinach, 1s. 2d. on okra, and so on.

(d) Honey was used to sweeten coffee, and also as a medicine for sore throats.

(e) After Christina had her child, she bought a considerable number of oranges for herself and him on the advice of the Mission clinic.

(f) Somo belonged to a *djaŋgi*, which bought salt and oil and retailed them to members at rates cheaper than those in the open market. Of the 18s. 6d. spent on salt, about 7s. 1d. worth was given away to kin and friends, exclusive of what was used in cooking to entertain guests. Of the 52s. 10d. spent on oil, at least 6s. 2d. was given away to kin and friends, although both Somo and his wife received small gifts of oil from their guests.

(g) At Christmas, and also when entertaining important guests, Somo bought a few kolas, as well as wine (3s. 6d.) and beer (5s. 7½d.).

165

(h) Somo bought small quantities of firewood, as his wife required some for frying gari. The bundles of kindling brought in by her from the farm did not suffice for the purpose. Somo also had a brazier to warm the house in the evening, and spent 1s. 8d. on charcoal for it.

(i) Somo bought, over the full year, 3 lengths of cloth at a total outlay of 33s., a headtie for 5s., shoes for 14s. 6d., and underwear for 7s. 6d. for his wife, Christina.

(j) He bought a shirt for himself, and in addition spent 6s. on shoe repairs. But it is noteworthy that the household received gifts of cloth and shoes from Christina's sister and mother, and also friends (see footnotes (ll), (mm) and (pp) below).

(k) Mburong (brother's son to Somo) often helped on the farm and received food, clothes, etc. for his work.

(l) Somo paid 6s. a year in fees for his own son Isaac, and 6s. for a relative, Bunila.

(m) The horse was bought from a Fulani, but was not broken in. Somo thought it would be useful later for riding to outlying coffee farms and to Bamenda Station.

(n) Somo intended to breed rabbits and sell the meat in the local market, but his first experiment failed and he gave up the idea.

(o) The amount cited above was spent on cement, wood, etc., for styes and does not include the value of cement received on credit from Bambui (see footnote (z) below).

(p) When Somo began raising pigs he had not sufficient food from his own farm, and, throughout 1947, he purchased large quantities of cocoyams, cassava, sweet potatoes, and skim milk. During 1948 his outlay would not have been so heavy as he would have the crops grown on his own farm.

(q) Christina lost 2s. in the market. On another occasion Somo had to pay 20s. for a parcel for which he was responsible and which he had lost.

(r) Early in 1946 Somo received a loan of £15 from the N.A.T. for pig-raising, as his outlay on food alone for the pigs was considerable. By the beginning of 1947 he had repaid £7. During 1947 he paid off another £7, but only by drawing on his savings in the "bank" at Tabessob. With the help of a loan of £5 from a soldier friend he was able to meet other commitments.

(t) Many of the returned soldiers had a relatively large amount of cash and one of Somo's friends lent him £5. By mid-March Somo still had not repaid his debt.

(u) The cash outlay entailed for gifts to affines, kin, etc., should be compared with gifts in kind given from own stores which are listed in footnotes (ll), (mm), etc. Somo's father-in-law had never recognized the marriage as legal and refused to make his peace, even when Somo and his wife had a number of children. Therefore Somo had no commitments to him. Somo's mother-in law had left her husband several years previously and lived at Bamenda Station, but she occasionally visited her daughter in Kimbaw and was visited by her in Bamenda. In addition to ordinary hospitality, Somo and Christina gave Christina's mother 23s. 11d. in cash, relishes bought specially (2s. 3d.), a blanket (30s.) and cloth (7s.). From her they received only 2½d. in cash, but she gave a number of presents (see (ll) below).

(v) Christina's sister, Angela, was a teacher in the R.C.M. school at Shisong and was a frequent visitor at the house. Besides making many gifts to the family she occasionally sold gari for Christina at the Mission. During the year Christina gave her 5s. 6d. in cash, and bought especially for her ink, knitting needles, butter, etc. She also gave her presents of food (which I have listed in footnote (mm) below). From Angela Christina and her children received small sums of cash in addition to gifts in kind (see below).

(w) I have not tabulated separately the gifts made to other kin of Christina, since the value was relatively small. The main recipients were her sister, brothers, and mother's brother (who was a returned soldier). The latter received small presents of cash amounting to 3s. 8d. during the year, but in return he gave small sums amounting to 9s. 1d.

(x) Somo was a grandson of the Fon, and was expected to be generous in gifts to vikinto as well as to his own kin. When the Fon died, Somo sent 2s. 6d. worth of beef and porridge to the vikinto as well as buying 1s. 6d. worth of salt for them. However, on different occasions, he received, all told, 8s. in cash from the reigning Fon. To a wiinto, who had shared a hut in the palace with Somo's father's mother, Somo gave salt, pots, and cash to the value of 1s. 11½d., as well as food from household supplies amounting to 3s. 1d. Somo felt some responsibility for a father's sister who lived at Mbuluf village and was alone. During the year he gave her 3s. 1d. in cash, cloth for a pubic covering (worth 1s. 6d.) and tobacco (1d.)—in addition to 3s. 5d. worth of salt and oil drawn from household supplies. From her Christina received gifts of cocoyam, corn, potatoes, etc., amounting to 5s. 3d. in value. To another relative Somo made a number of gifts at marriage, providing him with 2s. worth of wine, and 6d. in cash for the bride, as well as maize, egusi, flour, tomatoes, etc., to the value of 3s. 5d. This same relative had previously assisted Christina with the sale of her gari in the market, and had received from her gifts of food amounting to 2s. 4d. in value.

(*y*) It is not possible here to cite the details of all gifts made to friends of Somo and his wife. The gifts were, on the whole, small in value. Noteworthy are those to the godmother of Christina's own mother, and especially to the godmother of Christina herself. The latter received a headtie worth 5*s*., and 5*s*. in cash, as well as sundry gifts of food from household supplies. The cash received from friends far exceeds that given away to friends, and the main explanation lies in the fact that Somo and his wife had many visitors, some of whom stayed for several days; teachers on holiday, masons, sawyers, government employees with temporary work in Kimbaw, and so on. These had their meals with the family but from time to time gave cash and food to their hostess. Thus Damon lived with the family for several weeks and gave, all told, 13*s*. 7*d*. cash, 5*s*. worth of beef, 9*d*. worth of oil, and so on. It is noteworthy that most of them handed over the money to Christina, since it was her responsibility to provide the meals. Occasionally small sums were given to the children. The expenditure on gifts to affines, kin and friends amounts to £6.14.10½. Cash gifts received from affines, kin and friends amount to £7.14.6.

(*z*) Somo's outstanding debts were relatively heavy, but it was arranged with Bambui Government Farm that he should hand over a certain proportion of the proceeds from the sale of pork during the year 1948. The £15, which he had in hand by the end of February 1948, would be required for household expenses, incidental expenses for the piggery, and settlement of other debts.

(*aa*) Government employees, Mission teachers and others in the ' higher ' income group occasionally bought small quantities of ground coffee from Somo. The sum entered above also included the sale of a case to a *fai* for 23*s*.

(*bb*) The coffee berries were sold at 5*d*. a lb. in Bamenda Station. The entry above represented net profit. The cost of transport has been included under expenditure in another column.

(*cc*) During the year Somo killed about 3 pigs, and retailed the pork in the market. A little was given away to friends, and some was kept for the household.

(*dd*) Somo bought kolas for 3*s*. 9*d*. and retailed them for 5*s*. 5*d*.

(*ee*) Somo bought soap from the U.A.C. for 10*s*. 8*d*., and retailed it in small pieces for 16*s*. 1*d*.

(*ff*) Salt was bought for 8*s*. 8*d*. and retailed for 10*s*. 6*d*. In my budget records, kept during my absence from Kimbaw during the rains, there was an entry for 29*s*. on salt bought for retail, but no details of sales. I have omitted this item from the budget.

(*gg*) Bananas were bought for 7*d*. and retailed for 8*d*.

(*hh*) During the year, Christina bought in small quantities each week cassava at a total outlay of £3.18.8. Sometimes she made starch and sold throughout the year 21*s*. 8*d*. worth; the balance of the cassava was prepared as gari and sold for £5.15.10½. Some of Somo's firewood was used when frying the gari.

(*ii*) Christina bought beans for 3*s*. 10*d*. and sold bean balls for 5*s*. 3*d*.

(*jj*) Christina bought maize for 7*s*. 10*d*. in order to brew beer. She sold the beer for 8*s*. 8*d*. On another occasion she sold 6*s*. 3*d*. worth of beer, brewed from maize from her own farm.

(*kk*) Christina bought knitting wool for 12*s*. and knitted a sweater, which she sold for 20*s*., and a cap for 4*s*. 6*d*.

(*ll*) Gifts in kind, drawn from household supplies, were frequently made to Christina's mother. They included salt and various vegetables to the value of 4*s*. 0½*d*., wine (6*d*.) and 2 cocks (4*s*.). Christina received from her mother cocoyam, salt and fish to the value of 3*s*. 10*d*., and a hoe worth 5*s*. Her mother also contributed to the purchase of some cloth by Angela for Christina (see footnote (*mm*) below).

(*mm*) Christina frequently gave gari, corn, yams, onions, tomatoes, meat, greens, and so on to her sister Angela, who lived at the Mission School. The estimated value was 12*s*. 10*d*. In addition Somo gave her a fowl (1*s*. 6*d*.), wine (3*d*.), and coffee (6*d*.), while Christina made her a present of some ear-rings and vaseline worth 2*s*., which she herself had received while on a visit to friends in Bamenda.

From Angela the family received groundnuts, oil, maize, etc. to the value of 6*s*. 11*d*.; two lengths of cloth for dresses (40*s*. 6*d*.), canvas shoes (10*s*. 6*d*.) for Somo, shoes (30*s*. 6*d*.) for Christina, a handkerchief (1*s*. 3*d*.) for Somo, soap worth 6*d*. and sewing thread (1*s*.). It should be noted that Angela was an unmarried teacher, earning a salary, and that she had no one immediately dependent upon her apart from her mother.

(*nn*) Again, I have not itemized all gifts in kind to other kin of Christina. Her mother's brother received gari and other food to the value of 1*s*. 9½*d*., and also a fowl (1*s*. 6*d*.), on his departure to Bamenda. While staying with the family in Kimbaw, he made gifts in kind to the value of 11*s*. 2*d*. They included honey (1*s*. 6*d*.); pork (9*d*.), bought specially for the children; a large calabash (2*s*.); a strip of cloth (6*s*.) for Somo's son; and so forth. It is worth noting that the value of all gifts (in cash and in kind) to wife's kin amounts to £5.10.1, as compared with the value of £6.14.6½ of all gifts in cash and in kind received from wife's kin.

(oo) See footnote (x) above. It should be noted that in cash and in 'kind Somo gave away gifts to the value of 40s. 8½d., and he received from his kin gifts in cash and in kind to the value of 23s. 3½d.

(pp) It is difficult to deal with the details here in terms of the individuals concerned. I therefore include an estimate of the total value of various types of commodities given and received. To his friends Somo gave during the year food (20s. 9d,), fowls (7s.), coffee (3s.), trinkets (1s. 6d.), soap (11d.), and a calabash (1s.). From their friends Somo and his wife received food (35s. 10½d.), fowls (5s. 6d.), beer and wine (7s. 11d.), soap (3s. 7½d.), cosmetics (5s. 8d.), firewood (2s. 6d.), clothes (24s. 6d.), household utensils (4s. 7d.), and a pipe (2d.). It should be remembered that many of the presents received were often handed on to friends or kin immediately, or a few weeks later. This applied particularly to foodstuffs, trinkets, soap, and smaller household utensils. Again, as might be expected, when a gift was received, some kind of return was made later. But a detailed discussion of such acts of reciprocity must be postponed for another publication.

(qq) Christina and Somo farmed, all told, 3.3 acres (exclusive of plots under coffee). Somo gave help to his wife on all the farms except that devoted to rizga. In September 1947 they obtained 31 vegati of maize from their farm, but only ½ kegati of finger millet. Some of the maize was used to feed the pigs, but Somo kept no records of the amounts involved.

(rr) Somo grew very large quantities of sweet potatoes and on the basis of some figures which he gave me, I estimated a harvest of 15,000 lbs. Much of the crop was used for food for the pigs. He sold about 2s. worth of potatoes.

(ss) About 3d. worth of dwarf beans was sold to Europeans.

(tt) Somo did not give much time to his plantains, and he sold only 1s. 10d. worth, or about 40lbs.

(uu) Some of Somo's largest profits from farm produce were derived from the sale of tomatoes, onions, etc. Most onions are imported from Northern Nigeria and sell at anything from 2d. to 6d. each. Their cultivation in Nsaw therefore offers considerable financial possibilities.

BUDGET 3

(4th March 1947 to 5th March 1948)

A.—EXPENDITURE AND INCOME IN CASH

EXPENDITURE	£	s.	d.	£	s.	d.
Food—						
bags of maize (*a*) ..	2	11	1			
maize flour (*b*)		2	3			
plantains		3	3½			
cassava			9			
gari		1	6			
potatoes		3	2			
beans		11	2			
cow-peas			11			
groundnuts ..		3	10			
spinach		1	0½			
egusi		3	7½			
pepper			3			
okra			3			
tomatoes			6			
onions			2			
				4	3	9½
meat	1	0	11½			
fish		7	0			
eggs			3			
salt		17	6			
oil	1	10	5			
				3	16	1½
Stimulants—						
wine for Christmas..		3	7			
House & Farm Replacements—						
basin		4	0			
cane basket ..		2	0			
4 beer calabashes ..		2	8½			
2 sleeping mats (*c*) ..		4	0			
blanket ..		11	0			
drying mat ..		1	0			
alarm clock (*d*) ..	1	0	0			
firewood (*e*) ..	1	4	7			
kerosene ..		1	0			
soap		1	1½			
				3	11	5
Clothes—						
cloth for wife & daughter		16	0			
shirt for son ..		10	6			
cap for husband ..		3	0			
shirt for sister's son (*f*)		7	6			
shorts for son ..		9	6			
2 shirts for son ..		14	0			
				3	0	6
Church dues—						
collection		1	0			
contribution cards— husband & wife ..		9	0			
				10	0	
School fees—						
for daughter ..		10	0			
for sister's daughter's son	1	13	0			
for 'son'		3	0			
books, etc. (*g*) ..		3	0			
				2	9	0
Carried forward :				17	14	5

INCOME	£	s.	d.	£	s.	d.
Sales of—						
plantains		6	3			
pineapples			8			
pears			5			
oranges		1	5			
egusi			7			
				0	9	4
120 lbs. coffee (*o*) ..				1	18	0
Earnings as builder—						
2 houses in Mbinkar area (*p*)	1	11	6			
house in Ndzendzef area	2	0	0			
house in Veka' akwi	1	19	2			
				5	10	8
bricks for Women's Centre (*q*) ..	4	0	0			
wages for bricklaying	5	15	0			
				9	15	0
fees from apprentice (*r*)				1	10	0
Husband's profits from trade—						
groundnuts (*s*) ..						
soap (*t*)		3	6½			
2 shirts (*u*)						
meat (*v*)		2	0			
				5	6½	
Wife's profits from trade—						
beer (*w*)				3	0	9½
Carried forward :				22	9	4

169

EXPENDITURE							INCOME					
	£	s.	d.	£	s.	d.		£	s.	d.	£	s.	d.

EXPENDITURE						
		£	s.	d.	£	s.	d.
Brought forward:					17	14	5
Miscellaneous—							
tax	..	5	0			
gunpowder (*h*)	..	7	0			
medicine, etc.	..	1	10			
djaŋgi (*i*) ..	..	15	4			
interest (*j*) ..	..	2	0			
losses ..	..	1	11			
				1	13	1
Gifts—							
to wife's kin (*k*)	..	8	10½			
to husb.'s kin (*l*)	.. 1	0	7			
to friends (*m*)	..	9	7			
				1	19	0½

INCOME						
		£	s.	d.	£	s.	d.
Brought forward:					22	9	4
Gifts—							
from wife's kin (*k*) ..		1	6			
from husb.'s kin (*l*)..			9			
from friends (*m*) ..		7	3			
					9	6

Expenditure for one year: £21 6 6½   Income for one year: £22 18 10

BUDGET 3

(4th March 1947 to 5th March 1948)

B.—ESTIMATED VALUE OF OUTLAY (INCLUDING CONSUMPTION) AND INCOME *IN KIND* FOR ONE YEAR

OUTLAY, ETC., IN KIND

	£ s. d.	£ s. d.
Gifts from own supplies—		
to wife's kin (*x*) ..	14 0	
to husb.'s kin (*y*) ..	1 13 1½	
to friends (*z*) ..	1 11	
		2 9 0½
Soap & kindling used		
by household ..		1 12 0
Value of crops kept for		
household		9 2 4

INCOME IN KIND

	£ s. d.	£ s. d.
Gifts received—		
from wife's kin (*x*) ..	8 3	
from husb.'s kin (*y*)..	6 8	
from friends ..	5 2	
from kin & friends when daughters returned home (*z*)	1 12 8½	
		2 12 9½
soap from Hausa ..	2 0	
kindling collected by wife & niece ..	1 10 0	
		1 12 0
Market value of crops kept for household—		
1,764 lbs. grain (*aa*)	3 8 4	
4,747 lbs. roots (*bb*)	3 1 10	
66 lbs. beans, etc. ..	4 5	
greens, etc. (*cc*) ..	10 4	
		7 4 11
Tended by husband—		
635 lbs. plantains (*dd*)	1 11 9	
pears, oranges, etc...	1 6	
10 lbs. coffee (*ee*) ..	4 2	
		1 17 5

Outlay, etc., in kind for one year: £13 3 4½

Income in kind for one year: £13 7 1½

Estimated expenditure, etc., for one year—

	£ s. d.	£ s. d.
in cash ..	..21 6 6½	
in kind ..	..13 3 4½	
		£34 9 11

Estimated income for one year—

	£ s. d.	£ s. d.
in cash ..	..22 18 10	
in kind ..	..13 7 1½	
		£36 5 11½

Cash income is 63% of gross income.
Value of wife's contribution is 33% of gross income.

171

BUDGET 3

Francis Lole and Elizabeth-Kila

Francis Lole is a man in his late fifties and lives in Mbonyaar Compound with his wife, Elizabeth-Kila. Both were Roman Catholics before they were married (see text). One adolescent daughter, Scholastica, is a Health-Visitor at Bamenda Station; the other, Emilia Woomila, was appointed to the same position in Kimbaw in October 1947 and she lived with her parents. The eldest and only son, Francis Kpuntir, recorded Lole's budget for me while I was in the west of the Province from February to September 1947, after which I took over the weekly records myself. Kpuntir left for the secondary school in Victoria just before Christmas. Lole had two other children,—a girl attending school and a second at home. He also gave food to, and received help from, Cletus (son of a deceased sister), and from Everestus (son of a deceased brother). With these two youths he made sun-dried bricks and constructed houses in Kimbaw. He had also taken under his wing Elizabeth-Djingla and Tume—two daughters of a brother who lived in Mvø hamlet. There were thus nine members in the household during most of the year.

In addition to bricklaying Lole also tended plantain and other fruit trees, some raffia which he had planted at Kingomen, and a small coffee plantation in Kimbaw. His wife, with some assistance from Elizabeth-Djingla, farmed 1.7 acres. She also brewed beer and sold it to *djaŋgis*.

NOTES

(a) Elizabeth had a good maize harvest in September 1947 but, even so, Lole occasionally bought bags of maize, especially during the rains of 1947 when stores were low.

(b) Elizabeth was rather sickly and Lole bought flour, gari and beans to save her the chore of grinding grain. Note the relatively high expenditure on relishes for soup.

(c) When Kpuntir left for school, Lole bought him a fine mat for 3s. The other, costing 1s. was for the household.

(d) When Lole secured the contract for the Women's Centre he bought an alarm clock to ensure waking early for the job!

(e) Firewood was purchased from the Government Plantation. Of this Elizabeth used about 5s. worth for brewing beer.

(f) Cletus, the sister's son, assisted Lole and in return received food, clothes and a little pocket money.

(g) Lole paid fees for Laurence but did not buy books or clothes because the boy was lazy and did not work in his spare time. Lole feared he might set a bad example to his own children if he received everything for nothing. Lole also paid fees for the youngest son of Djingla (inherited wife of the *fai*). He said he did it out of pity because he himself had just lost a child.

(h) The gunpowder was fired to celebrate the return of Lole's daughters from Nigeria. See (x) and (y) below.

(i) Lole belonged to four *djaŋgis*: he " cooked " one at Mbonyaar for 67s. and provided 3s. 6d. worth of beer, which he purchased from his own wife. He " cooked " a weekly *djaŋgi* at Ka for 29s. and provided wine (1s.) and beer (2s. 6d.). From a weekly *djaŋgi* at Ndzendzef he obtained 100s. and gave wine (3s. 6d.); and from a monthly *djaŋgi* at Ndzendzef he got 75s. and provided wine worth 3s. He gave 1s. 10d. of meat when the " bank " met. His wife was also a member of the Mbonyaar *djaŋgi* and was to receive about 40s. at the end of March.

(j) Lole had at one time 31s. 5d. in the " bank " but, by the beginning of 1947, he had only 27s. left. In April, and again in June, he withdrew 12s. and paid 1s. interest on each amount later.

(k) The sum of 8s. 10½d. represented the total cash outlay for a number of small gifts to Elizabeth's kin. I cite them in detail because they illustrate the type of occasion when gifts are made to affines. When a new *fai* was installed as head of the lineage of Elizabeth's mother's father, Lole bought salt (1s. 6d.) and fish (1s. 9d.). He also provided a cock (2s. 6d.) from his own poultry and sent these gifts to the new *fai*. When the *Fɔn* died in April 1947 Lole bought a small goat (4s. 6d.) and sent it to the *fai* who, in his turn, took it to the palace. The value of gifts in cash to the *fai* for the year was thus 7s. 9d.

The value of gifts in kind to affines is discussed in (*x*) below. During the year Lole and his wife spent 5d. on groundnuts for Elizabeth's brother's son; 6d. for a pot for Elizabeth's brother's wife. Total expenditure was 1s. 1½d., in addition to gifts from household supplies. Elizabeth received 1s. 6d. in cash from her brother as a return for the care she had lavished on his sick wife.

(*l*) Lole gave 1s. 9d. worth of salt and 3d. worth of flour to his sister who was a *wiinto*. When the *Fɔn* died in April Lole sent to *vikinto* fish (9d.) and meat (1s.), in addition to the fufu prepared by his wife. He gave a shilling to Cletus; and a hoe (4s.) to a wife of a deceased brother, and 3d. to her son. At Christmas he distributed 14s. 6d. in cash among kin and friends. I have allowed 8s. for kin. He also provided pork (3s.) for his daughter and her friends; and later 6d. worth of wine for a working-bee which she had organized for the clearing of her farm.

From his own kin gifts in cash were small. Elizabeth at the wedding of a girl at Ndzendzef received 9d. Lole's mother was a kinswoman of Ndzendzef.

(*m*) During the year Lole gave small sums of cash to friends, and at Christmas he distributed about 6s. 6d. in presents. He received two sums in cash from friends (4s. and 3s. 3d.). See (*z*) below.

(*o*) Lole's coffee plantation was just under an acre. He obtained 40s. for the berries but paid 2s. for transport to Bamenda.

(*p*) Lole obtained 9s. for supervising the construction of a small house in Mbinkar; he was also due to receive 22s. 6d. for another, but to date had been given only 12s. 6d.

(*q*) Lole received the contract to make bricks for the new Women's Centre on the outskirts of Kimbaw. He was given 12s. 6d. a 1,000 bricks, but out of this he had to pay labourers 12s. which left him with a profit of 6d. His total profit from the bricks was 72s. 6d., plus an extra 7s. 6d. as payment for rough shelters for the bricks.

(*r*) The apprentice agreed to pay Lole 60s. for instruction in bricklaying. The training-was completed but Lole had received only 30s.

(*s*) Lole bought 2 bags groundnuts for 9s. to retail but he made nothing on the transaction.

(*t*) Lole bought a bar of soap for 1s. 1½d. to sell in small quantities, but made only a halfpenny on the deal.

(*u*) Meat was bought for 6s. and retailed for 8s.

(*v*) Two shirts cost 13s. 6d. and were sold by Lole for 17s.

(*w*) Every week Elizabeth bought one or two bags of maize and brewed beer for two *djaŋgis*. Her outlay on maize for the year was £7-2-4½, and her sales amounted to £10-3-2.

(*x*) I cite in detail gifts to Elizabeth's kin. When a new *fai* was installed as head of the patrilineage of Elizabeth's mother (see (*k*) above), Lole sent one of his own cocks (2s. 6d.). When the *Fɔn* died Elizabeth sent fufu and greens to the wives of the new *fai* who then handed the food to the *vikinto*. The value of gifts in kind to the new *fai* were thus 3s. 6d.

At the time of the *Fɔn's* death Lole also sent one of his own cocks to Fai-o-Ki, father of Elizabeth, who in turn handed it on to the palace. The brother of Elizabeth also received a cock (2s. 6d.) and later pineapples and bananas (9d.) and salt (6d.). When her sister-in-law was ill in hospital Elizabeth visited her daily, taking food to the value all told of 4s. Elizabeth's sister was given 3d. worth of salt.

But Lole's affines made some return for these gifts. When his daughters arrived from Nigeria, he and wife received potatoes (6d.) and eggplant (2d.) from the wives of Fai-o-Do (head of Elizabeth's mother's patrilineage). Elizabeth's own brother sent firewood (3d.) and two fowls (3s.); while her brother's wife occasionally sent food—e.g. yams (1s. 6d.), potatoes (9d.), corn (6d.), plantains (4d.) and fufu (1s.),—total value being 4s. 1d. Elizabeth's brother's daughter at Ketiwum sent potatoes (3d.).

(*y*) I shall not itemize all gifts made to Lole's own kin. They consisted in the main of small quantities of cooked food, beer, meat, and firewood. Late in the year he sent a large cock (3s.) and egusi (7d.) to his daughter at Bamenda. He gave his adolescent son, Kpuntir, 2 tin spoons (1s.), a fork (6d.), 2 basins and a cup (4s.), a pillow case (2s.), a blanket (8s.) and a small suitcase (10s.) from among the household possessions to take to school in Victoria.

(*z*) Lole and his wife received small quantities of food from his kin in the compound. When the daughters returned from Nigeria both kin and friends came forward with gifts. Lole said he could not remember all the individuals concerned, but the total cash value of

16 fowls, meat, wine, eggs, flour, groundnuts, salt, cocoyam and so on was about 32*s*. 8½*d*. My records of gifts in kind to friends are incomplete as Lole and wife were apt to be reticent about acts of hospitality.

In the mass of detail the balance of gifts has been obscured. Gifts in cash and in kind to Elizabeth's kin amounted to 22*s*. 10½*d*. Gifts in cash and in kind received from her kin amounted to 9*s*. 9*d*. Gifts in cash and kind to the kin and friends of Lole amounted to 65*s*. 2½*d*.; while gifts received amounted to 45*s*. 10½*d*.

(*aa*) Elizabeth harvested 17 *vegati* of maize in September 1947, and 3¾ *vegati* of finger millet in January 1948.

(*bb*) Elizabeth, with the help of her husband's niece, cultivated a relatively large *rizga* plot and obtained approximately 1,728 lbs. of roots; but she had only two small patches of sweet potatoes and not many trifoliate yams.

(*cc*) Elizabeth sold 7*d*. worth of *egusi* which I have deducted from the value of relishes.

(*dd*) Lole did most of the weeding of the fruit plantations. I have estimated a crop of 760 lbs. (worth 38*s*.) of which about 125 lbs. were sold.

(*ee*) Lole and his wife liked coffee which they drank very weak and without sweetening. The bulk of the crop was sold in Bamenda Station.

BUDGET 4

(6th October 1947 to 5th March 1948)

A.—EXPENDITURE AND INCOME IN CASH

EXPENDITURE	£ s. d.	£ s. d.	INCOME	£ s. d.	£ s. d.
Food—			*Sales of*—		
oil	6 4		plantains	10	
salt	10½				
cowpeas	1		44 bundles of thatch-		
meat	2 10		ing grass (*g*) ..	12 7	
groundnuts	3½		25 bundles of firewood	12 6	
egusi	3	10 8			1 5 11
House & Farm Replace-			*Profits from sale of*—		
ments—			kolas (*h*) ..	1 6	
basket (*a*)	3		honey (*i*) ..	3	
matches	2		tobacco (*j*) ..	6	
soap	2				2 3
seed-yams (*b*) ..	1 0	1 7			
			Gifts—		
			from wife's kin (*f*) ..		3
Clothes—					
for husband (*c*) ..	2 3				
Miscellaneous—					
wine for *djaŋgi* (*d*) ..	1 6				
Gifts—					
to husb.'s kin (*e*) ..	1 0				
to wife's kin (*f*) ..	1 0				
Expenditure for 5 months:		18 0	Income for 5 months:		£1 8 5

Estimated budget from 6th March to 6th October 1947

	£ s. d.		£ s. d.	£ s. d.
Food—		*Sales of*—		
staples, oil, etc. (*k*) ..	17 0	plantains (*o*) ..	1 8	
		fowls	6 0	
Farm & house replace-				7 8
ments	7 0			
Clothes—(*l*)	10 0	*Profits from trade*—		
Miscellaneous—		kolas (*p*)	2 0 0	
tax	5 0	rock-salt, etc. ..	10 0	
djaŋgi (*m*)	2 0			
incidental	5 0			
Gifts—				
to wife's kin (*n*) ..	4 0			
Estimated expend. for 7 months: £2 10 0		Estimated income for 7 months: £2 17 8		
Estimated expend. for one year: £3 8 0		Estimated income for one year: £4 6 1		

175

BUDGET 4

(March 1947 to March 1948)

OUTLAY, ETC., IN KIND	£ s. d.	£ s. d.
Gifts from own supplies—		
to wife's kin (*r*) ..		2 0
to husband's kin ..		1 0
Soap & kindling used by household ..		1 12 0
Value of crops & other self-produced supplies used by household ..		6 15 9

INCOME IN KIND	£ s. d.	£ s. d.
Gifts received—		
from wife's kin (*r*) ..		5 0
from husband's kin..		1 0
Soap from Hausa ..		2 0
Kindling collected by wife	1 5 0	
and by husband ..		5 0
Market value of crops kept for household & produced by wife:—		
1,105 lbs. grain (*s*)..	1 16 0	
3,795 lbs. roots ..	2 9 4	
66 lbs. beans, etc. ..	4 5	
greens, etc.	7 10	
		4 17 7
produced by husband—		
150 lbs. plantains (*t*)		7 6
fowls		6 0
5 bundles thatching grass		1 8
2,000 mud bricks ..		1 0 0

Outlay, etc., in kind for one year: £8 10 9	Income in kind for one year: £8 10 9

Estd. expenditure, etc., for one year—	£ s. d.	£ s. d.
in cash ..	.. 3 8 0	
in kind ..	.. 8 10 9	
		£11 18 9

Estd. income for one year—	£ s. d.	£ s. d.
in cash ..	.. 4 6 1	
in kind ..	.. 8 10 9	
		£12 16 10

Cash income is 33% of gross income.

Value of wife's contribution is 48% of gross income.

BUDGET 4

Kibu and Dzøøndzøiy

Kibu of Djem Compound is a man in his thirties, and has one wife, Dzøøndzøiy. Both are ex-Christians and they have two children living with them,—a daughter aged about 6 years, and a son aged about two years. A third child, a boy, lives with Dzøøndzøiy's mother at Mbam.

Dzøøndzøiy worked 1.4 acres in 1947 without assistance, apart from the clearing done by her husband and his help with the maize and millet harvest. She neither traded nor visited the market. Kibu headloaded kolas to Mayo Daga about 3 times a year, but during the period—October to March—he made no journeys as he was busy cutting thatching grass and firewood, and making mud-bricks for a house he intended to build in about a year's time. He belonged to two *djaŋgis:* one at Djem and another at Kinga, a neighbouring compound. I recorded his budget weekly from 6th October 1947 to 5th March 1948. During that time he was sick for several days and did not visit the market. He occasionally sold plantains, thatching grass, kolas and honey locally.

NOTES

(*a*) A basket bought for the millet harvest.

(*b*) Kibu gave his wife 1*s.* to buy seed-yams at Mvø as her own had been spoilt by insects.

(*c*) Kibu bought a Munshi loincloth to wear when working. He had cash in hand from the *djaŋgi* which he had " cooked " a week previously.

(*d*) Kibu cooked *djaŋgi* for 15*s.* on the 1st February 1948.

(*e*) Kibu sent a mat for the ceremonies of a relative who had just died.

(*f*) On the 15th November Dzøøndzøiy's mother came from Mbam for a visit. On her departure Kibu bought for her meat (9*d.*) and a condiment (1*d.*). He also gave 2*d.* to her companion. See also footnote (*r*) below. On the 18th January Dzøøndzøiy visited her mother at Mbam, and her father gave her 3*d.* to buy salt.

(*g*) During the dry season Kibu cut 49 bundles of grass. He said he would keep 5 for house repairs.

(*h*) During this period Kibu bought small quantities of kolas amounting to 19*s.* He was keeping these for a journey to Mayo Daga in April.

(*i*) Kibu bought honey for 3*s.* 9*d.* and sold it for 4*s.*

(*j*) Kibu bought tobacco in Memfu and sold it for 2*s.* 3*d.* I have estimated 6*d.* profit as I have no record of the purchase price.

(*k*) I have allowed 7*s.* for oil; 1*s.* 6*d.* for salt; 1*s.* for meat; and 7*s.* 6*d.* for staples and greens

(*l*) Dzøøndzøiy wore only a strip of baft (2*s.*) as pubic covering. Kibu possessed 3 large loin cloths, a tunic and a cap.

(*m*) Kibu " cooked " *djaŋgi* for 40*s.* in the rainy season.

(*n*) A man with Kibu's income would normally spend about 5*s.* a year on gifts to wife's kin.

(*o*) Kibu did not have many plantain trees so sales were small.

(*p*) Kibu made 3 journeys a year to Mayo Daga carrying 1,000 kola nuts each time, which he said he bought for 15*s.* and sold for 30*s.* But he incurred expenses for food and canoe transport and his estimated profits for 3 journeys were only 40*s.*

(*q*) While in Mayo Daga he bought rock salt or blankets and retailed them for about 10*s.* profit.

(*r*) Dzøøndzøiy's mother, when visiting Kimbaw, brought a hoe (1*s.* 6*d.*) for her grandchild; sugar cane (1*d.*); beef (6*d.*) for her grandson; and 2 farm bags (1*s.* 4*d.*) for her daughter. See also footnote (*f*). Dzøøndzøiy on the 18th January took her mother maize flour (6*d.*).

(*s*) Dzøøndzøiy harvested 7 *vegati* of maize in 1947 and 6 *vegati* of millet.

(*t*) The approximate cash value of 200 lbs. plantains was 10*s.* and I have estimated that 50 lbs. were sold during the year.

BUDGET 5

(6th October 1947 to 5th March 1948)

A.—EXPENDITURE AND INCOME IN CASH

EXPENDITURE	£ s. d.	£ s. d.	INCOME	£ s. d.	£ s. d.
Food—			*Sales of—*		
oil	6 8		plantains	3 10½	
salt (a)			2 goats (7s. each) ..	14 0	
meat	6		28 bundles of fire-		
groundnuts	5½		wood (g)	14 0	
		7 7½			1 11 10½
Household & farm replace-			*Profits from—*		
ments—nil			kolas (h)		2 0
Miscellaneous—					
diviner (b)		1			
djaŋgi (c)		2 6			
Gifts—					
to wife's kin (d) ..	4 0				
to brother's affines (e)	6				
to husb.'s kin (f) ..	1 0				
		5 6			
Expenditure for 5 months:		15 8½	Income for 5 months:		£1 13 10½

Estimated budget from 6th March to 6th October 1947

EXPENDITURE	£ s. d.	£ s. d.	INCOME	£ s. d.	£ s. d.
Food—			*Sales of—*		
oil, salt, etc. (i) ..		14 0	plantains (n) ..	6 0	
			fowls	6 0	
House & farm replace-			goats (o)	10 0	
ments (j)		3 0			1 2 0
Clothes (k)		10 0	Profits from kolas ..		10 0
Miscellaneous—					
tax		5 0			
djaŋgi (l)		2 0			
incidental		5 0			
Gifts—					
to wife's kin (m) ..		5 0			
Estd. expenditure for 7 months: £2 4 0			Estd. income for 7 months: £1 12 0		

	£ s. d.	£ s. d.		£ s. d.	£ s. d.
Estd. expenditure for one year	15 8½		Estd. income for one year	1 13 10½	
	2 4 0			1 12 0	
		£2 19 8½			£3 5 10½

178

BUDGET 5

(March 1947 to March 1948)

B.—ESTIMATED VALUE OF OUTLAY (INCLUDING CONSUMPTION) AND INCOME *IN KIND* FOR ONE YEAR

OUTLAY, ETC., IN KIND	£ s. d.	£ s. d.	INCOME IN KIND	£ s. d.	£ s. d.
Gifts from own supplies—			*Gifts received—*		
to wife's kin (*p*) ..	8 0		from wife's kin ..	2 0	
to husband's kin ..	1 0		from husb.'s kin ..	1 0	
		9 0			3 0
Soap & kindling used by household ..		1 12 0	Hausa soap	2 0	
			Kindling collected—		
Value of crops & other			by wife 1	5 0	
self-produced supplies			by husband ..	5 0	
used by household ..		8 9 9			1 12 0
			Fowls	6 0	
			Goats 1	4 0	
					1 10 0
			Market value at harvest of crops kept for house & produced by wife—		
			729 lbs. grain (*q*) .. 1	3 9	
			3,544 lbs. roots .. 2	5 9	
			66 lbs. beans & cu-curbits ..	4 5	
			greens, etc.	7 10	
					4 1 9
			produced by hus-band—		
			1,230 lbs. plantains (*r*)		3 2 0
			farm baskets made by husband		2 0
		£10 10 9			**£10 10 9**

	£ s. d.	£ s. d.		£ s. d.	£ s. d.
Estd. expenditure for one year—			Estd. income for one year—		
in cash	2 19 8½		in cash	3 5 10½	
in kind ..	10 10 9		in kind ..	10 10 9	
		£13 10 5½			**£13 16 7½**

Cash income is 23.8% of gross income.

Value of wife's contribution is 39% of gross income.

179

BUDGET 5

Mawo and Biy-Djem

Mawo of Djem Compound is in his late forties and is a pagan. He had formerly two wives, but one died and the other left him and went to Ndop with another man in 1940. Mawo's son is about 12 years' old and lives with him. A younger daughter stays with her mother's mother at Kikai Kilaki. Until he married again in 1946 Mawo arranged for the young girls of Djem compound to tend his kitchen-gardens, and he himself looked after his plantain groves and goats. He is not nearly so energetic a trader as his younger brother, Kibu,—possibly because his commitments are less heavy.

In 1946 he married Biy, a pagan from Kiyan. She became pregnant at the end of 1946 but had a miscarriage. She was again pregnant in September 1947, and Mawo decided to send her to the maternity clinic at Shisong. She went in January 1948, but returned to the compound on the 22nd February because the date had been miscalculated! During the weeks when she was at the Mission, Mawo gathered firewood and took it to her. He gained his main income from the sale of goats, plantains, and fowls, and occasional retailing of kolas. He was a jovial man who belonged to two *djaŋgis* and also attended *mfu* and another society in Mamu area each week, where he generally managed to obtain a little wine. I recorded his budget weekly from the 6th October to the 5th March, and have estimated his expenditure and income for the preceding 7 months in 1947.

NOTES

(a) I have no record of salt bought during the 5 months, although I generally mentioned salt when inquiring about purchases on market-day. Two weeks before I began recording the budget Mawo had spent 6d. on salt. He himself remarked on several occasions that he used less than other people.

(b) Mawo paid one penny to a diviner to consult the omens about his wife, Biy, who was pregnant. The diviner advised him to have a sacrifice performed by the *fai* of Biy's lineage at Kiyan, and another performed by the *fai* of her mother's mother's lineage at Mbam (see footnote (d) below.)

(c) Mawo ' cooked ' *djaŋgi* at Viya in December 1947 and collected £2. He provided wine to the value of 2s. 6d.

(d) See (b) above. Having consulted the diviner on the 2nd January, Mawo took 2 fowls (2s. 6d.) and a small goat (3s. 6d.) from his own farmyard to the *fai* of his wife's lineage. In addition he bought palm oil (1s.) and gave it to the *fai* of his wife's mother's mother's lineage for a sacrifice on behalf of Biy. On the 13th January he bought a fowl (1s. 6d.) and sent it to his wife's father. On the 15th November, the 25th December and the 8th January he sent each time a calabash of wine (total cost 1s. 6d.) to the *fai* of Biy's lineage.

(e) On the 2nd December Mawo bought a calabash of wine (6d.) for the *fai* of the widow of his brother who was ' cooking ' *mfu.*

(f) Mawo on the 11th February bought a mat to send to a kinsman for mortuary ceremonies.

(g) Mawo did not collect thatching grass because he said it gave him skin disease.

(h) Mawo bought kolas only once during the recorded period of 5 months,—namely 1,000 large nuts for 20s., which he sold for 22s. I estimated that he made about 12s. profit a year retailing kolas.

(i) An estimated expenditure of 8s. for salt and oil; 1s. for meat; and 5s. on staples and condiments.

(j) Biy, as a recently married woman, had a good supply of utensils and tools and expenditure was therefore small on such items in 1947.

(k) Biy, a pagan, wore a strip of baft costing 2s. Mawo spent little on clothes as he already possessed 2 large loin cloths, a tunic and cap.

(l) Mawo belonged to the Djem *djaŋgi* which he ' cooked ' for 20s. during the rains. I estimated 2s. for the cost of wine for the occasion.

(*m*) It is difficult to estimate the cost of articles given to wife's kin. Mawo was very vague but emphasized that he had given salt, oil, meat and wine several times in the year.

(*n*) Mawo had a very large grove of plantains and usually sold one or two bunches a week. As his wife's harvest of grain and roots was good he was not dependent on plantains for food in the house.

(*o*) Mawo said he sold about 4 goats a year at prices ranging from 5*s*. to 7*s*.

(*p*) See (*d*) above. I have allowed a further 2*s*. for gifts in kind from household supplies made earlier in the year.

(*q*) Biy farmed 1.3 acres. In September 1947 she obtained 4½ *vegati* of maize; and, in January 1948, 4 *vegati* of finger millet.

(*r*) The estimated weight of plantains was 1,430 lbs., and their value £3–12–0; but some fruit (10*s*.) was sold in the market.

BUDGET 6

(28th September 1947 to 26th February 1948)

A.—EXPENDITURE AND INCOME IN CASH

EXPENDITURE

	£ s. d.	£ s. d.
Food—		
oil (*a*)	8 10	
salt (*b*)	5 5	
groundnuts	3	
meat	3 9	
bagged maize (*c*) ..	12 9	
		1 11 0
Stimulants—		
tobacco		1
House & farm replacements—		
cowpea seed ..		1½
Clothes—		
khaki shirt for husb. (*d*)		15 0
Miscellaneous—		
bank interest (*e*) ..	3 4	
beer (4*s.*) & wine (1*s.*) for *djaŋgi* ..	5 0	
		8 4
Expenditure for 5 months:		£2 14 6½

INCOME

	£ s. d.	£ s. d.
Sales of—		
plantains	1 6½	
honey (*f*)	4 6	
hen	1 6	
trapped guineafowl	6	
		8 0½
Sales of—		
thatching grass (*g*) ..	14 7	
firewood	6	
raffia poles (*h*) ..	8 0	
		1 3 1
Gift to child		1
Profits from—		
salt retailed (*i*) ..	2 0	
kerosene (*j*)	1 10 6	
cassava gruel (*k*) ..	1	
		1 12 7
Commissions for sales for others		1 0
Income for 5 months:		£3 4 9½

Estimated budget from
27th February 1947 to 28th September 1947

EXPENDITURE

	£ s. d.	£ s. d.
Food—(*l*)		1 10 4
House & farm replacements		5 0
Cloth for wife		2 0
Miscellaneous—		
tax	5 0	
bank interest ..	3 4	
djaŋgi wine	3 0	
incidental (*n*) ..	10 0	
		1 1 4
Estd. expenditure for 7 months:		£2 18 8

	£ s. d.	£ s. d.
Estd. expenditure for one year	2 14 6½	
	2 18 8	
		£5 13 2½

INCOME

	£ s. d.	£ s. d.
Sales of—		
plantains (*o*) ..	8 6	
honey	5 6	
fowls	4 6	
		18 6
wine (*p*)	1 0	
kolas (*q*)	2 0	
		3 0
Profits from—		
retail of salt & kerosene (*r*)	1 15 0	
commissions ..	1 0	
		1 16 0
Estd. income for 7 months:		£2 17 6

	£ s. d.	£ s. d.
Estd. income for one year	3 4 9½	
	2 17 6	
		£6 2 3½

BUDGET 6

(February 1947 to February 1948)

B.—ESTIMATED VALUE OF OUTLAY (INCLUDING CONSUMPTION) AND INCOME *IN KIND* FOR ONE YEAR

OUTLAY, ETC., IN KIND	£ s. d.	£ s. d.	INCOME IN KIND	£ s. d.	£ s. d.
Gifts—			*Gifts*—		
to husb.'s kin (*s*) ..		1 0	from husb.'s kin and friend's (*s*) ..		1 0
Soap & kindling used in house		1 7 0	Hausa soap	2 0	
			Kindling collected by wife	1 5 0	
Value of crops consumed by household	4 3 9				1 7 0
Other supplies produced by husb. for household		1 1 8	Market value at harvest of crops produced by wife—		
			307 lbs. grain (*t*) ..	11 6	
			1,219 lbs. roots (*u*) ..	15 1	
			35 lbs. beans & cucurbits	1 11	
			greens, etc... ..	5 3	
					1 13 9
			crops produced by husb. for house—		
			800 lbs. plantains (*v*)	2 0 0	
			coffee seedlings (*w*) ..	10 0	
					2 10 0
			Goods supplied by husband—		
			10 bundles grass ..	2 8	
			500 mud bricks ..	5 0	
			beehive	1 0	
			fowls	6 0	
			palmwine	3 0	
			raffia poles	2 0	
			guineafowls	2 0	
					1 1 8
		£6 13 5			£6 13 5

Estd. expenditure for one year—				Estd. income for one year—			
	£ s. d.	£ s. d.			£ s. d.	£ s. d.	
in cash	5 13 2½			in cash	6 2 3½		
in kind	6 13 5			in kind	6 13 5		
		£12 6 7½				£12 15 8½	

Cash income is 48% of gross income.

Value of wife's contribution is 24% of gross income.

BUDGET 6
Tanye and Biy-Menggu

Tanye of Menggu Compound is a pagan in his thirties and has one wife, Biy, who is also a pagan. She has had one miscarriage and lost one child. The third is about 18 months old and she carries him to the farm each day as she is unable, except occasionally, to find a nursemaid. Biy herself is rather sickly and has no assistance on the farm. Her parents live in the distant village of Nkor and, during the year under review, never visited her. At the end of 1946 she was deprived of two large farms, and cultivated only 0.46 acre from February 1947 to February 1948, as compared with 1.2 acres in the previous farm season. She has one close relative in Kimbaw, her mother's sister (wife of a *kibai*), whom she sometimes visits on a rest day. She also accompanies her husband to the *djangi* at Mbonyaar on Sundays, and sits with the women there although she makes no financial contribution to the meeting. Tanye regularly retails kerosene and salt which he buys in the local market. He looks after the kola trees of his deceased father and, in addition, has charge of some raffia belonging to a *fai* of Meluf. I recorded his budget weekly from the 28th September 1947 to the 28th February 1948, but on two market-days he did not trade (owing to sickness), and on a third occasion he was away from Kimbaw for 4 days and did not return until the late evening of market-day. He belonged to 2 *djangis*.

NOTES

(a) The expenditure on oil was high for a small household but oil was bought from the ' bank ' at Mbonyaar.

(b) Expenditure on salt was considerable but, like palm oil, it was bought about once a month at 1s. 2d. a time from the ' bank ' at Mbonyaar. Tanye was reticent about it, but I think he disposed of some in the market.

(c) Biy's harvest of grain was small. Tanye bought 2 bags of maize for 4s. on the 9th December; two more bags at 4s. 6d. on the 10th January; one for 2s. on the 11th February, and another for 2s. 3d. on the 19th February.

(d) Tanye made a larger profit than usual on the kerosene (see main text) on the 11th February and celebrated by buying khaki cloth for himself, a fowl (2s.), and beef (3d.) for the household. His pagan wife wore only a small strip of baft (cost included in the preceding 7 months), while his small son wore nothing at all.

(e) Tanye had 31s. 5d. in the ' bank ' at Mbonyaar. In October 1947, and again in January 1948, he drew out 20s., repaying the amount later with 1s. 8d. interest each time. On the 12th October 1947, he ' cooked ' *djangi* for 60s. He spent 5s. on refreshments for members. Earlier in the year he had ' cooked ' *djangi* at the Nfoomi Gham's for 40s.

(f) Tanye had 3 beehives and sold honey 4s. 6d. Profits for the year were estimated at 10s.

(g) Ten bundles of thatching grass were kept for repair of 2 huts and store in the compound. The remaining 49 bundles were valued at 3½d. each.

(h) Tanye looked after raffia and disposed of 8s. worth of poles to a local builder. Estimated value of poles kept for home repairs was 2s.

(i) Salt was bought for 24s. (2 bags) and retailed for 26s.

(j) Tanye bought kerosene for £4–16–2 and retailed it in pint bottles for £6–6–8. His profits were larger than usual because he obtained one tin at cost price from me.

(k) Biy was given 4d. by her husband to buy cassava for trade. She made gruel and sold it for 5d.

(l) I have allowed 5s. 10d. for oil; 2s. for salt; 2s. for meat; 6d. for groundnuts for child; and 20s. for staples.

(n) After the death of his first two children, Tanye consulted a diviner when the third child was born and was advised to avoid all contact with his wife's kin until the child could walk. He therefore made no gifts to his affines during the period under survey.

(o) Tanye had a very large grove of plantains and normally he would derive 10s. a year from the sale of the fruit.

(*p*) Small perquisites of palmwine were obtained in return for his work as *ngaaruu* for a *fai*. Some he sold, and some was consumed by him and his friends.

(*q*) Tanye looked after some kola trees and received for his labour a few small nuts.

(*r*) On the basis of his budget recorded for 5 months I estimated that Tanye made approximately 1*s*. 3*d*. a week from retailing salt and kerosene in small quantities. This gives an annual income of 56*s*. 9*d*., but in the year under review it amounted to 67*s*. 6*d*. (See (*j*)).

(*s*) I have one record of food (3*d*.) contributed to feast at the building of a house of a kinsman of Tanye.

(*t*) In September 1947 Biy obtained only 3½ *vegati* of maize and later about 10 lbs. of finger millet. By the end of January she had only a small quantity kept for seed.

(*u*) Biy did not plant sweet potatoes, and had only a small area under *rizga* and yams.

(*v*) Estimated crop was 1,000 lbs. plantains, value 50*s*. Approximately 800 lbs. were consumed by household.

(*w*) Tanye had started a small coffee plantation a year previously.

BUDGET 7

(6th October 1947 to 5th March 1948)

A.—EXPENDITURE AND INCOME IN CASH

EXPENDITURE	£	s.	d.	£	s.	d.
Food—						
bags of maize (*a*) ..	1	1	5			
potatoes			1½			
greens			1			
cassava			8½			
groundnuts		2	7½			
				1	4	11½
salt (*b*)		7	10			
oil		11	10			
meat		5	9			
				1	5	5
Stimulants—						
tobacco (*c*)					3	3
House & farm replace-ments—						
2 pots			1½			
hoe for child ..		1	6			
basket			1			
knife			1			
hoe handle			1			
knitting needles ..			1			
soap		1	2½			
firewood (*d*) ..		3	2½			
				6	4½	
Clothes—						
necklace (*e*) ..						6
School fees—annual—						
for son		12	0			
books, etc.		3	6			
				15	6	
Gifts—						
to husb.'s kin (*f*) ..		4	0			
to wife's kin ..		5	0			
				9	0	
Miscellaneous—						
'interest' (*g*) ..					2	6
hospital card ..						2
Expenditure for 5 months:				**£4**	**7**	**8**

INCOME	£	s.	d.	£	s.	d.
Sales from—						
eggs						2½
Profits from wife's trade—						
cassava gruel (*h*) ..		2	6			
bean balls (*i*) ..			3			
beer (*j*)			1			
					2	10
Profits from tailoring—						
clothes sold (*k*) ..	3	11	6			
sewing		13	9			
				4	5	3
Income for 5 months:				**£4**	**8**	**3½**

Estimated budget from 6th March to 5th October 1947

	£	s.	d.	£	s.	d.
Food (*m*)				2	5	0
House & farm replace-ments					6	0
Clothes (*n*)				3	0	0
Miscellaneous—						
tax		5	0			
bank 'interest' (*o*)..		5	0			
djaŋgi (*p*)		7	6			
gifts to affines (*q*) ..		7	0			
incidental		3	0			
				1	7	6
Expenditure for 7 months:				**£6**	**18**	**6**
Estd. expenditure for year:				**£11**	**6**	**2**

	£	s.	d.	£	s.	d.
Sale of fowls					6	0
Profits from wife's trade ..					3	2
Husband's earnings—						
clothes sold	3	4	6			
sewing	3	4	3			
				6	8	9
Income for 7 months:				**£6**	**17**	**11**
Estd. income for one year				**£11**	**6**	**2½**

BUDGET 7

(March 1947 to March 1948)

B.—ESTIMATED VALUE OF OUTLAY (INCLUDING CONSUMPTION) AND INCOME *IN KIND* FOR ONE YEAR

OUTLAY, ETC., IN KIND	£ s. d.	£ s. d.
Gifts from own supplies—		
to husb.'s kin (*r*) ..	2 0	
to wife's kin (*s*) ..	10 0	
to friends (*t*) ..	1 0	
		13 0
Soap & kindling used by household ..		1 11 0
Work for Mission ..		9 0
Value of crops & other self-produced supplies used by household		6 6 9½

INCOME IN KIND	£ s. d.	£ s. d.
Gifts received—		
from husb.'s kin (*r*)..	2 0	
from wife's kin (*s*) ..	5 0	
from friends (*t*) ..	1 0	
		8 0
Soap from Hausa ..	1 0	
Firewood collected by wife & daughter ..	1 10 0	
		1 11 0
Work at Mission for contribution cards by wife & husb. (*u*) ..		9 0
Fowls	6 0	
500 mudbricks (*v*) ..	5 0	
		11 0
Market value at harvest of crops produced for household by wife & daughter—		
445 lbs. grain (*w*) ..	15 5½	
4,720 lbs. roots (*x*) ..	2 18 1	
110 lbs. beans & cucurbits ..	5 0	
greens, etc.	11 9	
coffee-seedlings ..	5 0	
510 lbs. plantains (*y*)	1 5 6	
		6 0 9½

£8 19 9½   £8 19 9½

Estd. expenditure, etc., for one year—	£ s. d.	£ s. d.
in cash ..	..11 6 2	
in kind ..	.. 8 19 9½	
		£20 5 11½

Estd. income, etc., for one year—	£ s. d.	£ s. d.
in cash ..	..11 6 2½	
in kind ..	.. 8 19 9½	
		£20 6 0

Cash income is 55% of gross income.

Value of wife's contribution is 39% of gross income.

187

BUDGET 7

Nicholas Ngee and Margaret Labam

Nicholas Ngee of Ka Compound is in his forties. Both he and his wife, Margaret Labam, are Roman Catholics, and have a large family of 7 children, the two youngest being twins and aged about 2 years. Margaret is in her thirties and, with the assistance of her daughter (Natasha, aged 14 years), works 2.1 acres. One son (aged 16 years) is at the R.C. school at Shishong, but returns for week-ends and holidays. Nicholas is a tailor and works each day in a small stall in the Hausa market, but occasionally goes to the Mbiami market (5 hours' walk distant) in the hope of augmenting his earnings. He has a bad goitre, is sickly, and is unable to give his wife much assistance on the farm. She even looks after the tiny coffee-plantation started in March 1947. She and Natasha earn a few shillings a year from petty trade in cooked foodstuffs, but the profits are devoted to the purchase of greens, groundnuts, baskets, and odd trinkets. Nicholas belongs to two *djaŋgis*—one at Mbonyaar and one in his own compound. He also contributes to the Mbonyaar ' bank '. During the period, 6th October 1947 to 5th March 1948, there were three occasions when he did not attend the market; but quite apart from this his earnings were small, compared with the earlier part of the year, because custom falls off during the dry season. I recorded the budgets of Margaret and Nicholas during the period mentioned above; and have given an estimate of expenditure and income for the preceding 7 months.

NOTES

(a) The yield of maize in September 1947 was very poor, and by the end of January only a little was left for seed (see main text). From the 7th November Nicholas bought, on an average, one bag of hulled maize a week.

(b) The expenditure on salt and oil was relatively high but Nicholas sent some of these commodities to his wife's kin.

(c) Nicholas smoked while sewing in the market. His expenditure on tobacco earlier in the year, however, was less.

(d) The mudbrick house was large and draughty and small bundles of firewood were purchased for heating.

(e) Margaret usually processed food for trade but the selling was done by Natasha, the daughter, who was sometimes allowed to keep part of the money. She bought a necklace and knitting needles. Her father gave her an old sock and, by unravelling the wool, she knitted a skimpy sweater!

At Christmas in 1947 Nicholas gave his wife a dress worth 21s. and a headtie (5s. 6d.). Natasha received a dress worth 6s., and each of the sons received a pair of shorts, worth 2s. Total value 38s. 6d., but the cloth had been bought early in 1947 and involved no cash outlay at the time.

(f) On the 15th November Nicholas bought 2 fowls (1s. 6d. each) and 2 calabashes of palmwine at 6d. each and presented them to the new sub-lineage head. His expenses to his own kin were thus heavier than normally. The amount expended on gifts to wife's kin was difficult to estimate. Nicholas said that in one year he gave salt and oil to the value of 14s., but about 8s. worth of this was drawn from household supplies, previously purchased at Mbonyaar. I have estimated a cash outlay of 3s. for the 5 months. In addition he spent 1s. on palmwine every two months for his affines.

(g) Nicholas belonged to Mbonyaar ' bank ' and on the 7th October, and again on the 27th January, he drew out 30s. He paid 2s. 6d. interest when he returned the first amount after 2 months.

(h) Margaret bought small quantities of cassava at a total cost of 4s. She made gruel and sold it for 6s. 6d.

(i) Margaret bought dwarf beans for 1s. 6d., made bean balls, and sold them for 1s. 9d.

(j) Margaret bought maize (3d.), brewed beer and sold it for 4d.

(k) During this five month period when I recorded his budget, Nicholas bought cloth to the value of 61s. 9d. During this same period he also ' cooked ' the Ka *djaŋgi* for 29s., and

188

drew out sums from the bank to meet this heavy expenditure. From his own budget and his statements about earnings, I estimated that he made on an average 3s. a week profit on the cloth made into garments. In addition he earned about 1s. 9d. a week from sewing for people who provided their own cloth.

(m) I have allowed 20s. for cost of staples, and 25s. for oil, salt, meat and groundnuts.

(n) See (e) above. In addition to the clothes mentioned, Nicholas also provided his schoolboy son with shorts and a shirt (6s. 6d.). I have allowed an expenditure of 15s. for clothes for himself.

(o) On the 22nd April, and also on the 17th June 1947, Nicholas drew out 30s. from the bank, and paid a total of 5s. interest.

(p) At the beginning of May 1947 Nicholas ' cooked ' the Mbonyaar djaŋgi for £4, and provided wine and beer to the value of 5s. The remaining 2s. 6d. should have been included in the budget for the last 5 months when he ' cooked ' the Ka djaŋgi.

(q) See (b) and (f) above.

(r) When /e-o-Ka was installed as sub-lineage head, Margaret cooked extra food to the value of 9d. for the guests. On another occasion she gave cocoyam (3d.) to the wives of her husband's kinsman, who was having a house built. I have allowed an outlay in kind to the amount of 2s. for the whole year; and a similar amount for income in kind. She was given a hoe-handle by Alphonse who lived in the coupound.

(s) In addition to about 8s. worth of salt and oil from household supplies, Margaret and Nicholas estimated that they gave food to the value of about 2s. a year to Margaret's kin when they visited Kimbaw. But, on the other hand, Margaret also received gifts from her relatives.

(t) Margaret was given a farmbag (9d.) at Christmas, and I have allowed another 3d. for odd gifts.

(u) Margaret and her husband worked for short periods at the Mission in order to make the payment for their contribution cards.

(v) At the end of 1946, Nicholas had built a sun-dried mudbrick house for his family, so he had no outlay for repairs during 1947. In his spare time he made a few bricks and said he might sell them later.

(w) In September, 1947, Margaret harvested only 4½ vegati of maize; and in January, 1948, only ¾ kegati of finger millet.

(x) Margaret's yam harvest at the end of 1946 was diseased, so she did not plant any yams in February, 1947.

(y) Margaret and Natasha weeded a small grove of plantains, but there was no surplus of fruit for sale. In addition, Margaret tended a few coffee plants which had been set about March, 1947.

BUDGET 8
(28th September 1947 to 5th March 1948)
A.—EXPENDITURE AND INCOME IN CASH

EXPENDITURE

	£ s. d.	£ s. d.
Food—		
bags of maize (a) ..	10 8	
maize flour (b) ..	1 0	
beans	2 8½	
potatoes ..	1 7	
okra	1	
groundnuts	1 5½	
		17 6
salt	7 8	
oil	9 11½	
meat	7 1	
		1 4 8½
Stimulants—		
wine for Christmas..		6
House & farm replacements—		
2 pots	1 1	
millet mat ..	6	
3 baskets ..	1 6	
cowpea seed ..	2	
soap	1 7	
firewood ..	3	
		5 1
Clothes for son (c) ..		2 6
Church dues—		
contribution cards ..	4 6	
collection	2	
		4 8
School fees—		
for son (d)	6 0	
books, etc. ..	1½	
		6 1½
Miscellaneous—		
hospital card ..	2	
' interest ' (e) ..	2 6	
djaŋgi wine (f) ..	3 0	
		5 8
Gifts—		
to wife's kin (g) ..	5 6	
to husb.'s kin (h) ..	6	
		6 0
Expenditure for 5 months:		**£3 12 9**

INCOME

	£ s. d.	£ s. d.
Sales of—		
plantains	3 4½	
pineapples (i) ..	5	
eggs	4	
fowl	1 6	
		5 7½
Profits from wife's trade—		
cassava (j)	3	
bean-balls (k) ..	1	
		4
Profits from—		
clothes sold (l) ..	2 18 0	
sewing (m)	1 8 10	
		4 6 10
Gifts—		
from wife's kin (g) ..	1 2	
from friends (h) ..	½	
		1 2½
Income for 5 months :		**£4 14 0**

Estimated budget from 6th March to 27th September 1947

	£ s. d.	£ s. d.
Food (n)		1 12 0
House & farm replacements (o)		6 6
Clothes (p)		3 0 0
Church dues		4 9
School fees, etc. ..		7 0
Miscellaneous—		
tax	5 0	
interest (q)	5 0	
djaŋgi wine (r) ..	11 0	
incidental ..	10 0	
		1 11 0
Gifts—		
to wife's kin (s) ..		7 0
to husb.'s kin ..		1 0
Expenditure for 7 months:		**£7 9 3**

	£ s. d.	£ s. d.
Sales of—		
plantains	4 7½	
pineapples	7	
pears	1 0	
fowls	4 6	
coffee (t)	7 6	
		18 2½
Wife's trade		6
Profits from—		
clothes sold ..	3 16 6	
sewing (u)	2 4 6	
		6 1 0
Gifts—		
from wife's kin ..		1 0
from husb.'s kin ..		1 0
Income for 7 months:		**£7 1 8½**

	£ s. d.	£ s. d.
Estimated expenditure for one year ..	3 12 9	
	7 9 3	
		£11 2 0

	£ s. d.	£ s. d.
Estimated income for one year ..	4 14 0	
	7 1 8½	
		£11 15 8½

BUDGET 8

(March 1947 to March 1948)

B.—ESTIMATED VALUE OF OUTLAY (INCLUDING CONSUMPTION)
AND INCOME *IN KIND* FOR ONE YEAR

OUTLAY, ETC., IN KIND

	£ s. d.	£ s. d.
Gifts from own supplies—		
to wife's kin (*v*) ..	2 6	
to husb.'s kin and others (*w*) ..	6 0	
		8 6
Soap & kindling used in household		1 9 6
Value of crops & other self-produced supplies kept for household		8 11 5

INCOME IN KIND

	£ s. d.	£ s. d.
Gifts received—		
from wife's kin (*v*) ..	2 6	
from husb.'s kin & others (*w*) ..	3 0	
		5 6
Hausa soap	2 0	
Firewood collected—		
by wife ..	1 5 0	
by husband ..	2 6	
		1 9 6
Fowls		6 0
Market value at harvest of crops produced by wife—		
1,083 lbs. grain (*x*)..	1 15 6	
6,086 lbs. roots (*y*) ..	4 0 0	
90 lbs. beans & cucurbits	3 4	
greens, etc.	11 1	
630 lbs. plantains (*z*)	1 11 0	
		8 0 11
produced by husband—		
130 lbs. plantains ..		7 6

	£10 9 5		£10 9 5

	£ s. d. £ s. d.		£ s. d. £ s. d.
Estd. expenditure for one year—		Estd. income for one year—	
in cash 11 2 0		in cash 11 15 8½	
in kind 10 9 5		in kind 10 9 5	
£21 11 5		£22 5 1½	

Cash income is 52% of gross income.

Value of wife's contribution is 44% of the gross income.

BUDGET 8

Thomas Kintarir and Yeduda Wirsungnin

Thomas Kintarir of Mbonyaar Compound is a Roman Catholic and is in his early forties. He has four young children, and the eldest son attends the Mission school during the day but sleeps at home. Yeduda Wirsungnin, his wife, is in her early thirties and cultivates a total holding of 1.8 acres without assistance, except for some help from her mother-in-law at the harvest of cereals. In addition, she weeds most of the plantains (retaining the right to dispose of the fruit), and looks after the small coffee-plantation belonging to her husband. She occasionally sells plantains and pineapples; more rarely she buys beans and cassava to cook and retail in the market. Her earnings are negligible.

Thomas formerly headloaded kolas to Yola, but a few years ago he became a tailor. During my stay in Kimbaw he sewed in his own house in the compound. It was a wattle and daub structure, but he had lined the walls with pith matting and furnished it with tables and chairs. It served also as a meeting-house for the men when they assembled for *djangi* on Sundays. On market-day Thomas had a small shelter in the market-place where he treadled his machine. He gave very little assistance with the clearing of farms, but sometimes brought in some kindling for the household. He belonged to the *djangis* of Ka and Mbonyaar. To the latter he also contributed small sums on behalf of his wife, and he was a member of the ' bank '. I recorded his budget for 5 months (i.e. 20½ Nsaw weeks). The budget for the preceding 7 months has been calculated on the basis of the later expenditure and income, and also from general statements made by Thomas in regard to his earnings.

NOTES

(a) Yeduda still had 3 *vegati* maize and 5¾ *vegati* millet at the end of January, 1948, but Thomas, with an eye to eking out supplies, occasionally bought bags of maize during the dry season when they were cheap.

(b) Yeduda worked long hours on the farm and, to conserve her energy, she sometimes used flour and beans bought by her husband instead of grinding corn.

(c) During this period Thomas did not buy clothes for his wife or himself.

(d) The fees covered tuition for 6 months. The cost of books for the year has been entered in the preceding 7 months.

(e) Thomas, on the 7th October and again on the 27th January, 1948, took out 30s. from the Mbonyaar ' bank ', where he had 31s. 5d. in savings. He repaid the first amount after two months with 2s. 6d. interest.

(f) Thomas usually paid in 6d. a week in his wife's name to the Mbonyaar *djangi*. In October 1947, she ' cooked ' *djangi*, but Thomas took the money and provided wine and beer for members at outlay of 3s.

(g) In November Yeduda attended the marriage of a kinswoman. She took *fufu* (3d.), and Thomas also gave her 3s. in cash (for the bride) and meat worth 2s. 6d. Yeduda was presented with 1s. 2d. by the groom and his kin, and she bought with it 2 pots for 8d. and a wash bowl (5d.).

(h) Thomas bought a calabash of palmwine (6d.) for his brother, Maurice, who ' cooked ' *djangi*. The halfpenny income was a gift to Yeduda's daughter, who spent it on ground-nuts after having first asked Yeduda's permission.

(i) Note that the pineapples and plantains came from Yeduda's own plantation and that she not only sold them but kept the money for further trade and the purchase of relishes.

(j) Yeduda several times bought small amounts of cassava at a total value of 7½d. As she had no time and patience to make gruel, she merely boiled them and sold them for 10½d.

(k) Yeduda bought beans and made bean-balls. Her outlay was 7½d. and her earnings 8½d.

(l) During this period Thomas was selling clothes made from cloth bought earlier in the year. He purchased the cloth at a total outlay of 37s. 6d. From his own statements and actual earnings I estimated that he obtained, on an average, 3s. profit a week during the year.

192

(*m*) Customers sometimes provided their own cloth for Thomas to make up into garments. He charged from 7*d*. to 1*s*. a garment according to type and size. He made on an average 1*s*. 9*d*. a week. These profits (see also footnote (*l*) above) are exclusive of the cost of machine maintenance,—e.g. oil (2*s*.), thread and needles (2*s*.). He said a reel of thread lasted about 1½ to 2 Nsaw weeks and cost him about 5*s*. to 6*s*. a year.

(*n*) I have allowed 10*s*. for staples; 5*s*. for salt; 12*s*. for oil; and 5*s*. for meat. Thomas obtained salt and oil from the Mbonyaar ' bank '.

(*o*) I have allowed 2*s*. for soap, and the balance for tools and utensils.

(*p*) I have allowed 25*s*. for dress and headtie for wife; 20*s*. for clothes for husband; and 15*s*. for Munshi cloth, shorts and shirts for the 3 eldest children. The youngest wore nothing at all.

(*q*) Thomas, in April, 1947, and again in June, withdrew 30*s*. from the ' bank ' and repaid the sums with 5*s*. interest.

(*r*) Thomas ' cooked ' the Ka *djaŋgi* early in September, 1947, for 32*s*. and provided wine and beer to the value of 3*s*. 6*d*. Earlier he had ' cooked ' the Mbonyaar *djaŋgi* for approximately £4. I am not sure of the exact amount but his weekly contributions were similar to those of Nicholas Ngee (see budget No. 7). He spent 7*s*. 6*d*. on beer and wine.

(*s*) Thomas, like most Nsaw men, was vague about the exact value of gifts to affines over a year. But, with his income, it would be from 10*s*. to 15*s*. a year. I have allowed 12*s*. 6*d*.

(*t*) Thomas had ¼ acre under coffee, but Yeduda did most of the weeding and the yield was poor.

(*u*) Estimate based on recorded earnings for the later period. See footnote (*m*) above.

(*v*) The only record which I made of a gift of food to Yeduda's kin in the last 5 months is a basket of *fufu* (3*d*.) for the marriage in November. But from time to time her mother's sister, who was a *wiinto*, visited the compound and was given food. During this same period, Yeduda was given yams worth 4*d*. by the *wiinto*, and a basket of long yams (*viruŋ*) worth about 6*d*. by her own mother.

(*w*) During the last 5 months of the year Yeduda twice provided *fufu* for a house-building feast; at Christmas she gave about 5*d*. worth of *fufu* to members of the compound, and Thomas gave beer (4*d*.). When the child of his brother, Maurice, was ill, Thomas sent meat (6*d*.) from his own supplies. I think he also gave a fowl to the daughters of his ' brother ', Lole, when they returned from Nigeria.

(*x*) Yeduda could not remember exactly how many *vegati* of maize she harvested but, on the basis of the size of her farm as well as the quantity of grain still in store by the end of January, I estimated there were about 7 *vegati*. I was present for the millet harvest and counted and weighed the baskets. There were 5¾ *vegati*.

(*y*) Yeduda was an indefatigable worker and, unlike most women working single-handed, she had 3 plots (total 842 sq. yards) under *rizga*.

(*z*) I estimated a total harvest of 770 lbs. of plantains from Yeduda's own groves, but of this about 140 lbs. would be sold during the year. The plantains tended by Thomas were consumed by the household and distinguished from those belonging to Yeduda.

BUDGET 9
(6th October 1947 to 5th March 1948)
A.—EXPENDITURE AND INCOME IN CASH

EXPENDITURE

	£ s. d.	£ s. d.
Food—		
bags of maize (a) ..	12 6	
greens, etc. (b) ..	3 0	
groundnuts	3 1½	
		18 7½
salt (c)	8 0	
oil	11 5	
meat	11 4	
		1 10 9
Stimulants—		
beer		7
House & farm replacements—		
cowpea seed ..	4	
3 calabashes ..	1 0¼	
blanket	18 0	
soap	2	
		19 6¼
Clothes—		
dress for wife (d) ..	17 6	
wrap for daughter ..	4 0	
cloth for son ..	3 6	
cloth for husb. ..	4 9	
		1 9 9
Tools—		
file, etc. (e)	9 7½	
solder (f)	6 0	
		15 7½
Miscellaneous—		
worm powder ..	1 0	
'interest' (g) ..	3 4	
		4 4
Gifts—		
to husb.'s kin (h) ..	3 0	
to wife's mother (hh)	3	
to friends	2 3	
		5 9
Expenditure for 5 months:		**£6 4 11½**

INCOME

	£ s. d.	£ s. d.
Sales of—		
eggs	6	
pineapples	2	
		8
Profits from wife's trade—		
cassava (i)	1 1½	
beer (j)	1 4	
		2 5½
Husband's earnings—		
gunpowder (k) ..	8 6	
smithing (l) ..	1 15 10	
		2 4 4
Income for 5 months:		**£2 7 5½**

Estimated budget from 6th March to 6th October 1947

EXPENDITURE

	£ s. d.	£ s. d.
Food (m)		1 3 6
House & farm replacements		6 6
Clothes— for husband ..		10 0
Miscellaneous—		
tax	5 0	
'interest' (n) ..	3 4	
djangi wine (o) ..	11 6	
church dues (p) ..	4 6	
incidental	5 0	
gifts	2 0	
		1 11 4
Expenditure for 7 months:		**£3 11 4**
Estd. expenditure for one year		**£9 16 3½**

INCOME

	£ s. d.	£ s. d.
Sales of—		
fowls	6 0	
pineapples	6	
		6 6
Profits from— wife's trade		5 7
Husband's profits—		
gunpowder	11 6	
smithing	7 4 2	
		7 15 8
Income for 7 months:		**£8 7 9**
Estd. income for one year		**£10 15 2½**

BUDGET 9

(March 1947 to March 1948)

B.—ESTIMATED VALUE OF OUTLAY (INCLUDING CONSUMPTION) AND INCOME *IN KIND* FOR ONE YEAR

OUTLAY, ETC., IN KIND	£	s.	d.	£	s.	d.	INCOME IN KIND	£	s.	d.	£	s.	d.
Gifts from own supplies—							*Gifts received—*						
to husb.'s kin (q) ..		4	6				from husb.'s kin (q)		4	6			
to wife's mother (r)..		3	0				from wife's mo. (r) ..		3	0			
to friends (s) ..		2	0				from friends (s) ..		2	0			
					9	6						9	6
Soap & kindling used by household ..				1	12	0	Soap from Hausa ..		2	0			
							Kindling collected by						
Value of crops & other self-produced supplies used by household				6	7	9	wife & daughter ..	1	5	0			
							by husband ..		5	0			
											1	12	0
							Work at mission for contr. cards of husb. & wife for 6 months		4	6			
							hoe-handles made by husband (t) ..			2			
							Fowls		6	0			
												10	8
							Market value at harvest of crops produced by wife and daughter—						
							595 lbs. grain (u) ..	1	0	0			
							4,719 lbs. roots (v) ..	3	1	9			
							110 lbs. beans & cucurbits		5	0			
							greens, etc.		11	4			
							340 lbs. plantains ..		19	0			
											5	17	1
				£8	9	3					£8	9	3

	£	s.	d.	£	s.	d.		£	s.	d.	£	s.	d.
Estd. expenditure for one year—							Estd. income for one year—						
in cash		9	16	3½			in cash		10	15	2½		
in kind		8	9	3			in kind		8	9	3		
				£18	5	6½					£19	4	5½

Cash income is 56% of gross income.

Value of wife's contribution is 43% of gross income.

BUDGET 9

Alphonse Fannso and Clara Yaya

Alphonse Fannso of Ka compound is a Roman Catholic as is also his wife, Clara Yaya, and their five children. The eldest daughter Julia, aged about 16 years, is a child of Clara's first marriage. The first husband had died and, as his kin did not look after her, Clara left their compound and married Alphonse despite their opposition. She is thus a *wiiy-o-tʃɛmin* and Alphonse has no commitments to her kin. The children born to Alphonse are all much younger than Julia, and one is a babe in arms.

Clara, with the assistance of Julia, farmed 2.1 acres but the maize and millet harvests for 1947 were poor, so the outlay on staples was heavier than normally. Alphonse, during the weeks beginning 18th January and 11th February, gave considerable help to his wife in clearing new plots. Clara occasionally made cassava gruel for Julia to sell in the market. Just before the end of my tour she began to brew beer for sale in order to augment the family income.

Alphonse was a smith who repaired guns, pots, and pans, and sold gunpowder as a side-line. He had a rough shelter near the market where he worked but, during the 5 months when I kept his budget, he was ill with fever early in December, and again from the 25th December to the 6th January. There were also two weeks (30th October and 7th November) when I did not see him, so his budget was less complete than that of the other men.

NOTES

(a) Clara's harvest of maize and millet was poor and, by the end of January, she had only ½ *kegati* maize and 2 *vegati* millet for the household. Between the 1st December and the 11th February Alphonse bought 6 bags of hulled maize.

(b) The expenditure on relishes was heavy but, while at Mbiami market, Alphonse bought a bag of dried okra for 2s., as greens on the farm were scarce.

(c) Alphonse obtained salt about once a month from the Mbonyaar ' bank ', and it is probable that he sold some and gave a little away to his wife's mother who was in the leper settlement at Kimbaw.

(d) Just before Christmas Alphonse bought a dress for 12s. for his wife; and at Christmas he bought her a headtie (4s. 6d.); and in the New Year a Munshi cloth for 1s.

(e) At different times Alphonse bought a stool (2½d.) for use while working; a tool basket (3d.); a second-hand file (4s.), and a fretsaw (5s. 2d.).

(f) He bought 1s. worth of solder; and later a boy-scout buckle for 5s. which he said he would smelt down.

(g) Alphonse had 31s. 5d. in savings in the Mbonyaar ' bank '. On the 7th October, and again on the 27th January, he drew out 20s., and paid a total of 3s. 4d. interest.

(h) When a sub-lineage head was installed in the compound, Alphonse provided salt, oil, etc., to the value of 3s. See (q) below.

(hh) Owing to the fact his wife Clara was a *wiiy-o-tʃɛmin*, Alphonse did not make gifts to his father-in-law; but, from time to time, he gave his mother-in-law salt and oil from household supplies. During the period he bought 6d. worth of oil specially for her. In addition he gave two parcels of salt to friends.

(i) Clara occasionally bought small amounts of raw cassava for 2s. 0½d. and cooked cassava gruel which she retailed for 3s. 2d.

(j) Clara was given 5s. by Alphonse to buy maize for beer, which she sold for 6s. 4d.

(k) Alphonse bought gunpowder by the cigarette-cup at 4s. 6d., and estimated that he made 6d. profit by retailing it in egg-cups at 6d. each. On one occasion he spent 24s. on gunpowder; but by March, 1948, had sold only 8s. 6d. worth. He made about 20s. profit per year.

(l) Alphonse made approximately 4s. a week from the repair of pots, pans, hoes, etc.,—his largest earnings being derived from the repair of dane guns, which brought him in about

196

5s. a-piece. I estimated that he made about £9 a year from his craft. The period during which I personally recorded his budget was not typical, as there were interruptions for the ceremonies connected with the succession of a sub-lineage head, Christmas, farm clearing, and illness.

(m) I have allowed 10s. 6d. for salt and oil; 2s. for meat; 1s. for groundnuts; and 10s. for staples. Note that Clara had better farm land. than the wife of Nicholas Ngee of the same compound.

(n) On two occasions Alphonse withdrew 20s. from the bank.

(o) Alphonse 'cooked' the Ka *djaŋgi* for 29s. and provided 5 calabashes of wine (2s. 6d.), and 2 of beer (1s.). The remaining 8s. should really be included in the succeeding 5 months when he provided 4 calabashes of wine (2s.) and 12 calabashes of beer (6s.) for the Mbonyaar *djaŋgi*, which he 'cooked' for £3. This amount enabled him to meet expenses incurred at the time. He also withdrew savings from the bank.

(p) Clara paid for her contribution card by profits from trade.

(q) When the sub-lineage head was installed, Alphonse gave one of his own fowls (1s. 6d.), 2 sticks of firewood (2s.), and food. The firewood was originally given to him by a kinsman at Ketiwum village.

(r) Clara took food, salt, and oil to her mother at the leper camp. She also looked after her mother's small farm at Shisong and took the produce to her, though she retained a portion for herself.

(s) I have allowed 2s. for food given to friends, especially those at Mbonyaar. On one occasion Clara gave Melalia honey (3d.) and a pineapple.

(t) Fai-o-Mbonyaar had a tree cut down for timber for a bridge over Ro-Kimbaw. The helpers received some of the branches, and Alphonse made two-hoe-handles.

(u) Clara harvested 5 *vegati* of maize in September and later, in January, 2 *vegati* of finger millet.

(v) Clara was unsuccessful with her trifoliate yams in 1946 and did not plant any in 1947. But in 1948, she prepared a patch. She cultivated, with the help of her daughter, relatively large areas under *rizga* and sweet potatoes.

BUDGET 10
(6th October 1947 to 5th March 1948)
A.—EXPENDITURE AND INCOME IN CASH

EXPENDITURE	£ s. d.	£ s. d.	INCOME	£ s. d.	£ s. d.
Food—			*Sales of*—		
okra & other relishes			plantains (g) ..	4 1½	
(a)	9		pears	2 0	
groundnuts	7		oranges	1 0	
		1 4	sugar cane	4	
meat	7 1				7 5¼
oil	8 0				
salt	5 10		coffee (h)		10 0
		1 0 11			
House & farm replace-			*Wife's trade profits*—		
ments—			cassava gruel (i) ..		2
wool kindling for flint	1				
cowpea seed ..	10½		Husband's wages as		
4 baskets	1 0½		caretaker (j) ..		6 10 0
broom	1				
food calabash ..	7				
pot	2				
kerosene tin (b) ..	3 0				
soap	3¼				
		6 1½			
Clothes—					
necklace (c) ..	1 0				
cloth for son ..	1 6				
		2 6			
Church dues—					
contribution cards ..		4 6			
Miscellaneous—					
hospital cards &					
medicine	5				
'interest' (d) ..	2 1				
djaŋgi wine (e) ..	3 0				
		5 6			
Gifts—					
to wife's kin (f) ..		4 6½			
Expenditure for 5 months:		**£2 5 5**	**Income for 5 months:**		**£7 7 7¼**

Estimated budget from 5th March to 5th October 1947

	£ s. d.	£ s. d.		£ s. d.	£ s. d.
Food (k)	1 9 0		*Sales of*—		
House & farm replace-			plantains	5 6	
ments (l)	7 4		pears	1 0	
Clothes (m)	2 10 0		oranges	1 0	
Church dues	4 6				7 6
Miscellaneous—					
tax	5 0		Fowls		6 0
'interest' (n) ..	2 8				
djaŋgi wine (o) ..	6 0		Wages for 7 months ..		9 2 0
incidental	10 0				
		1 3 8	Wife's trade profits ..		6
Gifts—					
to wife's kin (p) ..	10 0				
to husb.'s kin ..	5 0				
		15 0			
Estd. expenditure for 7 months:		**£6 9 6**	**Estd. income for 7 months:**		**£9 16 0**
Estd. income for one year:		**£8 14 11**	**Estd. income for one year:**		**£17 3 7¼**

BUDGET 10

(March 1947 to March 1948)

B.—ESTIMATED VALUE OF OUTLAY (INCLUDING CONSUMPTION) AND INCOME *IN KIND* FOR ONE YEAR

OUTLAY, ETC., IN KIND	£ s. d.	£ s. d.		INCOME IN KIND	£ s. d.	£ s. d.
Gifts from own supplies—				*Gifts received—*		
to wife's kin (*q*) ..	2 6			from wife's kin (*q*) ..	2 6	
to husb.'s kin & friends (*r*) ..	3 0			from husb.'s kin & friends (*r*) ,.	3 0	
		5 6				5 6
Soap & kindling used by household ..		1 12 0		Soap from Hausa ..	2 0	
				Kindling collected—		
Value of crops & other self-produced supplies kept for household		9 16 10		by wife	1 0 0	
				by husband .,	10 0	
						1 12 0
				Fowls		6 0
				Market value at harvest of crops produced by wife—		
				2,167 lbs. grain (*s*) ..	3 11 3	
				5,436 lbs. roots ..	3 13 4	
				120 lbs. beans & cucurbits	5 10	
				450 lbs. plantains (*t*)	1 2 6	
				greens, etc.	17 11	
						9 10 10
		£11 14 4				£11 14 4·

	£ s. d.	£ s. d.			£ s. d.	£ s. d.
Estd. expenditure for one year—				Estd. income for one year—		
in cash ..	.. 8 14 11			in cash ..	..17 3 7½	
in kind ..	..11 14 4			in kind ..	..11 14 4	
		£20 9 3				£28 17 11½

Cash income is 59% of gross income.

Value of wife's contribution is 39% of gross income.

199

BUDGET 10

Maurice Nyingka and Audelia-Kilar

Maurice was a man of Mbonyaar Compound who was a Roman Catholic and was in his late thirties. He was literate and kept the accounts for the 'bank' and *djaŋgi*. He had two small children, the younger being about 2 years' old. His wife, Audelia-Kilar, was in her twenties and an indefatigable worker. With the assistance of her mother (whom she assisted in return) she farmed 3.9 acres, most of the plots being within 30 minutes' walking distance of the compound. She tended plantains, pine-apples, pear and orange trees, and sold a portion of the produce. Only once during the 5 months (when I was recording the budget) did she traffic in cooked foods. She preferred to give her time to the farm.

Maurice was a caretaker of the Government Resthouse at Kikai and received 26s. a month. Apart from tending a small coffee-plantation, he rarely assisted his wife on the farm. He usually returned late in the evening from Kikai, and was far more reticent than the other men about his expenses and income. His wife was under the impression that he earned only a few shillings a week; and, on more than one occasion, said he had no money! He himself would often say towards the end of the month that he lacked cash and he would not admit he had savings. He belonged to two *djaŋgis* and contributed to the 'bank'. I attempted to record his budget for 5 months, but for two weeks I did not see him at all, and his records were less complete than those of other men. His wife had, by Nsaw standards, a good wardrobe and the family used a relatively large quantity of salt, oil, and meat, compared with the rest of the Compound.

NOTES

(a) Audelia had exceptionally large farm plots and there was no need for her husband to buy extra foodstuffs. Ninepence was expended on okra (2d.), davadava (2d.), and egusi (5d.).

(b) Maurice bought an empty kerosene tin for his wife to use as a water container.

(c) Audelia bought the necklace for herself from her trade earnings.

(d) Maurice had 25s. in the Mbonyaar 'bank'. In October, and again in January, he withdrew 25s. He repaid the first amount and 2s. 1d. interest.

(e) Maurice belonged to the monthly *djaŋgi* which he 'cooked' for 55s. He spent 3s. on wine, and his wife brewed beer to the value of 1s. from her own maize.

(f) Maurice bought his wife's mother a headtie (4s. 6d.) and, on a later occasion, tobacco (½d.). His cash expenditure was probably higher but I have no other records.

(g) Audelia tended plantains and other fruit trees, disposed of the produce, and kept the money for relishes, trinkets, and baskets.

(h) Maurice earned 10s. from the sale of 30 lbs. of coffee berries. In March, 1948, he had a 60 lb. case of berries for which he hoped to obtain 20s., less 2s. for transport.

(i) Audelia bought cassava (4d.) and made gruel, which she sold for 6d. In my records there is also a purchase of 4d. worth of cassava which she said she would make into gruel, but the sale is not in my notes and I have omitted the purchase.

(j) Maurice earned 26s. a month.

(k) I have allowed 10s. for oil; 6s. for salt; 5s. for meat; but it is probable expenditure was higher on these items. My estimates have been based on the recorded budget and also the expenses of other men.

(l) I have allowed 1s. 8d. for purchase of thatching grass for roof repairs, as Maurice's regular employment did not give him time to collect grass in the dry season.

(m) Cloth and headties for Audelia would cost 30s., while clothes for Maurice and the small child would amount to another 20s.

(n) During the rains Maurice withdrew, in April, 12s. from the 'bank'; and 20s. in June. Interest amounted to 2s. 8d.

200

(*o*) Maurice belonged to the Mbonyaar *djaŋgi* and I estimated that he ' cooked ' it for 60s. Through an oversight on my part I did not get the exact amount, but I have used his weekly payments as a guide.

(*p*) Maurice as a regular wage-earner would have more demands made upon him by his affines than most men.

(*q*) In the last period Audelia gave cooked food, worth 10*d*., to her mother. Another 9*d*. worth of food was for the marriage feast of a kinswoman.

(*r*) Maurice gave one of his own fowls to his brother's daughter when she returned from Nigeria. On other occasions his wife gave gifts of food worth 3½*d*. Maurice received meat (6*d*.) from his half-brother, Thomas; and meat (1½*d*.) from his half-brother, Lole.

(*s*) In September, 1947, Audelia reaped 15 *vegati* of maize; in January, she harvested 10½ *vegati* of finger millet.

(*t*) I estimated that Audelia obtained 650 lbs. plantains from her groves, but about 200 lbs. were sold per annum as she did not have to rely on the fruit as a supplement to the larder in the hungry period.

BUDGET 11

(24th February 1947 to 27th February 1948)

A.—EXPENDITURE AND INCOME IN CASH

EXPENDITURE	£	s.	d.	£	s.	d.
Food—						
groundnuts			11½			
meat (a)		2	5			
oil (b)		7	7.			
salt (c)			2			
					11	1½
House & farm replacements—						
2 pots			10			
3 knives			3			
farm bag			6			
3 stools			9			
2 hoes for daughters (d)		3	6			
3 baskets			7½			
razor blade			1			
raffia storebin ..		1	6			
cowpea seed ..			6			
					8	6½
Ornaments—						
camwood (e) ..			3			
necklace (f) ..			3			
						6
Miscellaneous—						
hospital card ..						2
Gifts—						
shirt to daughter's son		3	0			
soap to daughter ..			3			
salt for sister (g) ..			6			
pot stand for friend (h)			6			
					4	3

INCOME	£	s.	d.	£	s.	d.
Sales of—						
plantains		8	10			
beans (l)			9			
sweet potatoes ..			1			
					9	8
Miscellaneous—						
cash in hand (Feb., 1947) (m) ..					5	0
Gifts—						
from son-in-law (i)..		1	0			
from friends (j) ..		8	8			
at marriages (k) ..		1	5			
					11	1

	£	s.	d.
Expenditure for one year:	£1	4	7
Income for one year:	£1	5	9

BUDGET 11

(February 1947 to February 1948)

B.—ESTIMATED VALUE OF OUTLAY (INCLUDING CONSUMPTION) AND INCOME *IN KIND* FOR ONE YEAR

OUTLAY, ETC., IN KIND	£ s. d.	£ s. d.	INCOME IN KIND	£ s. d.	£ s. d.
Gifts from own supplies—			*Gifts received—*		
Ceremonial—			*Ceremonial—*		
flour sent to 3 marriages (*n*)	2 4		food, wine, at 3 marriages (*n*) ..	1 6	
flour to sister's daughter who had a child (*o*) ..	9		beans from sister's daughter (*o*) ..	3	
flour to palace when *Fon's* wife had twins (*p*)	1½		salt & oil from palace (*p*)	6	
flour to husb.'s br. wife for *mfu* (*q*) ..	5		food & wine at *mfu* (*q*)	2	
					2 5
beer & food to friends at Xmas (*r*) ..	8½		*Ordinary—*		
		4 4	from daughter—		
			fufu, kolas, camwood (*s*)	4	
Ordinary—			camwood, tobacco, meat, groundnuts, farm bag (*t*) ..	1 2¼	
to daughter in October (*s*)	1 7½				1 6¼
food to sick daughter (*t*)	8		meat, salt, oil from husband (*v*) ..	7 2	
food & beer for assistants clearing farm & harvesting guinea corn (*u*) ..	1 8½		salt, meat, soap, etc., from friends ..	2 0	
		4 0	firewood from husb. brother's son ..	4	
eggs, fowl to friends		2 3	Soap from Hausa ..	2 0	
			Kindling collected by Kengeran & ch...	1 10 0	
Soap & firewood used by household ..		1 12 0			1 12 0
			Fowls		7 6
Value of crops & other self-produced supplies kept for household		14 14 1½	Market value at harvest of crops produced by Kengeran & 2 daughters—		
			2,465 lbs. grain (*w*)	4 3 0	
			11,306 lbs. roots (*x*)	7 15 6	
		£16 16 8½	120 lbs. beans & cucurbits (*y*) ..	5 1	
			greens, etc.	19 0	
	£ s. d.	£ s. d.	530 lbs. plantains (*z*)	1 1 2	
Expenditure for one year—					14 3 9
in cash	1 4 7				
in kind	16 16 8½				
		£18 1 3½			

		£16 16 8½

Approximate cash income of husband, wife and children is 37% of gross income.

Value of wife's contribution is 40% of gross income.

	£ s. d.	£ s. d.
Income for one year—		
in cash	1 5 9	
in kind	16 16 8½	
		£18 2 5½

But, wife and children are almost self-supporting. If husband's income is excluded, then Kengeran's cash income represents 6% of her gross income.

BUDGET 11
Kengeran

Kengeran is a granddaughter of the *Fɔn* and one of the inherited wives of Fai-o-Djem. She is in her late forties, is frequently ill with coughs and fever, but is a keen and skilled farmer. Her household is a large one and includes an adult daughter, Mbaina (who has a son aged about 3 years), an adolescent daughter, Kisife, and a younger daughter. Wisiiy. Two grandchildren also live permanently with Kengeran; finally, there is another adult daughter who spends periods of 3 to 4 months at a time in the household. Kengeran, Mbaina and Kisife cultivate 17 plots, all on Djem land and totalling 4.5 acres. During the rains in 1947 Kengeran bought her youngest daughter, Wisiiy, a hoe and began to teach her to farm. Kumi, son of a deceased brother of the *Fai*, occasionally helps with the heavy clearing and receives gifts of food.

Kengeran receives a little salt and oil from her husband, but this is insufficient, and she disposes of plantains in the market to gain cash for necessaries, including utensils and tools. The actual selling is usually done by one of the daughters, but Kengeran decides what is to be purchased with the earnings. During my absence from Kimbaw, Kengeran's budget was recorded by the son of Vincent Kwangha, but there was little information on gifts in kind. However after September 1947, I returned to Kimbaw and kept complete records. Unfortunately, I was unable to record the budget of the *Fai*, who was extremely evasive about sales and purchases; but I counted his kola trees, raffia stands, and goats, and estimated his cash income was about £15 to £16 a year, and was derived from the sale of kolas (£10), palmwine (70s.), raffia poles (10s.), and goats (20s.). Cash gifts from affines were, I think, small and possibly balanced by the *fai's* outlay on gifts for his own wives' kin.

NOTES

(a) Kengeran had a very large farm and did not require to buy staples during the rains. She bought 8d. worth of beef in March, 1947, and 1s. worth of fish and 6d. meat in June, and 3d. worth in February, 1948. From her husband—see footnote (v) below—she received 8d. worth of fish in March, 1947, and 8d. worth in September. During the dry season her daughters caught 12 bush rats worth about 2d., and nine little fish worth about 1d.

(b) The expenditure on oil was heavy but the household was a large one and received only about one penny worth from the *fai* each week, or about 4s. worth a year.

(c) The cost of salt was small but Kengeran received about 1s. 10d. worth a year from her husband (most men would have given more), and occasional gifts from friends.

(d) Kengeran bought a hoe for 2s. 6d. for Kisife, and a small one for 1s. for Wisiiy. Usually the provision of such tools is the husband's responsibility, and the same applies to the raffia store-bin listed below.

(e) The camwood was bought for the young girls of the family when they attended marriage ceremonies.

(f) Kengeran wore only a baft pubic covering, as did her daughters with the exception of the second eldest who occasionally visited the family. The necklace was purchased for Kengeran.

(g) Kengeran gave Kisife 6d. worth of salt and 9d. worth of flour to take to a sister's daughter who had just borne a child in another village.

(h) Kengeran received 6d. from a friend and bought with it a calabash stand which she then passed on to a *fai*. He was a friend who frequently helped Kengeran with gifts of food in times of scarcity.

(i) Kengeran spent some time looking after a sick daughter in another village. Her son-in-law presented her with 6d. after each visit and her own daughter made gifts in kind. See footnotes (s) and (t) below.

(j) Kengeran received small sums in cash from various friends.

(k) Kisife and Mbaina (Kengeran's daughters) went to three marriage ceremonies and took gifts of maize flour,—see footnote (n) below. They in their turn received on one occasion 11d., and on another 6d. which they spent on groundnuts, camwood and bananas.

204

(*l*) Kengeran depended mainly on the sale of plantains for her cash income; but she had a good crop of beans in 1947 and sold 9*d*. worth. With this money and an extra 3*d*. she bought fish for the household.

(*m*) On the 24th February, 1947, Kengeran had 5*s*. which she had received from a European.

(*n*) Kisife attended three marriages: that of a relative of Kengeran's co-wife, Yuliy; that of her sister's husband's sister at Melim; and that of a maternal relative. On the first occasion she took 6*d*. worth of flour; on the second, 1*s*. 6*d*. worth of flour; and on the third 4*d*. worth.

(*o*) Kisife took flour when she went to greet a cousin who had borne a child.

(*p*) One of the wives of the Fon bore twins, and Kengeran, along with other relatives of the Fon, took food to the palace. She received oil and salt at the feast.

(*q*) Kengeran gave flour to Elizabeth-Bika of Djem who was a daughter of Fai-o-Dzem. The latter ' cooked ' *mfu*, and his relatives and their friends contributed food for the feast in his compound.

(*r*) Although Kengeran was a pagan she distributed beer (6*d*.) and food to Christian friends at Christmas. She received gifts in kind—cloth, meat, salt and oil—from me but I have not recorded these items in her budget.

(*s*) In October, 1947, Kengeran visited her daughter at Melim and stayed a few days. She took 1*s*. 6*d*. worth of flour and 1½*d*. worth of plantains. She was given *fufu*, kolas (3*d*.) and camwood (1*d*.) to bring home.

(*t*) When her daughter was ill Kengeran stayed with her. She took 5*d*. worth of trifoliate yams, orchid root (1*d*.) and maize (2*d*.). When she left, her daughter gave her a farm-bag (8*d*.), meat (3*d*.), camwood (1*d*.), and tobacco (½*d*.). Her son-in-law gave her 6*d*.

(*u*) Kengeran, with her daughters, went to help her married daughter at Melim harvest guinea corn. She took with her yams (4*d*.) and cocoyams (1½*d*.). Later she helped clear a new farm for the daughter, and brewed 8*d*. worth of beer and cooked 3*d*. worth of porridge for the workers.

(*v*) As I did not record the budget of Kengeran's husband, the *Fai*, I have included here his contributions to her household. The value of the salt and oil is an estimate based on my observations over a period of weeks; the actual value of the meat was noted in Kengeran's own budget.

(*w*) From her farms Kengeran (and her daughters) obtained 21 *vegati* of maize in September, and 8 *vegati* of finger millet in January.

(*x*) Kengeran sold only 1*d*. worth of sweet potatoes.

(*y*) The amount cited here is exclusive of 9*d*. worth of dwarf beans sold to obtain money for the purchase of fish.

(*z*) Kengeran had such good crops of cereals and roots that she was not so dependent as other women on plantains to augment household supplies.

BUDGET 12

(24th February 1947 to 29th February 1948)

A.—EXPENDITURE AND INCOME IN CASH

EXPENDITURE	£ s. d.	£ s. d.	INCOME	£ s. d.	£ s. d.
Food—			*Sales Profits—*		
beans (*a*)	2 10		maize porridge (*k*)	14 7½	
maize flour	3 1½		bean-balls (*l*)	2 7½	
maize	6		cassava gruel (*m*)	2 9½	
spinach	6				1 0 0½
cassava	8½				
egusi	7½		*Gifts—*		
food (*b*)	6		from friends (*i*)		6 9
		8 9½	from kin (*j*)		7 3
oil (*c*)	3 9				
meat (*d*)	1 11				
salt (*e*)	2 0				
		7 8			
House & farm replacements—					
pot	2				
farm bag	7				
millet basket	3				
cowpea seed	1				
beer for thatchers (*f*)	2 0				
		3 1			
Church dues—					
contribution card	3 0				
collection	1				
		3 1			
Miscellaneous—					
hospital card	2				
djaŋgi beer (*g*)	2 0				
trade loss (*h*)	2 2½				
		4 4½			
Gifts—					
to friend (*i*)		0 0 6½			

Expenditure for one year:	£1 7 6½	Income for one year:	£1 14 0½

BUDGET 12

(February 1947 to February 1948)

B.—ESTIMATED VALUE OF OUTLAY (INCLUDING CONSUMPTION) AND INCOME *IN KIND* FOR ONE YEAR

OUTLAY, ETC.	£ s. d.	£ s. d.	INCOME	£ s. d.	£ s. d.
Gifts to friends—			*Gifts from friends—*		
food & beer at Christmas		2 10	salt	1 2	
food for housebuilding		3	onion ..	2	
potatoes, eggs, *fufu*, fruit		1 3	honey & pineapples	4	
			dress & headtie (*n*) ..	15 0	
					16 8
Soap & kindling used in house		1 6 6	*gifts from mother—*		
			yams	9	
			bambarra nuts ..	3	
Value of crops and gifts used for household		5 10 11			1 0
			gifts from brothers—		
			meat	3	
			oil	11	
			salt	9	
					1 11
			Hausa soap		1 6
			Kindling collected by Melalia		1 5 0
			Market value at harvest of crops produced by self—		
			680 lbs. grain (*o*) ..	1 3 3	
			3,866 lbs. roots ..	2 11 2	
			60 lbs. beans & cucurbits ..	2 11	
			greens, etc.	9 4	
			180 lbs. plantains ..	9 0	
					4 15 8
		£7 1 9			£7 1 9

	£ s. d.	£ s. d.		£ s. d.	£ s. d.
Estd. expenditure, etc., for one year—			Estd. income for one year—		
in cash	1 7 6½		in cash	1 14 0½	
in kind	7 1 9		in kind	7 1 9	
		£8 9 3½			£8 15 9½

Cash income is 19% of gross income.

BUDGET 12

Melalia Shikiy

Melalia Shikiy is a Roman Catholic in her thirties who has two sons but no husband. She formerly lived with her mother at Meluf Village and still has farms and a storehouse there. But several years ago she moved to Kimbaw and was granted the use of a hut in Mbonyaar, where she was distantly related to Francis Lole. Her mother and Lole's belonged to different lineages of the Ndzendzef clan.

Melalia's two sons are at school, but one pays for his own fees and clothes and occasionally assists his mother with gifts of money; a relative pays the fees for the other son. Melalia farms 1.3 acres, some of the plots being on Mbonyaar land, some on her father's land at Meluf, while the rest are at Shisong Village and have been " begged " from strangers. She has about 50 plantain trees at Mbonyaar, but relies mainly on the retailing of processed foods for money with which to buy salt, oil, utensils, tools and clothes. She belongs to the Mbonyaar *djaŋgi*, contributing 6d. a week when she can afford it, otherwise her son pays for her. In February 1948 she ' cooked ' *djaŋgi* for 40s.

Melalia is a keen farm worker although she often suffers from chest trouble. During my absence from Kimbaw, her budget was recorded for me by Lole's son and it is, I think, incomplete in so far as not all gifts in kind have been entered. Also her earnings for the year are not typical because the market was closed to women by the Fon for 10 market-days. Melalia during the year made two long journeys, one to Fumban in the French Cameroons, and one to Bamenda Station.

NOTES

(a) In July, 1947, the *Fon* closed the market to women and Melalia was left with 6d. worth of beans and 2s. 6d. worth of flour, which she had intended to use for trade. She consumed them, but this increased the amount she would normally spend on food for the household. The market was opened again to women on the 6th October, 1947.

(b) Melalia had to go to Bamenda Station in mid-February and she spent 6d. on food, although she was given hospitality and gifts by friends.

(c) The amount spent on oil is small by Nsaw standards, but Melalia received some from kin; and her son also occasionally provided some.

(d) On Christmas Day, 1947, Melalia bought 1s. 3d. worth of meat for herself, her sons and visitors.

(e) Note that supplies of salt were also augmented by gifts from kin and friends.

(f) Melalia bought maize (2s.) to brew beer for relatives who were repairing her storehouse at Meluf. Such expenditure would normally be met by the male head of the household.

(g) When Melalia ' cooked ' *djaŋgi* in February, 1948, she bought maize (2s.) and brewed 7 calabashes of beer (value 3s. 6d.) for members.

(h) When visiting Fumban Melalia bought palm kernels (6s. 2d.), which she sold for 3s. 11½d. and so lost on the deal.

(i) Potatoes (5d.) and eggs (1½d.) were bought as a gift for a friend. Melalia received sums of cash from friends when in Bamenda Station.

(j) Melalia's brother and Lole occasionally gave her 3d. or 6d., and the total recorded in her budget was 1s. 3d. But I have added another 6s. to this as a contribution on her behalf by her son to *djaŋgi*. She herself did not know the exact amount but said he helped her when she had earned nothing from trade.

(k) Melalia used to buy 1s. to 2s. worth of maize flour early on market day, return to the house, prepare porridge with it, and sell this in the market later. Her profits ranged from 4d. to 1s. 6d. and were, on an average, 8d. a week. Her total expenditure on flour for the year was 29s. 4½d., and her total takings 44s. She used greens from her own farm for the relish.

(*l*) When flour was dear, she bought dwarf beans, boiled and ground them, and rolled them into balls, flavoured with condiments. Her total outlay on these was 4s. 4d. and her takings 6s. 11½d.

(*m*) Her expenditure on cassava was 3s. 8d. She made gruel and sold it for 6s. 5½d.

(*n*) When she visited Fumban she was given a dress and headtie by friend.

(*o*) In September, 1947, she obtained 6¼ *vegati* of maize; in January, she harvested 1½ *veg ati* of finger millet.

NOTES ON BUDGETS 13 TO 16

Three of the women, Yuliy, Vindjan and Yadiy (nos. 13, 14 and 15), are co-wives of Kengeran (no. 11) and married to Fai-o-Djem. As I have mentioned previously, I was unable to obtain details of the expenditure and income of the *Fai*, but he gave the three women small quantities of salt and oil regularly, as well as providing more costly tools and utensils. They, on their side, did not trade frequently in the market, but occasionally disposed of plantains, sugar cane, and so on, when they required small articles or wished to augment their supply of oil. Their households were smaller than that of Kengeran and their basic needs therefore more limited. I recorded their diminutive sales and purchases over 5 months, and have included them here because they are very typical of the pattern of petty trade engaged in by the great majority of Nsaw women. But I have not considered it worthwhile to estimate their budgets for a full year, or to work out gross outlay and income in kind. I refer the reader to my discussion of standards of living in Ch. VII for some estimate of the minimum expenditure incurred by their husband on their behalf.

The fourth woman, Sui (no. 16), was an elderly widow, nominally in the care of her late husband's brother. But she, on her side, never farmed or cooked for him and he, for his part, did not provide her with salt or oil. She sold plantains and engaged in the retail of small quantities of groundnuts, kolas, and so forth, and had the reputation of being a keen trader. Unfortunately, during the 5 months when I was in Kimbaw in my second tour, she injured her foot on the 9th December and was laid up until the middle of January. She did not trade then and her earnings were therefore not typical of a normal year. During my first tour I kept some records of her sales, and estimated that she made about 10s. to 12s. a year.

BUDGET 13

(28th September 1947 to 27th February 1948)

EXPENDITURE AND INCOME IN CASH

EXPENDITURE	£ s. d.	£ s. d.	INCOME	£ s. d.	£ s. d.
Food—			*Sales of—*		
oil (a)	2 0		plantains	4 7	
meat	3		sugar cane ..	4	
groundnuts ..	3				4 11
		2 6			
			Trade profits—		
Tobacco (b)		½	maize flour (d)		1
Farm & house replacements—			*Gifts—*		
cowpea seed	2		from relative (c)		6
firewood	2				
		4			
Miscellaneous—					
camwood for daughter ..		2			
Gifts (c)					
Expenditure for 5 months:		3 0½	**Income for 5 months:**		5 6

BUDGET 13

Yuliy

Yuliy is in her fifties and is an inherited wife of Fai-o-Djem. She has one adolescent daughter, Wirngoran, living with her, and together they farm 1.9 acres. She herself suffers from bronchial complaints and was twice incapacitated with pleurisy in 5 months. She had a few plantain trees and relies on Wirngoran to sell the surplus fruit. I recorded her budget for 5 months.

NOTES

Yuliy and her daughter harvested crops to the value of £7-3-9 (exclusive of 6s. worth of plantains) from 1.9 acres. In September, 1947, they obtained 8½ *vegati* of maize, and in January, 1948, 5 *vegati* of finger millet. I estimated that the gross weight of their grain was 1,147 lbs.; and of roots, 6,490 lbs. They had, compared with Kengeran and Vindjan, only a few plantain trees and probably obtained about 200 lbs. of fruit per year. I think they sold a little over half in order to purchase oil, meat, and tobacco.

(a) Yuliy obtained one pennyworth of oil (one-eighth pint) a week from the *fai*, and about one ounce of salt. Most of her trade earnings went to the purchase of oil.

(b) Yuliy smoked a pipe, and relied on friends and kin for tobacco.

(c) As far as I am aware Yuliy made no gifts involving a cash outlay to relatives and friends, but once she presented flour (1s.) to women of her father's compound for the celebration of a marriage. She and her daughter received in return wine, food, and a little meat. At another marriage—that of an affine of Kengeran—she sent 1s. worth of flour, and received food, wine, and 6d. in cash. Fai-o-Luun, her father, held a mortuary dance and she gave 9d. worth of flour. Finally, she presented ½d. worth of porridge to a friend at Christmas.

(d) Wirngoran bought 7d. worth of maize to brew beer, but she ground it into flour and retailed it for 8d., making 1d. profit.

BUDGET 14

(28th September 1947 to 27th February 1948)

EXPENDITURE AND INCOME IN CASH

EXPENDITURE	£ s. d.	£ s. d.	INCOME	£ s. d.	£ s. d.
Food—			*Sales of—*		
groundnuts	2½		plantains	3 0	
egusi	1		sugar cane	1	
		3½	pears	1	
					3 2
tobacco	4½				
House & farm replacements—					
2 pots	9				
6 baskets (a) ..	1 2				
cowpea seed ..	4				
		2 3			
Miscellaneous—					
bead thread for daughter	1				
pencil for son ..	1				
		2			
Gifts (b)	Nil				
Expenditure for 5 months:		3 1	Income for 5 months:		3 2

BUDGET 14

Vindjan

Vindjan is an inherited wife of Fai-o-Djem and is in her forties. She has one adolescent son living in another house in Djem compound, and two younger children— a boy and a girl—living with her. The boy attends the Basel Mission school and his fees and clothes are paid for by the *Fai*. The young daughter had just begun to experiment in farming in 1947. Vindjan had a married daughter living in another part of Kimbaw, and they formed a working team and cultivated together 5.2 acres. The crops were divided at harvest. I have exact figures for the maize and millet harvest retained by Vindjan for her own use, but no figures for her daughter's other crops. In September 1947 she obtained 10½ *vegati* of maize (892 lbs.) for herself, and in January 1948, 4½ *vegati* (382 lbs.) of finger millet. The grain at market value at harvest was worth 42s. 9d. I have estimated that Vindjan's share of the root crops was 8,074 lbs., and valued at £6–2–5. Pumpkins, beans, greens, and other relishes were worth about 24s. 9d., while 680 lbs. of plantains accounted for another 34s. Vindjan also had 2 small avocado pear trees from which about 3d. worth of fruit was eaten as snacks by the children, and 3d. worth sold. The total value of all crops was about £11–4–2.

NOTES

(a) Vindjan bought several baskets just before the millet harvest.

(b) Vindjan did not spend cash on gifts, but at a housebuilding in her father's compound she contributed 9d. worth of flour. During a funeral she gave her mother tobacco (1d.), and at Christmas she gave the brother of her deceased husband 4d. worth of beer brewed from her own maize. She occasionally received from him tobacco—about 3d. worth a year—; and from her own kin small amounts of wine, meat, and foodstuffs. She had two daughters who were married and lived in another tribe, and so did not receive anything from their respective husbands. Her other married daughter in Kimbaw was a *wiiy-o-t/emin* and Vindjan received very little from the husband. I have one record of a gift of 2d. worth of meat.

211

BUDGET 15
(28th September 1947 to 27th February 1948)

EXPENDITURE AND INCOME IN CASH

EXPENDITURE	£ s. d.	£ s. d.	INCOME	£ s. d.	£ s. d.
House & farm · replacements—			*Sales of—*		
knife	1		plantains		3½
farm bag	7		beer brewed from		
basket	2		maize		6
cowpea seed ..	1				
		11			
Miscellaneous—					
bead thread ..		½			
Expenditure for 5 months:		**11½**	**Income for 5 months:**		**9½**

BUDGET 15
Yadiy

Yadiy is about 35 years of age and has four young children.   She is the wife of Fai-o-Djem.   One son attends school and is given clothes by the *Fai*, his father.   Yadiy received, I think, more salt and oil than the other co-wives, with the exception of Shubuka who was particularly favoured by the *Fai*.   She had only a few plantain trees and little in the way of a surplus for petty sales.   She farmed 1.4 acres unassisted and had no time to trade.   Her kin lived in a neighbouring compound at Kinga.

NOTES

Yadiy obtained 5 *vegati* (425 lbs.) of maize in September, 1947, and 3¾ *vegati* (318 lbs.) of millet in January, 1948.   Their total value at harvest was about 24s. 4d.   I estimated that she obtained 4,068 lbs. of root crops, worth 53s. 3d. ; and pumpkins, beans, greens and other relishes worth 10s. 4d.   She had only a few plantains with a crop of fruit of about 30 lbs. (1s. 6d.).   In a year she might sell 10 lbs. fruit for about 6d. or 9d.   The total value of all crops was approximately £4–12–4.   The only gifts of which I have a record is 6d. worth of salt and oil, received at the palace on the occasion of one of the wives of the *Fɔn* giving birth to twins.   But it is my impression that she obtained small quantities of salt and oil from her parents at Kinga compound.

BUDGET 16

(28th September 1947 to 27th February 1948)

EXPENDITURE AND INCOME IN CASH

EXPENDITURE	£ s. d.	£ s. d.	INCOME	£ s. d.	£ s. d.
Food—			*Sales of*—		
oil	9		plantains	1 9½	
meat	1½		egg-plant	2	
salt	6		kola nuts	3	
groundnuts	2				2 2½
porridge	1				
		1 7½	*Profits from trade*—		
Farm replacements—			kolas (*a*)	Nil	
cowpea seed ..		4	commissions (*d*) ..		1¼
Miscellaneous—					
trade loss (*b*) ..	2½		*Gifts*—		
hospital card ..	2		at marriage (*e*) ..	9	
		4½	from boy of com-		
Gifts—			pound	1½	
groundnuts (*c*) ..		1			10½
Expenditure for 5 months:		2 5	Income for 5 months:		3 2½

BUDGET 16

Sui

Sui was an elderly widow of about 50 years who lived in Djem. Her eldest son was of *n/ilaf* status, since Sui's own father was a *tanto*. She farmed 1.07 acres and relied on her earnings from petty trade to buy salt, oil, and utensils, etc. Her sister was a Christian, and Sui, though remaining a pagan, adopted her sister's example in wearing apparel. During the year when I was in Kimbaw she bought no dresses, but was saving up to buy a Munshi wrap. Her earnings for the 5 months were not typical, as she injured her foot and did not trade for a month. Earlier in the period she had attended a number of ceremonies and did not go to the market regularly. I estimated that her earnings in a normal year would be from 10s. to 12s. She had one other son who was frequently absent from Kimbaw and who, according to her, made no monetary contribution to the household.

While Sui was incapacitated by her accident, the wife of the brother of Sui's deceased husband helped her with the millet harvest. She obtained 2¼ *vegati*. In September she harvested 6 *vegati* of maize (510 lbs.). The value of her entire grain harvest was 23s. 8d. Root crops (3,876 lbs.) were worth 50s. 10d., and pumpkins, beans, greens, etc. worth 11s. 1d. Her plantain grove was relatively large and she consumed about 800 lbs. fruit in her household and in small gifts to kin and friends. She sold the remainder of the crop for about 10s. in the market.

NOTES

(*a*) Sui once bought 3d. worth of small kolas and sold them for 3d.

(*b*) Sui bought a bag of groundnuts for 1s. 2¼d., and sold them by the cigarette-cup. She lost 2¼d. on the deal.

(*c*) While ill Sui persuaded 2 young girls in the compound to sell some plantains for her in the market. They obtained 3½d. and received from Sui groundnuts (1d.) as a reward.

(*d*) Sui occasionally sold small quantities of food for women unskilled in trading, and usually received ½d. commission for her pains.

(*e*) Sui, on the occasion of a marriage in her father's compound, gave flour (2s.). She obtained 9d. in cash from the groom, and also beef (3d.). When her father's kinsman built a house at Shup village, Sui contributed porridge (2d.). She received meat and wine worth 2d. When a maternal relative was ill, Sui sent porridge (1d.). Finally, when her father ' cooked' *mfu*, Sui gave flour (6d.). She obtained food, wine, and meat to the value of about 6d.; but, on the return home from the feast, knocked her foot against a sharp twig and was incapacitated for a month.

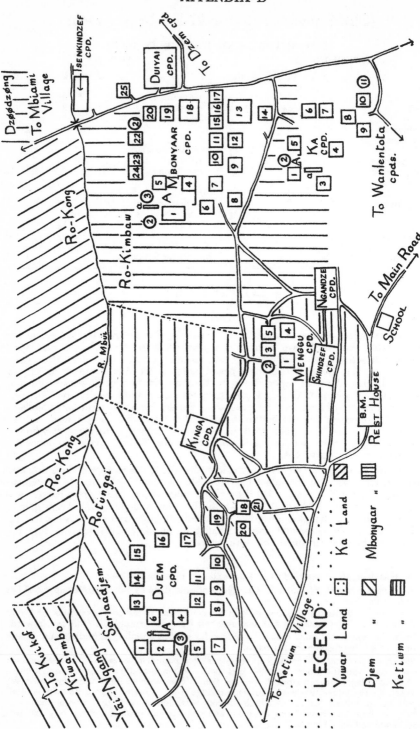

Sketch plan of section of Veka'akwi area (Kimbaw).

OCCUPANTS OF COMPOUNDS IN SKETCH PLAN

No.	Occupants	Relation to Compound Head	Remarks
A	*Mbonyaar Compound* —	—	Inner courtyard of Fai-o-Mbonyaar, compound head.
a	—	—	Gravestones of lineage heads of Mbonyaar.
1	Fai-o-Mbonyaar.	—	—
2 & 3	Fai-o-Mbonyaar.	—	Store huts.
4	Shemsum.	Senior inherited wife.	Also has the title of *yelaa*.
5	Wanaka.	Own wife.	Also resident is own child and young sister.
6	Fhshwaa.	Inherited wife.	Also resident is granddaughter.
7	Djingla.	Inherited wife.	—
8	Fhshwaa.	Inherited wife.	Hut belongs to Clement (see 9) but inhabited by his mother, Fhshwaa, during 1947 until hut no. 6 built.
	Clement Mbinkar	Father's brother's son.	Unmarried.
10	Yeduda Wirnsungnin, wife of Thomas Kintarir.	Father's brother's son's wife.	Four children also resident. Yeduda is son's wife to Fhshwaa (no. 6).
11	Thomas Kintarir.	Father's brother's son.	Hut contains 2 rooms—one for work and entertainment; one for sleeping.
12	Yirbongka.	Father's brother's daughter.	Kibong (divorced daughter) also resident.
13	Kaberry.	—	Hut owner is Sylvester Ndjodzeka (see 24), but hut occupied by Kaberry in 1946, and 1947-48.
14	Kaberry.	—	Kibong (see 12) owns hut, but lent it to Kaberry for kitchen.
15	Camilla Labam.	Father's brother's daughter.	Camilla is widowed sister to Lole (18) who built hut for her.
16	Elizabeth-Kila, wife of Francis Lole.	Father's brother's son's wife.	Hut used as kitchen by Elizabeth, and as bedroom by young children.
17	Francis Lole.	Father's brother's son.	Store room.
18	Francis Lole.	Father's brother's son.	Hut has 4 rooms and used as sleeping quarters by Lole, wife and older dependants.

No.	Occupants	Relation to Compound Head	Remarks
	Mbonyaar Compound-cont.		
19	Bertha Yiyi.	Father's brother's son's wife.	Bertha a widow. Also resident is her niece.
20	Maurice Nyingka.	Father's brother's son.	Wife and 2 children also resident.
21	Melalia Shikiy.	—	Store hut.
22	Melalia Shikiy.	—	Two sons also resident. Melalia is a maternal relative of Lole (no. 18).
23	Mbinkar.	Father's brother's son.	Unmarried son of Djingla (no. 7).
24	Sylvester Ndjozeka.	Father's brother's daughter's son.	Sylvester is son of Yirbongka. Also resident are his wife and 2 children.
25	Barnabas Shadze.	Father's brother's son.	Also resident—wife and 2 children.
	Ka Compound		
A	—	—	Inner courtyard of /e-o-Ka, compound head.
a	—	—	Gravestones of sub-lineage heads of Ka.
1	/e-o-Ka.	—	Dwelling hut.
2	/e-o-Ka.	—	Store hut.
3	Biy.	Mother.	—
4	Joseph.	Brother.	Unmarried, and son of Biy (3).
5	Yekong.	Inherited wife.	Mother of Nicholas Ngee (7).
6	Alphonse Fannso.	Father's brother's son.	Wife and children also resident.
7	Nicholas Ngee.	Father's son.	Son of Yekong (5). Wife and children also resident. Hut contains 2 rooms.
8	Casimir Nening.	Father's son.	Wife, Elizabeth Keh, also resident.
9	Beatrice Kwanteng, wife of Gabriel.	Father's son's wife.	Uses hut as kitchen and sleeps in 10.
10	Gabriel Kondjo.	Father's son.	Husband to Beatrice (9) and full brother of Casimir (8).
11	Gabriel Kondjo.	Father's son.	Store hut.
	Menggu Compound		
1	Tanye.	—	Compound head.
2	Tanye.	—	Store hut.
3	Biy.	Wife.	Small child resident. Hut used as kitchen and bedroom.
4	Bibiana Kiya, wife of Mathias Ngam.	Brother's wife.	Hut used as kitchen by Bibiana, and as bedroom by 3 children.
5	Mathias Ngam.	Brother.	Hut used as store and sleeping quarters by Mathias and wife (4).

216

No.	Occupants	Relation to Compound Head	Remarks
A	*Djem Compound* —	—	Inner courtyard of Fai-o-Djem, compound head.
a	—	—	Gravestones of lineage heads.
1	Fai-o-Djem.	—	Sleeping quarters.
2	Fai-o-Djem.	—	Hut used for entertainment.
3	Fai-o-Djem.	—	Store hut.
4	Yuliy.	Senior inherited wife.	Hut shared with daughter, Wirngoran.
5	Kengeran.	Inherited wife.	Hut shared with 6 dependants.
6	Shubuka & Yadiy.	Wives.	Hut shared with children.
7	Kumi.	Own brother's son.	Unmarried.
8	Djo'kem, wife of Gughe.	Father's son's wife.	Hut used as kitchen and bedroom.
9	Gughe.	Father's son.	Hut used as sleeping quarters by Gughe and small son.
10	Vindjan.	Deceased father's wife.	Hut shared with 2 young children.
11	Kumbu.	Father's brother.	Sleeping quarters for Kumbu and son, Mbinkar.
12	Semtur, wife of Kumbu.	Father's brother's wife.	Kitchen and sleeping hut for Semtur and daughter.
13	Fai-o-Djem.	—	Reserved mainly for performance of the *rum* ritual.
14	Wiramo'on.	Father's son.	Unmarried son of Vindjan (10).
15	Sui.	Father's son's widow.	Sui was formerly married to full brother of Mawo (16).
16	Mawo.	Father's son.	Hut used as kitchen and bedroom by Mawo and wife, Biy.
17	Kibu.	Father's son.	Kibu is full brother of Mawo (16). Hut shared with wife, Dzøndzøiy; and 2 children.
18	Vincent Kwangha.	Father's son.	Full brother of Gughe (9). Hut used as sleeping quarters by Vincent and young sons.
19	Maurice.	Father's son's son.	Unmarried son of Kwangha (18).
20	Elizabeth-Bika, wife of Vincent Kwangha.	Father's son's wife.	Hut used as kitchen and bedroom by Elizabeth and daughters and grandchild.
21	Vincent Kwangha.	Father's son.	Store hut.

INDEX

(32623) Wt. P3066—5930 750 9/52 G.S.St.

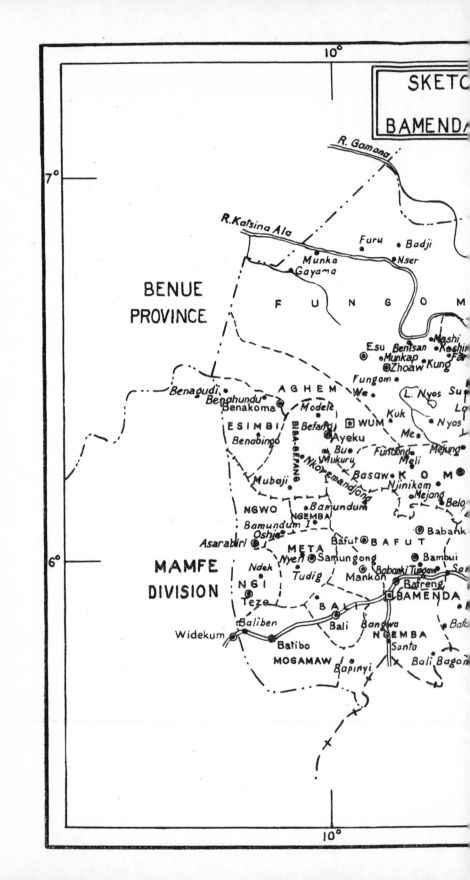

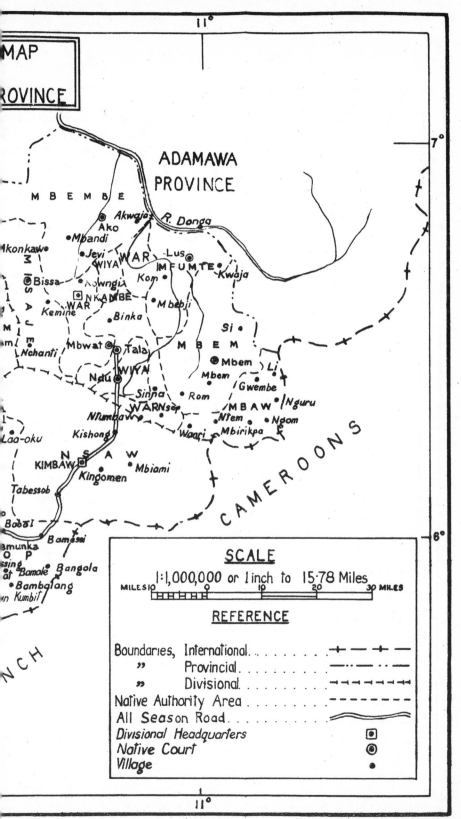

MAP

ROVINCE

ADAMAWA
PROVINCE

M B E M B E

Akwaja   R. Donga
Ako
Mbandi
Mkonkaw   Jevi   WAR   Lus
WIYA   IMFUMTE
Bissa   Kowngi   Kom   Kwaja
NKAMBE
WAR   Mbebji
Kemine   Binka
Mbwat   Tala   Si
Nchanti   M B E M   Mbem
WIYA   Li
Ndu   Mbem
Sinna   Rom   Gwembe
WARNser   MBAW   Nguru
Nfumbaw   Ntem   Ngom
Laa-oku   Kishong   Waari   Mbirikpa

N S A W
KIMBAW
Kingomen   Mbiami
Tabessob

Boбol
Bamesi
bmunka
O P
sing   Bamole   Bangola
Bambalang
n Kumbi

NCH

C A M E R O O N S

SCALE

1:1,000,000 or 1inch to 15·78 Miles

MILES 10   0   10   20   30 MILES

REFERENCE

Boundaries, International . . . . +— +—
     "   Provincial . . . . —·—·—
     "   Divisional . . . . ◄—◄—◄—◄
Native Authority Area . . . . — — — —
All Season Road . . . .
Divisional Headquarters   ▣
Native Court   ◉
Village   ●

A7748 Fosh & Cross Ltd., London

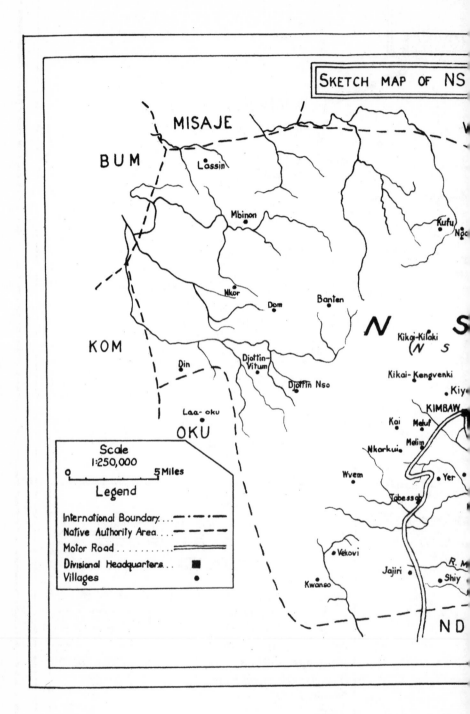

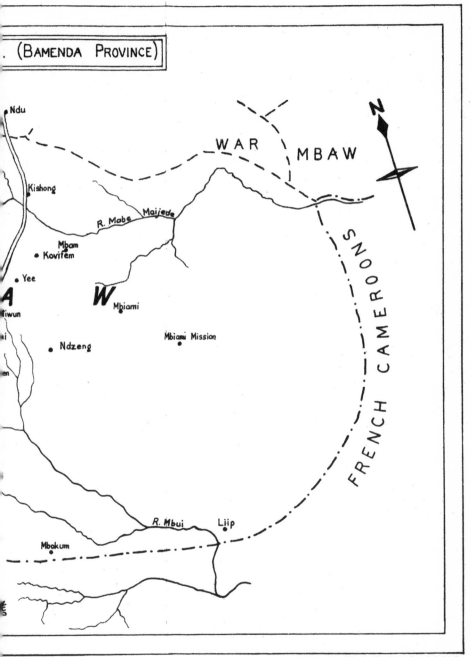

(BAMENDA PROVINCE)

Ndu

WAR MBAW

N

Kishong

R. Mabe Maijede

Mbam
Kovifem

Yee

A

iwun

W Mbiami

Mbiami Mission

Ndzeng

en

FRENCH CAMEROONS

R. Mbui Liip

Mbakum

A7748   Wt.P.3066   K6   3/52   Gp.959   Fosh & Cross Ltd., London